On Crime, Society, and Responsibility in the Work of Nicola Lacey

On Crime, Society, and Responsibility in the Work of Nicola Lacey

Edited by

IYIOLA SOLANKE

OXFORD
UNIVERSITY PRESS

OXFORD
UNIVERSITY PRESS

Great Clarendon Street, Oxford, OX2 6DP,
United Kingdom

Oxford University Press is a department of the University of Oxford. It furthers the University's objective of excellence in research, scholarship, and education by publishing worldwide. Oxford is a registered trade mark of Oxford University Press in the UK and in certain other countries

First Edition published in 2021

Impression: 1

Published in the United States of America by Oxford University Press
198 Madison Avenue, New York, NY 10016, United States of America

British Library Cataloguing in Publication Data

Data available

Library of Congress Control Number: 2020944790

ISBN 978–0–19–885268–1

DOI: 10.1093/oso/9780198852681.001.0001

Printed and bound by
CPI Group (UK) Ltd, Croydon, CR0 4YY

Foreword: An Ambivalent Affair, but Worth the Effort

Susanne Baer[*]

A Festschrift, or *liber amicorum*, is a book honouring a respected person—the honouree—often an academic. It is presented during their lifetime, as an edited volume and usually with contributions from the honouree's colleagues, former pupils and, if they are lucky and managed to meet and keep them, friends. The Festschrift is a German tradition that eventually travelled to many places around the world. As such, it is an early and particular form of peer review. So far so good. But since the honouree of this volume is Nicola Lacey, a prolific and world-renowned academic, one cannot end here. In the humble attempt to emulate her intellectual practice, one must contextualize how acts, whether it be the law as a criminal sanction, a code, a compositum (the rule of law) or a theory (positivism according to HLA Hart), or in our case a Festschrift, are (to be) read, what norms govern them, which institutions they form, and what interests drive them.

A Festschrift is much more than a book. First and foremost, it may be understood as a product born in a historically grown realm of intellectual homosociality, that of men. As such, the Festschrift has no mother but is sexed, just like the subject of law.[1] Specifically, the reception of a Festschrift, even more so than its production, is an 'authoritative activity culturally marked as feminine'. This is how Nicola Lacey described the format of the inaugural lecture. When she was confronted with that task, she spoke 'as a subject of the unspeakable sex, exercising the apparently impossible right of speaking on the unspeakable subject of sex'.[2] In this volume, some do the same. For Lacey, this was the responsible choice, compatible with the focus of this volume and much of her work, on responsibility, but it may also be described as a what I see as a typical critical move of elegant, of graceful, and seemingly effortless (Hanna Pickard, in this volume) subversion.

To follow the honouree's intellectual route, the Festschrift must be situated in its political economy, just like the law.[3] As such, the Festschrift is the incarnation

* Justice of the German Federal Constitutional Court, Professor of Public Law and Gender Studies at Humboldt Universität zu Berlin

1 Nicola Lacey, 'On the Subject of Sexing the Subject …' in Ngaire Naffine, and Rosemary J Owens (eds), *Sexing the Subject of Law* (Law Book Company 1997) 65.

2 Nicola Lacey, 'Unspeakable Subjects, Impossible Rights: Sexuality, Integrity and Criminal Law' (1998) 11(1) Canadian Journal of Law & Jurisprudence 47.

3 Nicola Lacey, The Prisoners' Dilemma: Political Economy and Punishment in Contemporary Democracies (Cambridge University Press 2008); 'Political Systems and Criminal Justice' (2012)

of the canon, yet another product of and for the citation cartel, another example of the 'Matthew effect' (as coined by Robert Merton *and* Harriet Zuckerman) that governs much academic recognition. I assume that, similar to the gendered nature of criminalization,[4] the function and practice of the Festschrift is remarkably pervasive across systems. It serves to perpetuate a white homosocially masculine utter lack of diversity, most certainly in legal studies with its proximity to power, and it informs a taken-for-granted abundance of self-inflation, also specifically male, in its hegemonic form. Taking this into account, a Festschrift dedicated to a critical thinker runs the risk of a performative contradiction. Although critical analysis should in fact be the default state of research, it is not, and thus must still be emphasized in describing the work of the honouree. Given this, her Festschrift must depart from that socio-homo-hegemonic canon and context, which makes it an ambivalent, and if we are lucky, eventually a subversive, affair.

Yet regarding the law, this is so often the case. Rights are an ambivalent affair, a 'call of the sirens' as exposed many years ago by Carol Smart.[5] According to Lacey, we 'must understand the limitations as well as the potential', and consider 'the interaction between legal, political, economic and cultural institutions as key factors in shaping'[6] law and rights. This requires us to then also consider what a Festschrift really does, its limitations and potential.

Departing from the tradition, a Festschrift is, then, also a space for, and fills time with, dialogue and it gathers attempts to speak a common language which the honouree, as stated in another context, considers worth the effort.[7] After all, the genre of a Festschrift was conceived to celebrate someone some people consider great, and indeed grand and inspiring enough to honour them with an extra piece of writing, with a mix of recognition and revelation. So if you are lucky, you find original pieces, and you even find pieces that engage the work as well as the person at the centre of attention. Festschrift contributions that do indeed queer the canon are more than book reviews, and they offer more than an entertaining recollection of encounters. Instead, contributions to this Festschrift are subjective but not about the writer, are generous and intellectually in love but not blind, are inspired and

65(1) Current Legal Problems 203; 'Punishment in the Perspective of Comparative Political Economy' ('Bestrafung in der Perspektive der Komparativen Politischen Ökonomie') (2012) 44 Kriminologische Journal 9: with David Soskice and David Hope, 'Understanding the Determinants of Penal Policy: Crime, Culture and Comparative Political Economy' (2018) 1 Annual Review of Criminology 195.

[4] Nicola Lacey, Women, Crime and Character: From Moll Flanders to Tess of the d'Urbervilles (Oxford University Press 2008). For a recent take, see 'Women, Crime and Character in Twentieth Century Law and Literature: In Search of the Modern Moll Flanders' *LSE Legal Studies Working Paper* No. 20/2017.

[5] Carol Smart, *Feminism and the Power of Law* (Routledge 1989).

[6] This is taken from the summary of an analysis of rights from the perspective of legal gender studies, in Nicola Lacey, 'Feminist Legal Theory and the Rights of Women' in Karen Knop (ed.), *Gender and Human Rights* (Oxford University Press 2004) 13.

[7] Lacey 2004, see n. 6, at 55.

inspiring. They are not portraits either. As evidenced by Nicola Lacey's breathtaking biography of HLA Hart,[8] it is a rather demanding task to write them.

However, if this were the calling here regarding the honouree, one might want to start with a woman reading, and reading, and reading books in the sun, elegantly dressed to the occasion yet even more to herself and those who enjoy each other's presence, generous with others and with a clear focus of her own, filled with as many questions as with answers simultaneously, and laughing, a true joy. Iyiola Solanke has gathered people who know how such an academic is to be celebrated, in serious writings. So if you can, meet the honouree someday. For now, enjoy reading.

[8] Nicola Lacey, *A Life of HLA Hart: The Nightmare and the Noble Dream* (Oxford University Press 2004).

Table of Contents

List of Contributors

Andrew Ashworth, CBE, QC, FBA is Emeritus Vinerian Professor of English Law and Emeritus Fellow of All Souls College, University of Oxford.

Susanne Baer is Justice of the Federal Constitutional Court of Germany; Professor of Public Law and Gender Studies, Humboldt University Berlin; and James W Cook Global Law Professor, University of Michigan Law School

Antony Duff FBA, FRSE is Emeritus Professor in Philosophy at the University of Stirling

Lindsay Farmer FBA is Professor of Law at the University of Glasgow Law School

John Gardner FBA (1965-2019) was a Scottish legal philosopher. He held the chair of Jurisprudence at the University of Oxford from 2000-2016, before becoming Senior Research Fellow at All Souls College, Oxford, a position which he held at the time of his death.

David Garland FBA, FRSE, FAAAS is Arthur T. Vanderbilt Professor of Law and Professor of Sociology at New York University, and Professorial Fellow in Criminology at Edinburgh Law School

Emily Jackson, OBE, FBA is Professor of Law at the London School of Economics Department of Law

Arlie Loughnan is Professor of Criminal Law and Criminal Law Theory at the University of Sydney Law School

Ngaire Naffine is Bonython Professor of Law at the University of Adelaide

Alan Norrie FBA is Professor of Law at the University of Warwick Law School

Hanna Pickard is Bloomberg Distinguished Professor in the William H. Miller III Department of Philosophy and Berman Institute of Bioethics, Johns Hopkins University

Iyiola Solanke is Professor in EU Law and Social Justice at the University of Leeds School of Law

Lucia Zedner FBA is Senior Research Fellow, All Souls College and Professor, Faculty of Law, University of Oxford; and Conjoint Professor, Faculty of Law, UNSW, Sydney

Introduction

Nicola Lacey's Pioneering Work On Crime, Society, and Responsibility[1]

Iyiola Solanke

I had the pleasure and privilege to be guided by Nicola Lacey during my doctorate in the Law Department at the London School of Economics. My supervisor became my friend and over the years a mentor, a sponsor and an ally. Together with my co-supervisor, Damian Chalmers—who introduced us—she not only helped me to excavate und unwind the entangled relationship between law, politics, and society but also to navigate academia, a space that can be both lonely and precarious for a black woman. At both a personal and professional level, she is an excellent role model and image of who and what an academic can be. One contributor put it well:

> 'Thinking Big' is what comes to my mind when I think about Niki—that she has a big reach across disciplines, times and places, and big ideas. She is a generous thinker. She is also subversive, and gorgeous and charming. And so what we see is this lovely person willing to take it all on.

***

It was Rob Wintemute who planted the seed. We were at an inauguration event at the Hart offices in Bloomsbury. He, I, and Nicola Lacey stood together as he informed us that as her first doctoral researcher to receive a Chair, it was my responsibility to organize a Festschrift in her honour. Niki and I both looked at each other in horror—oh, no, we both agreed, why would we consider engaging with such an old-fashioned white male tradition. The conversation quickly moved on.

However, the comment stayed with me. If, as claimed by Horowitz, the Festschrift is a 'reward for the best and inspiration for the brightest',[2] why should Nicola Lacey, one of the most influential intellectual voices of the twentieth and

[1] Iyiola Solanke is Professor of European Union Law and Social Justice in the School of Law, University of Leeds and Academic Bencher of the Inner Temple.

[2] Irving Horowitz, 'The Place of the Festschrift in Academic Life' Scholarly Publishing, (1990) 21 (2), 77.

Iyiola Solanke, *Introduction* In: *On Crime, Society, and Responsibility in the Work of Nicola Lacey.* Edited by: Iyiola Solanke, Oxford University Press (2021). © The several contributors. DOI: 10.1093/oso/9780198852681.003.0001

twenty-first centuries, not have a Festschrift to honour and celebrate her contribution? After the shocking discovery that there had never been a common law Festschrift honouring a woman[3] my mind began to shift—this tradition needed reform and given her track record as a pioneer, it would be fitting if Nicola Lacey was the first woman to inspire a common law Festschrift.

Together with David Soskice, Lucia Zedner, Andrew Ashworth, and John Gardner, potential contributors were identified and we set to decide upon a theme. This was a challenge: Nicola Lacey has worked with so many and her work spans legal theory, legal history, feminist theory, political theory, political economy, criminal law, criminal justice, and more. She stands out in respect of her international influence and how many other disciplines she has closely encountered—philosophy, sociology, history, literature, economics, psychology, to name a few. In relation to theme, a decision therefore had to be made: either try to do justice to all of her work or to take a narrower focus. The former would demonstrate the breadth of her mind but might overshadow her distinctive voice. The former might also produce a comprehensive volume but lack a coherent theme. The latter would be more manageable but less comprehensive. A consensus emerged upon the latter and a suggestion arose to organize the book around the idea of responsibility.

The study of responsibility in criminal law and criminal justice is longstanding[4] and remains a key theme.[5] A review of scholarship in this area illustrates that researchers have taken up many different facets, from the age of criminal responsibility[6] to psychological enquiries[7] and more recent concerns such as corporate crime,[8]

3 Michael Taggart, 'Gardens or Graveyards of Scholarship? Festschriften in the Literature of the Common Law' (2002) 22(2) Oxford Journal of Legal Studies 227 at <https://academic.oup.com/ojls/article/22/2/227/1428873/Gardens-or-Graveyards-of-Scholarship-Festschriften>

4 Richard Sparks —Diminished Responsibility in Theory and Practic' (1964) 27 Modern Law Review 9. Jonathan Glover, *Responsibility* (Routledge 1970).

5 See e.g. Insanity and the Capacity for Criminal Responsibility' (2001) 5 Edinburgh Law Review 325; Victor Tadros, *Criminal Responsibility* (Oxford University Press 2005); 'The Scope and Grounds of Responsibility' (2008) 11 New Criminal Law Review 191; Victor Tadros, 'Poverty and Criminal Responsibility' (2009) 43 Journal of Value Inquiry 391.

6 Thomas Crofts, *The Criminal Responsibility of Young People* (Ashgate 2003); Claire Mcdiarmid, 'An Age of Complexity: Children and Criminal Responsibility in Law' (2013) 13(2) Youth Justice 145; Carl Elliott, 'Criminal Responsibility and Children: A New Defence Required to Acknowledge the Absence of Capacity and Choice' (2011) 75(4) The Journal of Criminal Law 289;

7 Stephen J Morse, 'Psychopathy and Criminal Responsibility' (2008) 1(3) Neuroethics 205; Arlie Loughnan and Tony Ward, 'Emergent Authority and Expert Knowledge: Psychiatry and Criminal Responsibility in the UK' (January–February 2014) 37(1) International Journal of Law and Psychiatry 25; Jill Peay, 'Mental Incapacity and Criminal Liability: Redrawing the Fault Lines?' (May–June 2015) 40 International Journal of Law and Psychiatry 25; Hanna Pickard, 'Choice, Deliberation, Violence: Mental Capacity and Criminal Responsibility in Personality Disorder' (May–June 2015) 40 International Journal of Law and Psychiatry 15.

8 Peter French, *Collective and Corporate Responsibility* (University of Columbia Press 1984); John Braithwaite and Brent Fisse 'The Allocation of Responsibility for Corporate Crime' (1988) 11 Sydney Law Review 468; Marc Bovens, *The Quest for Responsibility: Accountability and Citizenship in Complex Organisations* (Cambridge University Press 1998); Celia Wells, *Corporations and Criminal Responsibility* (Oxford University Press 2001); Ian B Lee, 'Corporate Criminal Responsibility as Team Member Responsibility' (2011) 31(4) Oxford Journal of Legal Studies 755.

cybercrime, genetics, sexual[9] and social behaviour.[10] This topic has long ceased to be the preserve of medics[11] and psychiatry,[12] and has for decades generated interdisciplinary research[13] from scholars in forensic science, law,[14] sociology, history, and philosophy.[15] These enquires are not limited to any one jurisdiction but are global in scope.[16] Nicola Lacey ranks alongside HLA Hart[17] and Antony Honoré[18] in developing approaches to understanding responsibility. Like these authors, the influence of her work has spread beyond academia to change the perception of responsibility amongst practitioners. This idea was met with approval by those who had agreed to contribute and, with the help of Jamie Berezin at OUP, a book proposal was drafted and positively received by external reviewers.

This collection of essays is therefore the outcome of a collaborative venture, which I had the pleasure to co-ordinate. Our objective was to produce a volume

[9] Lynne Henderson, 'Rape and Responsibility' (1992) 11 Law and Philosophy 127; Scott BURRIS and Matthew WEAIT, *Criminalisation and the Moral Responsibility for Sexual Transmission of HIV* (Global Commission on HIV and the Law 2014); Vanessa Munro and Carl Stychin (eds), *Sexuality and the Law* (Cavendish 2007).

[10] Elvin Balajanov, 'Setting the Minimum Age of Criminal Responsibility for Cybercrime International Review of Law (2 January 2018) 32(1) Computers & Technology 2; Stephen J Morse, Genetics and Criminal Responsibility' (2011) 15(9) Trends in Cognitive Sciences 378; Maria Isabel González-Tapia '"Bad Genes" & Criminal Responsibility' (March–April 2015) 39 International Journal of Law and Psychiatry 60; Roberto Tatarelli et al., 'Behavioral Genetics and Criminal Responsibility at the Courtroom' (April 2014) 237 Forensic Science International 40.

[11] Phillip C Knapp, 'Criminal Responsibility' (1 November 1915) 6(4) Journal of the American Institute of Criminal Law and Criminology 571; Charles A Mercier, 'Criminal Responsibility' (15 October 1904) 2(2285) The British Medical Journal 957; Lionel A Weatherly, 'Criminal Responsibility' (11 September 1926) 2(3427) British Medical Journal 501.

[12] Murray Ferguson et al., 'Criminal Responsibility Evaluations: Role of Psychologists in Assessment, Psychiatry' (1 February 2011) 18(1) Psychology and Law 79; Jillian Craigie, 'Against a Singular Understanding of Legal Capacity: Criminal Responsibility and the Convention on the Rights of Persons with Disabilities' (May–June 2015) 40 International Journal of Law and Psychiatry 6.

[13] See e.g. the International Journal of Law and Psychiatry special edition on responsibility and liability.

[14] Shazia Choudry, 'Corporal Punishment and Parental Responsibility' in Rebecca Probert, Jonathan Herring, and Stephen Gilmore (eds), *Responsible Parents and Parental Responsibility* (Hart 2009); Alan Bogg and Jonathon Herring, 'Addiction and Responsibility' in Jonathan Herring, Ciaran Regan, Darin Weinberg, and Phil Withington (eds), *Intoxication and Society* (Palgrave Macmillan 2012).

[15] Thomas Giddens, 'Criminal Responsibility and the Living Self' (2015) 9(2) Criminal Law and Philosophy 189; Michael Bayles, 'Character, Purpose and Criminal Responsibility' (1982) 1 Law and Philosophy 5.

[16] Samuel Adjorlolo et al., 'Criminal Responsibility and the Insanity Defence in Ghana: The Examination of Legal Standards and Assessment Issues' (2 September 2016) 23(5) Psychiatry, Psychology and Law 684; Tessa Grant et al. (eds), 'Criminal Responsibility in Autism Spectrum Disorder: A Critical Review Examining Empathy and Moral Reasoning' (2018) 59(1) Canadian Psychology/Psychologie canadienne, 65; Laura Grossi et al. (eds), 'An International Perspective on Criminal Responsibility and Mental Illness' (2017) 2(1) Practice Innovations 2; S Garvey, 'Canadian Scholars on Criminal Responsibility' (2015) 9(2) Criminal Law and Philosophy 351; Thomas Crofts, 'Reforming the Age of Criminal Responsibility' (2016) 46(4) South African Journal of Psychology 436; B Goy, 'Individual Criminal Responsibility before the International Criminal Court' (2012) 12(1) International Criminal Law Review 1.

[17] HLA Hart, *Punishment and Responsibility: Essays in the Philosophy of Law* (Clarendon Press 1968)

[18] Antony Honoré, 'Responsibility and Luck' (1988) 104 Law Quarterly Review 530; Antony Honoré, *Responsibility and Fault* (Hart 1999).

that serves the needs of scholarship in addition to celebrating an eminent scholar. Our hope is that the Festschrift will be regularly used in teaching and research across a range of disciplines. The volume offers a set of thought-provoking essays on the many facets of responsibility which can act as an entry point to those seeking an orientation to research in this area, connecting the work of Nicola Lacey to a new generation. At the same time, the essays can serve as a work of reference on responsibility, providing a guide to further research for more advanced scholars by raising questions that stimulate new projects. The essays span Lacey's cumulative body of work: each author brings a particular challenge and new ideas to bear on her work, touching upon important aspects of responsibility that are current in the scholarship: categorization, frameworks for understanding criminal responsibility and the relationships between them, women in criminal law, the history of criminal law, blameworthiness and ascriptions of responsibility, moral responsibility, the role of politics, and political economy.

***

The volume is divided into three parts. Part I focuses on Meta Approaches to Criminal Responsibility. It contains two essays that take up Lacey's work on categorization. Ashworth and Zedner develop her ideas on the operationalization of responsibility. Their chapter considers what Lacey calls the 'accumulation of conceptions or "technologies" of responsibility'[19] focusing on hybrid legal orders such as the ASBO with which the state seeks to instil habits of respectable citizenship and secure civil order. Ashworth and Zedner examine how new techniques of 'responsibilization' are grafted onto existing criminal laws designed to police 'irregular' citizens who occupy precarious places at the margins, such as youth, those engaging in anti-social behaviour, the poor, and the homeless. They conclude by considering the implications of these developments for the attribution of responsibility both in and outside the criminal law. Duff takes a different approach—starting from the same text, he considers Lacey's four frameworks for understanding criminal responsibility—capacity, character, outcomes, and risk—and discusses just what these changing 'conceptions of responsibility' are conceptions *of*, and what it is that changes between them. He concludes that the ultimate change is best understood not as a change in the conception of responsibility, but rather as an abandonment of responsibility (answerability), in favour of kinds of liability that are detached from responsibility.

Part II contains four essays focusing on Gender and Ethics in Criminal Responsibility. The first, by Ngaire Naffine, returns to Lacey's consideration of the central characters in criminal law. Her paper interrogates the practice of theorizing

[19] Nicola Lacey, *In Search of Criminal Responsibility* (Oxford University Press 2016).

by criminal law scholars and takes issue with the dominant figure in the canon—'the criminal actor understood as a freestanding individual to whom responsibility can be properly assigned in a court of law, and who can be treated as an autonomous unit, removed from his group affiliations'. She sets this against the demographic or social model of the criminal person, the characters 'treated as members of a population that have certain criminal or law-abiding propensities rather than as separate distinct autonomous individuals'. Arguing that the English criminal law of rape adopts the former figure—'in effect, men are designated the exclusive class of persons at whom the law is directed'—she considers the work of legal philosopher John Gardner to elucidate how criminal law theorists who subscribe to this individualist model tackle a 'law which acknowledges its population of concern'.

It is perhaps appropriate that the word is immediately given to John Gardner. The second essay in this section engages directly with Lacey's enduring hesitancy about blame. In her later work, co-authored with Hanna Pickard, Lacey separated blame from responsibility, and explored ways in which responsibility could be assigned without blaming. Their suggestions have centred on the possibility of forgiveness. While admiring her humane instinct to urge us to do less blaming, Gardner interrogates what drives this instinct: is it possible to embrace forgiveness while holding those one forgives to be blameworthy or does forgiveness preclude blameworthiness? For him this makes the deeper puzzle about blameworthiness itself: what is it for, why does it matter, and what is its place in the architecture of the human condition? He argues that 'only when one works out why it matters that someone is blameworthy does one begin to show why people should ever do any blaming'. He suggests that the importance of blameworthiness is genuinely mysterious and concludes that while Lacey shares the same worries as Bernard Williams, they are not the right worries.

The theme of blame continues in the following essay by Hanna Pickard. While Gardner highlighted its moral purposes, Pickard examines the psychological function of blame and the consequences of responsibility ascriptions in relation to the crime of rape. Her essay draws upon recent work in the philosophy and science of causal cognition to argue that responsibility ascriptions, like explanations, are tethered to interests and perspectives: descriptive and prescriptive background norms affect not only what counts as a satisfying explanation of why something happened, but also who is singled out as the bearer of responsibility for what happened. She supports this argument using material taken from in-depth qualitative interviews with convicted rapists and empirical studies of the attitudes and factors that result in 'victim-blaming' within the general population, to detail the descriptive and prescriptive norms of rape culture. She suggests that use in court of a woman's violation of pervasive rape culture norms boomerangs blame for those violations on to her—as opposed to him—as the bearer of responsibility for what happened. She concludes that the 'psychological function and consequences of responsibility ascriptions may therefore contribute to the grotesque and persistent failure of the courts to convict and appropriately sentence rapists'.

Part II closes with an essay by Alan Norrie where he engages with Lacey's question on how legal forms of responsibility are generally configured. Norrie identifies two kinds of guilt and considers how the retributive theory of punishment sits in relation to them. He calls the two forms 'early' and 'mature', where the former entails a punitive and persecutory attitude of condemnation to a perpetrator and the latter an account which emphasizes restoration or atonement through making good. To develop these, Norrie draws on two lines in psychoanalytic theory, Melanie Klein's object relations approach, and the Hans Loewald and Jonathan Lear development of the later Freud's structural theory in terms of an ontology of love. He argues that retributivism tends to the punitive and persecutory but that an alternative guilt which is restorative and atoning might inform another retributive theory, one that is mature in its understanding of how serious violation should be addressed.

Part III, on Criminal Responsibility in Historical and Political Context, opens with an essay by Arlie Loughnan. Loughnan takes up another strand of Lacey's work by offering a reflection on time and space and criminal responsibility. She introduces the concept of 'interstitial space' as an analytical device to advance critical thinking on responsibility for crime. She suggests that the intellectual sphere of comparative jurisprudence around the turn of the twentieth century is an historical example of an interstitial space and argues that such interstitial spaces form part of the story of the development of ideas of responsibility for crime. Her examination of the first decades of the life of a key institutional text of comparative jurisprudence, the *Journal of the Society of Comparative Legislation*, shows that discussion of crime, punishment, and criminal justice encompassed an informative debates on responsibility for crime, with comparative jurisprudence revealing the connection between criminal responsibility and broader ideas about 'civilization' and 'progress', which themselves reflected power relations between states.

In answer to Lacey's identification of difficulties with interest analyses of law, Emily Jackson then turns attention to the interests that lurk behind ascriptions of responsibility. She argues that the core justification for the UK's 'blanket ban' on assisted suicide—namely that it is necessary in order to protect 'the vulnerable'—has tended to obscure two other important sets of interests. First, it has served to marginalize the interests of patients who are not vulnerable, and who have been used to exercising considerable control over their lives. There is evidence from countries which have legalized assisted dying that it is this non-vulnerable group of patients who are its principal users. Second, the core justification for the 'blanket ban' has deflected attention away from the interests of the medical profession itself, which in the UK has a long tradition of organized and powerful opposition to assisted suicide.

The final two essays engage with Nicola Lacey's work on political economy. Farmer sets the themes of criminalization and responsibility against the background of political economy. Drawing upon Lacey's analysis of variations in penal practices from the perspective of political economy in *The Prisoners' Dilemma*

(2008), he hones in on a central theme in her work—the development of criminal responsibility which links responsibility practices in modern criminal law to the interests and institutions central to the development of modern western capitalism. His essay explores the meaning and critical potential of the concept of political economy—how it is used by Lacey, the different traditions that she draws on—and what the perspective and theory of political economy contributes to our understanding of criminal law. He seeks to deepen the relevance of political economy to the analysis of criminal responsibility by exploring how the development of the modern conception of English criminal law in the early nineteenth century was itself shaped by contemporary understandings of political economy. In exploring the ways in which theories of political economy shaped the modern criminal law in this period, he opens up new possibilities for exploring connections between criminal law, criminal responsibility, and political economy—and thus for critical criminal law theory.

Finally, David Garland assesses Lacey's work on punishment and comparative political economy. He traces the trajectory of that work, describing how she was the first to bring the 'varieties of capitalism' framework to bear on the central questions of comparative penology and how she then proceeded to use an expanded version of the framework to develop an original explanation of American penal exceptionalism. The essay assesses this project by examining the theoretical fit between her political economy framework and the institutional characteristics of systems of criminal punishment, paying particular regard to the causal mechanism hypotheses that underpin her account.

On the following pages the reader will therefore discover engaging essays interrogating and furthering aspects of Lacey's scholarship on categorizations, characterization and the ethics of responsibility, or indeed intellectual methods—her encouragement to think across disciplines, time, and space and her refusal to adopt the traditional method of conceptual analysis in criminal law.

***

Alongside the joy and benefit that this book may hopefully bring to the honoree, its contributors, and readers, we remember with sadness Professor John Gardner who died in 2019, tragically young. Despite the difficult circumstances, he completed his chapter: it is poignant that his last essay was a tribute written in honour of the woman who taught him and was his long term mentor. Gone but not forgotten, he remains loved and his memory treasured.

Conspicuously absent from the list of contributors to this volume is another of Nicola Lacey's colleagues who died much too young—Professor Mike Redmayne. Had he not died in 2015, there is no doubt that he would have made an important contribution to this book. He enhanced the lives of everyone who worked with him and loved him. He continues to be hugely missed.

PART I

META APPROACHES TO CRIMINAL RESPONSIBILITY

1

'Technologies of Responsibility'

Social Order, Disorderly Citizens, and the State

Andrew Ashworth and Lucia Zedner[1]

1. Introduction

Academic scholarship on criminal responsibility has long been the domain of criminal law theory and of general jurisprudence. Nicola Lacey has made major contributions to both fields. Throughout her career, she has insisted that criminal responsibility is not solely a question of philosophy but one that should be addressed in its political, social, and economic context. Lacey's contextual approach attends to the ways in which criminal responsibility is mediated through the legal process and practices of criminal justice and allows for a more grounded account of the manner and means by which the state holds citizens to account for wrongdoing. In so doing, it draws attention to the centrality of the state–citizen relation, the demands the state places upon citizens and the protections offered in return, both against predation by others and, through due process and fair trial rights, against unwarranted state interference in citizens' lives.

In her superb and hugely important monograph, *In Search of Criminal Responsibility*, Nicola Lacey identifies four historically dominant conceptions of criminal responsibility—character responsibility, capacity responsibility, outcome responsibility, and, more recently, the rise of risk responsibility. She explores their historical development over the course of the past three centuries, tracing their rise, influence, decline, and resurgence. Lacey emphasizes the close intersection between these dominant paradigms of responsibility and the wider institutional conditions within which they are applied:

> there is a core to the idea of responsibility, a core related to the idea of human agency and accountability for conduct which acts as a constant thread amid shifting theories of responsibility over time and space. But this core is a relatively small one, and the inflection which it is given by varying social and institutional

[1] Andrew Ashworth is Emeritus Vinerian Professor of English Law and Emeritus Fellow of All Souls College, University of Oxford. Lucia Zedner is Senior Research Fellow, All Souls College and Professor, Faculty of Law, University of Oxford, and Conjoint Professor, Faculty of Law, UNSW, Sydney.

Andrew Ashworth and Lucia Zedner, *'Technologies of Responsibility'* In: *On Crime, Society, and Responsibility in the Work of Nicola Lacey.* Edited by: Iyiola Solanke, Oxford University Press (2021). © The several contributors.
DOI: 10.1093/oso/9780198852681.003.0002

> conditions and practical imperatives is so decisive that no theorist of criminal responsibility can afford to ignore it.[2]

This chapter takes up the challenge laid down by Lacey to explore these social and institutional conditions and, in particular, the legal strategies and measures with which the state seeks to instil habits of respectable citizenship and secure civil order. It draws upon Lacey's ground-breaking historical exploration of the changing relations between the individual and the state, and it addresses her contention that one can chart the history of a growing state 'confidence in the possibility of shaping the habits and dispositions of citizenhood'[3] through the criminal law and other legal measures. One intriguing conclusion of her analysis is that:

> We are seeing not so much a replacement of one paradigm of responsibility by another, but rather an accumulation of conceptions or 'technologies' of responsibility, as new legitimation problems and resources emerge without necessarily obliterating older ones.[4]

Lacey's insightful exploration of the use and significance of different 'technologies' of responsibility allows her to examine the means by which the state seeks to compel individuals into conformity with prevailing notions of the responsible subject or the 'good' citizen.

Our chapter takes up Lacey's influential ideas to examine, in section 2 below, the immediate background to these technologies in changing relations between the individual and the state. In section 3 we explore these technologies more closely, focusing on the array of civil, hybrid civil-criminal, and administrative orders introduced under the Anti-social Behaviour, Crime and Policing Act 2014 (ASB Act) to compel civility among those deemed disorderly. In section 4 we consider how far these new technologies fulfil their role of preserving civil order and how far they depart from basic principles of justice and fair procedure. Section 5 reflects on Lacey's claim that these technologies signal a growth in state confidence in shaping citizenhood to ask whether they might be better understood as attempts to apply regulatory fixes to the considerable challenges of modern state governance. These include the retreat from welfarism, the economic impact of globalization, greater public demand for state intervention in social relations, and limits to the capacity of criminal law to ensure conditions of 'social peace'. Section 6 concludes the chapter by observing that attempts to induce compliance among marginalized citizens overlook their incapacity or will to fulfil the demands imposed

[2] Nicola Lacey, *In Search of Criminal Responsibility: Ideas, Interests, and Institutions* (Oxford University Press 2016) 186–7.

[3] Ibid., 53.

[4] Ibid., 203.

upon them. Despite their promise to create responsible citizens, these technologies might better be seen as rights-eroding, character-based strategies of policing and crime control.

2. Changing Relations between the Individual and the State

In her monograph, *In Search of Criminal Responsibility*, in a section on 'Changing Relations between the Individual and the State', Lacey considers 'the increasing ambition of the state's governance of its population' historically and, as we noted above, she observes the growth of state confidence in shaping the citizen's habits and dispositions through criminal justice, as well as by more conventional welfare, education, and healthcare provision.[5] Lacey's interest in the state–citizen relation follows naturally from her longstanding exploration of the penal role of the state, and enquiry into what underpins state authority to criminalize, police, and punish, and the extent, limits, and justifications for the exercise of the state's coercive powers. Thus in her first major monograph, *State Punishment: Political Principles and Community Values*, Lacey identified punishment as 'a prima facie morally wrongful exercise by state officials of state power' that self-evidently required justification and raised further questions 'about the proper relationship between the state and its citizens'.[6] The hypothetical social contract is an enduring motif of liberal political theory which rests on the claim that the state alone has the capacity to guarantee civil order and stability, in return for which promise of protection citizens undertake to obey the law and submit to state authority, so long as it respects human rights. The birth of modern democracy saw sovereign state authority overlaid by the ideal of a democratic political community to which the individual is held accountable through prosecution, trial, and punishment,[7] as well as through informal mechanisms of community involvement. This largely theoretical account of the changing relationship between state and citizen calls for closer factually grounded scrutiny of the laws and legal institutions by which social order is mediated, of precisely the sort that much of Lacey's scholarship has supplied.[8]

An important focus of Lacey's more recent works has been the historical development of a criminal justice system founded upon individual accountability and state promotion of laws and measures that hold citizens to expectations of

[5] Ibid., 53–4.

[6] Nicola Lacey, *State Punishment: Political Principles and Community Values* (Routledge 1988) 14.

[7] Antony Duff, 'Responsibility, Citizenship and Criminal Law' in Antony Duff and StuartGreen (eds), *The Philosophical Foundations of the Criminal Law* (Oxford University Press 2011) 105–48.

[8] See e.g. Nicola Lacey, 'Institutionalising Responsibility: Implications for Jurisprudence' (2013) 4(1) Jurisprudence 1; Nicola Lacey, 'Social Policy, Civil Society and the Institutions of Criminal Justice' (2001) 26 Australian Journal of Legal Philosophy 7.

responsible citizenhood. As she points out, 'the project of securing civil order was itself premised on a very particular, modern construction of criminal law's subjects as responsible agents'.[9] Yet, the expectation of responsibility was not confined to criminal law alone. Lacey observes of the emergence of modern capacity-based governance that, '[n]ew regulatory institutions of governmental control, including but not restricted to criminal justice, assumed an ability to incentivize the formation of habits of good citizenship.'[10] Important too is the changing role of the community and of citizens in mediating between the state and the individual: Lacey identifies that 'a primary gatekeeper between social behaviour which might be defined as criminal and the process of formal criminalization is the ordinary citizen'.[11] It is the citizen who commonly reports a suspected offence and who thus acts as trigger to the criminal process, and, as we discuss in section 3 below, the community is increasingly empowered to inform criminal justice policy, for example by exerting influence on Police and Crime Commissioners and through legal instruments such as the Community Trigger.[12] State exercise of its police power is thus complicated by the expansion of the so-called 'policing family' to embrace ever greater civilian involvement.[13]

Facilitating community and individual involvement in crime control not only expands the power of non-state actors but also increasingly obliges them to take up quasi-police roles by imposing positive requirements upon individuals to report their fellow citizens for unlawful conduct and even mere transgressions of civil order. English criminal law now contains several offences of failure to report offending (or suspected offending) behaviour, failure to prevent offences, and failure to protect vulnerable individuals.[14] These may be seen as forms of 'active citizenship',[15] resulting from a 'responsibilization' of individuals and companies,[16] which in effect constitutes them as a primary crime-preventive agency. In terms

[9] Lacey, *In Search of Criminal Responsibility* (n. 2) 140.

[10] Lacey, *State Punishment* (n. 6) 143.

[11] Lacey, *In Search of Criminal Responsibility* (n. 2) 18.

[12] Trevor Jones, Tim Newburn, and David J Smith, 'Democracy and Police and Crime Commissioners' in Tim Newburn and Jill Peay (eds), *Policing: Politics, Culture and Control* (Hart Publishing 2012) 219–44; Kevin J Brown, 'The Community Trigger for Anti-Social Behaviour: Protecting Victims or Raising Unrealistic Expectations?' (2015) Criminal Law Review 488.

[13] The growth of private security has also had a very significant impact on the state's role, but it is beyond the scope of this chapter. See e.g. Ian Loader and Adam White, 'How Can We Better Align Private Security with the Public Interest? Towards a Civilizing Model of Regulation' (2016) 10 Regulation & Governance 1; Lucia Zedner, 'What Is Lost When Punishment Is Privatised?' in Tom Daems and Tom Vander Beken (eds), *Privatising Punishment in Europe?* (Routledge 2018) 167–86. This fragmentation of state power has implications also for punishment, see Nicola Lacey, 'Penal Practices and Political Theory: An Agenda for Dialogue' in Matt Matravers (ed.), *Punishment and Political Theory* (Hart Publishing 2000) 152–63, 159–62.

[14] Andrew Ashworth *Positive Obligations in Criminal Law* (Hart Publishing 2015).

[15] Andrew Ashworth, 'Positive Duties, Regulation and the Criminal Sanction' (2017) 133 Law Quarterly Review 606.

[16] Pat O'Malley, 'Responsibilization' in Alison Wakefield and Jenny Fleming (eds), *The Sage Dictionary of Policing* (Sage 2009) 276–8; Pat O'Malley, 'Risk, Power, and Crime Prevention' (1992) 21(3) Economy and Society 252–75.

of legal doctrine, the technology of responsibility being employed here is criminal liability for omissions—a controversial tool of English criminal law, even when the nature of the duty is clearly spelt out.[17]

Beyond these more recent examples of active citizenship, the citizen has long been recognized as a central figure in criminal law theory and in scholarship on criminalization. As Duff has observed, the citizen is the subject *whom* the criminal law addresses and it is citizens collectively *by whom* and *to whom* the citizen offender is called to account.[18] Citizenship figures centrally also in the constitutional relationships that underpin the state's authority to define and enforce the criminal law,[19] and the ways in which laws more generally define the rights and duties of citizens.[20] Lacey's own important contributions to these debates over several decades make clear the dual nature of the state–citizen relation in which the state stands both as protector and also as a major threat to individual liberty. While acknowledging that 'crime violates the duties of citizenship',[21] Lacey observes that 'the power to convict and punish represents the most vivid exercise of state force in relation to individual citizens'.[22] For this reason, she insists that 'criminal justice practices should be designed so as to recognise and respect the rights and responsibilities of all members of the community to the greatest degree which is compatible with a similar respect for others'.[23] This principle of equal respect further requires that criminal justice practices should be 'capable of being applied in an equitable and non-discriminatory way to members of different social groups' and in such a way as to respect social difference.[24] As Lacey's more recent work recognizes, the principle of equal respect is breached, both in form and practice, by the framing and discriminatory application of criminal laws and legal measures, not least the 'technologies of responsibility', which are a growing feature of contemporary crime control and social order. In order to understand just how these technologies are designed to operate, it is necessary to delve into the detail of the relevant legislation. Thus section 3 considers some of the more important measures introduced by the ASB Act that now govern responses to anti-social behaviour, before going on in section 4 to consider more critically the import and implications of these technologies.

17 Andrew Ashworth, 'A New Generation of Omissions Offences?' (2018) Criminal Law Review 354.

18 Antony Duff, 'Inclusion and Exclusion: Citizens, Subjects and Outlaws' (1998) 51 Current Legal Problems 241: Antony Duff, 'A Criminal Law for Citizens' (2010) 14(3) Theoretical Criminology 293.

19 Malcolm Thorburn, 'The Constitution of Criminal Law; Justifications, Policing and the State's Fiduciary Duties' (2011) 5 Criminal Law and Philosophy 259.

20 Ely Aharonson and Peter Ramsay, 'Citizenship and Criminalization in Contemporary Perspective' (2010) 13(2) New Criminal Law Review181, 181.

21 Lacey, 'Social Policy (n. 8) 19.

22 Ibid., 8.

23 Ibid., 13.

24 Ibid., 13–14.

3. The Technologies of Anti-Social Behaviour Legislation

New 'technologies of responsibility' have proliferated, in large part, as a consequence of the emergence of a new form of responsibility 'founded in risk'.[25] As Lacey acknowledges, risk responsibility 'equates to a more inchoate version of outcome responsibility',[26] that has been promoted by the development of actuarial tools of risk assessment and practices of prevention aimed at averting future harms.[27] These technologies are typically located in civil and administrative channels (albeit often backed by criminal punishment on breach) that do not require the 'stringent set of legitimating requirements for state criminalization and punishment' set by capacity responsibility.[28] As we shall see, although technologies of responsibility conform most closely with risk responsibility, they have the effect of reviving conceptions of character responsibility attribution that, as Lacey observes, are 'based on newly institutionalized forms of bad character'.[29]

The trend towards the 'responsibilization' of citizens to protect their persons, families, and property, and to contribute personally to crime prevention, for example through neighbourhood watch schemes, is well documented.[30] Less well observed is the degree to which this trend has also served as a form of social sorting that purports to distinguish decent, law-abiding citizens of 'good character' from those designated 'uncivil' or 'disorderly'. Ramsay has argued that the ideology of 'vulnerable autonomy', that has been applied to crime victims and all responsible citizens, stood behind moves to target anti-social behaviour under the Crime and Disorder Act 1998.[31] The ideology of vulnerability, he suggests, informed the state's commitment to target incivility, combat public anxiety, and provide reassurance with the ostensible aim of bringing about civic renewal.[32] The detrimental impact of anti-social behaviour on quality of life, particularly for those living in densely populated areas of inner cities, should not be dismissed as unimportant. Nor should the limitations of the criminal law in relation to minor but persistent incivilities be underestimated. However, the result of the 1998 Act was a significant

25 Lacey, *In Search of Criminal Responsibility* (n. 2) 46.
26 Ibid.
27 Andrew Ashworth and Lucia Zedner, *Preventive Justice* (Oxford University Press 2014).
28 Lacey, *In Search of Criminal Responsibility* (n. 2) 27.
29 Ibid., 103.
30 Pat O' Malley, 'Risk and Responsiblity' in Andrew Barry, Thomas Osborne, and Nikolas Rose (eds), *Foucault and Political Reason: Liberalism, Neo-Liberalism and Rationalities of Government* (UCL Press 1996) 189, 200; David Garland, *The Culture of Control: Crime and Social Order in Contemporary Society* (Oxford University Press 2001) 124–7.
31 Peter Ramsay, *The Insecurity State: Vulnerable Autonomy and the Right to Security in the Criminal Law* (Oxford University Press 2012) ch. 5.
32 Ibid. See also Andreas von Hirsch and AP Simester (eds), *Incivilities: Regulating Offensive Behaviour* (Hart Publishing 2006); Phil Edwards, 'New Asbos for Old?' (2015) 79(4) The Journal of Criminal Law 257.

erosion of legal protections for those subject to the Anti-Social Behaviour Orders (ASBOs) it introduced. ASBOs could be imposed in the civil process even though breach of the order was an offence punishable by imprisonment for up to five years.[33] These orders attracted considerable critical attention because they significantly expanded state police powers, allowed courts (applying civil law principles) to create personal criminal codes for individuals, undermined the protections of the criminal process, and targeted those who were already marginalized or vulnerable.[34] Nonetheless, the ASBO proved to be a powerful model for the subsequent proliferation of civil, hybrid civil-criminal, and administrative preventive orders.[35]

Mounting criticism of the ASBO led to its abolition by the ASB Act 2014; but, as Lacey demonstrates, the 2014 legislation deploys a range of other 'technologies of responsibility',[36] some of them entirely new. The first of the ASB Act's major themes was to create a more suitable and effective method of dealing with anti-social behaviour; its second major theme was to empower those subjected to anti-social behaviour to demand remedial action, as part of a broader agenda of 'putting victims first'.[37] In a bid to improve upon the technology of the ASBO, it was replaced by two forms of order. One is the Anti-social Behaviour Injunction,[38] which can be sought from the County Court, High Court, or (in the case of under-18s) the Youth Court; the court must be satisfied that the respondent has engaged or threatens to engage in anti-social behaviour, and that it is 'just and convenient' to grant the injunction to prevent the respondent from engaging in anti-social behaviour. The test of 'just and convenient', common to many injunctions, is far less demanding than the previous requirement that the order be 'necessary'; and the definition of anti-social behaviour still turns on the vague phrase 'conduct that has caused, or is likely to cause, harassment, alarm or distress' or, in housing cases, the even more expansive test of 'conduct capable of causing nuisance or annoyance to any person'.[39] Breach of the injunction is a contempt of court, and as such can attract up to two years' imprisonment.

[33] Andrew Ashworth, 'Social Control and Anti-Social Behaviour: The Subversion of Human Rights?' (2004) 120 Law Quarterly Review 263; Peter Ramsay, 'What Is Anti-Social Behaviour?' (2004) Criminal Law Review 908; Elizabeth Burney, *Making People Behave: Anti-Social Behaviour, Politics and Policy* (Willan Publishing 2005); Ashworth and Zedner, *Preventive Justice* (n. 27) 78–84.

[34] Peter Ramsay, 'Substantively Uncivilized Asbos' (2010) Criminal Law Review 761; Andrew Ashworth and Lucia Zedner, 'Preventive Orders: A Problem of Under-criminalization?' in Antony Duff et al. (eds), *The Boundaries of the Criminal Law* (Oxford University Press 2010); Craig Johnstone, 'After the Asbo: Extending Control over Young People's Use of Public Space in England and Wales' (2016) 36(4) Critical Social Policy 716.

[35] Ashworth and Zedner, 'Preventive Orders: A Problem of Under-criminalization?' (n. 34).

[36] Lacey, *In Search of Criminal Responsibility* (n. 2) 103–5.

[37] Home Office, *Putting Victims First: More Effective Responses to Anti-Social Behaviour* Cm 8367 (The Stationery Office 2012) at <https://assets.publishing.service.gov.uk/government/uploads/system/uploads/attachment_data/file/228863/8367.pdf>.

[38] ASB Act 2014, s. 1. See also Edwards, 'New Asbos for Old?' (n. 32) 262–5.

[39] ASB Act 2014, s. 2.

The second new order replacing the ASBO is the Criminal Behaviour Order (CBO).[40] Whereas the ASB Injunction can be made by a civil court (except where the respondent is under 18), the CBO can only be made on conviction by a criminal court. That court must be satisfied, to the criminal standard of 'beyond reasonable doubt', that the offender has caused or is likely to cause harassment, alarm, or distress, and that making the order would help to prevent further such acts. The order may stipulate prohibitions and/or requirements, any breach of which is punishable with up to five years' imprisonment.[41] These two orders, the ASB Injunction and the CBO, have been drafted in response to some of the criticisms of the ASBO. The CBO is confined to criminal proceedings and requires the criminal standard of proof. The Injunction is basically a civil remedy, although the requirement that the order be merely 'just and convenient' sets the bar problematically low.

The two orders take anti-social behaviour seriously, and are consistent with Ramsay's 'vulnerable autonomy' thesis already discussed,[42] which leads to the second theme of the Act, namely to empower those who are subjected to anti-social behaviour. Part 6 of the Act, entitled 'Local Involvement and Accountability', seeks to tackle persisting problems of anti-social behaviour at the local level by giving powers to local communities to demand action and to express their views through 'community representatives'.[43] The framing architecture of the Act devolves power and responsibility to local actors by requiring local police, councils, and landlords to respond to community concerns. The ASB Review (s. 105 ASB Act), or Community Trigger as it is better known, gives those who are subject to persistent anti-social behaviour the right to demand a formal case review and imposes an obligation on local officials to consult local police and relevant local bodies (including providers of social housing) and to disclose information requested by them in connection with the review.[44]

The Community Remedy (s. 101 ASB Act) also 'gives victims a say' in respect of community resolution disposals and conditional cautions.[45] The Statutory Guidance accompanying the 2014 Act describes the Community Remedy as 'a list of actions which may be chosen by the victim for the perpetrator to undertake in consequence of their behaviour or offending'.[46] The privileging of victim choice arises from an obligation on local councils to consult with the community as to 'what punitive, reparative or rehabilitative actions they would consider

[40] ASB Act 2014, s. 22.
[41] ASB Act 2014, s. 30.
[42] Ramsay, *The Insecurity State* (n. 31); see text at n. 31 above.
[43] ASB Act 2014, s. 101(5)(c) and s. 101(9).
[44] ASB Act 2014, Sch. 4.
[45] Home Office, *Anti-Social Behaviour, Crime and Policing Act 2014: Anti-Social Behaviour Powers Statutory Guidance* (Home Office 2017) 2 at <https://assets.publishing.service.gov.uk/government/uploads/system/uploads/attachment_data/file/679712/2017-12-13_ASB_Revised_Statutory_Guidance_V2.1_Final.pdf>
[46] Ibid., 12.

appropriate',[47] and in each individual case to invite the victim 'to choose an appropriate action', which the relevant officer should accept unless it is thought inappropriate.[48] Significantly these disposals are described as 'out of court punishments', a term that inappropriately applies the term 'punishment' to penalties imposed without formal proof of criminal liability or court proceedings. In practice, as the statutory guidance reveals, these disposals are not offender but victim-orientated. Their aim is to provide 'an important safety net for victims of persistent anti-social behaviour and those who may be most vulnerable' and to find 'a solution for the victim' 'while ensuring that the victim receives appropriate support'.[49] Yet as Lacey observes, although these provisions claim to involve community representatives, they actually give voice to 'basically whoever the police think represent the community'.[50]

While these community resolutions are designed to divert less serious offences from the trial process in cases where the perpetrator admits the behaviour or offence in question, such diversion comes at a cost. Diversion side-steps the criminal process, disregards the presumption of innocence (i.e. the obligation on the prosecution to prove criminal liability beyond all reasonable doubt), and circumvents the defendant's right to a fair trial under Article 6 of the European Convention on Human Rights (ECHR).[51] The use of the term 'victim' throughout the Statutory Guidance casually disregards the fact that no crime has been proven and no defendant found guilty of any offence, yet the Guidance requires that 'the welfare, safety and well-being of victims must be the main consideration at every stage of the process'.[52] Indeed, the Guidance even refers expansively to the future 'potential vulnerability' of victims.[53] This focus on the welfare and well-being of putative or potential victims comes at the obvious cost of due regard to the welfare, needs, and vulnerabilities of those who are the targets of the preventive orders introduced by the Act—the ASB Injunction and the CBO, described above.

This expanded notion of vulnerability was arguably driven partly by the introduction of locally elected Police and Crime Commissioners (PCCs) in 2010 who, as 'the voice of the people', have given new salience to local and community concerns.[54] Initiatives such as the PCCs and the later extension of police powers to

[47] Ibid., 12.
[48] Ibid., 13, applying ASB Act 2014, s. 102(4).
[49] Ibid., 3.
[50] Lacey, *In Search of Criminal Responsibility* (n. 2) 104–5. ASB Act 2014, s. 101(5)(c) specifies 'consultation with whatever community representatives the local policing body thinks it appropriate to consult'.
[51] Ryan Goss, *Criminal Fair Trial Rights: Article 6 of the European Convention on Human Rights* (Hart Publishing 2014).
[52] Home Office, *Anti-Social Behaviour, Crime and Policing Act 2014* (n. 45) 17.
[53] Ibid., 17.
[54] Fraser Sampson, 'Hail to the Chief?—How Far Does the Introduction of Elected Police Commissioners Herald a US-Style Politicization of Policing for the UK?' (2012) 6(1) Policing 4.

civilian volunteers[55] gave practical weight to popular concerns about civic disorder and insecurity.[56] The influence of community and voluntary organizations has further promoted 'citizen-led policing' that similarly tends to be focused on parochial concerns and quick to defend the perceived interests of the 'law-abiding majority' against the 'disorderly'.[57] Protection of the vulnerable therefore features prominently in recent developments in policing, and in both the new preventive orders (ASB Injunctions and CBOs). In addition, the new forms of community involvement (Community Remedy Documents and the Community Trigger), introduced by the ASB Act, shift the balance of power from those defined as 'disorderly' towards those described as 'victims,' aiming to give reassurance to the vulnerable and the potentially vulnerable.

These themes are further pursued in Part 4 of the ASB Act, entitled 'Community Protection,' which provides the legislative framework for the Community Protection Notice (CPN) and the Public Spaces Protection Order (PSPO). The CPN has attracted less popular concern and academic attention than some of the other new ASB powers, but it is no less problematic.[58] The CPN may be imposed in the case of conduct deemed by the local authority to be unreasonable and to have 'a detrimental effect, of a persistent or continuing nature, on the quality of life of those in the locality'.[59] The CPN may require individuals to refrain from such conduct or require them to do specified things or take steps to achieve specified results. Failure to comply is a criminal offence punishable by a fixed penalty notice of up to £100 or, on summary conviction, a level 4 fine (currently up to £2,500). The power to impose a CPN extends to a wide cast of actors including council officers, police, police community support officers, and social landlords. Although, formally, those issuing the Notice must first give a written warning and allow enough time for the individual to deal with the matter (s. 42(5)), this safeguard is undercut by the Statutory Guidelines, which allow that it 'could be a standard form of words, adaptable to any situation—for instance, a pre-agreed form of words that can be used by the officer on the spot'.[60] The result is to delegate very considerable summary powers to local council officials, allowing individual officers to impose CPNs—in effect giving them 'the power to act as legislator, judge and jury in relation to the conduct of private citizens'.[61]

55 Under the Policing and Crime Act 2017, see <https://www.hja.net/policing-crime-bill-proposals-give-new-powers-police-volunteers-reform-pre-charge-bail-raise-civil-liberties-concerns/>.

56 Sampson contends the introduction of PCCs creates 'the danger that local policing becomes driven by populist concerns about already marginalized groups' in Sampson, 'Hail to the Chief? (n. 54) 13.

57 See further Lacey, *In Search of Criminal Responsibility* (n. 2) 105, in which she argues that evidence from the United States shows that local control of criminal justice results in regulations being used disproportionately against the poor, with powers being used disproportionately by the privileged.

58 The Manifesto Club, 'CPNs: The Crime of Crying in your own Home' (2016) at <http://manifestoclub.info/cpns-report/>.

59 ASB Act 2014, s. 43(1)(a).

60 Home Office, *Anti-Social Behaviour, Crime and Policing Act 2014* (n. 45) 42.

61 The Manifesto Club, 'CPNs: The Anarchy of Arbitrary Power' (2017) at <http://manifestoclub.info/cpns-the-anarchy-of-arbitrary-power/>.

Even more controversial are PSPOs, set out in s. 59 of the ASB Act 2014, which may apply to a specified public space where an activity has had or is likely to have a 'detrimental effect on the quality of life of those in the locality', and which is or is likely to be 'persistent or continuing'.[62] The order may be purely preventive since the conduct need not yet have had a detrimental effect nor need it have persisted. The activity must further be 'unreasonable' and the restrictions imposed must be justified to prevent it from continuing, occurring, or recurring. PSPOs are administrative preventive orders[63] that may prohibit specified activities, require specified things to be done, or both. They may apply to specified persons or to all those in the designated space, at specified, or at all, times. The powers under PSPOs are very broad: activities prohibited range from the plausibly anti-social—dog fouling, abusive language, or abuse of alcohol—to activities more suggestive of individual need or poverty, such as lying down, rough sleeping, urinating in public, and begging. Some prohibitions appear discriminatory, such as prohibiting youths from gathering in groups of two or more.[64] The 'detrimental effect' of other activities targeted by existing PSPOs, such as busking, skateboarding, playing ball games, swimming, fishing, and even feeding birds, is more debatable.[65] Breach of any term of the order 'without reasonable excuse' (s. 67) may result in a Fixed Penalty Notice or prosecution for a criminal offence punishable by a fine (currently up to £1,000), non-payment of which may result in imprisonment.

PSPOs target and exclude those engaging in incivilities from public space and public life. In so doing there is a risk that PSPOs perpetuate an existing trend towards summary justice that undermines the protections owed to citizens under the criminal process,[66] not least because their prohibitions and requirements are set out in overly broad and vague terms that fail to provide fair warning and make compliance difficult. Moreover, the orders can be enforced by local officials, volunteers, and even private security agents, as well as police, without proper evidence or due process protections. Given that urban public spaces are disproportionately inhabited by the young, the poor, and the homeless, the impact of PSPOs potentially falls most heavily on already vulnerable and marginalized populations. These orders formally apply universally to all those within a designated area. However, in content and in application, they target particular groups who are judged otherwise incapable of fulfilling the expectations of civility but with precious little regard to

[62] See Kevin J Brown, 'The Hyper-Regulation of Public Space: The Use and Abuse of Public Spaces Protection Orders in England and Wales' (2017) 37(3) Legal Studies 543.

[63] On preventive orders see Ashworth and Zedner, *Preventive Justice* (n. 27) ch. 4.

[64] Such a prohibition has been applied to parts of the city of Oxford. See Lucia Zedner, 'Policing Civility in Public Space and the Exclusion of "Uncivil" Citizens' in Olivier Beaud (ed.), *La Citoyenneté Comme Appurtenance Au Corps Politique* (Editions Panthéon-Assas 2021).

[65] <http://manifestoclub.info/wp-content/uploads/2016/02/Data-PSPOs-passed.pdf>.

[66] Andrew Ashworth and Lucia Zedner, 'Defending the Criminal Law: Reflections on the Changing Character of Crime, Procedure, and Sanctions' (2008) 2 Criminal Law and Philosophy 21, 24–31.

their capacity to comply with the conditions imposed.[67] Nor do these orders do anything to tackle the underlying social, addiction, or mental health problems that lead some people to live much of their lives on the street.[68]

This section has surveyed just some of the more prominent technologies of responsibility introduced by the ASB Act. But as Selmini and Crawford point out, 'rather than operating in isolation, such novel administrative tools often form interconnected parts of a larger whole—a "regulatory ecosystem"—which interacts with the wider socioeconomic and political landscape'.[69] In the next section, we explore further the interrelation between these tools, as well as their interaction with the background social and political conditions of their deployment, in order to delve further into the question of how these orders frame and alter relations between state and citizen.

4. Technologies of Responsibility, Social Peace, and the Good Citizen

In political and legal theory, it is often said that the state exists to provide—or at least to offer some assurance of—what is variously called 'social peace', 'civility', or 'civil order'. MacCormick, for example, argues that the role of the institution of the criminal law is to underpin and enforce conditions of civility and good order and to impose restraints upon human interaction thought necessary for peaceful coexistence. He argues that 'the most basic demand citizens ought to make of criminal law is that it contributes to securing conditions of civility and social peace'.[70] The claim here is that to commit a crime is to violate the conditions of social peace.[71] However, the difficulty is to define social peace, to secure consensus as to what constitutes civility or reasonable enjoyment of public space, and to craft legal provisions that preserve civil order without unduly curtailing individual liberty. While the aims of the ASB Act 2014, considered in section 3 above, might be said to promote social peace, the technologies of responsibility deployed in this legislation may be thought to accede too readily to community demands and place too little weight on individual liberty or a person's capacity for compliance.

As we saw in section 3 above, both the ASB Injunction and the CBO turn on evidence that a person's behaviour caused or was likely to cause 'harassment, alarm

[67] Rossella Selmini and Adam Crawford, 'The Renaissance of Administrative Orders and the Changing Face of Urban Social Control' (2017) 23 European Journal on Criminal Policy and Research 1, 6.

[68] Zedner, 'Policing Civility' (n. 64) (see n. 57).

[69] Selmini and Crawford, 'The Renaissance of Administrative Orders' (n. 67) 4.

[70] Neil MacCormick, *Institutions of Law: An Essay in Legal Theory* (Oxford University Press 2007) 221.

[71] Anthony E Bottoms, 'Civil Peace and Criminalization' in R Antony Duff et al. (eds) *Criminalization: The Political Morality of the Criminal Law* (Oxford University Press 2014) 232.

or distress', a much-used but still imprecise term. It seems that, at a minimum, the causing of 'harassment, alarm or distress' must involve some 'emotional disturbance or upset' on the part of the putative victim.[72] One key question is whether the causing of 'harassment, alarm or distress', thus defined, is a sufficiently significant wrong to justify either criminalization or the imposition of one of the preventive orders created by the ASB Act 2014, such as the ASB Injunction or the CBO. In other words, the question is whether the terms 'harassment, alarm or distress' are too vague to support such powerful preventive orders, or whether (if they do not fail the vagueness test) they draw the line of responsibility too low.

Similar questions may be asked about the other form of anti-social behaviour addressed by the 2014 Act: 'conduct capable of causing nuisance or annoyance to a person in relation to that person's occupation of residential premises'.[73] It would seem that the ASB Injunction and the CBO are attempts by the state to 'shape the habits and dispositions of citizenhood', of the sort that Lacey has described,[74] by using preventive orders to target behaviour identified as 'disorderly' and to sanction those who persist in engaging in it. Seen this way, these 'technologies of responsibility' consist of preventive orders that are based on nebulous standards of liability and yet are backed up by punitive sanctions. Failure to comply with the terms of an ASB Injunction constitutes a contempt of court, punishable with imprisonment up to a maximum of two years; failure to comply with the terms of a CBO is a criminal offence with a maximum sentence of five years' imprisonment. Thus, although the term 'technology' might seem to imply a coolly neutral, mechanistic approach, these technologies of responsibility have considerable punitive bite.

Similar problems arise in respect of other parts of the 2014 Act. Both the CPN (applicable to persons) and the PSPO (applicable to specified places) pertain to conduct or activity that has, or is likely to have, a 'detrimental effect, of a persistent or continuing nature, on the quality of life of those in the locality'. These orders have similar features in that they entail a vague but even less demanding standard of liability, and the consequences of failure to comply with the terms imposed are correspondingly less harsh, inasmuch as they involve financial penalties and not imprisonment. However, the CPN and the PSPO, as well as the ASB Injunction and the CBO, can be said to valorize a particular conception of civility that is friendly to respectable citizens, to the interests of commerce, the affluent consumer, and the well-heeled worker, but markedly less tolerant of those who do not or who, often for reasons of destitution, substance abuse, or mental incapacity, are unable to conform.

[72] *R(R) v. DPP* (2006) 170 JP 661; see further David Ormerod and Karl Laird, *Smith, Hogan and Ormerod's Criminal Law 15th ed* (Oxford University Press 2018) ch. 31.6.1.
[73] ASB Act 2014, s. 2(1(b).
[74] Lacey, *In Search of Criminal Responsibility* (n. 2) 53–4.

Lacey rightly recognizes that 'several of these new forms of preventive order impose what is in effect a form of highly targeted status liability'.[75] Individuals whose lifestyles, habits, or activities are deemed to contravene prevailing notions of civility and who, in consequence, are found to fall into the class of uncivil or disorderly citizens are subject to a growing raft of prohibitions, positive conduct requirements, and exclusion from prescribed public spaces—resulting in 'serious social effects, for example on homelessness'.[76] Moreover, the orders discussed in this chapter are far from isolated examples. Rather they are symptomatic of a growing number of criminal, civil, administrative, and regulatory measures that play an increasingly legalized, even punitive role in social ordering.[77] As Lacey wryly concludes, the underlying assumption appears to be 'if we can simply detain or "take out" enough of [those of "bad" character] the world will be a safer place for those of "good character"'.[78] There is, it would seem, a fragile line between conduct- and character-based liability.

While, as Lacey observes, the 2014 Act 'significantly pushes outwards the terrain of hybrid and *de facto* criminalization',[79] it sits alongside other expansions of the criminal law such as the creation of pre-inchoate offences that 'push the boundaries of criminalization back in time'.[80] It was argued in section 2 above that the criminal law is also being used to alter the relationship between individuals and the state, notably by the expansion of offences of omission. This is part of the drive towards active citizenship: it is evident in the criminalization of failures to report offences, failures to prevent crimes, and failures to protect vulnerable individuals.[81] It is also evident, as noted in section 3 above, in the provisions of the 2014 Act that impose a duty on each local policing body to draw up a 'Community Remedy Document', creating the individual victim's power to select a community remedy to be carried out by the 'anti-social person', and introducing a 'Community Trigger', to force a review of the response to anti-social behaviour locally. Whereas the new generation of omissions offences *requires* active citizenship, the enhanced role of the 'victim' in the 2014 Act consists largely of *powers* to be exercised by the 'victim' in respect of the 'anti-social person'. Once again, these are different technologies of responsibility, situated in different political contexts; notably, in respect of the 2014 Act, the agenda of giving 'victims' a voice. This twin-pronged approach is consistent with O'Malley's observation that responsibilization has involved simultaneously

[75] Ibid., 159.
[76] Ibid., 104.
[77] See further R Kelly *Behaviour Orders: Preventive and/or Punitive Measures?* (DPhil, University of Oxford 2019). On the development of similar technologies across Europe, see European Journal on Criminal Policy and Research Special Issue: 'The Renaissance of Administrative Orders and the Changing Face of Urban Social Control' (2017) 23(1).
[78] Lacey, *In Search of Criminal Responsibility* (n. 2) 154.
[79] Ibid., 104.
[80] Ibid., 102.
[81] Ashworth, 'A New Generation of Omissions Offences?' (n. 17) 354–64.

imposing new obligations upon citizens and yet also empowering them to make more demands of the justice system.[82]

One aspect of the technologies of responsibility employed by the 2014 Act is that some of them diverge egregiously from basic principles of justice. Not only is the 'Community Remedy Document' to be drawn up by the local policing body, having consulted whatever community representatives the local policing body thinks appropriate and conducted whatever other public consultation is thought appropriate—a formulation that bestows enormous discretion on the police—but the enforcement of CPNs and PSPOs is placed in the hands of the local authority and their officers, or may even be sub-contracted to private companies. As Lacey observes of these provisions:

> These extend discretionary power well beyond criminal justice agencies, in a decentralizing move which is remarkably reminiscent of some of the features of the *ancien regime* system which was swept away in the eighteenth century.[83]

Given the relatively vague standards of behaviour deployed in the 2014 Act ('detrimental effect on quality of life'; 'harassment, alarm or distress'; 'nuisance and annoyance'), the discretionary elements in the enforcement of the legislation loom even larger. Moreover, there appears to be no framework of accountability for the use of these powers. By contrast to existing byelaws, the government chose not to introduce central oversight or reporting requirements for PSPOs on the grounds of seeking to 'reduce bureaucracy'.[84] As a consequence, it is difficult to know exactly how and in what ways PSPO powers are used in practice, a state of affairs that impedes transparency and accountability.

What we have described so far is a range of technologies of responsibility deployed in the 2014 Act. On the one hand, there are preventive orders based on vague standards of liability and reinforced by the criminal law with more or less severe sanctions, some of the orders being enforced by local officials. On the other hand, there are different technologies of responsibility within the criminal law, notably pre-inchoate offences and crimes of omission. A further technology is that which empowers victims to select the community resolution in the particular case, enabling the case to be dealt with by diverting it from the criminal process—thus sparing the defendant the stigma and sanctions of the formal process but also bypassing the protections of due process and the defendant's fair trial rights.

[82] In addition, of course, to the more conventional usage of holding offenders responsible for their actions. O'Malley, 'Responsibilization' (n. 16) 276–7.

[83] Lacey, *In Search of Criminal Responsibility* (n. 2) 104. Similar observations are made in Lucia Zedner, 'Policing before and after the Police: The Historical Antecedents of Contemporary Crime Control' (2006) 46(1) British Journal of Criminology 78.

[84] See Brown, 'The Hyper-Regulation of Public Space' (n. 62) 558.

5. State Confidence in Shaping Citizenhood

Having delved deeper into the intricacies of just some of the technologies of responsibility being currently deployed, we can return to consider whether, as Lacey suggests, their use demonstrates growing state 'confidence in the possibility of shaping the habits and dispositions of citizenhood' through the criminal law and other legal measures. This suggestion raises several possibilities.

First, the proliferation of laws and measures that target conduct and character may be reflective less of growing confidence in legalism than of a loss of faith in more traditional mechanisms of socialization. That is, resort to legal measures may be driven less by belief in their superior regulatory capacity than by recognition of the decline of investment in welfare provision, healthcare, education, and family services. The post-war Welfare State is commonly portrayed as a period of benign state assistance to those in need, but there has always been a strongly regulatory aspect to welfare, and its provision was partially restricted to those considered 'deserving' of state aid.[85] Furthermore, public assistance was often made contingent on individuals' ability and willingness to abide by prescriptive criteria of respectability: as Koch has observed, post-war recipients of council housing were obliged to abide by 'moralistic criteria of upkeep and cleanliness' or risk losing their homes.[86] While the commitment to 'shaping habits and dispositions of citizenhood' through governmental intervention thus has a longer history, the state's capacity to do so is significantly altered by the decline of the Welfare State.

Garland famously suggested that the 'collapse of faith in correctionalism began a wave of demoralization', which gave rise to a new culture of repressive crime control.[87] Lacey has challenged his 'counsel of despair', however, on the grounds that many countries manage to sustain a more moderate penal politics in the post-welfare era.[88] This was, as Lacey acknowledges, rather less true in the United Kingdom. Following the 2008 financial crisis, a political commitment to austerity led to the imposition of stringent funding cuts on social services. These cuts left the police and the criminal justice system to deal with many of the consequences of diminished welfare provision, not least increased poverty, alcohol and drug addiction, and a growing population of rough sleepers many of whom had been discharged from institutional care, and required the police to do so with diminished

[85] David Garland, *The Welfare State: A Very Short Introduction* (Oxford University Press 2016) chs 4 and 6; Insa Koch, *Personalizing the State: An Anthropology of Law, Politics, and Welfare in Austerity Britain* (Oxford University Press 2018) 38, 39–44.

[86] Ibid., 42.

[87] Garland, *The Culture of Control* (n. 30) 61.

[88] Nicola Lacey, *The Prisoners' Dilemma: Political Economy and Punishment in Contemporary Democracies* (Cambridge University Press 2008) 25.

resources. Arming the police and other officials with powers to impose coercive behaviour orders may be a cheap technological fix, but the hurdles to conformity faced, for example, by the homeless in cities with insufficient social housing and inadequate hostel provision, raise the question whether state confidence in such technologies is misplaced.[89]

Secondly, increasing resort to criminal law and to preventive orders may be indicative less of growing state confidence than the adverse impact of globalization. As Lacey has herself observed, globalization has made national economies increasingly interdependent and has diminished state sovereignty with the result that 'in an increasingly unpredictable and culturally disembedded world, these dynamics have led to a greater resort to criminal justice policy as a tool of social governance'.[90] However, as Lacey has also been careful to note, the manner in which this shift plays out varies considerably depending on differences in political economy and national culture. Thus, a co-ordinated market economy, such as the Netherlands, with relatively stable structures of investment and a highly co-ordinated governmental structure is more likely to develop a relatively inclusionary criminal justice policy.[91] However, a liberal market economy such as Britain, with a more individualistic social structure and less interventionist government, is more likely to rely upon more exacting, and potentially more exclusionary, legal measures of the sort described above.[92]

Thirdly, whereas confidence in shaping the habits and dispositions of citizenhood through legal measures might be thought indicative of faith in the power of expertise, it is generally recognized that trust in expert knowledge has instead declined.[93] In its place we see the growth in influence of populism, the increased empowerment of 'victims', and greater weight given to local preoccupations and concerns.[94] Successive UK governments have declared their willingness to prioritize the interests of 'decent people ... to respect and courtesy'[95] and to take a less tolerant view of those who do not conform.[96] Resort to criminal laws and other legal measures designed to regulate the social conduct and habits of the young, the

89 Terry Skolnik, 'Homelessness and the Impossibility to Obey the Law' (2016) 43(3) Fordham Urban Law Journal 741; Jeremy Waldron, 'Homelessness and Community' (2000) 50(4) University of Toronto Law Journal 371.

90 Lacey, *The Prisoners' Dilemma* (n. 88) 25.

91 Ibid., 58.

92 Ibid., 59.

93 Ian Loader, '"Fall of the Platonic Guardians": Liberalism, Criminology and Political Responses in England and Wales' (2006) 46(4) British Journal of Criminology 561

94 Ramsay, *The Insecurity State* (n. 31) ch. 5.

95 <http://webarchive.nationalarchives.gov.uk/20070306080821/http://www.respect.gov.uk/>.

96 In 2010, the then Home Secretary Theresa May said, 'Some people seem to believe anti-social behaviour is just a bit of a nuisance—a fact of modern life—but I believe it is time for us to stop tolerating it. Anti-social behaviour ruins neighbourhoods and can escalate into serious criminality, destroying good people's lives.' Teresa May 'Moving Beyond the ASBO' (July 2010) at <https://www.gov.uk/government/speeches/crime-home-secretarys-speech-on-moving-beyond-the-asbo-28-july-2010>.

poor, the marginalized, and the homeless thus appear less as signs of state confidence than of declining mutual regard and trust, and growing political and public intolerance of anti-social behaviour. As such, resort to regulatory laws and preventive orders appears less indicative of state confidence, than a direct response to populist demands to respond to wider social and economic problems. Under public pressure to do something about disorder, government has responded with the cheap, technical fix of behavioural orders and the promise that these measures empower local officials to prescribe standards of conduct, and to prohibit or even banish those who fail to conform.[97]

Fourthly, might the deployment of technologies of responsibility such as the preventive orders introduced by the 2014 Act, the new generation of omissions offences, pre-inchoate crimes, and so forth, be indicative of a governmental response to pressure to portray itself as effective in the field of social policy? Garland has pointed out that governments may not be able to regulate crime but they can certainly regulate punishment;[98] and Lacey adds that 'criminalization is symbolically decisive and does not require the creation of new institutional infrastructure'.[99] On this line of argument, the technologies of responsibility considered in section 3 have been deployed largely because they are low cost and politically attractive, particularly at times when the government appears otherwise unable to reduce rates of crime and anti-social behaviour. Anti-social behaviour is a problem that particularly blights the lives of the poor and vulnerable. However, targeting anti-social behaviour through negative proscriptions backed up by sanctions does little to address the underlying social problems of inner-city life, exacerbated by austerity politics, the retrenchment of state expenditure on welfare, and resultant structural deficits in housing provision, mental health, and social care. Thus the question remains whether protection against anti-social behaviour ought to take the legal form of the technologies of responsibility introduced under the 2014 Act. In answer, we are minded to recall Lacey's observation that 'the nature of criminal justice power may be seen as a telling index of how humane and civilised a society really is'.[100]

[97] Andrew Rutherford, 'Criminal Policy and the Eliminative Ideal' (1997) 31 Social Policy and Administration 5, 116–35; Jock Young, *The Exclusive Society: Social Exclusion, Crime and Difference in Late Modernity* (Sage 1999). On the United States see Katherine Beckett and Steve Herbert, *Banished: The New Social Control in Urban America* (Oxford University Press 2009); Katherine Beckett and Steve Herbert, 'Penal Boundaries: Banishment and the Expansion of Punishment' (2010) 35(1) *Law and Social Inquiry* 1.

[98] Garland has observed, 'There is an emerging distinction between the *punishment of criminals* which remains the business of the state (and becomes one again a significant symbol of state power) and the *control of crime*, which is increasingly deemed to be "beyond the state"'. Garland, *The Culture of Control* (n. 30) 120.

[99] Lacey, *In Search of Criminal Responsibility* (n. 2) 105.

[100] Lacey, 'Social Policy (n. 8) 8.

6. Conclusion

The emphasis of the 2014 Act was on providing 'fast and effective responses' to anti-social behaviour through informal, early intervention designed 'to reinforce the message that anti-social behaviour is not tolerated'.[101] The source of such thinking can be traced to the zero tolerance stance promoted by the, now largely discredited, 'broken windows' school of crime prevention.[102] Today, the primary target appears to have moved from broken windows to what might aptly be called 'broken people'.

Provisions such as the ASB Injunction, the CBO, the CPN and the PSPO directly target 'inadequate' or 'irregular' citizens who already occupy precarious places at the margins of society: youth engaging in anti-social behaviour, the poor, unemployed, the homeless, drug and alcohol dependents, and the mentally ill. They have been made the subject of legal orders that are designed to shape the 'habits and dispositions of citizenhood', but they are often applied to a population who do not or cannot fulfil the standards expected of the autonomous responsible citizen that is the presumed subject of liberal criminal law. Moreover, these diverse powers do not replace criminal laws but engraft new technologies of responsibility on to existing institutions of criminal justice to layer further burdens of conformity but offer little by way of support or the means to reintegration. Technologies of responsibility assume the ability of those targeted to conform to the legal requirements placed upon them, yet they hold individuals to standards of civility that may be difficult to meet in conditions of declining welfare provision and increasing deprivation. The high rates of breach only attest to the ineffectiveness of these measures as technical fixes to deeper socio-economic problems.

In her highly accomplished and illuminating tracing of the historical evolution of responsibility, Lacey acknowledges 'the subterranean survival of character',[103] and it is indeed evident that character is alive and well in the persistent characterization of individuals as 'anti-social' or 'disorderly' citizens. Arguably, the legal regulation of bad character has not merely survived but, by evading the criminal law and its attendant procedural protections, has led to the proliferation of measures that are less transparent, less well regulated, and yet scarcely less intrusive upon individual rights. Lacey has long made hugely important contributions to legal scholarship generally, to legal, feminist, and penal theory and, more recently, to legal history. Her historical research provides a fascinating account of the changing ways and means by which the state attributes responsibility and a timely reminder of the hazards of responsibility attribution based on character. In so doing,

[101] Home Office, *Anti-Social Behaviour, Crime and Policing Act 2014* (n. 45) 17.

[102] George L Kelling and Catherine M Coles, *Fixing Broken Windows: Restoring Order and Reducing Crime in Our Communities* (Free Press 1996). For a powerful counterblast to the broken windows thesis see, Bernard E Harcourt, *Illusion of Order: The False Promise of Broken Windows Policing* (Harvard University Press 2001).

[103] Lacey, *In Search of Criminal Responsibility* (n. 2) 148.

she lays bare the state's claim to be able to be able to create the responsible subject or the good citizen through legal 'technologies' alone and invites us to reflect more deeply on the use, and abuse, of law in late modern society.

Bibliography

Aharonson, E and Ramsay, P, 'Citizenship and Criminalization in Contemporary Perspective' (2010) 13 New Criminal Law Review 2

Ashworth, A, 'A New Generation of Omissions Offences?' (2018) Criminal Law Review 354

Ashworth, A, 'Positive Duties, Regulation and the Criminal Sanction' (2017) 133 Law Quarterly Review 606

Ashworth, A, *Positive Obligations in Criminal Law* (Hart 2015)

Ashworth, A, 'Social Control and Anti-Social Behaviour: the Subversion of Human Rights?' (2004) 120 Law Quarterly Review 263.

Ashworth, A and Zedner, L, 'Preventive Orders: A Problem of Under-criminalization?' in RA Duff et al. (eds), *The Boundaries of the Criminal Law* (Oxford University Press 2010)

Ashworth, A and Zedner, L, 'Defending the Criminal Law: Reflections on the Changing Character of Crime, Procedure, and Sanctions' (2008) 2 Criminal Law and Philosophy 21

Ashworth, A and Zedner, L, *Preventive Justice* (Oxford University Press 2014)

Beckett, K and Herbert, S, 'Penal Boundaries: Banishment and the Expansion of Punishment' (2010) 35 Law and Social Inquiry 1

Beckett, K and Herbert, S, *Banished: The New Social Control in Urban America* (Oxford University Press 2009)

Bottoms, AE, 'Civil Peace and Criminalization' in RA Duff et al. (eds), *Criminalization: The Political Morality of the Criminal Law* (Oxford University Press 2014)

Brown, KJ, 'The Hyper-regulation of Public Space: The Use and Abuse of Public Spaces Protection Orders in England and Wales' (2017) 37 Legal Studies 3

Brown, KJ, 'The Community Trigger for Anti-Social Behaviour: Protecting Victims or Rising Unrealistic Expectations?' (2015) Criminal Law Review 488

Burney, E, *Making People Behave: Anti-social Behaviour, Politics and Policy* (Willan Publishing 2005)

Duff, RA, 'Responsibility, Citizenship and Criminal Law' in RA Duff and S Green (eds), *The Philosophical Foundations of the Criminal Law* (Oxford University Press 2011)

Duff, RA, 'A Criminal Law for Citizens' (2010) 14 Theoretical Criminology 3

Duff, RA, 'Inclusion and Exclusion: Citizens, Subjects and Outlaws' (1998) 51 Current Legal Problems 241

Edwards, P, 'New ASBOs for Old?' (2015) 79 The Journal of Criminal Law 4

Garland, D, *The Welfare State: A Very Short Introduction* (Oxford University Press 2016)

Garland, D, *The Culture of Control: Crime and Social Order in Contemporary Society* (Oxford University Press 2001)

Goss, R, *Criminal Fair Trial Rights: Article 6 of the European Convention on Human Rights* (Hart Publishing 2014)

Harcourt, BE, *Illusion of Order: The False Promise of Broken Windows Policing* (Harvard University Press 2001)

Home Office, *Anti-social Behaviour, Crime and Policing Act 2014: Anti-social Behaviour Powers Statutory guidance* (Home Office 2017)

Home Office, *Putting Victims First: More Effective Responses to Anti-Social Behaviour* Cm 8367 (The Stationery Office 2012)

Johnstone, C, 'After the Asbo: Extending Control over Young People's Use of Public Space in England and Wales'(2016) 36 Critical Social Policy 4

Jones, T, Newburn, T, and Smith, DJ, 'Democracy and Police and Crime Commissioners' in T Newburn and J Peay (eds), *Policing: Politics, Culture and Control* (Hart 2012)

Kelling, GL and Coles, CM, *Fixing Broken Windows: Restoring Order and Reducing Crime in Our Communities* (Free Press 1996)

Kelly, R, *Behaviour Orders: Preventive and/or Punitive Measures?* (DPhil, University of Oxford 2019)

Koch, I, *Personalizing the State: An Anthropology of Law, Politics, and Welfare in Austerity Britain* (Oxford University Press 2018)

Lacey, N, *In Search of Criminal Responsibility: Ideas, Interests, and Institutions* (Oxford University Press 2016)

Lacey, N, 'Institutionalising Responsibility: Implications for Jurisprudence' (2013) 4 Jurisprudence 1

Lacey, N, *The Prisoners' Dilemma: Political Economy and Punishment in Contemporary Democracies* (Cambridge University Press 2008)

Lacey, N, 'Social Policy, Civil Society and the Institutions of Criminal Justice' (2001) 26 Australian Journal of Legal Philosophy 7

Lacey, N, 'Penal Practices and Political Theory: An Agenda for Dialogue' in M Matravers (ed.), *Punishment and Political Theory* (Hart Publishing 2000)

Lacey, N, *State Punishment: Political Principles and Community Values* (Routledge 1988)

Loader, I, 'Fall of the "Platonic Guardians": Liberalism, Criminology and Political Responses in England and Wales' (2006) 46 British Journal of Criminology 4

Loader, I and White, A, 'How Can we Better Align Private Security with the Public Interest? Towards a Civilizing Model of Regulation' (2016) Regulation & Governance 10

MacCormick, N, *Institutions of Law: An Essay in Legal Theory* (Oxford University Press 2007)

O'Malley, P, 'Responsibilization' in A Wakefield and J Fleming (eds), *The Sage Dictionary of Policing* (SAGE 2009)

O'Malley, P, 'Risk and Responsiblity' in A Barry, T Osborne, and N Rose (eds), *Foucault and Political Reason: Liberalism, Neo-Liberalism and Rationalities of Government* (UCL Press 1996)

O'Malley, P, 'Risk, Power, and Crime Prevention' (1992) 21(3) Economy and Society 252

Ormerod, D and Laird, K, *Smith, Hogan and Ormerod's Criminal Law 15th ed* (Oxford University Press 2018)

Ramsay, P, *The Insecurity State: Vulnerable Autonomy and the Right to Security in the Criminal Law* (Oxford University Press 2012)

Ramsay, P, 'Substantively Uncivilized ASBOs' (2010) Criminal Law Review 761

Ramsay, P, 'What is Anti-Social Behaviour?' (2004) Criminal Law Review 908

Rutherford, A, 'Criminal Policy and the Eliminative Ideal' (1997) 31 Social Policy and Administration 5

Sampson, F, 'Hail to the Chief?—How Far Does the Introduction of Elected Police Commissioners Herald a US-Style Politicization of Policing for the UK?' (2012) 6 Policing 1

Selmini, R and Crawford, A, 'The Renaissance of Administrative Orders and the Changing Face of Urban Social Control' (2017) 23 European Journal on Criminal Policy and Research 1

Skolnik, T, 'Homelessness and the Impossibility to Obey the Law' (2016) 43 Fordham Urban Law Journal 3
Thorburn, M, 'The Constitution of Criminal Law; Justifications, Policing and the State's Fiduciary Duties' (2011) 5 Criminal Law and Philosophy 259
von Hirsch, A and Simester, AP (eds), *Incivilities: Regulating Offensive Behaviour* (Hart Publishing 2006)
Waldron, J, 'Homelessness and Community' (2000) 50 University of Toronto Law Journal 4
Young, J, *The Exclusive Society: Social Exclusion, Crime and Difference in Late Modernity* (SAGE 1999)
Zedner, L, 'Policing Civility in Public Space and the Exclusion of "Uncivil" Citizens' in O Beaud (ed.), *La Citoyenneté comme appurtenance au corps politique* (editions Panthéon-Assas 2021)
Zedner, L, 'What Is Lost when Punishment is Privatised?' in T Daems and T Vander Beken (eds), *Privatising Punishment in Europe?* (Routledge 2018)
Zedner, L, 'Policing before and after the Police: The Historical Antecedents of Contemporary Crime Control' (2006) 46 British Journal of Criminology 1

2

Searching for Criminal Responsibility

What Are We Looking for?

Antony Duff[1]

1. Introduction

Nicola Lacey's 2016 book, *In Search of Criminal Responsibility*,[2] brings together some of the central themes of her work over the last two decades: it provides an argument for a particular kind of cross-disciplinary methodology in criminal law theory, but also an exercise in such theorizing to explicate 'the idea of responsibility' in English criminal law—more precisely, the 'broad trends' that can be discerned in the 'alignment[s]' of the 'multiple patterns of responsibility-attribution' in the history of English criminal law [viii]. It thus offers both a richly complicated history of central dimensions of English criminal law, and a challenge to those who theorize criminal law, including especially those engaged in normative theorizing. The challenge is to take the history seriously, and to recognize that what we are theorizing is a set of institutions with such a history, whose present condition and structure must therefore be understood in terms of that history; normative theorizing must be 'accountab[le] to actual practices of criminal responsibility' [179], since it claims 'to offer an account of the implicit normative structure of an actually existing social practice' [185]. Thus if we are to theorize criminal responsibility, we cannot appeal to the ahistorical analyses that philosophers often offer—analyses of 'a concept of responsibility whose validity or conceptual appropriateness is assumed to transcend place and time and which need not satisfy any particularly rigorous criteria of fit with social practices' [6]. We must instead understand responsibility by looking at its roles within particular social practices—in the case of criminal responsibility, within the institutional practices of criminal law: for we can come to understand what responsibility 'is' only by understanding what it is 'for' [2]—its functions within those practices; and as those functions change, so too do conceptions of responsibility. What emerges from this historical inquiry is not, Lacey argues, a single, coherent, concept(ion) of criminal responsibility, but

[1] Thanks to Iyiola Solanke for helpful editorial comments on an earlier draft.
[2] Nicola Lacey, *In Search of Criminal Responsibility: Ideas, Interests, and Institutions* (Oxford University Press 2016); bare page references will be to this book.

Antony Duff, *Searching for Criminal Responsibility* In: *On Crime, Society, and Responsibility in the Work of Nicola Lacey.*
Edited by: Iyiola Solanke, Oxford University Press (2021).
DOI: 10.1093/oso/9780198852681.003.0003

a set of 'multiple and philosophically inconsistent conceptions of responsibility' [vii], which interweave in complex ways, and two or more of which might sometimes coexist in states of uneasy compromise. If we are to understand these multiple conceptions, and the relationships between them, we must attend to their histories, and to the influences (particularly the 'ideas, institutions, and interests') that formed them.

There is much to be said about this methodological challenge: about the ways in which philosophical and normative theorizing about 'criminal law' cannot but be theorizing about particular, historically contingent, practices of criminal law; about the ways in which such theorizing must be historically informed; about the possibility of normative theory, and the extent to which such theory must be accountable to actual practice.[3] However, I will not take up these issues directly here. I want instead to respond to Lacey's claims about the changing conceptions of responsibility that she finds in English criminal law: not to deny those claims, but to argue that they need to be qualified in the light of a more complex conceptual schema than she provides. To that end, I will say a bit in section 2 about what these changing 'conceptions of responsibility' are conceptions *of*; in section 3 I will discuss just what changes between these different conceptions; and in section 4 I will argue that the final change, which Lacey describes as the development of a conception of 'responsibility as founded in risk' [46], and as marking a 'resurgence of character-based mechanisms' [162], is best understood not as a change in the conception of responsibility, but rather as an abandonment of responsibility (as both Lacey and I understand it), in favour of kinds of liability that are detached from responsibility.

2. Multiple Conceptions of What?

'[M]ultiple and philosophically inconsistent conceptions of responsibility' [vii] must be, in some sense, conceptions of the same thing—or else they cannot be inconsistent. This is not to say that responsibility is some kind of metaphysical entity or Platonic form, existing outside all human practices, and awaiting our fallible attempts to analyse it: but if we are to say that conceptions of Φ are inconsistent with each other, we must be able to identify a shared object of which they are all conceptions. However, Lacey argues, it is a mistake to start by focusing on what responsibility 'is—its conceptual contours and moral foundations': we must instead first ask 'what it is for—its social roles, meaning and functions', or 'what it has been "for" at different times and in different places' [2]. This is a version of the Wittgensteinian

[3] On this issue, see Chloe Kennedy, 'Immanence and Transcendence: History's Role in Normative Legal Theory' (2017) 8 Jurisprudence 557; Alan W Norrie, 'Criminal Law and Ethics: Beyond Normative Assertion and its Critique' (2017) 80 Modern Law Review 955.

slogan that 'meaning is use':[4] if we are to understand a concept, we must see what role(s) it plays in the practices in which it is used. To find the common core of criminal responsibility, that of which these multiple conceptions are all conceptions, we must look at its roles or functions within the practice of criminal law.

Lacey's initial answer to the 'for' question is that criminal responsibility 'is best thought of as a set of ideas that play two major roles in the development of modern criminal law: legitimation and coordination' [2]. But that is clearly not the right sort of 'for' account to help us see what responsibility 'is': for different sets of ideas could serve the aims of legitimation and coordination, not all of which would plausibly count as ideas of responsibility. However, Lacey has a particular type of legitimation in mind: the 'ideational frameworks' that structure our understandings of criminal responsibility have 'implications for ... the accountability or answerability of [agents] and the conditions of that answerability'. They thus help to answer 'the question of legitimation': 'what is seen as justifying the calling to account of individuals or other bodies in the name of the criminal process' [25]. This helps us identify the '"core" of the idea of responsibility' [186], and thus the 'is' of criminal responsibility.

That 'core' is 'related to the idea of human agency and accountability for conduct', and 'acts as a constant thread amid shifting theories of responsibility over time and space'. But it is a 'relatively small' core, given different 'inflection[s]' by 'varying social and institutional conditions and practical imperatives' [186–7]: if we are to understand criminal responsibility, we therefore cannot look only at this core, but must attend to those different inflections—to the more concrete ways in which the idea of criminal responsibility is worked out in different contexts and at different times. Part of the point here is that this core is not a descriptive core: 'responsibility' does not serve to describe some feature of the world. It is rather 'a normative device—a matter of construction and ascription' [203]. This reflects one of Lacey's premises: 'criminal responsibility is a practice of attribution' [vii]: it 'encompasses a set of doctrinal rules and principles', or 'all the rules which shape how the legal system attributes a particular act or omission to a particular individual or group' [1].

I will argue in what follows that this 'core' is rather more substantial than Lacey allows; and that if we take the idea of accountability seriously, we will see that some of the changes in criminal law that she traces should be understood as changes not in the law's conception of responsibility, but in the extent to which it takes responsibility as accountability seriously. Accountability is indeed Lacey's main concern: conceptions of responsibility legitimate 'the calling to account of individuals ... in the name of the criminal process (or the state)' [25]. She also argues that to understand the changing contours of criminal responsibility we must look

[4] Ludwig Wittgenstein, *Philosophical Investigations* (trans. GEM Anscombe, Blackwell 1963) § 43; see Lacey, 203.

beyond the formal criminal process, to other aspects of the institutional practices of criminal law—to the criminal law in action. I will turn to that argument in section 4, where I will argue that once we broaden our view in that way, we will see that one of the changes that Lacey identifies in our criminal law is best understood as marking a shift from accountability towards attributability.

We should first note an important difference between accountability and attributability: to attribute something (for instance an action or omission) to a person is not necessarily to hold her accountable for it.[5] This difference can be seen in the provisions in English law for those who are unfit to plead. If a defendant is so mentally disordered at the time of his trial that he cannot understand or respond to the charge against him, or advise his lawyer, or play a comprehending part in the proceedings, he must be found 'unfit to plead', in which case his trial is barred:[6] even if he was sane and competent at the time of the (alleged) crime he cannot now be tried. But his unfitness does not bar every kind of inquiry into his conduct: although he cannot be tried, an inquiry is still held in court, the evidence that would have figured in a trial is examined, and the jury must determine 'whether they are satisfied ... that he did the act or made the omission charged against him as the offence'. If they are thus satisfied, he will not be convicted: they instead 'make a finding that the accused did the act or made the omission charged against him as the offence'; and the court then makes a suitable order (to hospital, to guardianship, to supervision and treatment) or discharges him.[7] If the jury make that finding, they attribute the offence to the defendant, as his action; but he is not held accountable for it, since given his disorder he is incapable of accounting, of answering, for his actions.[8] So too, when a defendant is found 'Not guilty by reason of insanity',[9] it is proved that he committed the offence charged (which is why the verdict is not simply 'Not guilty'), and thus that it can be attributed to him; but if he was at that time non-responsible because disordered, he cannot be held accountable, called to answer, for his actions.

We can focus here on accountability: for it is accountability that is purportedly central to criminal responsibility, as shown by the importance of fitness to plead; if attributability were all that mattered, a defendant's incapacity at the time of the trial would not bar the trial. I will also focus for the moment on accountability as it figures in a criminal trial, where defendants are formally held accountable (or found

[5] The classic distinction between attributability and accountability was drawn by Gary Watson: 'Two Faces of Responsibility' in his *Agency and Responsibility* (Oxford University Press 2004) 260; I adapt it here for my purposes.

[6] See Criminal Procedure (Insanity) Act 1964, s. 4; David Ormerod and Karl Laird, *Smith, Hogan and Ormerod's Criminal Law* (15th edn, Oxford University Press 2018) 281–90.

[7] Criminal Procedure (Insanity) Act 1964, ss. 4A–5A.

[8] 'The aim of such a hearing is to test the evidence rather than to hold D to account' (Ormerod and Laird, *Criminal Law* (n. 6) 286).

[9] Trial of Lunatics Act 1883, s. 2 (as amended); see Ormerod and Laird, *Criminal Law* (n. 6) 290–307.

not to be accountable) for alleged crimes, since that is where the central features of accountability are displayed most clearly.

A further distinction will also be important in what follows: between accountability and liability.[10] If it is proved at her trial that a defendant committed the crime charged, she is held accountable for that crime: which is to say that she is called upon to account—to answer—for it. But that is not yet to say that she is criminally *liable* to be convicted and punished for that crime: for she might offer an exculpatory account—a justification or excuse that shows either that the commission of the crime was in that particular context permissible, or that she should not be condemned for its admittedly wrongful commission. To say that she is accountable for the crime is, rather, to say that she is liable to conviction and punishment for it *unless* she can offer an exculpatory account: proof of the commission of a crime warrants a presumption of liability; but that presumption can be defeated by a defence. (Hence the significance of the distinction between offences and defences: proof of the commission of the offence proves accountability; but only in the absence of any defence does this lead to liability.)

If we are concerned with accountability, we must ask what we can be (held) accountable for, under what conditions, by and to whom, and with what implications if we cannot provide a satisfactory answer. If we instead focus on liability, we must ask what we can be held liable to or for, on what basis, and at whose hands. In the context of criminal law, and in the formal context of the criminal trial, we can say that we are properly held accountable for the proved commission of a crime; that a theory of criminal responsibility aims to tell us how crimes, the objects of responsibility, should be defined, and what the conditions of responsibility should be; that we are called to answer to our fellow citizens by the polity to which we belong; and that the implication of failing to provide an exculpatory answer is liability to conviction and punishment for that crime (and to the further 'collateral consequences' of conviction).[11] As for criminal liability, the simple answer is that we are liable to conviction and punishment (and their collateral consequences) on the basis of proof that we are accountable for a crime, and failed to provide an exculpatory defence; and that the direct results of liability are imposed by officials acting in the name and on behalf of the polity.

As with criminal responsibility, understood as accountability, so with criminal liability, we must also ask whether it operates beyond the formal context of the criminal trial: does it encompass a wider set of liabilities, including liabilities not grounded in a formal finding of criminal accountability? I will argue that what

[10] I previously drew this as a distinction between responsibility and liability (R Antony Duff, *Answering for Crime* (Hart Publishing 2007) ch. 1.

[11] See further Duff, *Answering* (n, 10); *The Realm of Criminal Law* (Oxford University Press 2018; ch. 3.3 deals with the status of non-citizens in the polity). On collateral consequences, see Zachary Hoskins, *Beyond Punishment? A Normative Account of Collateral Restrictions on Offenders* (Oxford University Press 2019).

Lacey identifies as a change in conceptions of responsibility to one of 'responsibility as founded in risk' [46] can also be understood as a change in the conditions of criminal liability, and a disconnection of such liability from responsibility understood as accountability: liability to various kinds of coercion under the aegis of criminal law is no longer grounded in accountability (although it may be grounded in attributability). There is nothing very novel about liability that is 'criminal', in that it is imposed under the aegis of the criminal law, or in relation to matters that concern the criminal law, but that is not grounded in accountability: someone found to be unfit to plead, or 'Not guilty by reason of insanity', is thereby rendered liable to various kinds of coercive measure, most obviously to detention;[12] but, I will argue, what the phenomena that Lacey identifies as exemplifying 'responsibility as founded in risk' display is a growing tendency to impose such liability independently of any proof of criminal accountability.

I return to liability in section 4: but we must first get clearer about responsibility understood as accountability.

3. What Changes?

One obvious question about accountability concerns who, what kind of being, is (or can be properly) held accountable: what is it to be an accountable agent in the eyes of the criminal law? That is not, however, Lacey's central concern in this book: her concern is rather with the ways in which, conditions under which, or purposes for which, people are held criminally responsible.[13] But we must distinguish different questions here. One concerns the objects of responsibility: for what can we be held accountable? Another concerns the conditions of responsibility: given what conditions can we be thus called to account?[14] In the context of criminal responsibility, we must also ask what kinds of evidence are allowed to be relevant to establishing responsibility—a point that Lacey emphasizes [38–40]: for although the meaning of *X* is not determined by the evidence that is taken to bear on its proof (we can work out what counts as good evidence for *X* only once we know what *X* is), the role that *X* plays in our practices is connected to the methods by which we take it to be proved. When Lacey talks about the different conceptions of criminal responsibility, we must therefore ask whether what changes is an

[12] See Criminal Procedure (Insanity) Act 1964, ss. 5–5a (as amended).

[13] But see at 25, 136–7, 140–4, 182 (she has written much on this elsewhere). See Lindsay Farmer, *Making the Modern Criminal Law: Criminalization and Civil Order* (Oxford University Press 2016) ch. 6.

[14] On objects and conditions of responsibility, see Douglas N Husak, 'Does Criminal Liability Require an Act?' in R Antony Duff (ed.), *Philosophy and the Criminal Law* (Cambridge University Press) 60, 67–75; R Antony Duff, 'Virtue, Vice and Criminal Liability' (2002) 6 Buffalo Criminal Law Rev 147, 155–60.

understanding of the objects of responsibility, or of its conditions, or only of what kinds of evidence are relevant.

Take first the idea of responsibility as grounded in 'character'—a recurring theme in this book as in Lacey's earlier work.[15] 'Character' can mean different things, and one objection to Lacey's talk of 'the resurgence of character' [147] is that the 'surge' in the latter part of the twentieth century is not a 'resurgence' of character as understood in the eighteenth century, but the rise of something different. One common point is admittedly that 'character' can in both contexts be understood in personal or in social terms. That is, it could be understood as consisting in features of the person herself; or in her reputation or standing in the relevant social context.[16] The latter meaning is most obviously relevant to character as evidence, but I focus here on the former. Character as a feature of the person can be understood in quite rich, traditional terms as a matter of the person's virtues and vices, of her dispositions of thought and feeling, of her goals and values: that is how some 'character' theorists of criminal law understand it, and is perhaps how it was understood in the eighteenth-century context. But when we turn to the 'resurgence' of character, we find a different, much more minimal, conception of character, as consisting only in patterns of conduct, or a 'propensity' to commit certain kinds of offence, as displayed in prior commissions of such offences. Thus Mike Redmayne's justly celebrated book, *Character in the Criminal Trial*,[17] is primarily about the admissibility of evidence of prior convictions to support the prosecution's case at trial. So too, when the Criminal Justice Act 2003 relaxed the rules on the admissibility of 'bad character' evidence in trials, it defined 'bad character' in behavioural terms, as a matter of 'misconduct', or a 'disposition towards' it (s. 98); and although 'misconduct' is defined with disturbing breadth to cover not just 'the commission of an offence', but also 'other reprehensible behaviour' (s. 112(1); [154–6]), the focus is still on conduct as constituting 'character'. A richer idea of 'character' is indeed at work in sentencing [63–4], and perhaps also in instances of 'status responsibility', such as the offence of 'loiter[ing] or solicit[ing] ... for the purpose of prostitution' as 'a common prostitute':[18] but even then we must ask whether there is more to being 'a common prostitute' than a particular pattern of behaviour—regular (and generally known) soliciting. Perhaps the newer category of 'terrorist' comes closer to classical conceptions of character [152–3]: to say that someone is a terrorist is to comment not merely on their patterns of conduct, but on their lasting motivation

[15] See especially Nicola Lacey, *Women, Crime, and Character: From Moll Flanders to Tess of the D'Urbervilles* (Oxford University Press 2008); 'Psychologising Jekyll, Demonising Hyde: The Strange Case of Criminal Responsibility' (2010) 4 Criminal Law & Philosophy 109.

[16] The latter meaning was evident when Victorian employers dismissed servants 'without a character': see e.g. Oscar Wilde's *Lady Windermere's Fan*, Act 1 (Duchess of Berwick: 'I caught him winking at my maid, a most pretty, respectable girl. I dismissed her at once without a character'). Lacey also brings out this meaning of 'character', e.g. at 38–9.

[17] Mike Redmayne, *Character in the Criminal Trial* (Oxford University Press 2015).

[18] See Street Offences Act 1959, s. 1; Lacey, 63.

for acting thus: but this brings us to 'risk', to which I return below; we need note here only that insofar as people are held criminally responsible as presenting a risk to others, it is again not clear what notion of 'character' is in play.

A further point should be noted about 'character': there is a difference, albeit only one of degree, between judgments of the character of a person and judgments of the character of their actions. This is clearly seen in the case of motives as bearing on criminal responsibility, an obvious instance of which is 'hate crime' legislation under which a specified motive can aggravate an underlying offence:[19] when the law attends to *D*'s motivation, it is attending to the deeper meaning of *D*'s action, and thus inevitably to an aspect of *D* himself; but it is not explicitly attending to *D*'s character as consisting in *D*'s relatively stable or lasting dispositions of thought and feeling; nor can *D* gain an acquittal by arguing that a racially motivated attack was 'out of character'. So it is misleading to say that '[a]nalytically, the distinction between evaluation of an act and evaluation of the character of the actor is clear' [36]: evaluations of acts are often evaluations of actions as performed by this actor; the change from evaluating (only) actions to evaluating actors' characters is a move along a spectrum from a relatively shallow judgment of the action to a much deeper judgment that sets that particular action in the richer context of the actor's life.

If we are to talk of criminal responsibility as grounded in 'character', we must ask what notion of 'character' is in play, and also what kind of grounding is in play: is 'character' the *object* of responsibility—that for which we are responsible; or a *condition* of responsibility, so that we are held responsible for something else (for an action, most plausibly) on condition that it was suitably related to character; or only *evidence* of responsibility for something else —evidence that *D* was responsible for the commission of the crime? If character is the object of criminal responsibility, the criminal acts that form the formal focus of a criminal charge are not the real substance of criminal liability: they serve as evidence for the character traits that really concern the criminal law. But if character is a condition of criminal responsibility, then what we are held accountable for, and convicted and punished for, is a criminal action—although only if that action is suitably related to some aspect of our character.[20]

Lacey is well aware of the distinction between character as object or condition and character as evidence, and notes the way in which that analytically clear distinction is blurred in practice, so that *D*'s 'bad character' becomes integral to her criminal responsibility, rather than evidence of it [38–40]; but she is less sensitive to the distinction between character as the object of responsibility, and character as a condition of responsibility. She talks sometimes as if character is the object of

[19] See e.g. Crime and Disorder Act 1998, ss 28–32; Lacey, 150.

[20] Compare the difference in conceptions of criminal attempts, between the view that what we are properly held accountable for is the action that constitutes the attempt, and the view that the law is really concerned with the dangerous disposition that the attempt reveals (see American Law Institute, *Model Penal Code and Commentaries* (American Law Institute 1985) Part I §§ 3.01 to 5.07, 323).

responsibility [e.g. 34–5]: what we are to be condemned for is bad character, perhaps on condition that it is revealed in criminal action. But she also cites Tadros as a 'character' theorist, and for Tadros character arguably functions not as the object, but as a condition, of responsibility: that is, an agent is responsible for an action, on condition that 'it reflects on the agent *qua* agent'.[21]

Why does it matter whether what we are (really) held accountable for, and are convicted and punished for, is a character trait, or the action that the law defines as criminal? It matters partly because if character is an object of responsibility, we confront the problematic question of whether we can legitimately be held responsible for our character, for being the kinds of people we are [see 37], whereas if character is only a condition of responsibility we can ask when we can be responsible for our actions without having to worry about responsibility for character. But it also matters whether what we are accused of, and what we are condemned for if we are convicted, is an aspect of our character, or what we have done. It matters both as far as labelling is concerned (does conviction label me as the author of a wrongful action, or as a bad person?), and for sentencing, insofar as an offender's sentence reflects a judgment of the seriousness of the offence of conviction: if character is the object of responsibility, my sentence can properly be aggravated, or mitigated, by the seriousness of the character defect displayed in my conduct; but if it is only a condition of responsibility, the seriousness of my crime should be assessed purely by considering the criminal action for which I am formally convicted.

The importance of the distinction between objects and conditions of responsibility is also evident if we turn to the next two ideas or patterns of criminal responsibility that Lacey picks out: 'capacity' and 'outcome'. Our capacities (our 'powers of understanding and self-control' [27], of effective practical reasoning) are not of course the objects of criminal responsibility: we are not held responsible for possessing them. Their possession is a condition of criminal responsibility: we cannot be held responsible if we lack them. What we are on this view held responsible for is the way in which we exercise, or perhaps fail to exercise, these capacities: most obviously for the choices we make, since on a standard view it is in choosing to act that we display our rational practical capacities; also perhaps for failures to choose (omissions) when we could and should have chosen to act (offences of negligence can be seen as offences of omission—failing to take care that one could and should have taken). Now a view of this kind, that what we are properly held responsible for are the choices we make, is familiar in twentieth-century criminal law theory as a paradigm example of 'subjectivism';[22] but it is not clear how far it ever structured criminal law doctrines and practice, as distinct from criminal law theory (even 'to

[21] Victor Tadros, *Criminal Responsibility* (Oxford University Press 2005) 8; see Lacey, 34.

[22] Andrew Ashworth's theoretical writings in the latter part of the last century provide a very good example of this species of subjectivism: see e.g. Andrew J Ashworth, 'Belief, Intent and Criminal Liability' in John Eekelaar and John Bell (eds), *Oxford Essays in Jurisprudence*, 3rd Series (Oxford University Press 1987) 1.

a lesser extent' than theory [30]). For as Lacey herself puts it, the questions that courts must answer still have to do not just with what choice the defendant made (with what she intended to do or realized that she would or might bring about), but with what she brought about in the world: for instance, 'Did the defendant cause the victim's death? If so, did s/he do so with intent to cause death or grievous bodily harm?' [30]. Even when the law defined offences 'in the inchoate mode',[23] it required action as a (formally) core constituent of the offence: it never reflected the strictly subjectivist conception of criminal responsibility as being for, and only for, the choices we make; if it were to do so, and even if it would still require some *actus reus* as proof of the criminal choice, it would define all offences in the inchoate mode—it would not distinguish attempted from completed crimes, or dangerous conduct that caused the relevant harm from equally dangerous conduct that fortuitously did not cause the harm.

This suggests that an 'outcome' conception of criminal responsibility was closely related to the 'capacity' conception: even when a capacity conception was prominent, the production of a relevant outcome in the world was still essential to criminal responsibility—even if that outcome was not the completed mischief at which the law was aimed, but the risk of such a mischief, or conduct constituting an attempt to cause it. There are three ways in which we can combine outcome and capacity.

First, we could say that choice (or failure to make a choice) is the object of responsibility, but that a condition of responsibility is that that choice result or be expressed in overt conduct that has an impact on the world: this condition might be added for evidential reasons (because only given overt conduct do we have the kind of evidence that can be non-intrusively secured and relied on by courts), or because a liberal state ought to attend to its citizens' choices only when they impact on the shared public world.

Second, we could say that responsibility is for outcomes, but that it is a further condition of responsibility that the outcome was caused by the defendant's choice, or by a failure to exercise the capacity for choice:[24] for, we might say, it is unjust to hold a person responsible for an outcome if that condition is not satisfied. When Lacey talks of 'outcome-responsibility of the hybrid kind' [59], we might thus see this 'hybrid' as instantiated more widely than she supposes: the difference between 'the terrain of the "real crime" which preoccupied text book writers', in which capacity held sway, and the 'intellectually siloed (yet empirically growing) area of "regulatory crime"' in which there is 'a reliance on outcome responsibility' [145], is not that outcome responsibility was not relevant to the former, but that

[23] See Andrew J Ashworth, 'Defining Criminal Offences without Harm' in Peter Smith (ed.), *Criminal Law: Essays in Honour of J C Smith* (Butterworths 1987) 7.

[24] Although omission-based responsibility is not always for outcomes that we failed to prevent or negligently caused; it might be for the very failure to take care, whether or not that failure resulted in harm.

the constraints set by the requirements of 'capacity' were weakened in the latter area. They might be weakened, for instance, by changing from a requirement that the prosecution prove an outcome caused by an exercise of practical capacity (for instance that 'the defendant cause[d] the victim's death ... with intent to cause death or grievous bodily harm' [30]), to a weaker requirement that the prosecution prove the outcome (for instance that *D* '[sold] to the purchaser's prejudice any food which [was] not of the nature or substance or quality demanded by the purchaser'), leaving it to *D* to offer a defence of lack of capacity or of fair opportunity to avoid producing that outcome (for instance that she exercised all 'due diligence' to avoid it);[25] and then to a system of strict liability, which does not even allow for such defences.

Third, we could posit a unitary conception of responsibility as being for actions—actions now understood as consisting in the exercise of rational capacities in ways that impact on the shared social world:[26] on this view 'outcome' (the result that defines an action as the action it is) and 'capacity' (as exercised in action) are both aspects of the object of responsibility.

Here again, the difference between objects and conditions matters. If choice is the object of responsibility, and even if some outcome is required as a condition, then both the label that comes with conviction and the severity of the sentence should depend on the choice made by the offender: I should (as 'subjectivists' argue) be held culpable in just the same way whether or not my choice produced its intended or expected result; my penal desert should likewise be determined purely by reference to my choice, and not to the actual outcome of my action. If instead what I am held responsible for is the outcome, or the action of which that outcome was the result, that is what labels me (not as one who chose to harm, but as one who harmed), and that is what partly determines the seriousness of my crime and my penal desert. Insofar as both substantive law and sentencing practice consistently made outcomes crucial, we can say (contrary to Lacey's account of the dominance of a capacity-based conception) that our criminal law has never operated with a conception of (the exercise of) capacity as the object of criminal responsibility.

Turning finally to risk, as central to the fourth conception of responsibility, we can again see the importance of distinguishing objects from conditions of responsibility; we also find features that suggest a move away from making responsibility, understood as accountability, the main basis of criminal liability. Lacey talks at one point of 'attribut[ing] responsibility for risk' [47]. If that is what the law is doing, then 'risk' is the object of responsibility, and it is natural to suppose that risk is now a matter of the risk created by particular actions: we are accountable for the risks of harm that our actions create. But that is not a distinct conception of responsibility, since it can be fully captured within the 'capacity-outcome' model: risk is

[25] See Food Safety Act 1990, ss 14, 21; and generally, Ormerod and Laird, *Criminal Law* (n. 6) 170–4.
[26] See Duff, *Answering* (n. 10) ch. 5.

the outcome for which we are held responsible, on condition that we created it by exercising our capacities for rational action (or failed to prevent it when we could and should have done so); this marks an admittedly significant change in the range of objects of responsibility, but not in the conception of responsibility. There are, however, at least two other ways in which risk might be relevant, if not to criminal accountability, then to criminal(-like) liability.

First, risk or its avoidance might figure neither as the object, nor as a direct condition, of responsibility, since we can be responsible for actions that do not create the relevant risk, but as the rationale for the creation of criminal offences. We create a regulation, whose breach is then criminalized, in order to prevent some kind of harm and the risk of its occurrence: but although what justifies the regulation is that it is an efficient way of reducing risk, and thus of preventing harm, the conduct that it prohibits will not always itself be harmful or dangerous; nor will it be a defence to show that although my conduct breached the regulation, it did not create an unreasonable risk of the relevant kind of harm. This is a feature of many so-called *mala prohibita*: if I break the speed limit, or drive a car that has not passed the required safety test, I might not in fact create the kind of risk that these legal regulations aim to reduce, and I might know this to be so; but I will still be liable to conviction of a criminal offence, because I have broken a regulation that was justified as an efficient and not unreasonably burdensome method of reducing risk. Here again, we do not have a different conception of responsibility. A capacity-outcome model still holds good, in that liability requires both a relevant outcome (the breach of the regulation) and the capacity to avoid that outcome (though that requirement might be weakened in the ways noted above); what has changed is not the law's conception of responsibility, but views about what kinds of conduct should be criminalized.[27]

Second, risk might be seen as inhering not in the criminalized action, but in the agent (or, we might better say, the person), who is subjected to special criminal measures because he is judged to be dangerous; that is why Lacey talks of a resurgence of character in this context, since dangerousness is now seen as a characteristic of the person that makes him dangerous in the future. Here, however, it becomes less clear that we are dealing with 'responsibility for risk', or indeed with criminal responsibility understood as accountability. The obvious point to notice is that dangerousness of character does not typically figure formally in the criminal trial as a reason to convict a defendant, either as part of what he is convicted of (as part of the object of responsibility), or as a condition of conviction for an offence that does not formally involve character (as one of the conditions of responsibility). Even with offences related to terrorism, such as those concerning membership of or support for a 'proscribed organisation', or the possession of items 'for terrorist purposes',[28] it need not be proved that

[27] See further Duff, *Realm* (n 11) chs 2.3, 7.5.
[28] See Terrorism Act 2000, ss 11–12, 57.

the defendant is a 'terrorist' in the sense of having a commitment to terrorist ends as a lasting character trait. The examples that Lacey offers of responsibility grounded in 'the apprehension of risk' [46], and as marking the (re)surgence of a particular version of character-based responsibility, are not primarily examples of criminal offences: instead, she cites 'the new penology', policing, pre-trial procedures and sentencing, provisions for dealing with mentally disordered people and with immigration, various kinds of preventive detention, sex offender registers, a range of civil preventive orders that may be backed by the criminal law,[29] and profiling [46–8, 61–4, 102–4, 157–61, 169–73]. Thus for just one instance among others, section 23 of the Anti-Terrorism, Crime and Security Act 2001 made provision for the detention of 'a suspected international terrorist' who could not be deported, and the definition of 'suspected international terrorist' in section 21 was clearly aimed not at one who might engage in one-off acts of terrorism, but at those with a more lasting commitment to terrorist aims: but the provisions for such detention were not provisions for holding suspected international terrorists accountable, in a criminal court, either for their terrorist actions or for being terrorists; instead, they abandoned any attempt to deal with such people through the formal criminal process of holding them to account for their alleged wrongdoing—the practice of responsibility as accountability.[30]

Lacey has a firm reply to this criticism—a reply that leads us to another central theme of the book. If we are to understand the changing ideas and patterns of criminal responsibility, she insists, we must not focus solely on the formal attributions of responsibility displayed in the law's formal definitions of offences and in the formal verdicts of criminal trials: we must instead attend to 'the patterns of responsibilization *as realised in criminalization practices as a whole*' [62]; we must analyse 'practices of responsibility-attribution within the context of criminalization overall' [151]. Now this insistence on examining the law in action, rather than focusing only on the 'law in the books' or in the formal verdicts of criminal courts, is clearly both right and important: if we are either to understand, descriptively or analytically, what kind(s) of role criminal law plays in a society's life, or argue, normatively, about the role(s) it should play, we must attend to the whole set of practices that make up the 'criminal law' as a distinctive kind of institution, and to the actual workings of those practices rather than only to their formal rules and doctrines. However, what is much less clear is whether when we turn our gaze to this broader canvas we are still looking at patterns of responsibility-ascription—at least if we understand responsibility as accountability.

[29] See Andrew J Ashworth and Lucia Zedner, *Preventive Justice* (Oxford University Press 2014) esp. ch. 4.

[30] As Lacey notes [63, n. 84] these provisions were held to violate human rights in *A v. Secretary of State for the Home Department* [2004] UKHL 56; they were removed by s. 16 of the Prevention of Terrorism Act 2005, and finally replaced by TPIMs in the Terrorism Prevention and Investigation Measures Act 2011.

4. Accountability and Liability

Liability to conviction and punishment, imposed and determined by a criminal court, depends formally on accountability: defendants are convicted if and because they have been proved to be accountable, answerable, for a criminal offence, and have failed to provide an exculpatory account of their conduct; they are sentenced to a punishment that is for that offence—that is, its imposition is justified by that proved and non-exculpated accountability. Other types of criminal liability are also formally determined by, or depend on, accountability: penalties of various kinds can be imposed by prosecutors or by the police, without a criminal charge or a criminal trial; the police can dispose of cases by a formal caution.[31] Such provisions formally depend on accountability if they require a formal admission of guilt by the alleged offender,[32] and they informally depend on accountability if they in fact assume guilt: they can therefore be seen as ways of holding (supposed) offenders accountable without the costs and burdens of a trial.

We can also note a further way in which liability to criminal punishment is determined by accountability: not for the offence for which the defendant has been convicted, but for her previous conduct. When a defendant's criminal record is treated, formally or informally, as an aggravating factor in sentencing, her penal liability is determined not just by the specific crime for which she is held accountable at her trial but by the previous crimes for which she was held accountable at previous trials: because, it might be said, those prior crimes serve to aggravate her culpable responsibility for her latest crime; or because she is held accountable not just for her latest crime, but for her failure to correct her ways or to respond as she should to her previous punishments.[33]

Even if we attend only to the criminal process of trial and sentencing, however, we can see ways (identified by Lacey) in which liability becomes more or less detached, formally or substantively, from accountability. Thus in sentencing, an offender might be sentenced to an extended period of detention because he is taken to be 'dangerous',[34] but he is not now being held responsible, in advance, for the future danger that he would supposedly present to others if released; we should instead see such provisions as more like those for mentally disordered offenders who are judged to be dangerous, such as the 'restriction orders' that courts can add

[31] For such provisions in English law, see Andrew J Ashworth and Mike Redmayne. *The Criminal Process* (4th edn, Oxford University Press 2010) ch. 6.

[32] Which is not always the case: thus in Scotland, for instance, prosecutor fines do not require an admission of guilt; see Peter Duff, 'The Prosecutor Fine' (1994) 14 Oxford Journal of Legal Studies 565.

[33] We need not engage here in the debate about whether or how prior record can justify an enhanced sentence: for a useful set of readings, see Julian Roberts and Andreas von Hirsch (eds), *Previous Convictions at Sentencing* (Hart Publishing 2010).

[34] See e.g. the provisions for indefinite 'imprisonment for public protection' (IPP) in the Criminal Justice Act 2003, ss 224–30 (see Lacey, 160), now replaced by provisions for 'extended determinate sentences' (Legal Aid, Sentencing and Punishment of Offenders Act 2012, ss 122–8); also the Scottish provisions for 'Orders for Lifelong Restriction' under the Criminal Justice (Scotland) Act 2003, Part 1.

to hospital orders that they make for convicted defendants who are judged to be dangerously mentally disordered.[35] In such cases, a person is (held to be) liable to detention because he is judged to be dangerous, and one could see dangerousness as a matter of 'character' (though not the kind of character that figured in criminal responsibility in the eighteenth century, on Lacey's account): but this is not to say that the sentencing court is holding the defendant responsible, accountable, either for the threat that he is taken to pose to others, or for the 'character' traits in virtue of which he is judged to be dangerous. This is, we might say, liability grounded in attributability rather than accountability:[36] dangerousness, that is, is attributed to the offender as a reason for detaining him; but it is not something for which he is being held accountable.

Plea-bargaining is another arena in which we can see a move away from responsibility as accountability in the substantive operations of criminal justice (though not in its formal rules or principles)—at least or most evidently in the way that plea-bargaining has developed in the United States [183–4]. Formally, of course, plea-bargaining is concerned with responsibility as accountability: by pleading guilty, the defendant admits accountability for the commission of the crime, admits that she can offer no defence, and thus accepts liability to conviction and punishment. But a central objection to the contemporary practice of plea-bargaining is that it has lost any meaning it might once have had as a formal admission or confession of guilt: it becomes simply a formal move in the game, signifying acceptance of the terms of the bargain that was agreed between defence and prosecution. A *reductio ad absurdum* of this practice is found in the notorious *Alford* plea, when the US Supreme Court upheld the conviction of a defendant who said in the course of pleading 'Guilty': 'I'm not guilty but I plead guilty'—in order, he said, to avoid the threat of the death penalty if he went to trial.[37] When this happens, criminal liability to conviction and punishment has become substantively detached from any serious concern with responsibility understood as accountability: a defendant is now allowed to deny that she is accountable for the crime while still formally pleading 'Guilty'.[38] What we see here is thus not a change in the conception of criminal responsibility, but an abandonment of the dependence of criminal liability to conviction and punishment on a justified ascription of responsibility-accountability. It is not a formal abandonment, since lip service is still paid to the dependence of criminal conviction and punishment on responsibility as accountability; but it is a de facto, albeit concealed, abandonment.

[35] See Mental Health Act 1983, ss 37, 41; Ashworth and Zedner, *Preventive Justice* (n. 29) 210–11 (and 214 on discussions about 'Dangerous and Serious Personality Disorder').

[36] See at nn 5–9 above.

[37] *North Carolina v. Alford* 91 S. Ct 160 (1970).

[38] In fairness to the Alford Court, one reason it gave for upholding Mr Alford's conviction was that there was strong evidence of his guilt: but see Allison D Redlich and Asil Ali Özdogru, 'Alford Pleas in the Age of Innocence' (2009) 27 Behavioral Sciences and the Law 467.

I have focused so far on criminal liability to conviction and punishment. However, once we look beyond the formal institution of the criminal trial, to 'patterns of responsibilization *as realised in criminalization practices as a whole*' [62], or to 'practices of responsibility-attribution within the context of criminalization overall' [151], we will find other forms of criminal liability—liabilities to other kinds of imposition or coercion under the aegis of the criminal law, or in relation to matters that intimately concern the criminal law, some of which also detach liability from accountability. One example is that of pre-trial remands in custody—which Lacey mentions among 'risk and character-based patterns of criminal responsibility attribution' [103, 159–60].

If a defendant is remanded in pre-trial custody, on the grounds that if left free he would be likely to abscond, or interfere with witnesses, or commit offences,[39] this is a matter of averting perceived risk: the court's judgment will be informed by its view of the defendant's character, since it 'shall have regard to', *inter alia*, his 'character, antecedents, associations and community ties', and his 'record as respects the fulfilment of his obligations under previous grants of bail in criminal proceedings'.[40] But he is not being held accountable *for* those perceived risks: the risk or danger is attributed to him, but he is not being called to answer for posing it. Here again, then, we find liability—liability to detention under the aegis of the criminal law—that depends on attributability rather than on accountability. Another example was noted above: the provisions for the detention of suspected terrorists.[41] The process by which a 'suspected international terrorist' was subjected to detention was not one through which he was called to answer or to account for his alleged terrorist activities (as was highlighted by the fact that he might not even be allowed to see the evidence on the basis of which detention was sought): a dangerous disposition to terrorism was attributed to him, but he was not being treated as an accountable agent who should be called, and allowed, to answer the accusation of terrorism.

Other examples that Lacey discusses are more complicated—particularly the examples of 'civil preventive hybrid orders' such as ASBOs and their successors [103–5, 159–61].[42] Once such an order is made, the person against whom it is made is held criminally responsible for breaching its conditions, and such responsibility can be understood in terms of some kind of outcome-capacity model:[43] the object of responsibility is, at least formally, the breach of the order, which the defendant supposedly had the capacity to avoid (though there must of course remain a suspicion that the defendant is being substantively sentenced not just for breaching the order, but for the anti-social or otherwise criminal conduct it was intended to prevent). But that is a peculiar object of criminal responsibility—the breaching of an individualized order,

39 See Bail Act 1976, Sch. 1.
40 Bail Act 1976, Sch. 1, para. 9.
41 Anti-Terrorism, Crime and Security Act 2001, s. 23; see at nn 29–30 above.
42 And see Ashworth and Zedner, *Preventive Justice* (n. 29) ch. 4.
43 See at nn 24–6 above.

which can be seen as creating an 'individualized offence' [153];[44] and the significant change lies in the expanding provisions for the making of such orders—orders that count formally as civil rather than criminal orders, but that bring those against whom they are made within the reach of the criminal law. The making of such orders depends on allegations, or suspicions, or even judgments, of past criminal conduct, whose future repetition they are to prevent: but even if the process through which they are made requires proof of such past conduct to the criminal standard,[45] it is not a process in which the person is held to account for, or called to answer the accusation of, such conduct. Instead, that conduct, and the risk of its repetition, is attributed to her; that attribution renders her liable to have new prospective responsibilities imposed on her (to obey the requirements specified in the order); and she is held criminally responsible, criminally accountable, for any breach of those new responsibilities.

Here again, the development to which Lacey points is better understood, not as a change in conceptions of criminal responsibility as accountability, but rather as a shift away from a focus on accountability as the necessary basis of criminal liability. Formally, of course, the person's liability to criminal conviction and punishment does depend upon accountability for the breach of the provisions of the preventive order: in that way such orders are quite unlike provisions for the detention of those judged to be dangerous, in which accountability plays no part. Nonetheless, such liability is grounded in an imposition of new responsibilities, which is itself grounded in an attribution of criminal conduct for which the person is not called, and is not allowed, to answer: liability—to the imposition of such responsibilities, and thus also to conviction and punishment for their breach—is substantively detached from accountability.

This detachment is clearly exemplified in the 'Terrorism Prevention and Investigation Measures' (TPIMs) that may be imposed on those whom the Home Secretary is 'satisfied, on the balance of probabilities' are or have been 'involved in terrorism-related activity'.[46] Such orders impose 'requirements, restrictions and other provision[s]' on those subject to them,[47] and it is a criminal offence to breach their terms: that is, they impose new, and individualized, prospective responsibilities, whose breach is criminalized. Liability to conviction for breach of such an order does thus depend on responsibility understood as accountability: the person

[44] See Victor Tadros, 'Justice and Terrorism' (2007) 10 New Criminal Law Review 658, 683–5.

[45] As was true of ASBOs, following the decision in *R (McCann) v. Manchester Crown Court* [2003] 1 AC 787 —though the court also made clear (at 808) that whilst it must be proved that the person had 'acted … in an anti-social manner, that is to say, in a manner that caused or was likely to cause harassment, alarm or distress' to others outside his household, i.e. that he acted in a way that constituted the conduct element of an offence under ss 4A–5 of the Public Order Act 1986, no *mens rea* need be proved.

[46] Terrorism Prevention and Investigation Measures Act 2011; see Lacey, 161. These replaced Control Orders, which required only 'reasonable grounds for suspecting' involvement in terrorism (Prevention of Terrorism Act 2005, s. 2(1)).

[47] Terrorism Prevention and Investigation Measures Act 2011, s. 2(2); Control Orders had been described as imposing 'obligations' on those subject to them (Prevention of Terrorism Act 2005, s. 2(1)), thus making explicit the way in which such orders impose new prospective responsibilities.

is formally summoned to answer a charge that he contravened a TPIM, and has the chance to argue that he had a 'reasonable excuse' for doing so.[48] Liability to the imposition of such an order, however, does not depend on accountability: it requires only an attribution of terrorist involvement.

Does it matter whether we describe the kinds of development discussed in this section as Lacey describes them, as changes in the conception of responsibility with which the criminal law operates; or as I have suggested we should describe them, as marking a detachment of liability from responsibility understood as accountability? After all, we can agree on the need 'to resist [this] resurgence of character-based mechanisms which foster the most dangerous aspects of criminalization and punishment as forms of social power' [162], even if we differ about just how that 'resurgence' should be analysed. Furthermore, if attributability is itself a kind of responsibility, perhaps 'the aretaic face of responsibility',[49] and if the 'mechanisms' discussed here involve attributions of criminality or dangerousness, they are still mechanisms of responsibility: so we are still dealing with changing conceptions of criminal responsibility —with, in this case, a movement from accountability to attributability. However, describing these changes in the way I suggest helps to make clearer just what they involve, and why they are so 'dangerous': they endanger the liberal understanding of how the state should see and treat its citizens—an understanding that is (or should be) central to our conception of political legitimacy.

A preliminary, but suggestive, point to notice is that whilst practices of attribution might display 'the aretaic face of responsibility', they can easily become detached from ideas either of virtue or moral character, or of what we could recognize as responsible agency. Thus if the jury determines that someone who is unfit to plead 'did the act or made the omission charged against him as the offence', or finds the defendant 'Not guilty by reason of insanity',[50] this is in one obvious sense an exercise in 'attribution': the conduct that constituted the offence is attributed to the defendant as something she did. But such attributions are not attributions of criminal responsibility: rather, they are attributions of non-responsible agency (or, in the case of one who is unfit to plead, of agency that might not have been responsible agency) to one who is found not to be a responsible agent.[51]

The crucial point, however, concerns the centrality of accountability to our understanding of the state's appropriate relationship to its citizens.[52] As Lacey puts it, 'citizen criminal law ... responds to subjects invested with rights', as distinct from 'enemy criminal law', which 'treats its objects as dangers to be managed'

48 Terrorism Prevention and Investigation Measures Act 2011, s. 23(1).
49 See Watson, 'Two Faces of Responsibility' (n. 5) 267.
50 See at nn 6–9 above.
51 As Lacey notes [28, n. 5] in the case of insanity.
52 And to those who live within its territory without being (formally) citizens: see n. 11 above.

[158–9].[53] A central right that 'subjects' should be able to claim as citizens is the right to be treated as responsible agents, and central to that right is the right to be treated as agents who can answer for themselves and their conduct. We think that we can justifiably detain without their consent those who are dangerously mentally disordered, in order to protect them and others from what they might do: but that is because their mental disorder, we believe, undermines their status as responsible agents; they cannot be held accountable for their deeds. 'Enemy aliens' might be liable to be detained in wartime, either en masse or if judged individually to present a risk:[54] such detention involved attribution —the attribution of dangerous or 'disloyal' attitudes; but it was not based on accountability—those subjected to it were not called to answer to a charge of disloyalty. In both cases, those detained are precisely not treated as responsible citizens: the mentally disordered because they are not responsible, and 'enemy aliens' because in the crisis of war they are not seen or treated as citizens, or even as respected guests. But that is not, we (liberals) think, how a state should treat its citizens: if they are suspected of wrongfully harmful or dangerous conduct, they should be called to answer, held to account for it; and the criminal law, if structured by a conception of responsibility as accountability, is one way in which citizens can thus be held to account.[55] That is what is lost when criminal liability, or liability related to criminal law in the way that preventive orders and detention are, is detached from accountability; that is why the 'resurgence of character-based mechanisms' that Lacey identifies is such a 'dangerous aspect[]' of contemporary practices of 'criminalization and punishment' [162].

I have argued that we can gain a clearer understanding of the changes that Lacey describes by distinguishing attributability from accountability, accountability from liability, objects from conditions of responsibility, and liability that is grounded in accountability from liability that is not thus grounded; I have also argued that we can see more clearly the nature of what she calls the 'resurgence of character-based mechanisms', or the emergence of 'a hybrid pattern and practice of responsibility based on a combination of [risk or danger] and a new sense of bad character' [147] if we see it not as a new, hybrid form of responsibility as accountability (which is how both she and I understand the 'core' of responsibility), but as a detachment of criminal (or criminal-like) liability from accountability. Nothing in what I have said is meant to cast doubt on the main features of her argument in this richly

[53] Drawing on Günther Jakobs' notorious distinction: Günther Jakobs, 'Bürgerstrafrecht und Feindstrafrecht' (2004) Höchstrichterliche Rechtsprechung Strafrecht 88; see also the references in Lacey 158, n 65.

[54] For a summary of British internment practices in the Second World War, see the report in The National Archives at <https://blog.nationalarchives.gov.uk/blog/collar-lot-britains-policy-internment-second-world-war>. Captured enemy combatants were also, of course, liable to be detained in prisoner-of-war camps.

[55] Another important aspect of accountability is that to hold someone accountable is also to commit oneself to attend to the account that they give: for accountability is (should be) a reciprocal matter. That is not how criminal trials in fact often operate; but that is just one way in which our practice betrays its professed principles.

stimulating book: my aim has rather been to show how that argument can be made clearer by drawing various conceptual distinctions among different aspects of 'responsibility' and related concepts.

Bibliography

Ashworth, AJ, 'Belief, Intent and Criminal Liability' in J Eekelaar, and J Bell (eds), *Oxford Essays in Jurisprudence*, 3rd Series (Oxford University Press 1987)

Ashworth, AJ, 'Defining Criminal Offences without Harm' in P Smith (ed.), *Criminal Law: Essays in Honour of J C Smith* (Butterworths 1987)

Ashworth, AJ and Redmayne, M, *The Criminal Process* (4th edn, Oxford University Press 2010)

Ashworth, AJ and Zedner, L, *Preventive Justice* (Oxford University Press 2014)

Duff, P, 'The Prosecutor Fine' (1994) 14 Oxford Journal of Legal Studies 565

Duff, RA, *The Realm of Criminal Law* (Oxford University Press 2018)

Duff, RA, *Answering for Crime* (Hart Publishing 2007)

Duff, RA, 'Virtue, Vice and Criminal Liability' (2002) 6 Buffalo Criminal Law Review 147

Farmer, L, *Making the Modern Criminal Law: Criminalization and Civil Order* (Oxford University Press 2016)

Hoskins, Z, *Beyond Punishment? A Normative Account of Collateral Restrictions on Offenders* (Oxford University Press 2019)

Husak, DN, 'Does Criminal Liability Require an Act?' in RA Duff (ed.), *Philosophy and the Criminal Law* (Cambridge University Press 1998)

Jakobs, G, 'Bürgerstrafrecht und Feindstrafrecht' (2004) Höchstrichterliche Rechtsprechung Strafrecht 88

Kennedy, C, 'Immanence and Transcendence: History's Role in Normative Legal Theory' (2017) 8 Jurisprudence 557

Lacey, N, *In Search of Criminal Responsibility: Ideas, Interests, and Institutions* (Oxford University Press 2016)

Lacey, N, 'Psychologising Jekyll, Demonising Hyde: The Strange Case of Criminal Responsibility' (2010) 4 Criminal Law & Philosophy 109

Lacey, N, *Women, Crime, and Character: From Moll Flanders to Tess of the D'Urbervilles* (Oxford University Press 2008)

Norrie, A, 'Criminal Law and Ethics: Beyond Normative Assertion and its Critique' (2017) 80 Modern Law Review 955

Ormerod, D and Laird, K, *Smith, Hogan and Ormerod's Criminal Law* (15th edn, Oxford University Press 2018)

Redlich, AD and Özdogru, AA, 'Alford Pleas in the Age of Innocence' (2009) 27 Behavioral Sciences and the Law 467

Redmayne, M, *Character in the Criminal Trial* (Oxford University Press 2015)

Roberts, J and von Hirsch, A, (eds), *Previous Convictions at Sentencing* (Hart Publishing 2010)

Tadros, V, 'Justice and Terrorism' (2007) 10 New Criminal Law Review 658

Tadros, V, *Criminal Responsibility* (Oxford University Press 2005)

Watson, G, 'Two Faces of Responsibility' in *Agency and Responsibility* (Oxford University Press 2004)

Wittgenstein, L, *Philosophical Investigations* (trans. GEM Anscombe, Blackwell 1963) § 43

PART II

GENDER AND ETHICS IN CRIMINAL RESPONSIBILITY

3

The Characters of Criminal Law

From Abstract Individualism to the Social Sexual Person

Ngaire Naffine[1]

My entire chapter is a tribute to the pathbreaking work of Niki Lacey over so many years. I have marvelled at her novel, imaginative thinking in feminist legal theory, political and social theory, and in criminal law and justice. I have been inspired by her many endeavours to make us see and think and feel differently about the society we live in. Her work has been dedicated to the pursuit of social and legal justice. It has been an inspiration. Her warmth and generosity, her intelligence and humour, have made her a treasure as a friend and as a feminist comrade in arms.

***

1. Introduction

Criminal law theorists necessarily start their theorizing with some idea of their subject: the person they believe criminal law is regulating. They rely on an implicit character, sometimes called a centre of responsibility, who is really the potential accused notionally addressed by criminal law, who can be singled out, have charges levelled against them, and assigned blame. Two main characters are conjured up in criminal law theory.

The dominant figure in the canon is the criminal actor understood as a free-standing individual to whom responsibility can be properly assigned in a court of law, and who can be treated as an autonomous unit, snipped out of his time and place and group affiliations, with their associated criminal proclivities, or law-abiding tendencies. This is a (deliberately and knowingly) thinly conceived individual, abstracted, and posited as universal and ahistorical, but actually historically liberal, in that he is taken to be a rational choosing agent. Hence an idea of human

[1] Bonython Professor of Law, University of Adelaide.

Ngaire Naffine, *The Characters of Criminal Law* In: *On Crime, Society, and Responsibility in the Work of Nicola Lacey.* Edited by: Iyiola Solanke, Oxford University Press (2021). © The several contributors.
DOI: 10.1093/oso/9780198852681.003.0004

beings, located in place and time, is assumed, even within this thin model of the person.[2] I shall call him Model 1.

Then there is **the demographic or social model of the criminal person**. Here our disciplinary characters are treated as *members of a population* that have certain criminal or law-abiding propensities rather than as *separate distinct autonomous individuals, treated on their own*, each making up their own mind about whether to offend. With the demographic model, the person has socially made inclinations and tendencies. And they come in categories of persons which represent real concerns for the state and impose an obligation on the state to offer an effective and tailored response. Here men and women immediately come to mind as they are so different in their patterns of offending.

Those who subscribe to this second model tend to be thinking of real historical and social people, located in places and contexts,[3] as well as people with bodies and sexes whose population membership behaviour is of practical concern to the criminal law, though criminal law is generally loath to express this, that is to specify its people of interest, preferring laws of generality. Again, they are thinking of men and women, people with a class, an age, a race, a group set of beliefs. Here the person is understood as a member of a group, of a population, possessing characteristics which matter to criminal law. I shall call this Model 2.

Most criminal laws operate on the basis of a Model 1 person, with an individual without social characteristics or context. Generally speaking criminal law does not treat its subjects as members of a group or class of concern. Its prohibitions are explicitly directed at so-called 'persons' or 'individuals'. But occasionally these population or demographic concerns are directly expressed in criminal laws, the intended class of persons is made explicit, and the interchangeable, almost fungible, individual as central character is abandoned. Criminal law takes a bead on its real subjects of interest and tries to respond appropriately to their perceived anti-social tendencies; to the threat they pose to the community. The English criminal law of rape is one such law. It still names men as the people of concern. In effect, men are designated the exclusive class of persons at whom the law is directed.

The English law of rape therefore poses a challenge for Model 1 individualists, requiring them to make some sense of this population-specific law, if they choose to engage with it as a subject of theory. You would therefore expect them to avoid

[2] On the abstracted person of criminal law see Alan Norrie, *Crime, Reason and History: A Critical Introduction to Criminal Law* (3rd edn, Cambridge University Press 2014) 26. See also Celia Wells and Oliver Quick, *Lacey, Wells and Quick, Reconstructing Criminal Law: Text and Materials* (4th edn, Cambridge University Press 2010) 95.

[3] For a sustained endeavour to locate criminal law's persons in their social and historical context see Lindsay Farmer, *Making the Modern Criminal Law: Criminalization and Civil Order* (Oxford University Press 2016). And on the historical development of the idea of the responsible subject see Nicola Lacey, *In Search of Criminal Responsibility* (Oxford University Press 2016).

such analysis but they do not. The crime of rape has been a remarkably popular topic for theoretical analysis.[4] So, when individualists write about the nature of rape and its law, it is highly revealing of their thinking about their own criminal law character, the individual, and about the other character, the member of a group of criminal concern. In this paper I take some of the work of legal philosopher John Gardner, who has written influentially about English rape law, to discover what an individualist does with a law which acknowledges its population of concern. What happens when the two paradigms are apparently in open conflict?

2. The Foreground and the Background Views

Though it complicates analysis, I must concede that Model 1 and Model 2 are not simply polar opposites: each operates with more than one view of the person. Each model has what I call a foreground and background view of its subject, which as I will show permit tacit agreements between adherents of the two approaches, not just antagonism. Thus the two models sit in an interesting relationship with one another, which allows for differences of opinion or at least mutual tolerance. I should also concede my preference for the social model, for Model 2, and my possible confirmation bias in this direction of explanation. This means that I am offering a riposte to Gardner and the other individualists who still abound in criminal law theory.

The Model 1 being is the strongly dominant character. And there is a reason for this. The dominant cultural model of the person in liberal democracies and in criminal law is still that of the individual, regarded independently of their defining population memberships, such as their sex, age, class, race, and religion. In criminal law and its theory he is conceived as a centre of decision-making, and a bearer of rights and duties and responsibilities etc. The Model 1 person has been around for some time, though he has been partially reinvented and reinvigorated for modern criminal law theory. He might even be considered a legal fiction, a conscious device for getting the processes of establishing responsibility going, an as-if being, to invoke Hans Vaihinger. For example he is presumed competent without further inspection. His thoughts are taken to be knowable to himself and to a court of law. He is deemed capable of making a choice and acting on it in a manner which will align to criminal responsibility, say the mental states of intention or recklessness.

Model 1 individuals are understood as discrete and interchangeable decisional units. Without this insertion of a person into the heart of things, it would be

[4] For an analysis of this preoccupation, and its perverse effects, see Ngaire Naffine, *Criminal Law and the Man Problem* (Oxford University Press 2019).

difficult to get the criminal law show on the road. *This is the foreground view. It entails thin rather than thick description of the person.*[5]

Most offences reflect this foreground view of the person of Model 1. They do not single out a group of concern, even when there is obviously one. More commonly the central legal character is called an 'individual' or 'person'. Even laws which initially have a class of person in mind, when first conceived, tend to succumb to the individual model by the time of enactment, so dominant is that model. For example the English offence of coercive control had men in mind, when first imagined, but ended up being about anyone.[6]

There have been infamous Model 2 laws which named their subjects of concern. The offence of gross indecency, now happily gone,[7] was once expressly aimed at a class of persons, at gay men. It was singling out certain men and certain forms of behaviour and proscribing and punishing them as offences against the state. English rape law persists in naming its subject of concern and so is a Model 2 law.

On what I call the foreground view, these two models of criminal law's person do not pose a necessary problem for one another—they can and do coexist. The Model 1 individual, thinly conceived as bearer of rights and duties, typically inhabits the formulation of criminal laws, which are about persons and individuals; the Model 2 theorists implicitly cede to Model 1. But even then Model 1 is not necessarily ousting the more social Model 2. For the Model 1 individual can be understood pragmatically as a formal device or as a compilation of legal elements. Law needs a unit of responsibility and analysis. It needs an addressee. It needs an idea of a person of sufficient generality to allow rights and duties to attach, to anyone, so that laws themselves can apply generally. It needs a legal fiction of a person, in some ways knowingly thought of as a legal device.

The elements of offences and defences that must be established or negated to create a criminal thus implicitly build upon the Model 1 idea of an artificial legal person. The elements are knowingly legal terms: they do not endeavour to reach deeply into the nature or psyche of individual persons, however they are conceived. Thus intention to perform some type of proscribed conduct is intention as law defines it and not necessarily what the accused thinks he is doing, in all its complexity. The criminal comes into being when the elements of the offence, legally defined, are found to be proven, rather than some deep personal set of meanings discovered or established, as the person experiences them. This satisfaction of the legal elements is enough of a person to serve at the foreground level. (The general population is poorly acquainted with this idea of a person which is why the decisions of criminal courts are poorly understood by the public at large.)

[5] Clifford Geertz, 'Thick Description: Toward an Interpretive Theory of Culture' in *The Interpretation of Cultures: Selected Essays* (Basic Books 1973) 3.

[6] See Evan Stark, *Coercive Control The Entrapment of Women in Personal Life* (Oxford University Press 2009).

[7] Though not until 2004 in England, by the Sexual Offences Act (2003).

Model 2, with its insistence that crime is committed more by some sections of the population than others, that it is patterned and unevenly distributed, and that this is commonplace knowledge, sits outside the Model 1 idea of the individual person, without tension or contradiction. For the Model 1 person, which is written into most criminal laws, is not trying to get down to rich psychological or social details, nor to establish or respond to broad propensities of different classes of people. It is not aiming for thick description, for a well-rounded view of the person, nor of their place in the community and what that place stands for, to them and to others. It is knowingly thinning out the individual so that it can indeed apply to anyone, so that there can be laws of generality. That is why this individual is something like Vaihinger's neglective fiction.[8]

In the interests of coherence, the individual of Model 1 sets aside or brackets the knowledge that crime is unevenly distributed; that it is associated with known populations and that criminal laws should possibly be aimed at their real targets. As a consequence, the known propensities of different groups are not factored into Model 1, nor into most criminal law, which typically depends on this model. Therefore perhaps the most important feature of crime—who tends to commit it—is simply left out of conceptions of the person in criminal law.

Though they are not necessarily in tension, it is common for these two approaches to criminal law's person to be thought of as oppositional and as residing within different schools or paradigms of thought, with different advocates and language games, even though the supposedly oppositional school is taken as a given. In the foreground the models can coexist, especially if the Model 2 advocates implicitly concede that the uses of Model 1 in criminal laws do not speak definitively or comprehensively about the nature of persons.

a. The Background Views

It is in the background views of what we are, of our natures, that real difficulties can arise for the discipline in talking across worldviews or ideological positions and in coming to grips with the social and historical nature of crime and its criminal populations. In the background understandings of the person there can emerge serious incompatibilities. For it is in the background that we find deeper theories of the person. We find metaphysics and the problem or tension is that the individualists and the demographic people tend to think of us quite differently, as fundamentally different creatures or creations.

In the background, Model 1 individualists typically subscribe to the classical liberal view of the person: that we are pre-social beings, whose natures are formed,

[8] Hans Vaihinger, *The Philosophy of 'As If'* (Kegan Paul 1924) 201–2.

somehow, before we enter society. John Stuart Mill, the committed individualist and liberal, expressed this view when he said 'Men are not, when brought together, converted into another kind of substance.'[9] In other words they are already themselves before they enter society and they stay that way once they get into the social world. This view of our persons, however, is one that has been doubted by so many disciplines, that it is difficult to sustain. I suspect that many individualists are fully apprised of this change in general thought and may incline towards the social view, even when their theories do not seem to reflect it.

But the individualists have another basis to their thinking, which is perhaps more defensible, morally and legally. It also marries well with their foreground view. Their other background view of the person is more moral than metaphysical. It is that it is desirable to treat each of us *as if* we were separate, distinct, rational, and responsible, for this is the conception of us that best respects us, never mind what we are really like.[10] This openly invented or manufactured view of the person is perhaps the best case for the individualist approach to our natures. To treat each of us as centres of moral responsibility, rationally and autonomously directing our own behaviour, is the dignifying way to think of ourselves and others. It is an ennobling fiction; and as with a formal legal fiction, it entails the endorsement of a known untruth, but for a particular purpose.[11]

It is common knowledge that those accused of crime, and certainly those who end up in prison, tend to be the least articulate, the most disadvantaged and marginalized, and even the most mentally disturbed. But these unfortunate truths are thought not to provide the best model of a responsible subject, one that law should invoke, if it is to hold us accountable for our thoughts and actions. An as-if person, a person of higher calibre than the average felon, is therefore substituted and then the blaming of persons also makes more sense; it is itself more morally defensible, lending greater integrity to the criminal justice system because it contains the idea that we blame only those who can shoulder such responsibilities.

In the other camp, made up of those who advance the social model of the person, Model 2, there is also a *background* view of our natures. To the social or population theorists, society forms us. We are made in (and even as) social relations, and so to understand us as persons we must understand our social memberships.[12] As the social historian EH Carr put it: 'Society and the individual are inseparable; they

[9] John Stuart Mill, *A System of Logic* (Harper and Collins 1882) vii, 1.

[10] See John Gardner, 'The Gist of Excuses' (1997) 2 Buffalo Criminal Law Review 1 who says as much. Antony Duff has also taken this view of us (thanks to Ian Leader-Elliott for this reminder.) RA Duff, *Answering for Crime: Responsibility and Liability in the Criminal Law* (Hart 2007) 87. And for a critical analysis of Duff see Ian Leader-Elliott, 'A Critical Reading of RA Duff, *Answering for Crime*' (2010) 31 Adelaide Law Review 47. See also Victor Tadros, *Criminal Responsibility* (Oxford University Press 2005) 2; AP Simester and Andrew Von Hirsch, *Crimes, Harms and Wrongs* (Hart 2011) 7.

[11] The knowledge that the fiction is indeed a fiction is vital to its definition according to Lon L Fuller, *Legal Fictions* (Stanford University Press 1967).

[12] See Ngaire Naffine, *Law's Meaning of Life: Philosophy, Religion, Darwin and the Legal Person* (Oxford University Press 2009).

are necessary and complementary to each other, not opposites ... That is an aspect of the truth.'[13] In direct reply to Mill, Carr asserts that 'the fallacy is to suppose that they [people] existed, or had any kind of substance, before being "brought together" [into society].'[14]

As Carr elaborates:

> As soon as we are born, the world gets to work on us and transforms us from merely biological into social units. Every human being at every stage of history or prehistory is born into a society and from his earliest years is moulded by that society. The language which he speaks is *not an individual inheritance*, (my emphasis) but a social acquisition from the group in which he grows up. Both language and environment help to determine the character of his thought; his earliest ideas come to him from others.[15]

To press home his point, Carr explains that

> the individual apart from society would be both speechless and mindless. The lasting fascination of the Robinson Crusoe myth is due to its attempt to imagine an individual independent of society. The attempt breaks down. Robinson is not an abstract individual, but an Englishman from York; he carries his Bible with him and he prays to his tribal God. The myth quickly bestows on him his Man Friday; and the building of a new society begins.[16]

b. The Missing Men

The two largest social clusters into which Model 2 theorists might want to divide humanity are men and women and these happen to be the clusters that have the largest bearing on crime and criminalization.[17] For criminal law, the biggest social and biological group of concern is—of course—the social class of men and so it is men who call for close attention by criminal law and its interpreters, though typically this has not been the case. In the social view of Model 2, men necessarily become men within society and what counts as a man is a social concept as much as a biological one. It changes over time and place. And it is a social concept in need of ongoing social investigation. Perhaps the obvious question to pose is 'What is

[13] EH Carr, *What is History?* (Penguin 1961) 31.
[14] Ibid.
[15] Ibid.
[16] Ibid., 31–2.
[17] This obvious fact, that crime clusters, tends to be better acknowledged by an adjacent discipline, criminology, but then criminologists are less in the business of considering how to draft principled criminal law of general application, which Model 1 theorists would be quick to point out.

it about the society of men which predisposes them to crime (as mainly men have defined it)?' And then perhaps, 'What sort of criminal law best responds to these criminal proclivities?' And perhaps also, 'is the crime problem a man problem?' and further still 'Should women, as taxpayers, have to bear the great financial burden on the state of the crime that men do?'[18]

The remarkably muted concern about this social population in criminal law scholarship is testimony to the power of Model 1: the individual model of the person. Criminal law thinking has tended to neglect its main subject of practical concern, men, preferring the analytical division of men into just one individual after another, as if they were equivalent to, and interchangeable with, women. But even the social model of the person has tended to treat men more as a natural than as a social category. Men have formed a remarkably invisible class; as if they were not beings with distinctively male social, economic, political, and legal attributes; and as if they were not distinguished, from the other sex, by their far greater criminal inclinations.[19] The focus on the abstract Any-Person individual turns a blind eye, perhaps knowingly, to the actual patterned and social nature of the conduct: that it is a feature of certain populations who behave in certain predictable ways, the most worrying being the social category comprised of young men who dominate violent crime.

c. The Uneasy Relation

Within criminal law and its theory, these two major working models of the person, Model 1 and 2 sit in an odd and interesting relationship with one another. Theorists, I argue, know of both approaches, whichever their leaning, and when theorists are advancing one view, because of their particular leanings as theorists, they are necessarily conscious of the other and may even presuppose it. Criminal law theorists tend to identify with one position or the other. Either they are inclined to a demographic/social model of the person or they presuppose a freestanding individual as either real or ideal model of the person for law.

These ideological and intellectual camps tend to be antagonistic or mutually neglectful. They tend to disparage the other. Typically they stick to their guns, and hold to their own view, and demonstrate a great reluctance to step across the border, or threshold, from one approach to the other, because the approach of the other, especially in the background view, can be deeply disturbing to their own approach. There is a genuine tension here, a pull in two directions—between asocial

[18] This is a question that has been posed by Grayson Perry, *The Descent of Man* (Allen Lane 2016) 74.

[19] See Ngaire Naffine *Criminal Law and the Man Problem* (Oxford University Press 2019) on the invisibility of men in criminal law theory.

and ahistorical abstraction on the one hand and social realism on the other - because different principles and perhaps also philosophical approaches are in play.

For those who subscribe to Model 1, there is a felt classical need to have a liberal individual at the centre of liberal criminal law, a rational autonomous choosing individual, the capacity for reason being their only salient characteristic; someone who can address and be addressed by the law, as a central and irreducible character or person of concern, in a sort of Strawson sense.[20] But then there is the practical legal knowledge, highlighted by proponents of Model 2, that for real people, not only are their social, legal, and economic classifications and their behaviour of interest patterned, grouped, and clustered, but they conduct themselves in different ways and this should be reflected in law. Thus criminal laws should be directed at actual criminal problems and classes of people.

Model 2 remains abstracted to a significant degree, though it is also figurative. But it is closer to the social reality of crime as it recognizes that criminal law needs to be directed at certain populations, the people who are more prone to engage in anti-social behaviour, even though law is required to apply generally and impartially. The need for general application is recognized but so is the social and sexed nature of crime. Feminists have been swift to make this point.[21]

Notwithstanding this powerful tendency for theorists to operate within their own camps, and to look askance at the other encampment, sometimes an open acknowledgement of the position across the border is unavoidable. And these moments of encounter are revealing. The criminal legal analysis of the English law of rape, a crime explicitly directed at men and therefore at a population, provides an intriguing and informative illustration of this encounter between the two schools because it has been undertaken by some influential individualists who have had to respond to the fact that this is not a crime about Any-Person individuals. It is a crime which sits more comfortably with Model 2. And yet it is a favourite crime for analysis by scholars from both sides and one surprisingly in which men, as men, may not feature strongly.

3. Gardner as the Case Study

To show the disconcerting effects of this moment of encounter between the individualist theorist and a population of practical concern, which is patently not operating as just so many individuals, I now examine some writing on the law of rape of John Gardner, who died tragically during the writing of this chapter.[22] I take two

[20] See PF Strawson, *Individuals: An Essay in Descriptive Metaphysics* (Routledge 1959)

[21] See especially and generally the criminal law scholarship of Nicola Lacey and most recently, *In Search of Criminal Responsibility* (Oxford University Press 2016).

[22] John Gardner was a robust, lively, and generous scholar. This riposte to his work is intended as a mark of respect of a fine intellect. I will retain the present tense when referring to John and his ideas.

papers which are linked, the latter a companion piece to the former, though they span nearly twenty years. I take: 'The Wrongness of Rape' first published in 2000, with Stephen Shute,[23] and its companion piece 'The Opposite of Rape' published in 2018.[24] It is illuminating to take papers so far apart in time because the author had considerable time to reflect on his intellectual commitments and to decide not to change them.

In Gardner's writing, we can view the work of an individualist and also a scholar whose natural setting is English law, though he strives to be a universalist. We can also observe his moves when he feels bound to acknowledge the social model within his nation's law of rape, of which he is inevitably aware: that this law and this behaviour is actually about the social class of men, not the individual. For women are individuals too and they are not the target of this law. Gardner's work is useful because he pushes his argument and analysis further than most, as a committed individualist, and he does this with confidence and flair.[25]

In essence, Gardner is wedded to the idea of the individual as central figure of criminal law, in both pieces, and yet he chooses a crime to exemplify his thinking which is historically, culturally, and legally tightly linked to particular populations, to classes of persons, rather than to individuals: to the class of men and further to certain subclasses of men. He tacitly takes the English law of rape, which is not only still directed at men, but which also precluded husbands from liability right up to the 1990s. And so, from the outset, he sets himself a hard problem. His Model 1 foreground view, of the individual as a sort of neutral rights and duty bearer—an Any-Person—which is in fact the starting point of most criminal laws, cannot be his starting point because the law he has chosen per se conforms to Model 2.[26] To wrench rape from men (Model 2) and instate this Any-Person individual (Model 1) is what he does, to a surprising degree, but not consistently so.

As much as he can, Gardner tries to get real men out of his analysis, and to make the neutral liberal choosing individual his central character; this is Model 1 in the background view. However Gardner conspicuously struggles with this and keeps having to defer to Model 2, because rape is very much a crime of place and time and men and their relations with women. Indeed, it has been about men for centuries.

[23] 'The Wrongness of Rape' was co-written with Stephen Shute in Jeremy Horder (ed.), *Oxford Essays in Jurisprudence, Fourth Series* (Oxford University Press, 2000). Apologies to Stephen Shute for my focus on Gardner.

[24] John Gardner 'The Opposite of Rape' (2018) 38(1) Oxford Journal of Legal Studies 48

[25] It could be said that he pushes things to a point where they take on some rather odd characteristics—in the 'The Wrongness of Rape' he does not even need a woman who is experiencing that wrong, who knows that it is happening to her, and this appears counterintuitive.

[26] Gardner has chosen a difficult crime, perhaps the hardest, for an individualist because rape is one of the most conspicuously male crimes, associated with real physical and social men. Within its conventional definition, it is committed by men, and those who can commit it are legally required to be men in England, requiring male genitalia and so to proceed as an individualist here is quite a feat.

The Wrongness of Rape

From the outset, in The Wrongness of Rape,[27] Gardner (and Shute) condemns the crime of rape as odious, as always and everywhere utterly wrong. His purpose is to explain why it is wrong. He declares that 'Arguably, rape is among those wrongs which are never excusable.'[28] He says this in the common knowledge that all husbands were excused from the crime until 1991 in his own country and that in England women remain outside of the scope of liability. He is therefore writing about rape both inside and outside the law.

Gardner sets out to explain what an individual has to do to commit this atrocity, which in his view is both a moral and a legal wrong; he wants to nail the thought, the act, and hence the wrong, as so many have tried to do before him. He does this by paring away what he takes to be all extraneous elements and trying to isolate the essence of the wrong, with an atrocious individual intent on committing this evil act. Even the content and variability of actual laws are implicitly not to the point. He alludes to rape laws, he slides between jurisdictions with their variable definitions of the crime, though their variability is skated over. His footnotes on the nature of rape may hail from Canada, the United States, or England.

Implicitly the positive law of rape, which is highly jurisdiction-specific, is extraneous to argument and purpose. The character of rape, it would seem, does not take its meaning from the law, even though his article is about rape law. So the foreground view of the individualists' individual, which typically concentrates on the formal legal rights and duties of persons, is both part of the discussion yet also set outside of this discussion.

And yet Gardner does repeatedly invoke 'the law'. He is writing as a lawyer, not as a philosopher who may well not have a close working knowledge of the formal ingredients of the crime. Gardner's purpose is to identify the essential wrong of rape that 'the law' everywhere should recognize.[29] But there is a continuous gravitation to actual social men and women, and indeed to England and English law. Though 'the criminal law' at times is treated as a free-floating thing, and offenders and their victims as simply individuals, for Gardner, in his analysis, the crime of rape is something nearly always inflicted by a man—he refers repeatedly to men as the offenders in his model—but not as a delimited class of persons. However to be a man is to be classified as one of a group; the individual is necessarily surrendered to the class. So then one should be obliged to ask, what is it about the class of men

[27] Originally published as John Gardner and Simon Shute, 'The Wrongness of Rape' in J Horder (ed), *Oxford Essays in Jurisprudence, Fourth Series* (2000). Republished as John Gardner 'The Wrongness of Rape' in John Gardner, *Offences and Defences: Selected Essays in the Philosophy of Criminal Law* (OUP 2007) ch. 1. Pagination is from this 2007 reprinting.

[28] Gardner 'The Wrongness of Rape' (n. 27) 1.

[29] This in Gardner's view is the worse wrong that one individual can do to another, whenever and wherever and whoever they are.

that makes them prototypical offenders? With this question, the conception of the crime is no longer about the thoughts and actions of the individual.

The drive to detach the crime from positive law and its positive sex-specific characters performing certain specific acts on others who are thereby harmed by the experience, is also evident in Gardner's choice of his '*pure* case' as one 'entirely stripped of distracting epiphenomena'[30] such as the victim's awareness of it, and the fact that it never comes to the law. He is quite clear about this: 'It is no objection that the question of the wrongfulness of this rape will never arise in any practical deliberation, such as the deliberation of a court, since *ex hypothesi* the rape will never come to light.'[31] The courts and their deliberations are cast out of his analysis.

And yet despite the reference to the 'basic, or essential, wrongness of rape',[32] outside of courts and laws, a particular legal cast of defendants and victims, one which belongs well within English law, is implicitly and explicitly invoked, with men as the offenders and women as the imagined victims. To wit, after a rape, '*She* may be traumatized, lose *her* trust in *men*.' Here we have men and women and their relations and a nod to the fact that men and women may lead very different lives in terms of their victimizing and being victimized.

But then the woman does become simply a person and so does the man. Thus to Gardner, 'Rape, in the pure case, is the sheer use of a person.... Rape is terrifying and humiliating... because the sheer use of a person, and in that sense the objectification of a person, is a denial of their personhood. It is literally dehumanizing.' Moreover 'all sheer use of human beings, all treatment of them merely as means, is *ab*use; and rape is the central case of such abuse'. Sex specificity is abandoned and his characters become individuals or persons. As he puts it, 'rape is, fundamentally, a crime of objectification, a crime of using a person as a thing'.[33]

The closest Gardner gets to linking his idea of rape openly to a particular law is to concede 'that although the mere use of people is a timeless evil, the elevation of penetrative non-consensual sexual violation to the status of special paradigm is a long-standing, but culturally conditioned application'.[34] What is being employed to penetrate and what is penetrated, both things normally specified in law, is not said. Nor is the culture that is conditioning the meaning and definitions of these acts made explicit.[35]

30 Gardner 'The Wrongness of Rape'(n. 27) 7.
31 Ibid., 8.
32 Ibid., 7.
33 Ibid., 27.
34 Ibid., 23.
35 He says also that 'rape is a crime of sexual violation according to its social meaning; and that social meaning is the meaning which is at the heart of rapes wrongness.' Ibid., 25. Now this statement might seem to take us to a particular society and its laws and to the sex-specific lives of men and women within it; perhaps to English society. But Gardner then retreats to the idea of the individual and their rights, and to the person. Men and women disappear and so too does location, culture, and society.

a. The Opposite of Rape

In Gardner's second paper entitled 'The Opposite of Rape', good sex is *conducted between individuals*, not men and women, or even men and men or women and women, and it is not simply the opposite of sexual subordination. It is not even something to which one consents, as that has too contractual a flavour, suggesting a type of standard contract with the more powerful party setting the standard terms. Instead good sex is more of a free-for-all, active, noisy, energetic enterprise, described as a matter of teamwork and undertaken with constant mutual agreement. It is an act of 'intense physical pleasure, of close affective engagement, of raw sexual chemistry, of playful experimentation, of satisfaction of sexual appetites'.[36] It can be likened 'to good ensemble playing by musicians, good ballroom dancing and good circus acrobatics'.[37] Throughout, Gardner accentuates the agency of the participants, indeed he recognizes their full liberal credentials.[38] Here is the background view of Model 1, strongly drawn.

Though Gardner stresses the importance of the wishes and communication of the participants, to emphasize and respect their autonomy, he locates his individuals in no-man's and no-woman's land. In this modern criminal law analysis, we can observe the central characters being abstracted—from the actual history of rape law and from modern rape laws. For Gardner, rape which is the opposite of good sex, 'is a *timeless* ritual of humiliation, degradation, and *dehumanisation*'.[39] In other words, rape does not take its meaning from a time, a place, and a people: or rather from the people of influence. The meaning of rape is 'timeless'. It has a Platonic form.[40] And by necessary implication, the perfect rape law would correspond with this real Platonic form of rape. It would nail this wrong.[41] This is the individual of Model 1.

The fact that few past or present rape laws are mentioned with any specificity again helps to secure this sense of timelessness and placelessness; the invocation of actual law, in any detail, would reveal that the offence of rape has varied enormously by time and place. It would also require analysis to focus on men and women and their changing roles over time. It would move us to Model 2, which Gardner does only briefly in this piece, and then quickly retreats.

36 Gardner 'The Opposite of Rape' (n. 24) 51.
37 Ibid., 51.
38 Ibid., 51.
39 Ibid., 50.
40 On the uses of Platonic forms in the writing of Gardner see Ngaire Naffine 'Moral Certainties of Rape and Murder' in Bernadette McSherry, Alan Norrie, and Simon Bronitt (eds), *Regulating Deviance: The Redirection of Criminalisation and the Futures of Criminal Law* (Oxford University Press 2009) 213.
41 This blanket human-to-human prohibition, in which men and women are interchangeable, both potential humiliators or humiliated, has never existed in English rape law. So Gardner is not theorizing about the criminal law of his own country. His timeless crime is somewhere else.

The degree of commitment to individualism is striking. Although he is explicitly and vividly writing about sex, at the same time Gardner abstracts the main characters from their sex. By this I mean that we are not meant to think of our legal subjects as necessarily men and women any more, only as human beings. Despite references by Gardner to the actual statistics of rape, revealing that much of it is a crime committed by men[42] and mainly directed at women, (i.e. Model 2) the nature of rape and the nature of its opposite—good sex—are seen in terms of just 'people', coming together, for intimate purposes in very bad or very good ways (Model 1).[43]

As Gardner makes clear, 'the heterosexual case' is his exemplar purely to retain 'simplicity' of analysis [56]. This sex of the subjects is not given an explicit history nor a body of historical or contemporary law. He bypasses the foreground view of individualism which can normally rely on laws directed at individuals or persons, not laws aimed at men and women. However, English rape law recalcitrantly invokes men not persons. It is explicitly directed at a class of persons and so poses an almost insuperable problem from the outset for a Model 1 theorist, for an individualist that is.

In this analysis, there are two individuals interested in human border-crossing, and these individuals could be anyone, of any sex, anywhere. And so 'if both parties correctly diagnose in each other the intention to have sex with each other on condition that the other has a like intention, we are not an unrealistically long way from concluding that they have the joint intention necessary for it to qualify as good sex'.[44] Gardner's individuals are simply persons deciding whether to enter the society of sexual relations, like Mill's individuals entering into social relations.

By detaching most of his analysis of rape, and its opposite, from actual laws, Gardner is doing something now characteristic of much modern criminal law scholarship, which is why I am spending some time considering his intellectual moves. He is extracting the crime from its broader setting: from its time, its place, and its culture, from real people and their patterns of behaviour, in fact from those things that have given it meaning, and still do.[45] Gardner does consider the concept of consent within rape laws; but he does not consider rape's status limitations and exemptions which is where the men and women of rape law are to be found.

The analysis sets aside, by silent fiat, most of those things which have made the crime of rape what it is. The history of legal thought about the nature of rape, which is after all a creation of criminal law, is on the whole treated as extraneous to

42 And after all, only a man can commit the offence of rape as a principal in England for obvious historical and social reasons.

43 Gardner does refer to 'heterosexual penetrative sex', in which 'the male and the female genitalia' are the 'principal instruments' but this is intended as just one of his models of sex within his overarching model of gender-neutral coition. Gardner 'The Opposite of Rape' (n. 24) 55.

44 Ibid.,55. What matters is their subjective intentions and communication of those intentions, though Gardner also countenances happy silence.

45 Wittgenstein would say that if we extract our words from their working usage, language goes on holiday, see *Philosophical Investigations*. Alison - Are publication details required here?

analysis. The different meanings of the crime over time, its legal inclusions and exclusions,[46] which continue to the present day, in different ways, are not of scholarly interest because there is a true meaning of rape to be found outside of time and history. To Gardner, rape is essentially a human-to-human humiliation which entails a 'dehumanisation'[47]—it is not about men and women and their very different social and legal histories and roles embedded within the English criminal law of rape.

With Gardner, there is an elegant modelling of the crime of rape and its opposite, 'good sex', which takes individualism to a new level and so, in some ways, makes it easier to observe. This intellectual exercise is reminiscent of economic modelling which also relies on abstractions from real men and women.[48] The analysis depends on a simplified model of humans and human sexual relations. As few elements as possible are used to build the positive models of rape and of good sex. Most significantly, men and women have lost their distinguishing features as men and women and have become sexless, genderless humans. Most of the features are removed which once mattered—such as sex, sexuality, and marital status. And yet some of these features still do, in fact, delimit the crime. What we are left with are humans with intentions and desires. This suggests a silent selection of what will be taken out of the model and what will be put in. This selection process is unfortunate because it takes out things which have been critical to the legal understanding of the nature of the crime (and its opposite). Fundamental information about how the crime has been formed, and by whom, is removed.

With choosing or desirous human beings selected as the basic units of analysis, we arrive at the classic character of modern liberal individualism. With these processes of selection and modelling, two modern liberal and equally powerful individuals emerge, making love, freed of centuries of misogynist thinking about men, women, and sex, and freed of actual law. Here is the background view of Model 1. It is Model 1 in metaphysical mode.[49] The process of selecting out leaves us with a model of idealized equal liberal relations between humans who, when they are doing the opposite of rape, are doing so in their own, freely chosen, liberal, world and they are doing so person to person; they are only incidentally sexed.

This degree of abstraction, of modelling, is almost impossible to visualize without men and women. It is a thought experiment which is not meant to be seen,

[46] Which have depended on sex, marital status, sexuality, even sexual history, and still do in some ways.

[47] The female rapist is therefore necessarily included, though again this does not reflect English rape law.

[48] See Allan Gibbard and Hal R Varian, 'Economic Models' (1978) 75(11) The Journal of Philosophy 664.

[49] To make love of course they do need bodies but these bodies are strangely bereft of detail: for much of the analysis there are no specified genitalia, despite the activities in which they are engaged. Consistently specified genitals would only complicate the analysis and of course immediately create sex specificity and sexed relations.

in the mind's eye, in any detail.[50] Given any visual content, inevitably, we start seeing men and women[51] (or perhaps men and men and women and women) doing certain things with certain parts of their bodies. And then the cultural and social significance of these relations starts creeping in. In this modern liberal legal analysis, everything resides in the thoughts and intentions of the individuals engaged in the relevant activities, who have no history and so no historical inequalities (e.g. they do not have the thoughts of socially powerful men or weaker women).

But actually this modern liberal individual is not freely chosen and freestanding. Rather he has his own history, running through Locke and Kant and Mill. And within this liberal history of the individual, women have been poorly individualized, as Carole Pateman has explained.[52] Indeed male individualism tended to presuppose the non-individuation of women. Even the good Mill saw the sexes differently and so did the mid-twentieth-century liberals: Norval Morris, Glanville Williams, and Colin Howard as I have shown elsewhere.[53]

And despite the endeavour to maintain an Olympian stance, any social or legal analyst is still stuck with the problem that there is no place outside of culture, outside of particular societies and their particular histories, from which to view those laws and crimes and make sense of them. Neither the analyser nor the analysed can be taken out of society. There is no Mount Olympus. We are always in the thick of things, though the analyser can reflect on their own location within the maelstrom, which will improve her analysis, as Thomas Nagel makes clear.[54]

And even when it seems that the people in legal contemplation, under examination, should be able to just slip away, do their own private intimate thing, entirely on their own terms, human to human as modern beings, away from the glare of law and society, society continues to define us. As the novelist and cultural critic, Angela Carter, put it:

> We do not go to bed in simple pairs; even if we choose not to refer to them, we still drag there with us the cultural impedimenta of our social class, our parents' lives, our bank balances, our sexual and emotional expectations, our whole biographies.[55]

What is taken to be 'good sex' and horrific rape, is not a matter of personal private invention or intention. On the contrary, men and women still go into the bedroom with law and society not only looking over the bed but also inhabiting the persons

[50] On the limitations of such thought experiments see Kathleen Wilkes, *Real People: Personal Identity Without Thought Experiments* (Oxford University Press 1988).
[51] Which is probably why 'penetrative heterosexual sex' is Gardner's exemplar of sex.
[52] Carole Pateman, *The Sexual Contract* (Stanford University Press 1988).
[53] Ngaire Naffine, *Criminal Law and the Man Problem* (Oxford 2009).
[54] Thomas Nagel, *The View from Nowhere* (Oxford University Press 1986).
[55] Angela Carter, *The Sadeain Woman: An Exercise in Cultural History* (Virago 1979) 9.

themselves. Particular individuals, with their own particular thoughts, cannot retreat from society and go to bed, to have sex of their own devise, subject only to their own imaginations and their private ongoing agreements and arrangement. Instead the individual takes their society, and their position and power within it, to the bedroom. The bed is therefore a highly public place and to understand what is going on in the bedroom, in its forced and consensual forms, we need to understand the place of men and women in society and in law and their respective histories.

To invoke Carter again:

> our flesh arrives to us out of history, like everything else does.... Although the erotic relationship may seem to exist freely, on its own terms, among the distorted social relationships of a bourgeois society, it is, in fact, the most self-conscious of all human relationships, a direct confrontation of two beings whose actions in the bed are wholly determined by their acts when they are out of it.[56]

There is a long history of criminal law which has given meaning to those acts, those people, and those relationships. The bedroom is truly crowded.

To return to Carr, and his thoughts on Robinson Crusoe, literature's classic discrete individual, fully removed from society; as Carr rightly observes, in truth Robinson was of his place and time. 'The lasting fascination of the Robinson Crusoe myth is due to its attempt to imagine an individual independent of society.' But the attempt fails. Robinson is actually 'an Englishman from York'; who brings with him his religion and his God.[57] And of course Robinson has a sex; he is a man not a woman, and this matters greatly to the viability of the story, though Carr makes little of this social feature. The lightening conflation of man and individual, by Carr himself, shows the tenacity of the individualist approach and its ready eclipse of men as a social class, even when it is a committed social theorist doing the analysis. A solitary man is quickly mistaken for a solitary individual; Carr does not quite see that all the impedimenta of his sex also accompanies Robinson to the island.

4. Conclusion

My further argument is also that any remaining sense that criminal law harbours a centre of solid principle, in which people are both respected and protected, depends on an unacknowledged movement between the Model 1 individualist conception of the person and the Model 2 of socially conceived people, imagined as men and women, as adults and children, as social and historical beings who need

56 Ibid., 9–10.

57 EH Carr, *What is History?* (Penguin 1961) 31–2

regulating in certain ways. This oscillation, typically not remarked upon, keeps the show on the road, in the sense that criminal law is still thought to address us as universal individuals but to deal with real social problems and people and populations. At least it is when it is thought to be doing its job well.

It also keeps the man problem at bay; and so poorly dealt with by the discipline. That is, the historical dominance of the discipline by men is unacknowledged, in favour of a studied scholarly neutrality: it is an Anyone who is formulating theory. As a consequence, the demands that men place on the criminal justice system as the more criminal sex are poorly incorporated into theory and also insufficiently incorporated explicitly into law, because abstract individualism countenances against it.

Instead there are unacknowledged movements between the two Models and also an assumption that there is no problem in doing this. So some of the time the background assumption is that men or women are the true subjects of concern, understood in certain ways, but the language used is that of the individual; or the explicit law reform treatment is of men and women and then the problem of the individual is left hanging.

For criminal law-making, its theorizing and justification to be intellectually honest and engage truthfully with its subjects, this tension must always be recognized, but it is not and this leads to some very odd thinking. Abstract individualism should be acknowledged as just that, as a legal means of achieving certain purposes and promoting certain principles, as an ideal type, as a device. It should not convey a sense that the individuals to whom it applies do not behave in patterned ways and that some groups are a much greater problem than others. The slide to the female pronoun when referring to the defendant in much contemporary scholarship conveys the idea, strongly, that sex does not matter. And recall that the offence of coercing and controlling behaviour designed for men ended up being drafted in a manner which concealed this fact. I suspect this often happens: the individual, as anyone, tends to trump the designation of the specific problem group.

Perhaps there is an inevitable tension in criminal law between the need to identify a wrong or harm which must be proscribed, at a level of generality and abstraction that it protects and proscribes everyone, and the need to deal with complex particular historical social problems and people? Even if there is, this too needs to be noted and factored into criminal legal thought. This has yet to happen.

Bibliography

Carr, EH, *What is History?* (Penguin 1961)
Carter, A, *The Sadeain Woman: An Exercise in Cultural History* (Virago Press 1979)
Gardner, J, 'The Opposite of Rape' (2018) 38(1) Oxford Journal of Legal Studies 48

Gardner, J and Shute, S, 'The Wrongness of Rape' in J Horder (ed.), *Oxford Essays in Jurisprudence, Fourth Series* (Oxford University Press 2000)
Geertz, C, 'Thick Description: Toward an Interpretive Theory of Culture' in *The Interpretation of Cultures: Selected Essays* (Basic Books 1973)
Gibbard, A and Varian, HR, 'Economic Models' (1978) 75(11) The Journal of Philosophy 664
Lacey, N, *In Search of Criminal Responsibility* (Oxford University Press 2016)
Naffine, N, *Criminal Law and the Man Problem* (Hart 2019)
Naffine, N, 'Moral Certainties of Rape and Murder' in B McSherry, A Norrie, and S Bronitt (eds), *Regulating Deviance: The Redirection of Criminalisation and the Futures of Criminal Law* (Oxford 2009)
Naffine, N, *Law's Meaning of Life: Philosophy, Religion, Darwin and the Legal Person* (Hart 2009)
Nagel, T, *The View from Nowhere* (Oxford University Press 1986)
Norrie, A, *Crime, Reason and History: A Critical Introduction to Criminal Law* (3rd edn, Cambridge University Press 2014)
Pateman, C, *The Sexual Contract* (Stanford University Press 1988)
Perry, G, *The Descent of Man* (Allen Lane 2016)
Strawson, PF, *Individuals: An Essay in Descriptive Metaphysics* (Routledge 1959)
Wells, C and Quick, O, *Lacey, Wells and Quick, Reconstructing Criminal Law: Text and Materials* (4th edn, Cambridge University Press 2010) 95
Wilkes, K, *Real People: Personal Identity Without Thought Experiments* (Oxford University Press 1988)
Wittgenstein, L, *Philosophical Investigations* (Macmillan 1953)

4
Why Blame?

John Gardner[1]

1. Blame Scepticism

> *The uneducated person blames others for their failures; those who have just begun to be instructed blame themselves; those whose learning is complete blame neither others nor themselves.*[2]

So says Epictetus, spelling out one tenet of Stoic thought: that blame, whether of oneself or another, has no place in a life wisely lived. To blame is unhealthy and dispensable. This tenet long endeared me to Stoicism. For I was, for many years, what Peter Graham calls a 'blame sceptic'.[3] That is not to say that I resiled from blaming. Rather, I blamed and then reproached myself for doing so. Since reproaching entails blaming, I thereby compounded my felony. And then, reproaching myself for compounding my felony, I compounded it some more.

Blame sceptics come in many stripes. Numerous and notorious among them are *responsibility sceptics*. They doubt whether anybody is ever responsible for anything. Rightly thinking that being responsible is a necessary condition of being blameworthy, they doubt whether blame is ever in order. Yet that is only the start of their troubles. Responsibility matters for so much more than blame. If I lack responsibility, what I do is no special concern of mine. Why, then, should I pay special attention to what I do? In particular, why should I pay special attention to the advice of responsibility sceptics and stop blaming? If I lack responsibility, it is no special concern of mine whether I blame or not. As you can see already, it is doubtful whether responsibility scepticism is a coherent position. Realizing this, some responsibility sceptics restrict their scepticism to 'moral responsibility', supposedly a special kind of responsibility that, if it existed, would be the one to open the way to blame. What the word 'moral' adds here is generally left unclear. Does it mean that our blame scepticism should be restricted to moral blame, and should not extend to the cases in which, for example we only have ourselves to blame for missing the last train home? Be that as it may, this 'moral responsibility' is very

[1] John Gardner (1965–2019) was Senior Research Fellow at All Souls College, Oxford.
[2] Epictetus, *Enchiridion*, ch. 5.
[3] Peter Graham, 'The Standard Argument for Blame Incompatibilism' (2008) 42 Noûs 697.

John Gardner, *Why Blame?* In: *On Crime, Society, and Responsibility in the Work of Nicola Lacey.* Edited by: Iyiola Solanke, Oxford University Press (2021). © The several contributors. DOI: 10.1093/oso/9780198852681.003.0005

commonly portrayed as a magical property of persons, possessed under conditions so ratcheted up by philosophical fantasists that scepticism about it is unavoidable. The lesson of their work is not that one should be a responsibility sceptic. Rather one should be a sceptic about philosophical fantasies according to which responsibility, moral or otherwise, requires possession of some magical property such as 'contracausal freedom'.[4]

Responsibility scepticism will not concern us further here. It is a blind alley. Blame sceptics of a more interesting stripe—I will call them *judgment sceptics*—are sceptics about standards, or some kinds of standards. Blamers, they say, purport to apply standards of rectitude that exist, and apply to those who are blamed, independently of the invocation, application, acceptance, endorsement (etc.) of those standards by the one who is blamed. No such independent standards exist, says the judgment sceptic, or at least none that are suitable to vindicate judgments of blameworthiness. Thus Bernard Williams writes:

> [W]e can blame a man (we may think) for neglecting his wife even though he has no motivation to be concerned about his wife. So if blame is necessarily connected with reasons, it seems to be necessarily connected with external reasons [reasons that exist independently of the agent's motivations]. Therefore, if there are no such things as external reasons for action, there is something suspect about blame.[5]

Here are two possible answers to Williams, each of which strikes me as both true and dispositive: (a) there are external reasons for action and (b) in judging someone blameworthy, one need not invoke external reasons for action. I will simply assume the truth of (a) here. Meanwhile, we already have an example of (b) to hand. 'You only have yourself to blame for missing the last train home' is commonly uttered to someone who was indeed motivated to catch the train. Blame is not *necessarily* connected to external reasons for action. At least some blame, then, seems to escape the Williams dragnet even if you agree with him that there are no such things as external reasons for action.

Judgment sceptics join responsibility sceptics in doubting whether anyone is ever blameworthy. *Standing-to-blame sceptics* differ in allowing that people can indeed be blameworthy. But they doubt the suitability of any of us to be the one who actually does the blaming. 'He that is without sin among you,' cautions Jesus in a standing-sceptical vein, 'let him cast the first stone.'[6] This is just one of several

[4] The best diagnosis of the slippage between ideas that draws people into this philosophical fantasy is probably Harry Frankfurt, 'Alternate Possibilities and Moral Responsibility' (1969) 66 Journal of Philosophy 829.

[5] 'Internal Reasons and the Obscurity of Blame' in Williams, *Making Sense of Humanity* (Cambridge 1995) 41.

[6] As GA Cohen says, 'the question, "Who can say what to whom?," goes largely unexplored in contemporary moral philosophy.' Cohen, 'Casting the First Stone: Who Can, and Who Can't, Condemn

flavours of blame scepticism in which problems are supposed to begin, not with the soundness of our judgments, but with the attitudes, emotions, or actions to which those judgments give rise. The underlying thought here is that actually *blaming* someone—whether that involves taking a certain attitude to her, feeling a certain way about her, or addressing or treating her in a certain way—involves optional further steps beyond a mere judgment of her blameworthiness. This formulation is already problematic. For perhaps *judging* someone blameworthy is also an optional further step beyond her merely being blameworthy? Could one not instead suspend judgment? 'Don't judge me', says the attention-seeker on social media, nervous that he may have crossed the limits of style or taste. Does this mean 'pay no attention' (an unlikely position for a social media attention-seeker!) or 'don't form any opinions' (how could I not?) or 'give me the benefit of the doubt' (isn't that judging?) . . . or what? We will have cause to return to this 'don't judge me' problem below. For now let's keep the making of bare judgments of blameworthiness out of the picture. Blaming, let's say for now, means going a bit further than that.

But how much further? Nicola Lacey and Hanna Pickard are *efficacy sceptics* about blame. Like the standing-to-blame sceptics they allow for blameworthiness but they caution against the move to blame itself. That is because they think that blaming is typically counterproductive. To say this, they have to assess it against some aim or aims. In the main they have responsibility-accepting and (thereby?) behaviour-improving aims in mind. But never mind that for now. For now our interest is in what, for them, counts as the blaming that we should be efficacy-sceptical about. They call it 'affective blaming':

> Affective blame, as we define it, is the range of hostile, negative attitudes and emotions that are typical human responses to blameworthiness. It can include, for instance, hatred, anger, resentment, indignation, disgust, disapproval, contempt and scorn, and can be manifest in any number of ways, including seeking retaliation, retribution, and vengeance.[7]

Here are three queries arising out of this passage.

(i) Lacey and Pickard lump 'attitudes and emotions' together. 'Affective' seems to be a good label for negative emotions of the blamer but a bad label for

the Terrorists?' in his posthumously published collection *Finding Oneself in the Other* (Princeton University Press 2013) 115, 119. This paper by Cohen, and his follow-up 'Ways of Silencing Critics' in the same volume, are welcome exceptions. A more recent exception that repays study is Macalester Bell, 'The Standing to Blame: A Critique' in D Justin Coates and Neal A Tognazzini (eds), *Blame: Its Nature and Norms* (Oxford University Press 2013).

[7] Nicola Lacey and Hanna Pickard, 'From the Consulting Room to the Court Room? Taking the Clinical Model of Responsibility Without Blame into the Legal Realm' (2013) 33 Oxford Journal of Legal Studies 1.

negative attitudes. In the light of what someone did, I can (dispassionately) lose faith in her or (dispassionately) lose admiration or respect for her.[8] Then I take an attitude towards her which lacks any affective ingredient. She is lowered in my estimation but I have no feelings on the subject. Here I am not merely judging her blameworthy. I am actually blaming her. But in what sense is the blame affective?

(ii) True, we may be disappointed in, or despair of, or despise those whom we blame. Then there is something affective going on. But are these really ways of blaming, or are they just possible emotional consequences of blaming? Couldn't I say 'I'll always blame him for what happened and that's why I'll always hate him'? Isn't blaming best thought of, then, as an intermediate (attitudinal) step between judging someone blameworthy and harbouring hostile feelings towards that someone? (Note that this is compatible with there being *some* emotions, such as remorse or vengefulness, that are partly constituted by the blaming attitude; something can exist in consequence of one of its constituents.[9])

(iii) The harsh ways of treating the person blamed that are listed at the end of the passage ('retaliation, retribution, and vengeance') are certainly 'typical ... manifestations' (and typical consequences) of the 'affective blame' described. However the blamer can in principle avoid the typical manifestations, unlike the typical emotions, by deciding to avoid them. One can be a blamer who is full of resentment, disgust, or scorn and yet not do anything to reveal or convey how one feels, or even that one blames, to the person blamed (or to anyone). True, concealment is easier if one does not have to fight against strong feelings. Still, one can make an effort to hide how one feels and often one succeeds. Myself, I often make the effort (e.g. when dealing with a cold caller) and sometimes but not always I succeed.

Of these, query (iii) is the most pressing. Perhaps what one conveys to the person blamed (or indeed to others) should be judged by its efficacy relative to some aim or aims. Efficacy is a suitable standard for judging actions, including expressive ones. But should the attitudes and emotions that one expresses be judged in the same way? Surely attitudes and emotions are to be judged by how they befit their objects, not by what they achieve?[10] One should love the loveable, trust the trustworthy, admire the admirable, regret the regrettable, be disgusted by the disgusting, give

[8] See George Sher, *In Praise of Blame* (Oxford University Press 2006) 88–9.

[9] Compare R. Jay Wallace, *Responsibility and the Moral Sentiments* (Harvard University Press 1994) 74. Wallace seems to run together the question of whether certain emotions are part-constituted by blame with the question of whether it would be odd to blame without experiencing at least one of them.

[10] Classic discussions of the question include Justin D'Arms and Daniel Jacobson, 'The Moralistic Fallacy: On the "Appropriateness" of Emotions' (2000) 61 Philosophy and Phenomenological Research 65 and Wlodek Rabinowicz and Toni Rønnow-Rasmussen, 'The Strike of the Demon: On Fitting Pro-Attitudes and Value' (2004) 114 Ethics 391.

credit for the creditable, and (by the same token) blame the blameworthy. The case of belief is similar: one should believe the believable (aka the credible). Of course it might be that a certain belief is giving one a lot of trouble, exposing one to ridicule, causing one to lose sleep, sending one off the rails, etc. But is that strictly speaking a reason against the belief, or is it only a reason to keep quiet about believing it, develop strategies to avoid losing sleep over it, etc.? This choice is too stark. There is an intermediate possibility. That a certain belief is troublesome is not a reason against the belief. Yet it is a reason to take steps to rid oneself of the belief—not merely to manage its negative effects. Even though the belief is fully in order *qua* belief, one has reasons to expunge it. Likewise, it seems, with troublesome attitudes and emotions, including blame and its cognates. Imagine that one's disposition to blame the blameworthy (or, say, to resent them or despise them) is interfering with one's work as a therapist or probation officer or social worker or schoolteacher. One option is to find a new line of work. But first one might try to contain one's disposition to blame, say by taking a closer interest in the blameworthy people one deals with, and learning to focus on something about them other than their blameworthiness.[11] True, one needs some such indirect strategy to contain attitudes and emotions that one still regards as befitting their objects. The unwelcome attitudes and emotions do not disappear merely because one realizes that it would be better if they did. Nor can one lose them simply by deciding to lose them. Yet they can at least sometimes be tackled, and the mere fact that they still befit their objects is not enough to make a conclusive case for holding onto them.

It is a long way, however, from here to the thesis that blame, even affective blame, is to be judged by its efficacy, where this means assigning some aim or aims to it. Attitudes and emotions do not have aims.[12] What has an aim, or often has an aim, is the expression or communication of an attitude or emotion. When Lacey and Pickard worry about the inefficacy of blame, then, they are not exactly blame sceptics, or even affective-blame sceptics. They are something more like *reproach sceptics*, where reproach is an expression of blame conveyed to the person who is blamed.[13] Reproach is the right kind of thing to be judged by its efficacy; blame, by contrast, is not. One could be a reproach sceptic even though one is an enthusiast for blaming. In fact one could be a reproach sceptic *because* one is an enthusiast for blaming. One might think that reproaching, being inefficacious, gives blaming an undeservedly bad name.

[11] For some more specific suggestions on how to contain a disposition to blame, see Lacey and Pickard, 'From the Consulting Room to the Court Room? (n. 7)22–4.

[12] The same point is made with respect to beliefs in David Owens, 'Does Belief Have an Aim?' (2003) 115 Philosophical Studies 283.

[13] They may also support *punishment-scepticism* if, as I suspect, one cannot punish without reproaching. As it happens, Lacey and Pickard do not agree that one cannot punish without reproaching. They aim to 'challenge[] the strong association between punishment and blame' (Lacey and Pickard, 'From the Consulting Room to the Court Room? (n. 7) 2). So in a surprising twist they aim to mount a rescue, not a critique, of punishment. Here I will not focus on this aspect of their thinking.

2. The Dispensability of Blame

I have considerable sympathy with Lacey and Pickard's reproach scepticism, and with the 'counterproductivity' case they make for it. But in this chapter I want to develop and test a second thesis that they advance less conspicuously, one that (if sound) would support a far-reaching blame scepticism. They say this:

> In keeping with the justice model, [our] model judges patients responsible . . . for wrongful or harmful conduct to the extent that they possess the relevant cognitive and volitional capacities in relation to it. But in contrast, it resists any corresponding tendency towards affective blame. Put simply, according to [our] model, blameworthiness, understood as responsibility . . . for wrongdoing, does not entail the 'worthiness' of affective blame.[14]

Although there is a lot going on in this passage, the core proposition seems to me to be this: inasmuch as blaming is not to be judged by its efficacy (but instead e.g. by its justice) there is nothing that blame gives us that responsibility without blame would not also give us. Once we are willing to hold ourselves and each other responsible, blaming can be dispensed with. As Epictetus thought, it has no place in a mature moral outlook.

Possibly I am reading Lacey and Pickard wishfully,[15] for the core proposition that I have just distilled captures my own longstanding qualm about blame, the one that originally attracted me to Epictetus' precept. One way in which I am clearly laundering the Lacey–Pickard position is this. *Pace* Lacey and Pickard, the dispensability objection (as I will call it) is not merely an objection to attitudinal blame and its associated emotions. It extends to judgments of blameworthiness too. The last sentence of the quoted passage, with its curious scare-quotes around 'worthiness', shows why. Being blameworthy *just is* being worthy of blame. If responsibility already gives us everything that we need, then not only our tendency to blame but our concern with blameworthiness must be superfluous. We can manage without the whole apparatus of blame-related thought, feeling, and action. Lacey and Pickard avoid this conclusion by equating blameworthiness with responsibility for wrongdoing. But this equation is a mistake. As they acknowledge in

[14] Ibid., 3.

[15] Here is one piece of evidence that suggests that I am. In the second major instalment of their joint work on the subject, Lacey and Pickard contrast blaming with forgiving, and speak up for forgiving: 'To Blame or to Forgive? Reconciling Punishment and Forgiveness in Criminal Justice' (2015) 35 Oxford Journal of Legal Studies 665. But forgiving, for Lacey and Pickard, is curtailing or forestalling blame. In a world in which blame is dispensed with, in the way that I have in mind, there is no role for forgiveness so understood. Both belong to the same redundant apparatus. Possibly, however, forgiving is not quite so closely connected with blaming as Lacey and Pickard suggest, and so could survive the end of blame. See Julia Driver, 'Wronging, Blame, and Forgiveness' (2017) 4 Oxford Studies in Agency and Responsibility 206.

other remarks,[16] I may be responsible for wrongdoing without being blameworthy. Most obviously, I may have an excuse for what I did. It is only if I am responsible for wrongdoing that the question of whether I have an excuse for it arises. If I am not responsible for it, then how come the wrongdoing is mine to excuse?

It is tempting to associate the dispensability objection with the question 'what is blame for?' If one were an evolutionary psychologist, that might be a well-formed question.[17] But not for us. What we seek here is not just any explanation for the fact that people blame, but an explanation that brings out the rational intelligibility of their doing so (if there is any rational intelligibility to be brought out). 'What is blame for?' is a bad way to ask for *that* kind of explanation. We already know why. Attitudes and emotions can be reasonable or unreasonable; they answer to reasons. But *qua* attitudes and emotions they are not to be assessed in terms of the value of having them. The reasons to which they answer are facts about their objects that make them befit those objects: one should despise the despicable, love the loveable, etc. If blaming the blameworthy is superfluous, then, that is not because there is no value in blaming. (Blaming might be, for example, cathartic or fun.) Rather, it is because blameworthiness is a pseudo-property of its objects that is conjured up only to give blame something to befit. The whole apparatus, according to the dispensability objection, is rationally mysterious. If only we could get past our psychological attachment to blaming, we would see: it does not matter who is blamed and therefore it does not matter who is blameworthy.

Now I am associating the dispensability objection with a different question: 'why does blame matter?' You may think that the answer to this question is obvious, and that the dispensability objection is therefore easily dismissed. Blame matters because adverse consequences for the blamed person, such as reproach and punishment, are attached to it by the blamed person and/or by others. I should care whether I am being blamed because, if I am blamed, the next thing you know I will be accused, admonished, guilt-tripped, prosecuted, denounced, shunned, etc. That answer, however, gets the problem back to front. We already need to know why blame matters apart from such adverse consequences if we are to find out why such adverse consequences should ever be attached to it. It cuts no ice that such adverse consequences will be attached to blame whether they should be or not. Recall: we are interested in the rational intelligibility, not the empirical psychology, of blame and its associated practices. Why should adverse consequences be attached to something that, apart from those adverse consequences, does not matter? If I should not care whether I blame you, or for that matter whether you are blameworthy, why should I care to reproach you or punish you or otherwise convey that

[16] e.g. Lacey and Pickard, 'From the Consulting Room to the Court Room?' (n. 7) 18: 'When a person is responsible for harm *and has no excuse*, they are blameworthy' (emphasis added).

[17] A 'naturalistic' treatment of the subject that makes sense of this question—at the price of a certain measure of critical abstention—is Victoria McGeer's 'Civilizing Blame' in the Coates and Tognazzini volume, *Blame: Its Nature and Norms* (n. 6).

I do or might blame you? Why is it not enough, in particular, just to acknowledge and mark your responsibility without judging you blameworthy, without blaming you, and without attaching any blame-conveying consequences?

This, it seems to me, is the challenge[18] posed by Bernard Williams in the following famous passage:

> The lorry driver who, through no fault of his, runs over a child, will feel differently from any spectator, even a spectator next to him in the cab, except perhaps to the extent that the spectator takes on the thought that he himself might have prevented it, an agent's thought. Doubtless, and rightly, people will try, in comforting him, to move the driver from this state of feeling, move him indeed from where he is to something more like the place of a spectator, but it is important that this is seen as something that should need to be done, and indeed some doubt would be felt about a driver who too blandly or readily moved to that position. We feel sorry for the driver, but that sentiment co-exists with, indeed presupposes, that there is something special about his relation to this happening, something which cannot merely be eliminated by the consideration that it was not his fault.[19]

'It was not his fault' is a synonym for 'he was not blameworthy in respect of it' (or, equivalently, 'he was not to blame for it'). The 'something special' that nevertheless connects him to the child's fate is the driver's responsibility. As already noted, some people like to say that, since the driver was not to blame, he was not *morally* responsible. But that, as Williams goes on to explain,[20] is a tendentious way to talk. Why should we (or the driver) care whether his responsibility is 'moral'? If 'moral responsibility' just is blameworthiness, then we are back at our original question: why should we (or the driver) care whether or not he was to blame? The question is pressing because, as Williams explains, the fact that the driver was responsible for what happened to the child already leaves its mark on his life, blameworthy or not. The various justifications and excuses that stand between him and blame are cold comfort. He may offer them. He may be bound to offer them. They may be accepted, agreed, endorsed. But, except inasmuch as they help to protect him from certain adverse consequences, what is the significance of these justifications and excuses? And if they have no significance apart from their ability to protect him from certain adverse consequences, then *how* do they serve to protect him against those consequences? Why would anyone care about anyone's (including their own) justifications and excuses?

[18] This challenge does not depend on, does not support, and does not resemble Williams' judgment-sceptical challenge to blame outlined above (see text at n. 5). In the passage quoted here Williams is not being even slightly judgment-sceptical.

[19] Bernard Williams, 'Moral Luck' in Bernard Williams (ed.), *Moral Luck: Philosophical Papers 1973–1980* (Cambridge University Press 1981) 20–28.

[20] Ibid., 39.

Here Williams gives us the dispensability objection in a nutshell, at least the version of it that always resonated with me. When we are responsible agents, and our actions have bad outcomes, that is bad enough already. Our lives are already blemished, sometimes even blighted. Various adverse consequences are already in the offing. Some relationships will never be the same; some debts will never be repaid; some negative feelings about what we did are bound to afflict us, and rightly so; some burdensome actions now have to be undertaken.[21] How does our blameworthiness make it any worse, or even any different? And if it does not, why blame?

3. How we Relate to Reasons

As these remarks reveal, any attempt to meet the dispensability objection has to begin not with blame but with blameworthiness. The key thing we need to establish is that, quite apart from whether we are actually blamed, it matters whether we are blameworthy. Once that is established, it will be a relatively short step to defending blame, for blame will be the attitude that befits the blameworthy. This formulation may seem to suggest, implausibly, that blameworthiness has logical priority over blame. But that is not what I have in mind. To understand what blameworthiness is, I agree, we already have to grasp what it is to blame someone. All that I am adding is that, to make the resort to blame rationally intelligible, we first have to grasp why it matters whether someone is blameworthy. In short: while blame has logical priority, blameworthiness has justificatory priority.

Although other currencies might serve equally well, I will attempt to explain why blameworthiness matters in the currency of reasons. At this point I have in mind not our reasons to blame, but rather the ways in which we fall short relative to reasons when we are blameworthy. And although our own actions are not the only things in respect of which we can be blameworthy, I will simplify by focusing on our blameworthiness in respect of our own actions. This already reveals an important necessary truth about blame and blameworthiness. Both are *of* someone *for* something. If out of the blue I say 'I blame Joe', an essential piece of information is missing. What do I blame Joe for? Similarly with 'Joe is blameworthy' and 'Joe is to blame'. For what? There is no such thing as being blameworthy 'in the air', to adapt a famous phrase from Pollock's *The Law of Torts*.[22] If I am asked what I blame Joe for, and I say 'oh, nothing in particular, I just blame him', then I am making no sense. Maybe I am making an esoteric joke. Contrast 'I trust Joe', 'Joe is to be trusted', 'Joe is trustworthy'. These already express complete thoughts. Part

[21] This is the main subject of my book *From Personal Life to Private Law* (Oxford University Press 2018).

[22] Sir Frederick Pollock, *The Law of Torts* (11th edn, Stevens 1920) 455. Pollock is talking about negligence, not blameworthiness.

of the mystery of blameworthiness and blame is why they are, so to speak, essentially localized in this way: why I cannot be blamed, or be to blame, if not *for* something. I hope that thinking about why blameworthiness matters in the currency of reasons, focusing on reasons for action, will help to unravel this mystery.

Consider, then, the three ways in which responsible agents might fall short in their actions, relative to the reasons that militate for and against their performing those actions.

a. Failure to Conform to a Reason

The most obvious failure relative to a reason for action is failure to do what the reason is a reason to do. There is a reason *r*1 to φ or to χ or to Ψ (let's say, doing any one of those things would please my aunt) but I do none of those things. Clearly this alone does not make me blameworthy. For everything that there is a reason for me to do, there is invariably at least one reason for me not to do it. That is not a conceptual truth but it is a fact of the human condition. To find me blameworthy we need to begin by thinking about how competing applicable reasons fare in their competition with each other. We need to ask whether reason *r*1, which I did not conform to, was *defeated* by reason *r*2, which I did conform to. I did nothing that pleased my aunt, but I did something (incompatible with pleasing my aunt) that saved a life. Here we might say that what I did was *justifiable*. As we shall see under sub-heading b. below, justifiability alone does not rule out blameworthiness. Nor, as we'll see under sub-heading c., does unjustifiability guarantee blameworthiness. Nevertheless justifiability is the place to start in exploring the subject.

My cursory example of a competition between reasons for action (aunt-pleasing vs. life-saving) is deliberately ecumenical. My verdict in the example (life-saving defeats aunt-pleasing) is compatible with various thoughts about how one reason defeats another. I should emphasize that very often there is no defeat. There are undefeated reasons on both sides and one is left with a choice of justifiable actions.[23] But when one reason does defeat another, we may be inclined to think at first in terms of weight. All else being equal I have a weightier reason to see a more beautiful city (say, Rome) than a less beautiful one (say, Detroit): the more beautiful city will bring more beauty into my life. But this is not the only way in which one reason may be defeated by another. Sometimes one reason holds a trumping or pre-empting force, such that it is capable of defeating another independently of weight. I promised to be a commentator at a conference in Detroit over that May weekend, so now unfortunately I have to miss my cousin's wedding in Rome. Could

[23] For some this happens only when the reasons have equal force; for others, it also extends to cases of incommensurability. For a good overview of the debate, see Timothy Macklem, 'Choice and Value' (2001) 7 Legal Theory 1.

a bare promise really add enough weight to tip the balance against a May family wedding in Rome, in favour of a mere conference comment in Detroit? Unlikely. More likely, the promise excludes the joys of the Rome trip, or some of them, from the balance.[24] The point of promising was to bind myself, to give myself an obligation to go to Detroit. It is not an absolute obligation; if my son is suddenly hospitalized with meningitis on the eve of departure it would surely be justifiable to pull out. But just to take up a later invitation to a more beautiful city for a more fun event? That does not cut the mustard in the same way. My existing obligation to the Detroit folks rules out my accepting the Rome invitation, never mind how attractive the Rome trip is made. Feel free to adjust the example. Make Rome better; make Detroit worse. At some point you realize that weight relative to competing reasons is not the only factor bearing on whether a reason is defeated, and hence whether nonconformity with it is justifiable.

Some people associate blameworthiness with breach of an obligation. But that is too narrow. Recall from section 1: 'You only have yourself to blame for missing the last train home'. You had no obligation to catch the last train or to get home at all. Nobody is waiting for you. But staying that extra few minutes at the pub was a stupid mistake. The only reason to stay (one last drink) was easily outweighed, hence defeated, by the main reason for leaving (one last train). That puts you, so to speak, in blame's way. True, there might well be doubts about my standing to blame you, when you tell me the story at work the next day. Yet you clearly do have standing to blame yourself: not for breaching any obligation to yourself, I hasten to add, but just for making such a stupid mistake. So although it is not for me to blame you, I might say, you only have yourself to blame.

b. Failure to Act for a Reason

Sometimes what I do is justifiable, yet unjustified. I do what an undefeated reason would have me do, but I do not do it *for* that reason. I do it for some other (defeated) reason. A classic example is found in the English criminal case of *R v. Dadson*.[25] Under the law of the time, a police constable was permitted to use lethal force against a felon *in flagrante delicto*, but not against the perpetrator of a mere misdemeanour. Stealing wood was treated as a felony only upon a third offence. Constable Dadson shot and killed a wood thief who, unbeknown to him, was a third-time wood thief. He pleaded the lethal force rule. The court denied its benefit to him. Why? Because one acts with justification, not only in English law but also in ordinary life, only if one meets what lawyers call a 'subjective' condition. Not

[24] This way of explaining what is going on is owed to Joseph Raz's famous analysis in *Practical Reason and Norms* (Hutchinson 1975) 35–48.

[25] (1850) 4 Cox CC 358.

only must there be an undefeated reason to do as one does; one must also do it *for that reason*. Here's another example, this time not from the law.[26] An arms dealer or an estate agent says: 'If I didn't do these terrible things, others would quickly fill the gap that I leave in the market and do even worse things. You're lucky to have me. I'm actually protecting you against the really bad guys out there.' We should reply: 'Is that why you're doing these terrible things? Are you doing them in order to stop other people doing worse things? If not, you are not offering a valid justification. You are just confirming that you are the villain we originally took you to be, and on top of that, a bare-faced evader of blame.'[27]

Justified action is action performed for an undefeated reason, not merely action that conforms to an undefeated reason.[28] In saying this we presuppose that ordinarily one's failure to act for a reason that applies to one, even an undefeated reason, is unobjectionable. Barring exceptional cases, not acting for a given reason is not a failure relative to that reason, for a reason calls only for conformity.[29] That justified action is action performed for an undefeated reason reflects an independent principle of rationality (aka reasonableness). Those who conform to this principle act blamelessly. As noted already, justifiability does not rule out blameworthiness, but justification does.

c. Failure of Sensitivity to a Reason

Our rationality is pervasively vulnerable to error. Frequently we treat defeated reasons as undefeated, or nonexistent reasons as existent. We take actions to be justifiable, or justified, when they are not, and we perform them accordingly. When our mistakes in such matters are themselves reasonable, we have excuses for what we do. An excused action, like a justified action, is blameless. But why? The quick answer is that when we are excused, we are duly sensitive to reasons and their force, even though we fail relative to them in other ways. The classic examples, also marked in the law, are those in which we act without justification owing to reasonable mistakes of fact, or reasonable but powerful emotions such as fear and anger. We act for what we have undefeated reasons to treat as undefeated reasons for what we do, but which in fact are not. In short, we do what we are justified in treating as justified.[30]

[26] The most exacting discussion of these cases is Jonathan Glover, 'It Makes No Difference Whether or Not I Do It' (1975) 49 Proceedings of the Aristotelian Society, Supplementary Volume 171.

[27] For further explanation see my *Offences and Defences* (Oxford 2007), chs 3 and 5.

[28] This proposition requires some interpretation to apply it to cases in which people act for multiple independent reasons. These need not detain us here.

[29] Joseph Raz, *Practical Reason and Norms* (2nd edn, Princeton University Press 1990) 178–82.

[30] For further explanation see Gardner, *Offences and Defences* (n. 27) ch. 6.

Some people extend the word 'excuse' beyond such cases to include a very different class of cases in which we are not responsible for our actions, for example actions borne of severe mental illnesses. When we are not responsible for our actions, we are not expected to be sensitive to reasons, or to act for them, or even to conform to them. We are exempt from rational assessment. The only objection I have to calling such an exemption an 'excuse' is that it is so far removed from the cases of excuse that interest us here. Here we are assuming responsible agency and considering those failures relative to reasons that are possible within the scope of responsible agency. One distinct type is a failure of sensitivity: one was not attentive or receptive enough to certain applicable reasons and made an error beyond the limits of excuse.

If Williams' lorry driver writes to the parents of the injured child, or visits the child in hospital, or sends flowers or toys, he may be exhibiting his sensitivity to some of the reasons that, alas, he did not conform to when he knocked the child down. The explanation for his nonconformity, he thereby asserts, was not his lack of sensitivity. That this point can be made *afterwards* reveals that sensitivity to reasons, unlike conformity to reasons, is conceived as a property of agents, not a property of individual actions. One might of course in one solitary action show a momentary insensitivity to some reason, constituting a puzzling aberration in an otherwise admirably sustained record of sensitivity to reasons of the same kind. The point is that (barring special cases where responsibility is lacking) such a momentary insensitivity still lies on the record of the agent even when it is an aberration. In such a case one can certainly say 'that wasn't like me' but one does not so easily get to say the responsibility-denying 'that wasn't me'.[31] For one did reveal, alas, what one is capable of, and thereby left a stain on one's reputation (or at any rate on the reputation that one deserves to have).

A fairly common view has it that blaming targets, as it were, the agent as opposed to the action. Blameworthiness on this view is insensitivity to reasons, never mind conformity with them.[32] But this is a simplification. As we noted already, an agent is to blame *for* an action. The action is being judged too. In what way? In the way that we have just been exploring. To be blameworthy in respect of a given action, a responsible agent must (a) have failed to conform to a reason in performing that action, and (b) not have been justified in so failing, and (c) not have been excused in so failing. The question of the agent's sensitivity to reasons arises, strictly speaking, only at stage (c). If by good fortune she conforms to undefeated reasons and also by good fortune acts for such reasons then her insensitivity to those or other reasons does not make her blameworthy. For in such a case there is nothing

[31] I am not sure that Nicola Lacey upholds the difference when she writes, in her *State Punishment: Political Principles and Community Values* (Routledge 1988) 71, that the criminal justice system should 'respond punitively only to actions which are in a real sense [the agent's] own'.

[32] A leading version of this view equates blameworthiness to 'subjective wrongness', following Derek Parfit's proposal in his *Reasons and Persons* (Oxford University Press 1984) 25.

to blame her for. So judging someone to be blameworthy is not a simple case of judging someone negatively. Rather, it is judging that something (in the cases that concern us here, an action) bears negatively on how someone is to be judged. In a familiar idiom, we judge that the action 'reflects badly' on the agent. Do we now judge her disloyal, dishonest, unreliable, mean-spirited, or what? That remains to be seen. All that is clear is that 'blameworthy' is not a further entry on the same list. Blameworthiness is not a negative trait of the agent, but rather the condition under which one or more negative traits of the agent are manifested (exhibited, displayed) in her actions.

We return to the social media attention-seeker who says 'don't judge me'. Could the request be to judge the faux-pas if one must, but not to judge the maker of it in the light of it? It is hard to see how that request could be honoured. It is not the same as a request to be forgiving or merciful or lenient, which one honours by judging someone to be blameworthy but then declining to blame or reproach or punish (as much as one otherwise would). 'Don't judge me' seems to be a request not to judge the maker of the faux-pas to be blameworthy. To honour that request one must grant, at least arguendo, that the faux-pas is justified or excused. As a rule, however, 'don't judge me' is uttered without any suggestion of a justification or excuse for the faux-pas. That being so, how can we avoid the conclusion that the faux-pas reflects badly on its maker? We may be reminded here of the Augustinian advice 'hate the sin, not the sinner'.[33] Fully generalized as a precept for life, I tend to regard that advice as an invitation to hypocrisy, but it can at least be implemented by the cultivation of a certain mindset. Suppose, however, that it were replaced with '*judge* the sin, not the sinner'. It is not clear how that advice could be implemented, leaving aside cases in which there is a valid justification or excuse for the sin. And in such cases the sin does not reflect badly on the sinner anyway, so the advice is otiose. It becomes: 'when the sinner cannot be judged by the sin, judge the sin, not the sinner (obviously)'.

4. Blame and Character

This necessarily abbreviated discussion may well make you think of what Lacey at one time called 'the character conception of responsibility'[34] but which, in the light of her work with Pickard, might better be renamed 'the character conception of blameworthiness'. As I just explained, being blameworthy is not a negative trait of the agent, but it is the condition under which one or more negative traits of the agent are manifested (exhibited, displayed) in her actions. When we say that

[33] St Augustine, *Letters 211–270* (trans. Teske, ed. Ramsay, New City Press 2005) 25 ('with love for the persons and a hatred for their vices').

[34] Lacey, *State Punishment* (n. 31) e.g. at 73.

someone is 'at fault' in their actions we mean that in their actions they manifest one or more of their faults (aka vices, flaws, deficiencies, shortcomings). Blameworthy people, we might then summarize, are people of *pro tanto* bad character.

It may strike you that this summary is too crude. To be blameworthy one must *manifest* one's fault; but surely one *has* the fault irrespective of whether one manifests it? Bad character, unlike blameworthiness, is a matter of sheer insensitivity to reasons; nonconformity does not come into it. But that is a mistaken view of character. Character traits exist only inasmuch as they are manifested. The action partly constitutes the trait.[35] Someone who so far never had the opportunity to act (dis)honestly is not yet (dis)honest, never mind how they might have acted had the opportunity for (dis)honesty presented itself. That is how a court is able to say that a criminal defendant, just found guilty of an offence, is of 'previous good character'. The picture is not that there was a hidden vice lurking there all the time, one that we only now got to see. The picture, which is indeed the right picture, is that until it was manifested, there was no vice: until one was insensitive to reasons *in failing to conform to them*, one's character was still unblemished. (It must be recalled here that we have artificially restricted ourselves throughout to thinking about blameworthy actions, which manifest practical faults. One's epistemic faults are manifested in one's beliefs, one's intellectual faults are manifested in one's reasoning, and so on. Still, each exists only inasmuch as it is manifested.)

This 'no character without manifestation' thesis is the flip side of the thesis, already advocated, that even a momentary nonconformity with reason, if unjustified and unexcused, counts against an agent's character. When someone says of such a lapse that it was 'out of character' we should not hear them to say that the lapse somehow does not count against the agent's character. On the contrary: the lapse shows what the agent is capable of, and her character is, in the relevant sense, a set of capacities. One may be interested for other reasons, of course, in whether the action was 'out of character'. If one is considering one's future relationship with the agent, for example, one might be tempted to forgive what one holds to be an unjustified and unexcused aberration. That can be true even with quite serious lapses. One infidelity might be forgivable with a bit of effort; two or three, starting to form a pattern, might be impossible to forgive. Forgiving, however, is not excusing. Excusing negates the judgment of blameworthiness, whereas forgiving presupposes the judgment of blameworthiness.[36] The forgiven action reflected badly on the agent, to be sure, but one manages not to hold it against him. Or put in other words: his character did not come out smelling of roses but one can still reconcile oneself, in one's attitude towards him, to what one discovered about his flaws.

[35] Compare Michael S. Moore, 'Choice, Character, and Excuse' (1990) 7 Social Philosophy and Policy 29, 47. Moore's objection to the constitutive view depends on the 'partly' being implicitly replaced with 'wholly' to yield what he calls 'the behavioural view', which is obviously false.

[36] A valuable discussion of the point is Lucy Allais, 'Wiping the Slate Clean: The Heart of Forgiveness' (2008) 36 Philosophy and Public Affairs 33.

Lacey's longstanding worries about the institutionalization in the law of the character conception stem principally from the evidence, which she has done so much to document, that thinking in terms of character can lead the law astray on these very points. Too easily, she thinks, the law may end up

> exhibit[ing] what we might call 'character essentialism' and 'character determinism'. In other words, it proceeds from a view of human character … and of identity as fixed, or at least as relatively stable; and it regards character as determining conduct.[37]

Lacey's 'character essentialism' is the mistaken thesis that character is necessarily temporally extended. It follows that there is no room for one-off aberrant actions that reflect badly upon my character, and so no possible case for showing forgiveness or mercy towards me in respect of blameworthy actions on the ground that are 'not like me'. That is because, for the character essentialist, there can be no such actions. Meanwhile, Lacey's 'character determinism' is a behaviourist exaggeration of the 'no character without manifestation' thesis. We might call it the 'character as sheer manifestation' thesis. It treats nonconformity with reasons as sufficient, not merely necessary, for bad character.[38] Hence it gives no quarter to excuses (and possibly not even to justifications). Sometimes Lacey gives the impression that the 'character conception' of culpability is at odds with what she calls the 'capacity conception'.[39] But once we rid ourselves of the twin errors of character determinism and character essentialism, it is doubtful whether this is true. The capacity conception seems to be just one attempt—personally, I am not enamoured of it[40]—to explain the difference between an action that exhibits bad character and one that does not. It attempts to do so by attempting to explain the difference between an excused action and an unexcused action in terms of the capacities and opportunities of the agent to avoid performing each.

Lacey tends to worry most about the potential of the character conception, in comparison with the capacity conception, to spread blame too widely and too harshly. But in one way the character conception is too restrictive. Our actions may reflect badly on us by manifesting our want of skill as well as our bad character. As Aristotle explains:

> [I]t is from the same causes and by the same means that every virtue is both produced and destroyed, and similarly every art; for it is from playing the lyre that both good and bad lyre-players are produced. And the corresponding statement

[37] Nicola Lacey, *In Search of Criminal Responsibility: Ideas, Interests, and Institutions* (Oxford University Press 2016) 35.

[38] Moore collapses these two theses in the passage cited above n .35.

[39] e.g. Lacey, *In Search of Criminal Responsibility* (n. 37) 59.

[40] See Gardner, *Offences and Defences* (n. 27) ch. 6.

> is true of builders and of all the rest; men will be good or bad builders as a result of building well or badly. For if this were not so, there would have been no need of a teacher, but all men would have been born good or bad at their craft. This, then, is the case with the virtues also; by doing the acts that we do in our transactions with other men we become just or unjust, and by doing the acts that we do in the presence of danger, and being habituated to feel fear or confidence, we become brave or cowardly.[41]

Here we see Aristotle articulate the 'no character without manifestation' thesis, as well as the thesis that actions may manifest traits of character without those traits being settled or stabilized in the person who manifests them. The same is true, as he notes, of skills and their absence. We are interested here in the negative cases, the cases of actions that went awry. For those are the cases in which the question of blameworthiness arises. Those, to put it another way, are the cases in which the question arises of whether the action reflected badly on the agent, such as to count as a manifestation of a fault, now understood as extending beyond her character flaws to include her technical failings, such as being a bad builder or a bad lyre-player.

5. Saving Blame from Dispensability

We judge human actions, or more generally the lives to which those actions belong. We also judge human agents, who are the people leading those lives. The two classes of judgments are not interchangeable. That you are leading a bad life (or acting badly) does not automatically make you a bad person (even *pro tanto*). It does so only inasmuch as the way you are leading your life reflects badly upon you. As soon as the question arises of whether the way you are leading your life (or anything else) reflects badly upon you, we are unavoidably concerned with blameworthiness. It follows that if people are to be among the possible objects of judgment, the dispensability objection to blame fails. You might think that people could be among the possible objects of judgment without judging that anything they do (or think or feel etc.) reflects badly upon them. But inasmuch as judging people means judging them in respect of their character or skill, that is false. For character and skill do not exist without actions (etc.) that manifest them, and actions manifest character or skill only if they reflect well or badly upon their agent. Accordingly we have no escape from judgments of blameworthiness, short of a comprehensive refusal to judge people as being of bad character or deficient skill. Such a refusal would clearly be a tall order. Would it even be possible? Can human beings implement

[41] *Nicomachean Ethics* 1103^{b}7ff.

'don't judge me' as an across-the-board self-denying ordinance? Not for as long as they seek relationships with people who are worth relating to, and try to be worthy of such relationships themselves. Not for as long as they engage with history, literature, and politics. Arguably, not for as long as they think of other people (and themselves) as people. These are all things that human beings, on at least some occasions, have reason to do.

Understanding this much should make us (and certainly has made me, over the years) less profoundly blame sceptical. Once we see that judgments of blameworthiness play an unavoidable role in the rational architecture of human life, it is a short step to rehabilitating blame. Blaming someone is taking the attitude towards her that befits her blameworthiness. It is losing faith in her, or losing admiration for her, or taking a dim view of her, or something like that. The move from judging someone blameworthy to blaming is subtle, but the possibility of forgiveness shows that it exists. The move from blame to blaming emotions is also short and subtle. The possibility of someone's being diminished in one's eyes, but only dispassionately, shows that it is there. The blaming emotions may be fitting but, as Lacey and Pickard point out, it does not follow that they are welcome. In some contexts and on some occasions they are better tamed. One of the reasons, emphasized by Lacey and Pickard, is that these emotions can motivate counterproductive or otherwise unjustified blaming actions, such as excessive reproaching or punishing. Such excessive actions, it seems to me, tend to give blame itself a bad name. The blame does not lie with blame, exactly, but with the ease with which people are driven to express blame in harsh and hostile ways. After all of these years I still cannot see the case for all this harshness and hostility. That is what is left of my blame scepticism. That one feels like coming down hard on somebody is no reason to do it. Even if such a hostile emotion is fitting, the fittingness of the emotion only makes the reaction excusable, not justifiable. It follows that the rest of us, including politicians, prosecutors, journalists, and so on, should not support the expression of the emotion but rather manage it.[42]

The problem, in short, is not so much that we live in a 'blame culture' but that we live in a 'call-out culture' where accusation, reproach, censure, and punishment run wildly out of control and can no longer be managed back into proportion by mediating institutions such as the criminal courts.

Niki Lacey's first book, *State Punishment*,[43] was written when I was lucky enough to be her undergraduate student in the mid-1980s. I was privy to some of the process. In this early work Niki was already grappling with many of the themes that I have traversed, all too cursorily, in the preceding pages. I was an enthralled and broadly sympathetic reader of *State Punishment* when it came out, and the book

[42] For wider application of this point see David Enoch, 'The Masses and the Elites: Political Philosophy for the Age of Brexit, Trump and Netanyahu' (2017) 8 Jurisprudence 1.

[43] Above n. 31.

did more than any other to set the thematic direction of my own academic work for the following twenty years (even though Niki and I always disagreed about various questions of approach). As Niki once said to me, we tend to work on the things that we find most difficult in our own lives, and for me the relevant difficulty, laid bare in her work, was always the difficulty with blame: I was a blamer myself, and in particular a self-blamer, but I could not see a good place for blame in the rational architecture of human life.

I struggled for those twenty years to tackle this worry, as Niki did, through critical engagement with the criminal law. I tried to find a rationale for all the blaming that we all do by starting from the way in which blame is institutionally expressed, captured, and managed, in the criminal justice system. I remained a blame sceptic throughout, moved mostly by what I have been calling the dispensability objection, which gave me a kind of abolitionist predisposition in respect of criminal punishment. That was healthy: every time I found something in the criminal law that I thought I could make sense of, I was on my guard. Was I being duped? But I later came to think that my blame scepticism was artificially nourished by my abolitionist predisposition, in a feedback loop that was by no means so healthy. Contrary to what Epictetus thought, blame itself is not the main problem, the main immaturity. Blame has an important place in the architecture of rational human life after all; just not where I had been looking for it. The main problem is with the *expression* of blame, and in particular with the Janus-faced way in which the criminal law must always seem to be endorsing harsh and hostile public blaming emotions, by giving expression to them, if it is going to be able to manage them. Up to a point, the law must cosy up with the mob if it is to enjoy any sustainable control over the mob's excesses.[44] In the last few years this problem has been overtaken, to some extent, by technological developments. Now the mob can bypass the criminal justice system with virtual impunity by use of Twitter and other online instruments of populist reproach and punishment, via a kind of Orwellian 'group hate'. Even in top form, the criminal justice system would be virtually powerless to manage any of this and, like other mediating institutions of the state, it is anyway limping along in a ramshackle condition owing to the hyperdependency of the state on the robber barons of high finance. A book called *State Punishment* could still usefully be written. But now the title would surely carry a more ironic and despairing ring.

Bibliography

Allais, L, 'Wiping the Slate Clean: The Heart of Forgiveness' (2008) 36 Philosophy and Public Affairs 33

[44] See the reflections in Gardner, *Offences and Defences* (n. 27) ch. 11.

Bell, M, 'The Standing to Blame: A Critique' in DJ Coates and NA Tognazzini (eds), *Blame: Its Nature and Norms* (Oxford University Press 2013)

Coates, DJ and Tognazzini, NA (eds), *Blame: Its Nature and Norms* (Oxford University Press 2013)

Cohen, GA, *Finding Oneself in the Other* (Princeton University Press 2013)

D'Arms, J and Jacobson, D, 'The Moralistic Fallacy: On the "Appropriateness" of Emotions' (2000) 61 Philosophy and Phenomenological Research 65

Driver, J, 'Wronging, Blame, and Forgiveness' (2017) 4 Oxford Studies in Agency and Responsibility 206

Enoch, D, 'The Masses and the Elites: Political Philosophy for the Age of Brexit, Trump and Netanyahu' (2017) 8 Jurisprudence 1

Frankfurt, H, 'Alternate Possibilities and Moral Responsibility' (1969) 66 Journal of Philosophy 829

Glover, J, 'It Makes No Difference Whether or Not I Do It' (1975) 49 Proceedings of the Aristotelian Society, Supplementary Volume 171

Gardner, J, *Offences and Defences* (Oxford 2007)

Gardner, J, *From Personal Life to Private Law* (Oxford University Press 2018)

Graham, P 'The Standard Argument for Blame Incompatibilism' (2008) 42 Noûs 697

Lacey, N, *In Search of Criminal Responsibility: Ideas, Interests, and Institutions* (Oxford University Press 2016)

Lacey, N, *State Punishment: Political Principles and Community Values* (Routledge 1988)

Lacey, N and Pickard, H, 'To Blame or to Forgive? Reconciling Punishment and Forgiveness in Criminal Justice' (2015) 35 Oxford Journal of Legal Studies 665

Lacey, N and Pickard, H, 'From the Consulting Room to the Court Room? Taking the Clinical Model of Responsibility Without Blame into the Legal Realm' (2013) 33 Oxford Journal of Legal Studies 1

Macklem, T, 'Choice and Value' (2001) 7 Legal Theory 1

McGeer V, 'Civilizing Blame' in DJ Coates and NA Tognazzini (eds), *Blame: Its Nature and Norms* (Oxford University Press 2013)

Moore, MS, 'Choice, Character, and Excuse' (1990) 7 Social Philosophy and Policy 29

Owens, D, 'Does Belief Have an Aim?' (2003) 115 Philosophical Studies 283

Parfit, D, *Reasons and Persons* (Oxford University Press 1984)

Pollock, F, *The Law of Torts* (11th edn, Stevens 1920)Raz, J, *Practical Reason and Norms* (2nd edn, Princeton University Press 1990)

Raz, J, *Practical Reason and Norms* (Hutchinson 1975)

Sher, G, *In Praise of Blame* (Oxford University Press 2006)

St Augustine, *Letters 211–270* (trans. Teske, ed. Ramsay, New City Press 2005)

Wallace, RJ, *Responsibility and the Moral Sentiments* (Harvard University Press 1994)

Williams, B, 'Internal Reasons and the Obscurity of Blame' in B Williams, *Making Sense of Humanity* (Cambridge University Press 1995)

Williams, B, 'Moral Luck' in B Williams, *Moral Luck: Philosophical Papers 1973–1980* (Cambridge University Press 1981)

5

Responsibility and Explanations of Rape

Hanna Pickard[1]

I first met Niki when we were colleagues together at All Souls College, Oxford. I was in my late thirties so not young, but I was, in a sense, young in my career: having taken a diversion from analytic philosophy into clinical practice, I was at that stage working to integrate these very different perspectives, and to develop a voice I could genuinely call my own. I could not believe my luck when Niki suggested we have lunch and then—after what would prove to be the first of many long and intense discussions washed down with a bottle of good white wine—that we co-author a paper together. A decade or so later, we're about to embark on our fifth. Writing with Niki has been one of the most wonderful intellectual experiences of my entire life. No one could ask for more in a co-author: erudite, rigorous, generous, dedicated, and with an intellect so penetrating and an understanding so broad in scope that she is like no one else I know. But for me, Niki did something more, and in truth more important. Philosophy is not known for its femininity. Prior to Niki, none of my significant teachers, mentors, or academic influences, had been a woman, and I had no clear conception how to be, at one and the same time, a woman and an academic. Niki modelled this with such grace and wit that it appeared effortless. It was transformative to work alongside her. She showed me how to be myself, simply by being herself. But I now know that, appearances notwithstanding, this was not in fact effortless on her part. Writing this chapter has given me occasion to read parts of Niki's work I was hitherto ignorant of. I was astonished to learn, from her inaugural lecture for her Chair in Law at Birkbeck College, University of London, published in 1998,[2] that, much like me, she had not been educated by women, but only by men, and was at that time in her career struggling to find a voice both feminine and professorial. How many more generations of academic women will be forced to experience this crisis of identity? Niki and my co-authored work has not been feminist in orientation, despite the fact that it is written by two women who are committed feminists. This chapter is feminist in orientation and it is about a very painful topic that Niki speaks to in that inaugural

[1] This chapter has been a long time in the making. I would like to thank Iyiola Solanke not only for providing me with the opportunity to write it, but also for her patience while I did; Josh Knobe, Niki Lacey, Iyiola Solanke, and Elanor Taylor for helpful comments and discussion; and Harvey Lederman, Ian Phillips, Jocelyn Pickard, and Zoë Pickard for their support through the writing process.

[2] Nicola Lacey, *Unspeakable Subjects: Feminist Essays in Legal and Social Theory* (Hart 1998) ch. 4.

Hanna Pickard, Responsibility and Explanations of Rape In: On Crime, Society, and Responsibility in the Work of Nicola Lacey.
Edited by: Iyiola Solanke, Oxford University Press (2021). © The several contributors.
DOI: 10.1093/oso/9780198852681.003.0006

lecture: the criminal law's grotesque and persistent failure to do justice to women who are victims of rape. I write it out of love, respect, friendship, and gratitude, for Niki as a woman and as an academic. Thank you for what you have given us all.

* * *

In Search of Criminal Responsibility: Ideas, Interests, and Institutions argues that one cannot understand what criminal responsibility *is* without attention to what it is *for*.[3] And what it is for—according to Lacey—is the legitimation and coordination of criminal law as an exercise of state power. Lacey therefore situates her analysis of criminal responsibility squarely within a sweeping view of the changing social, political, and economic contexts within which the criminal law has historically operated. This analysis reveals no one core idea of criminal responsibility capable of transcending time and place, but rather a series of distinct if historically overlapping ideas—each contributing, albeit in different ways, to criminal responsibility's crucial role of legitimation and coordination. These ideas of criminal responsibility pertain to character, capacity, outcome, and, in recent years, risk. Each idea is complicated and contentious—both in principle and in its practical manifestation within the criminal process—and each contributes in an equally complicated and contentious way to the legitimation and coordination of the criminal law. But, to crudely simplify the nuance of Lacey's theoretical and historical articulation of each of these ideas, they can be seen as props for the state's power to censure those who commit crimes and thereby to regulate social norms and behaviour in the following ways. Character legitimates censure in so far as the crime is expressive of an inherently vicious or criminal disposition; capacity is legitimating in so far as voluntary and autonomous wrong action reveals, if not always or inevitably a guilty mind, then at least a choice, or, alternatively, a reasonable opportunity to conform one's conduct to the law; actual outcomes of crime matter in so far as some harms are so violating of social or moral norms that regulating any and all conduct producing them is essential for the public good; risk matters in so far as there is a genuine probability of such a social or moral norm-violating outcome in future. For each of these legitimating ideas, establishing whether and to what extent they apply in any particular case coordinates and structures the criminal process, including the presentation of the evidence at trial in order to determine a verdict, as well as the nature of an appropriate sentence and its aftermath. Lacey narrates the development of our ideas and practices of criminal responsibility in the context of the ever-present need for regulatory state power to be legitimated and coordinated: this is the purpose for which they evolved and to which they must answer.

[3] Nicola Lacey, *In Search of Criminal Responsibility: Ideas, Interests, and Institutions* (Oxford University Press 2016).

Lacey's discussion is so rich and interdisciplinary that I cannot but gulp before suggesting that it contains an omission. But, in situating her analysis of criminal responsibility predominantly in relation to historically changing social, political, and economic contexts, her gaze is trained outside of the courtroom, as much if not more than within it. And, within the courtroom, criminal responsibility may have a further role that is less socio-political and economic, and more psychological. Or so I shall argue. Very schematically, the aim of this chapter is to begin to critically interrogate the psychological function and consequences of responsibility judgments and practices in the courts—much as our co-authored work has done in relation to judgments and practices of *affective blame*. As this omission characterizes our co-authored work as much as *In Search of Criminal Responsibility*, I start with a very brief account of that work as a backdrop to what follows.

Lacey and I have together argued for the value and viability of importing the clinical model of responsibility without blame that I have elsewhere articulated[4] into criminal law.[5] This model deploys an idea of responsibility linked firmly to capacity—as opposed to character, outcome, or risk—emphasizing the cognitive and volitional conditions necessary for determinations of responsibility. But the reason for this emphasis on capacity is not the usual backward-looking concern: to legitimate the imposition of 'hard treatment' for past wrongdoing and ensure offenders get their 'just deserts'. The reason is rather forward-looking: for it is only when an action is voluntary and autonomous—in the broadest sense—that it is possible for an individual to work to directly change their behaviour in future, and for interventions that target and support their agency—whether clinical or correctional—to be practically effective. This is one of the core values of capacity responsibility: agency matters to responsibility in the clinic—and arguably in the courtroom—not because it identifies when punishment is legitimate, but because it identifies when interventions aimed at behavioural change can make a difference.[6] But, this forward-looking goal can only be achieved if practices of holding

[4] Hanna Pickard, 'Responsibility without Blame: Empathy and the Effective Treatment of Personality Disorder' (2011) 18 Philosophy, Psychiatry, Psychology 209; Hanna Pickard, 'Responsibility without Blame: Philosophical Reflections on Clinical Practice' in KW M Fulford et al. (eds), *The Oxford Handbook of Philosophy and Psychiatry* (Oxford University Press 2013) 1134.

[5] Nicola Lacey and Hanna Pickard, 'From the Consulting Room to the Court Room? Taking the Clinical Model of Responsibility without Blame into the Legal Realm' (2013) 33 Oxford Journal of Legal Studies 1; Nicola Lacey and Hanna Pickard, 'To Blame or to Forgive? Reconciling Punishment and Forgiveness in Criminal Justice' (2015) 35 Oxford Journal of Legal Studies 665; Nicola Lacey and Hanna Pickard, 'The Chimera of Proportionality: Institutionalising Limits on Punishment in Contemporary Social and Political Systems' (2015) 78 Modern Law Review 216; Nicola Lacey and Hanna Pickard, 'A Dual Process Approach to Criminal Law: Victims and the Clinical Model of Responsibility without Blame' (2019) 27 The Journal of Political Philosophy 229.

[6] Pickard, 'Responsibility without Blame: Empathy and the Effective Treatment of Personality Disorder' (n. 4); Pickard, 'Responsibility without Blame: Philosophical Reflections on Clinical Practice' (n. 4). See too Gunnar Björnsson and Karl Persson, 'The Explanatory Component of Moral Responsibility' (2012) 46 Noûs 326; Gunnar Björnsson and Karl Persson, 'A Unified Empirical Account of Responsibility Judgments' (2013) 87 Philosophy and Phenomenological Research 611.

responsible and to account are fashioned so as to avoid what I have called *affective blame*, understood to include both stigmatizing and essentializing character judgments, and the hostile, negative emotions and associated reactions that all too typically accompany ascriptions of responsibility for wrongdoing. Affective blame, thus understood, undermines the potential of responsibility to effect behavioural change, precisely because of the psychological effect it has on the person who is blamed. Of course, the laws of human psychology are *ceteris paribus*: there will always be exceptions and individual differences. But affective blame typically—if not inevitably—makes people feel that they are worthless, hated, shunned—unfit for relationships and not welcome in our community. In consequence—and especially for those who, like many offenders, come from backgrounds of psychosocial adversity and have limited socio-economic opportunities—it can strip people of reason to hope or motivation to change.[7] Lacey and I have therefore aimed to articulate an idea of *criminal responsibility without affective blame*, and to sketch a corresponding set of criminal justice policies and practices, fit on the one hand for the purpose of holding to account, and on the other for the more rehabilitative and reparative ends which must stand alongside accountability in any modern conception of the criminal law which claims moral and political legitimacy.[8] In other words, we have argued for the great value of responsibility to the multiple purposes of criminal law provided it is divorced from the invidiousness of affective blame—the difference between them being rooted in their contrasting psychological functions and consequences.[9]

But responsibility judgments and practices also have psychological functions and consequences that are all too easily invidious in criminal justice contexts—especially when the crime in question is rape. To make this case, the chapter proceeds as follows. Drawing on recent work in the philosophy and science of causal cognition, I suggest in section 1 that responsibility judgments function in part like explanatory judgments. Part of what they are *for* is to provide a sense of understanding—indeed, closure. Responsibility ascriptions, like explanations, are naturally tethered to our interests and perspectives: they focus on all and only those causes that stand out as unusual and abnormal, relative to descriptive and prescriptive norms that work in the background. But this means that what stands out as unusual or abnormal depends on which norms we accept. Shifting the norms therefore not only affects what is likely to count as a *satisfying explanation of why something happened*, but who is singled out as the *bearer of responsibility for what happened*. Section 2 then sketches some of the descriptive and prescriptive norms of rape culture, extracted from in-depth qualitative interviews with convicted

[7] For further discussion see especially Lacey and Pickard, 'To Blame or to Forgive?' (n. 5).

[8] Ibid.

[9] For further discussion see especially Lacey and Pickard, 'From the Consulting Room to the Court Room?' (n. 5); Lacey and Pickard, 'A Dual Process Approach to Criminal Law' (n. 5).

rapists, and empirical studies of the attitudes and factors that result in 'victim-blaming' within the general population. Section 3 brings the discussion of section 1 and section 2 together. I explore how information about the victim introduced by the defence in rape trials can serve to shift the focus such that rape culture norms come to be at work in the background. This means that a satisfying explanation of why the rape occurred in the minds of members of the court—including both judges and juries—is likely to avert as much to what *she* did as to what *he* did—and that, correspondingly, responsibility ascriptions for rape are prone to involve *her* as much as *him*. In other words, I suggest that the criminal law's grotesque and persistent failure to find perpetrators of rape responsible is in part a predictable upshot of the explanatory function of responsibility, in combination with the pervasiveness of rape culture norms in our society. I conclude with some brief remarks about how responsibility as capacity is therefore poised to distort justice for women, until women's sexual autonomy and sexual integrity[10] is valued.

1. Responsibility, Causation, and Explanation

Traditionally in both philosophy and the law, it is not the concept of *explanation* that is linked to responsibility but of *causation*.[11] To take a classic example, suppose there is a fire in the house. What caused the fire? The full causal story includes many facts that we typically take for granted when we try to answer the question. For example, there can be no fire in absence of oxygen and combustible material. But, in most contexts, we do not cite these facts as part of what we often call 'the cause' of the fire. We rather point to an event that is both more specific and more salient to us. For example, the offender entered the house and set it alight using gasoline and a lighter: this is a case of arson. Assuming the presence of oxygen and the combustibility of the house, the cause of the fire is the offender's act. Given that the capacity conditions are met—the offender knew what they were doing at the time of the offence and the act was voluntary—the fact that the defendant was the cause of the fire is central to a finding of criminal responsibility.[12]

How do we select 'the cause' from all the other facts that are part of the full causal story? Within the philosophical literature, there is relatively clear consensus that, whatever the answer, the upshot is in no sense objective. John Stuart Mill states that we have 'no right' to single out one cause from others;[13] while David Lewis

[10] To use the concept Lacey rightly emphasizes in her inaugural lecture. See Lacey, *Unspeakable Subjects* (n. 2) ch. 4.

[11] For a review see Michael Moore, 'Causation in the Law' in Edward N Zalta (ed.), *The Stanford Encyclopedia of Philosophy* (Winter 2019 Edition) forthcoming at <https://plato.stanford.edu/archives/win2019/entries/causation-law/> UPDATE

[12] This general claim of course leaves unspecified the question of how the law in fact understands (and ought to understand) the notion of knowledge of action, voluntariness, and causation.

[13] John Stuart Mill, *A System of Logic, Volume I, Fourth Edition* (J.W. Parker and Son 1856) 361.

refers to the principles by which we distinguish 'the cause' from other causal factors as 'invidious'.[14] But the fact that our procedures are not objective does not mean that they defy description. Consider Fred Dretske's telling remark: 'I have nothing particularly original to say about how one identifies the cause of something from among the many events and conditions on which it depends. It seems fairly clear that this selection is often a response to the purpose and interests of the one doing the describing.'[15] This seems correct so far as it goes; but is there anything general that can be said about our purpose and interests in asking why something happened, and how these shape our causal reasoning?

Christopher Hitchcock and Joshua Knobe have put forward an original and intuitive proposal about how people in fact select the cause from all other causal factors, based on a synthesis and analysis of multiple empirical studies conducted over the past decades.[16] Simplifying somewhat, they argue, first, that our causal reasoning is on the whole guided by the goal of discovering successful interventions: 'In general, while causal structure identifies all of the factors that *could* be manipulated (either singly or in combination) to effect a change in the outcome, [what we select as] the actual causes are the factors that *should* be manipulated.'[17] In other words, we are often interested in why something happened because of the power this information gives us to shape future events: intervention is the purpose served by the concept of cause. Second, they suggest that the process of causal reasoning commonly proceeds through consideration of counterfactuals: we ask, would the outcome have occurred *if* a particular causal factor had not been present or had been significantly different?[18] Third, they argue that we assess which of the many factors *should* be manipulated—which counterfactuals are relevant to discerning an intervention—by identifying what about the causal story is *unusual or abnormal*.[19] In other words, we focus on the causal factors that stand out as *violations of our expectations* as determined by a combination of both descriptive and prescriptive norms, including norms which are statistical, functional, conventional, practical, moral—and, we might wish to add, legal. For these violations constitute a natural target for intervention, without requiring us *to disrupt any of the background descriptive or prescriptive norms*—which is unlikely to be expedient in practice, and which we may in addition view as problematic in principle.

14 David K Lewis, 'Causation' (1973) 70 The Journal of Philosophy 556; cited from his *Philosophical Papers, Volume II* (Oxford University Press 1986) 162.

15 Fred Dretske, *Explaining Behavior: Reasons in a World of Causes* (MIT Press 1991) 24.

16 Christopher Hitchcock and Joshua Knobe, 'Cause and Norm' (2009) 106 The Journal of Philosophy 587. For a contrasting empirical account of our procedure for cause selection in cases of negatively evaluated actions, see Mark D Alicke, David Rose, and Dori Bloom, 'Causation, Norm Violation, and Culpable Control' (2011) 108 The Journal of Philosophy 670.

17 Hitchcock and Knobe, 'Cause and Norm' (n. 16) 590.

18 This step in the proposal is similar to the classic *sine qua non* test for 'cause-in-fact' in criminal law.

19 This step in the proposal is similar to Herbert Hart and Tony Honoré's discussion in *Causation in the Law* (Clarendon Press 1959).

By way of illustration, return to the example of the fire in the house, and consider why in this case we might wish to select 'the cause' from all other causal factors. Given that the event in question is a harm, it is no surprise that the answer is intervention: we want to understand why it happened, so we can try to ensure it does not happen again.[20] Suppose now that we discover that the fire was not caused by an act of arson, but a random freak of nature: the house was hit by lightning. Does this point to an intervention to stop fires from occurring in future? The presence of oxygen in the atmosphere and the combustibility of the house are statistically normal features of the Earth's environment and dwellings respectively. If there hadn't been oxygen in the atmosphere, or if the house hadn't been combustible, then there wouldn't have been a fire. But, because these features are normal, they are relegated to the background: in principle, we keep unremarkable factors such as these fixed while conducting our inquiry; in practice, we have no ready means of changing them anyhow. In contrast, lightning, although a natural occurrence, is more out of the ordinary, statistically speaking, and so immediately emerges as a possible cause. Would the fire have occurred, if the house had not been hit by lightning? Like the case with oxygen and combustibility, the answer is no. But, could we have prevented the house from being hit by lightning? Unlike the case of oxygen and combustibility, it is immediately apparent that they answer is yes. We cannot stop lightning, but we can divert it. Had the house been equipped with a lightning rod, there would have been no fire. That is the lesson to be learned in this case from asking about the cause: we discover a way to potentially stop a fire in the house from happening again. The value of Hitchcock and Knobe's proposal is that it explains *how* we make this selection in relation to *why* we make it at all. We attend to those parts of the causal story that stand out as violations of descriptive or prescriptive norms and identify these as 'the cause', precisely because this puts us in the best position possible to effectively intervene to alter the outcome in future.

Suppose now that we revert to the example as originally presented: when we ask what caused the fire, the answer is that it looks like arson. The mere whiff of human agency brings with it an interest not just in determinations of causation but of responsibility. What is the purpose of determining responsibility? We may have backward-looking considerations primarily in mind: we may want to find out who caused the fire in order to know who to punish and blame. Or, we may have forward-looking considerations primarily in mind: we want to find out who caused the fire in order to intervene to ensure that the individual in question does not set a fire again. Notably, this forward-looking consideration is the rationale that Lacey and I employ in our joint work, as the basis for a form of criminal responsibility linked firmly to capacity, but without affective blame: just as our interest in causation may stem from concern with intervention for the sake of a better future,

[20] If the event under consideration is a good, we may wonder about the cause in the hope that the answer will allow us to try to intervene for the opposite reason, namely, to ensure it happens again.

so too may our interest in criminal responsibility. Of course, the offender would have been unable to set the fire if the atmosphere had been devoid of oxygen, the house had not been combustible, and it had not been easy to procure gasoline and a lighter. But these are statistically normal features. Their presence is to be expected: we take them for granted and relegate them to the background. Given this background, what explains why the fire occurred is that the offender knowingly and voluntarily set it. Not only *the act* of arson, but this *state of mind* itself, violates norms (e.g. statistical, moral, and legal) and stands out as such. But, in part because of this, and unlike the other causal factors that contributed to the fire, it is also a ready object of intervention. If the offender has a *change of mind* and determines not to set fires in future, then there will be no future fires of their making. We can therefore intervene to target their state of mind—through clinical, correctional, or other means—in order to try to secure this future.

My discussion thus far has been cast—at least predominantly—in the traditional terms of responsibility and causation. But the picture that has emerged is more naturally cast in terms of responsibility and explanation. As noted above, there is broad philosophical consensus that there is no objectivity in our causal selection process. Hitchcock and Knobe's proposal explains why. Causes are selected relative to norms of many varieties, which are held fixed in the background; but, unfix the norms, and you change which cause out of the many possible causal factors will be selected. To illustrate this point, vary the example. Consider a case not of arson, but of gun violence in modern America. Statistically, many Americans own guns.[21] Morally, plenty believe gun ownership is a right. Holding those stats and that right fixed, the cause of a death by shooting is the person who pulled the trigger: from this perspective, as the slogan goes, it is people who are bad, not guns. But, in contrast to the presence of gasoline and lighters in the country, plenty other Americans refuse to resign themselves to these gun statistics or believe there is any such right to gun ownership. Unfix these norms, and the cause of a death by shooting is as much the availability of guns as the individual who pulled the trigger. If they didn't have a gun—*which they shouldn't, and only do because of political and moral corruption*—then there wouldn't have been a shooting. *That* violation is as important to single out and to intervene on as any individual who pulls a trigger. From an objective perspective, neither of these violations is any more or less the cause of the death than any other of the myriad causal factors that constitute the full causal story in this case. But, depending on whether your interests and perspective embody norms supporting gun rights or gun reform, you are respectively likely or unlikely to be satisfied with an explanation of why the death occurred that fails to mention this further violation: whether an explanation strikes you as good or not depends, among other things, on where you are coming from. Correspondingly, depending

[21] Precise numbers of owners are difficult to estimate, but see The World Population Review of Gun Ownership by State 2019 at < http://worldpopulationreview.com/states/gun-ownership-by-state/>.

on whether your interests and perspective embody norms supporting gun rights or gun reform, you are respectively likely or unlikely to ascribe responsibility entirely to the individual shooter, with no consideration of wider moral and political context as (potentially) mitigating and (certainly) relevant: whether a responsibility ascription strikes you as fair or not depends, also, on where you are coming from. For, if the shooting is not the only violation that has come into focus, then both an explanation of why the death occurred, and an ascription of responsibility for the death, that omits the other salient violation will be missing an important part of the story—in neither case does it yield the understanding and closure you want and expect. Responsibility ascriptions, like explanations, are naturally tethered to our interests and perspectives: they depend not only on what we want to explain and why we want to explain it, but on what norms we assume as background. Shifting the norms therefore not only affects what is likely to count as a *satisfying explanation of why something happened*, but who is singled out as the *bearer of responsibility for what happened.*

In recognition of this parallel between responsibility and explanation, Gunnar Bjornsson and Karl Persson have made the striking claim that responsibility judgments *just are* explanatory judgments.[22] But one can acknowledge the point without going so far. What seems clear is that responsibility ascriptions can be sensitive to the same kinds of considerations that selections of cause are sensitive to, and so *function like* explanations. This similarity is fundamentally procedural: they both naturally focus on all and only those causes that stand out as unusual and abnormal, in virtue of violating accepted background norms. But it is also psychological: they both provide understanding and closure, marking the end of inquiry. Indeed, in the courts, this closure is marked explicitly by the verdict announcing a finding of guilty or not guilty, which signifies the end of the inquiry and resolution of the trial.

I believe it is important to acknowledge the similarity without endorsing the outright identification because it is possible for us to resist the temptation to allow

[22] Björnsson and Persson, 'The Explanatory Component of Moral Responsibility' (n. 6); Björnsson and Persson, 'A Unified Empirical Account of Responsibility Judgments' (n. 6). Simplifying somewhat, they argue for this claim in three ways. First, similar to the clinical model of responsibility without blame, they suggest that our practices of holding people responsible are forward-looking. they aim at preventing behaviour. But they argue that, if so, we should expect responsibility to be ascribed when the person's state of mind is a significant part of the explanation of the behaviour—the salient cause—otherwise our practices would be idle. Second, they point out that many everyday excuses function by showing how, in the particular case under consideration, a person's state of mind is not in fact a reliable or remarkable cause of their behaviour. Rather, they acted as they did because they were forced, coerced, ignorant, or even simply obeying the rules—excuses function to refocus our attention on explanations other than the person's state of mind as the cause of their behaviour. Third, through a detailed discussion, they show how conflicting philosophical intuitions about the nature and existence of moral responsibility can be explained by recognizing how different thought experiments foreground or background different interests and perspectives. Despite quibbling about their core claim, my discussion owes a great deal to Bjornsson and Persson's work; indeed, they allude to the possibility of applying their framework to explain victim-blaming in n. 16 of 'The Explanatory Component of Moral Responsibility'.

our responsibility ascriptions to mirror our explanatory judgments. For example, if the judge instructs the jury to ignore their personal view of gun rights or gun reform in deciding whether or not this defendant is responsible for the death, and instead to focus only on whether the defendant knowingly and voluntarily pulled the trigger—honing in on a narrow idea of responsibility as capacity only—I do not rule out that that the jurors are able to focus their minds and do just that—including those who believe that the moral and political context is (certainly) relevant and (potentially) mitigating. What I am suggesting is rather that our responsibility ascriptions—especially in so far as they embody forward-looking ends—are as a matter of fact *prone* to be influenced by explanatory considerations that are easy to manipulate—as I have tried to do by the way I developed the examples. As a result, we are all too easily led astray, by mechanisms such as rhetoric, allusion, dramatic framing, and even the simple introduction of a new piece of information, that serve to focus our attention on a new possible norm violation, and correspondingly, a new possible part of the explanation of *why* the event occurred and hence locus of responsibility *for* its occurrence.[23] Indeed, such manipulation is a hallmark of opening and closing statements in court, where prosecution and defence may try to tell the story of the crime so as to foreground or background respectively the defendant's part in explaining it, and, in consequence, his responsibility for it.

I shall now argue that this psychological tendency to tether responsibility ascriptions to what strikes us as a significant part of the explanation for why something happened poses a serious problem for justice for rape.

2. Rape Culture Norms

Let us begin with some statistics. The US National Intimate Partner and Sexual Violence Survey 2010 Summary Report states that one in five women has been the victim of rape or attempted rape;[24] the US Department of Justice reports that out of 1000 sexual assaults, 230 are reported to the police, 46 reports lead to arrest, 9 cases are referred to prosecutors, 5 cases result in felony convictions, and 5 convicted offenders are incarcerated.[25] Rape statistics are often the subject of controversy; and

[23] In a series of studies on victim-blaming as a general phenomenon, Laura Niemi and Liane Young found that assignments of blame could be manipulated simply by shifting the focus of the vignette from perpetrator to victim—while holding all the facts reported constant. They also found that victim-blaming was associated with what they label 'binding values', which include commitment to loyalty, authority, and purity, as oppose to 'individualizing values', which simply prohibit harm. Laura Niemi and Liane Young, 'When and Why we See Victims as Responsible: The Impact of Ideology on Attitudes towards Victims' (2016) 42 Personality and Social Psychology Bulletin 1227.

[24] National Intimate Partner and Sexual Violence Survey: 2010 Summary Report at <https://www.cdc.gov/violenceprevention/pdf/nisvs_report2010-a.pdf>.

[25] Rape Abuse and Incent National Network at <https://www.rainn.org/statistics/criminal-justice-system>. There has been recent outcry concerning the failure of police and prosecution to pursue those sexual assaults that are reported: see Barbara Hagerty, 'An Epidemic of Disbelief' (2009) The Atlantic 72.

it is unquestionably true that elements of this overall picture are hard to measure given low reporting rates combined with the failure of reporting to lead to arrest and prosecution. But the general trend is crystal clear: the odds of a woman being raped are high, while the odds of a man being convicted of rape are—to put it mildly—low.

Why do men rape—and why does our society so reliably fail to hold them to account for doing so? Here I consider just one potential part of what must ultimately be a multi-dimensional answer: rape culture norms, understood as cultural norms that function to enable and license rape. To examine these norms, I draw on two sources: the voices of convicted rapists themselves as documented by Diana Scully through in-depth qualitative interviews with 114 men, published in her book *Understanding Sexual Violence: A Study of Convicted Rapists*;[26] and empirical studies of the attitudes and factors that result in 'victim-blaming' within the general population.[27] Strikingly, the pictures that emerge from each of these sources match. Men who rape justify and excuse their actions by appeal to many of the same factors that the general public considers as mitigating of their responsibility; and a specific attitude towards women found in convicted rapists is also associated with victim-blaming among study participants.

Before describing these factors and attitude, it is worth drawing attention to why this alignment is important to recognize. There is a long history within psychiatry and popular culture alike of viewing rape as the expression of a kind of mental disorder—a 'sickness' or 'disease'.[28] This pathologization of rape has not in general been admissible as a defence in the criminal courts. But it has nonetheless served as what I should like to call a *cultural defence mechanism* against the recognition that, in our society, rape is *normal*. But normal it is. Recall that one in five women are victims of rape or attempted rape; now add the fact that 41 per cent of these woman are assaulted by an acquaintance.[29] Put these statistics together: roughly one in ten women experience rape or attempted rape at the hands of an acquaintance, which means that in all likelihood, we all know men who rape. Moreover, there is no clear evidence that rates of mental health problems are any different or higher among

Comparable statistics and a similar problem exist in the United Kingdom. See <https://www.theguardian.com/society/2019/mar/06/prosecution-rate-in-england-and-wales-falls-to-five-year-low>.

[26] Diana Scully, *Understanding Sexual Violence: A Study of Convicted Rapists* (HarperCollins 1990).

[27] For a comprehensive review see Claire R Gravelin, Monica Biernet, and Caroline E Bucher, 'Blaming the Victim of Acquaintance Rape: Individual, Situational, and Sociocultural Factors' (2019) 9 Frontiers in Psychology, Article 2422. I cite this review whenever the number of studies supporting a claim are too many to sensibly reference given the aims of this paper; many of the individual studies cited below are reported in this review, too. Obviously, other sources in addition to those I use here can also shed light on rape culture, e.g. depictions of rape in the media, literature, music, films, and, perhaps most of all, pornography.

[28] For discussion see Scully, *Understanding Sexual Violence* (n. 26).

[29] The National Intimate Partner and Sexual Violence Survey 2010 Summary Report at <https://www.cdc.gov/violenceprevention/pdf/nisvs_report2010-a.pdf>.

convicted rapists than other felons: rapists are not distinctively 'sick' or 'diseased'.[30] And although, like other violent felons, convicted rapists appear more accepting of violence than non-felons and non-violent felons alike, they do not report poor relationships with mothers, sisters, girlfriends, and spouses, or unusual sexual development or activity in childhood or adolescence, or a lack of sexual activity or sexual frustration prior to imprisonment.[31] On the whole, they consider themselves to be—and in many ways are—ordinary men. Indeed, research on the prevalence of and attitudes towards rape as *self*-reported[32] by male college students supports this outlook. In a sample of 6159 students, 1 out of 4 reported participating in acts of sexual aggression, including sexual contact (10.2 per cent), sexual coercion (7.2 per cent), attempted rape (3.3 per cent), and rape (4.4 per cent);[33] in a sample of 356 students, 28 per cent indicated some likelihood of raping[34]—a percentage that a separate study with a sample size of 172 students found to increase to 37 per cent if the students were given assurances that they would not be caught.[35] As feminist theorists have long insisted, much as we may not wish to acknowledge it, rape culture is *our* culture.[36] The striking alignment between the mindset characteristic of convicted rapists and the mindset found in ordinary study participants shines a spotlight on this fact. Men rape—and justify and excuse why they rape—in large part because the ideas about women and rape that they themselves report as motivating and explanatory are prevalent within our society. Rape and its rationale is not abnormal: it is culturally learned.[37]

Scully's analysis of the in-depth interviews she conducted suggests that rapists fall into two categories, *admitters* and *deniers*.

[30] Scully, *Understanding Sexual Violence* (n. 26).

[31] Ibid.

[32] Self-report is of course not an accurate measure. Given the assumption that the students are unlikely to report acts of, and willingness to engage in, sexual assault, real rates are likely to be higher. On the other hand, if the students felt that reports of acts and expressions of willingness were somehow *expected* of them, real rates are likely to be lower. Both possibilities support the idea that rape is *normal*, albeit in different ways.

[33] Mart Koss, Christine Gidycz, and Nadine Wisniewksi, 'The Scope of Rape: Incidence and Prevalence of Sexual Aggression and Victimization in a National Sample of Students in Higher Education' (1987) 55 Journal of Consulting and Clinical Psychology 162.

[34] John Briere and Neil Malamuth, 'Self-reported Likelihood of Sexually Aggressive Behavior: Attitudinal versus Sexual Explanations' (1983) 17 Journal of Research in Personality 315.

[35] Note that 20 per cent of these men indicated a likelihood greater or equal to midpoint on the rating scale; this was correlated with belief in a selection of rape culture norms (see below). Todd Tieger, 'Self-rated Likelihood of Raping and Social Perception of Rape' (1981) 15 Journal of Research in Personality 147.

[36] 'Rape is not committed by psychopaths or deviants from social norms—rape is committed by *examplars* of social norms ... Rape is not excess, no aberration, no accident, no mistake—it embodies sexuality as the culture defines it' (Andrea Dworkin *Our Blood: Prophecies and Discourses on Sexual Politics* (Perigree Books 1976) 45–6). See too Catherine Mackinnon, *Feminism Unmodified: Discourses on Life and Law* (Harvard University Press 1987), and *Toward a Feminist Theory of the State* (Harvard University Press 1989).

[37] The claim that it is culturally learned is supported by cross-cultural anthropological studies which, although limited, suggest that rates of rape are widely variable and correlated with measures of gender equality. See Scully, *Understanding Sexual Violence* (n. 26).

Admitters acknowledge that they raped. But they explain what happened in ways that distance themselves from the act and reduce their responsibility, thereby protecting them from an identity as *a rapist*:

> It's different from anything else I've ever done. I feel more guilt about this. It's not consistent with me. When I talk about it, it's like being assaulted myself. I don't know why I did it, but once I started, I got into it. Armed robbery was a way of life for me, but not rape. I feel like I wasn't being myself.[38]

Exculpatory themes that emerge from the interviews and serve this identity-protecting function include:

(i) Being under the influence of drugs and alcohol which 'made' them do it:

> [Alcohol] brought out what was already there but in such intensity it was uncontrollable. Feelings of being dominant, powerful, using someone for my own gratification, all rose to the surface.[39]

Multiple studies report that ordinary subjects also view intoxication as significantly reducing responsibility in perpetrators; the more intoxicated the perpetrator, the more study participants excuse his behaviour and do not hold him responsible.[40] On the other hand, in an all too predictable asymmetry, the more intoxicated the victim, the more she is perceived as responsible for the rape (see below).[41]

(ii) Going through a particularly difficult period characterized by emotional distress:

> My parents had been married for many years and I had high expectations about marriage. I put my wife on a pedestal. When I walked in on her, I felt like my life had been destroyed, it was such a shock. I was bitter and angry about the fact that I hadn't done anything to my wife for cheating. I didn't want to hurt her [the victim], only to scare and degrade her.[42]

Note that this quotation expresses a common motivation for rape identified by rapists: revenge for the actions of a particular woman taken out on women as a group. A minority of rapists not only explain their behaviour by appeal to

[38] Ibid., 129.
[39] Ibid., 124
[40] Gravelin, Biernet, and Bucher, 'Blaming the Victim of Acquaintance Rape' (n. 27).
[41] Ibid.
[42] Scully, *Understanding Sexual Violence* (n. 26) 127.

emotional distress at the time of the rape (as this man does), but in addition pathologize their state of mind, inferring that, because they raped, they must be sick. Study participants also show associations between victim blaming, and the belief that rape is due to male pathology and inability to control sexual urges, especially combined with 'female teasing' (see (iv) below).[43]

(iii) They are actually a 'nice guy'. As evidence of this, some men report being 'kind' to their victims even though they raped them, for example they tried to be gentle while raping, or they gave their victim money to get home after. Men who were convicted of gang rape may explain how they were led along by others:

> I'm against hurting women. She should have resisted. None us of were the type of person that would use force on a woman. I never positioned myself on a woman unless she showed an interest in me. They played to me, not me to them. My weakness is to follow. I never would have stopped [the car], let alone pick her up without the others. I never would have let anyone beat her. I never bothered women who didn't want sex: never had a problem with sex or getting it. I loved her—like all women.[44]

Deniers, in contrast, do not believe they are guilty of rape. Some—not all—acknowledge that what they did was not quite right; but they maintain it was justifiable in the circumstances. The majority of these justifications focus precisely on *features of the woman raped*, supposedly rendering the man's behaviour understandable in the context:

(iv) A range of so-called 'precipitating' factors figure in virtually all reports offered by deniers as legitimating their actions; in empirical studies, these factors are found to be strongly associated either with increased perception of victim responsibility, or reduced perception of perpetrator responsibility, or both.[45] These features of women include: dressing in a revealing way, sexual history and reputation, flirtatious or 'teasing' behaviour, going home with someone, being a sex worker or other jobs/factors seen as impugning character, and, as noted above, victim intoxication. The myth that 'nice girls' do not get raped but only women who in some way 'ask for it'—as supposedly evidenced by these factors—appears pervasive.

(v) Women say no when they mean yes. Although they may 'cry rape' afterwards, in truth they are consenting. This connects to the further belief expressed by many deniers that their victims did not themselves want to bring

[43] Barbara Krahé, Jennifer Temkin, and Steffen Bieneck, 'Schema-driven Information Processing in Judgements about Rape' (2007) 21 Applied Cognitive Psychology 602.

[44] Scully, *Understanding Sexual Violence* (n. 26) 129.

[45] Gravelin, Biernet, and Bucher, 'Blaming the Victim of Acquaintance Rape' (n. 27).

charges, and only did so because they were pressured to by other men, for example boyfriends and spouses:

> A man's body is like a Coke bottle, shake it up, put your thumb over the opening and feel the tension. When you take a woman out, woo her, then she says, 'no, I'm a nice girl,' you have to use force. All men do this. She said 'no' but it was a societal 'no,' she wanted to be coaxed. All women say 'no' when they mean 'yes' but it's a societal 'no' so they won't have to feel responsible later.[46]

(vi) Women like rape: they eventually 'relax and enjoy it'. This justification may be related to the previous one, in that rapists frame rape as sex, which women want but do not admit to wanting. It may also connect to the view expressed by many rapists, including in the quotation in (iii) above, that women *should* resist rape: this duty lies with them—while pushing a woman who says no to have sex is a man's prerogative. Connectedly, empirical studies demonstrate a correlation between depictions of women who forcefully resist rape, and ascriptions of perpetrator responsibility.[47] In both convicted rapists and study participants, women appear to be perceived as required to forcefully resist rape in order to escape the risk of being perceived either as consenting and/or as in part responsible.

(vii) Rape is a minor wrong if a wrong at all. Often this justification is linked to economic transactions that are traditionally gendered. In one study that manipulated the kind of date preceding an acquaintance rape, victim responsibility and perceived justifiability of the rape were highest when the date was expensive and the man paid.[48] This mode of reasoning is explicit in the following convicted rapist's justification of his behaviour:

> After I paid for a motel, she would have to have sex but I wouldn't use a weapon.[49] I would have explained I spent the money and if she still said no, I would have forced her. If it had happened that way, it would have been rape to some people

[46] Scully, *Understanding Sexual Violence* (n. 26) 104. The belief that 'no means yes' figures in Douglas Husak and George C Thomas's argument that men's mistaken belief in consent can be honest and reasonable and hence constitutive of a permissible defence (see n. 58). Husak and Thomas argue that empirical studies of 'token resistance' indicate there is a convention of women saying no but meaning yes; they see this convention as allowing the possibility of reasonable mistake. Douglas N Husak and George C Thomas, 'Date Rape, Social Convention, and Reasonable Mistakes' (1992) 11 Law and Philosophy 95.

[47] Gravelin, Biernet, and Bucher, 'Blaming the Victim of Acquaintance Rape' (n. 27).

[48] Susan Basow and Alexandra Minieri. 'You Owe Me": Effects of Date Cost, Who Pays, Participant Gender, and Rape Myth Beliefs on Perceptions of Rape' (2011) 26 Journal of Interpersonal Violence 479.

[49] Scully notes that the towering size and strength of this particular man makes it unlikely he needed a weapon to gain compliance.

> but not to my way of thinking. I've done that kind of thing before. I'm guilty of sex and contributing to the delinquency of a minor, but not rape.[50]

Note that neither admitters nor deniers report feeling remorse in the aftermath of raping or concern for the victim; most report feeling good. Deniers, unlike admitters, continue not to feel remorse even with the passage of time; but, of course, this is as expected: they deny there is much to feel remorse about.

Importantly, despite documenting the differences in exculpating belief and styles of reasoning among rapists, Scully nonetheless identifies a single attitude common to all rapists, admitters and deniers, alike: they are strongly committed to what she calls 'pedestal values'. Women are placed 'on a pedestal' but only insofar as they conform to very rigid standards of moral and sexual conduct, for example, they display none of the so-called 'precipitating' factors in (iv). Needless to say, few if any women meet 'pedestal' standards. Correspondingly, rapists identify with traditional stereotypes of male superiority and masculinity: off the pedestal, women are objects for male sexual use. One rapist who murdered his victim expresses this attitude very clearly:

> Rape is a man's right. If a woman doesn't want to give it, a man should take it. Women have no right to say no. Women are made to have sex. It's all they're good for. Some women would rather take a beating, but they always give in; it's what they are for.[51]

One cannot but hope that the majority of study participants would disagree with this chilling statement. Nonetheless, endorsement of traditional gender roles that maintain unequal status between women and men and place restrictions on women's roles and rights is significantly correlated with a willingness to blame victims and endorse rape culture norms in empirical studies.[52]

Drawing this discussion together, we can discern the following highly schematic norms that characterize rape culture:

Descriptive norms for women:

(1) Women engage in deception about wanting and consenting to sex [rape]
(2) Women enjoy forced or coerced sex [rape]

[50] Scully, *Understanding Sexual Violence* (n. 26) 111.
[51] Ibid.,166.
[52] Gravelin, Biernet, and Bucher, 'Blaming the Victim of Acquaintance Rape' (n. 27). Note that endorsement of politically conservative values is similarly correlated: Kathryn Anderson, Harris Cooper, and Linda Okamura, 'Individual Differences and Attitudes toward Rape: A Meta-analytic Review' (1997) 23 Personality and Social Psychology Bulletin 295.

Prescriptive norms for women:

(3) 'Nice girls' don't get raped: to communicate non-consent and/or avoid rape, women are required to conform to certain standards of dress, behaviour, status
(4) To communicate non-consent and/or avoid rape, women are required to forcefully resist rape
(5) Women 'owe' sex if they engage in traditionally gendered economic transactions

Descriptive norms for men:

(6) 'Nice guys' rape because something else 'made' them do it, for example emotional distress, pathology, peer pressure
(7) Men are unable to control their desire to rape when intoxicated

Prescriptive norms for men:

(8) Men have a right to sex [rape]
(9) Men are permitted to use pressure, coercion, and if necessary force to get sex [rape] given the descriptive norms for women (1) and (2) above

How widespread is adherence to these norms? It is not possible to answer this question definitively, but the good and bad in our surrounding culture seeps into us all, men and women, whether we like it or not: these norms may *influence* in absence of *overt adherence*. Certainly the failure of reported rape to be charged and prosecuted, and those rapists who are charged and prosecuted to be convicted, suggests rape culture norms are not confined to a small minority of the general population any more than rape reflects a pathological mindset attributable only to 'sick' rapists. Rape culture is part of our society—including, of course, the courts.

3. Failures of Responsibility: Rape Culture and Explanations of Rape in the Courts

In 2018 during a rape trial in Ireland, the defence lawyer for a twenty seven-year-old man charged with raping a seventeen-year-old girl in an alleyway asked: 'Does the evidence out-rule the possibility that she was attracted to the defendant and open to meeting someone and being with someone? You have to look at the way she was dressed. She was wearing a thong with a lace front.'[53] The defendant was unanimously acquitted by the jury.[54]

The story prompted outcry. Protests erupted—including in the Irish Parliament—and women posted pictures of their underwear under #IBelieveHer and #ThisIsNotConsent. But the story is hardly unique. The history of rape trials is replete with occasions where the defence introduces as evidence information about the victim's dress, sexual history and reputation, flirtatious or 'teasing' behaviour prior to the assault, whether they went home with the defendant, whether they forcefully resisted or 'complied' with rape, status as a sex worker or other kinds of jobs or factors that could be seen as impugning character, and state of victim (and defendant) intoxication. Recent media investigation of the low rates of arrest and prosecution of reported rapes suggests that police and prosecutors—like judges and juries—may be swayed by exactly these factors—and, ironically, by the fact that they expect judges and juries to be swayed by them.[55] In parallel, defendants may be portrayed by their lawyers as 'nice guys' of good character who have already suffered enough,[56] and whose life stands to be adversely affected by what in this context comes to be called a 'harsh' sentence but in any other context—on the assumption that rape is a serious crime, not a minor transgression—would be called a reasonable one.[57]

How does the introduction of such evidence function to exonerate defendants in the courts? No doubt, part of the answer is that it can be used to support a mistake of fact defence, in so far as it supposedly renders intelligible how the defendant could have had an honest and reasonable belief in consent. In the background is the belief that the defendant is a 'nice guy'—not the kind of man who would have non-consensual sex. By a purely subjective standard, information about the victim introduced by the defence can explain why he honestly believed she was consenting, *given the nature of that information combined with the fact that he adheres to or is significantly influenced by*

[53] *The New York Times*, 15 November 2018 at <https://www.nytimes.com/2018/11/15/world/europe/ireland-underwear-rape-case-protest.html>.

[54] *The Guardian*, 15 November 2018 at <https://www.theguardian.com/uk-news/2018/nov/15/thong-protest-in-belfast-raises-concerns-over-trials>.

[55] Barbara Hagerty, 'An Epidemic of Disbelief' *The Guardian* 6 March 2019 at <https://www.theguardian.com/society/2019/mar/06/prosecution-rate-in-england-and-wales-falls-to-five-year-low>.

[56] And so are treated with 'himpathy,' to use the phrase coined by Kate Manne in *Down Girl: The Logic of Misogyny* (Oxford University Press 2018). In this context, it is telling to note how the convicted rapist in the quotation above illustrating the general mindset of *admitters* expressed his suffering, thereby revealing the degree of his self-focus and failure to recognize the suffering of his victim: 'When I talk about it [rape], it's like being assaulted myself.'

[57] This indeed was a part of the judge's reasoning in the now famous case of Brock Turner, a Stanford University student convicted of three felonies: assault with intent to rape an intoxicated woman; sexually penetrating an intoxicated person with a foreign object; and sexually penetrating an unconscious person with a foreign object. Turner received a sentence of six months in prison (he served three months) and three years on probation; the judge also considered the fact he was intoxicated at the time of the assaults as a mitigating factor in sentencing. See *The Guardian* 14 June 2016 at <https://www.theguardian.com/us-news/2016/jun/14/stanford-sexual-assault-read-sentence-judge-aaron-persky>. Brock Turner is of course wealthy and white: rape culture norms intersect with class and race, and are unlikely to exculpate or mitigate in the same way when ethnic minority or otherwise marginalized men are accused of rape.

the relevant rape culture norms (1)–(5) above. Is such an honest belief reasonable? It depends, of course, on what it means for a belief to be reasonable. If a reasonable belief is one which the average person in the defendant's position would have believed—*and the average person in his position adheres to or is significantly influenced by the relevant rape culture norms (1)–(5)*—then information about the victim introduced by the defence and pertinent to those norms may indeed render his belief reasonable.[58] On the other hand, if a reasonable belief is judged in relation to moral norms that value the sexual autonomy and integrity of all people of all genders equally *and hence conflict with rape culture norms*—moral norms, it should be noted, that sexual offences laws purport to reflect—then the defendant's belief, however honest, is not reasonable.[59] Without disputing the importance of such evidence to the possibility of mistake of fact defences, I want nonetheless to suggest that it has a significant additional function in the courts, namely, to focus the search to understand *why the rape happened* on her part in the full causal story, not his.

The facts introduced by the defence pertaining to the victim typically reveal her as violating one or more of the women-specific norms characteristic of rape culture. The burden of section 2 of this chapter was to argue that such norms are a genuine part of our society—they are influential, even if we do not know that the majority of people explicitly adhere to them. The burden of section 1 of this chapter was to suggest that, as a matter of fact, we (implicitly or explicitly) treat norm violations as targets for intervention and select them as the cause that explains why something happened, and, correspondingly, where responsibility lies. Putting these together, introducing facts revealing the victim as violating rape culture norms—given the influence of these norms—focuses our attention on these facts as the causes that explain why the rape happened, and where the responsibility lies. The counterfactuals that then guide our reasoning—either implicitly or explicitly—are counterfactuals such as the following. If she hadn't been dressed that way, *then the rape wouldn't have happened*. If she hadn't flirted with him, *then the rape wouldn't have*

[58] Lacey explores precisely this kind of case as one among many examples of so-called 'cultural defences' in 'Community, Culture, and Criminalization' in Rowan Cruft, Matthew H Kramer, and Mark R Reiff (eds), *Crime, Punishment and Responsibility. The Jurisprudence of Antony Duff* (Oxford University Press 2012) 292. Note that, although my argument in this chapter focuses entirely on rape, its structure may apply more broadly across the criminal law.

[59] A long history of accepting mistake of fact defences and acquitting defendants charged with sexual assault on this basis suggests the latter interpretation of reasonableness is, to put it mildly, not common in the courts. One solution is to impose the latter interpretation on the courts—an imposition justified, arguably, by the purpose of sexual offences laws. Another solution is to reject mistake of fact defences in sexual assault, instead either requiring consent to be subject to positive and affirmative proof (Lucinda Vandervoort, 'Mistake of Law and Sexual Assault: Consent and *Mens Rea*' (1987–1988) 2 Canadian Journal of Women & the Law 233)—or, more radically, by making sexual assault subject to strict liability—responsibility as outcome only, to adopt Lacey's term—thereby removing any element of *mens rea*. An alternative solution—given the principled and pragmatic impediments to all these reforms—is to give up on the criminal courts altogether, and use civil suits as a way for women to get recognition and compensation for the wrong of rape. I have become increasingly convinced of the value and viability of exploring the possibility of reconceiving rape as a strict liability offence, thanks to discussions with Sarah Hirschfield.

happened. If she hadn't gone home with him, *then the rape wouldn't have happened.* If she hadn't been drunk, *then the rape wouldn't have happened.* If she had forcefully resisted rape, *then the rape wouldn't have happened.* Meanwhile, the defendant may be presented as *conforming* to male-specific norms characteristic of rape culture—for example, he is just a 'nice guy' who would never have done this if he hadn't been drinking with the boys—and so as in no way unusual or abnormal. She is the norm violator, not him. The explanatory focus is thereby shifted away from his motivation and behaviour—factors now relegated to the background of the full causal story—onto her motivation and behavior—factors now in the foreground as targets for intervention *to prevent rape.*[60] Given our tendency to tether responsibility ascriptions to what strikes us as a significant part of the explanation, the shift in explanatory focus from him onto her creates a shift in focus of responsibility from him onto her.[61] For the story has now been manipulated such that the explanation of why the rape occurred appeals to what she could—and should—have done differently.

Note that—in an all too familiar depressing turn—it may be true that, in some cases, these facts about her are indeed part of the full causal story. Perhaps this rapist only rapes women at home: it is true that she wouldn't have been raped if she hadn't gone to his home. The point is that the response to this counterfactual should not be to pass over to her some or all of the responsibility for the rape, but rather a resounding: *so what?* Even if her decision to go home with him is part of the full causal story of why the rape occurred, it is irrelevant to the question of whether he is criminally responsible for raping her, which ought to be answered by focusing our attention on him: what *he did* and—assuming *mens rea* is to be preserved as relevant to the crime (see footnote 58)—what was in his mind when he did it.

To make this as plain as possible, consider the preposterousness of comparable counterfactuals being judged relevant by the courts with respect to the crime of burglary. Suppose a woman is in her house, intoxicated and lying in her underwear on the sofa. A man sees her through the window and opportunistically views her vulnerability as conducive to burglary. He tries the door of the house and finds she has left it open. He walks in and takes her wallet in front of her eyes and then leaves. While he is robbing her, she says 'That's mine! Don't take it!' But she does not try to forcefully stop him. The following counterfactuals may well be true: If she hadn't

[60] In this respect, it is noteworthy that rape prevention strategies are inevitably directed at women, both in the public realm and in our collective parenting. I started teaching my daughters how to protect themselves against rape when they were about three. I am hardly unique in this respect. But how many parents of boys drill into them—not just at that age, but at any age—that they must always ensure that all sex is consensual?

[61] Does the fact that we teach women rape prevention strategies from such a young age therefore set them up to feel responsible should they get raped, no matter how much we simultaneously insist that, if anything does happen, it is in no way their responsibility, but entirely his? Given the extraordinary pervasiveness of self-blame among rape victims, I worry the answer is yes. To my daughters: I am sorry.

been lying intoxicated in her underwear, *then the burglary wouldn't have occurred.* If she hadn't left her door open, *then the burglary wouldn't have occurred.* If she had forcefully tried to stop it, *then the burglary wouldn't have occurred.* The point is that none of these counterfactuals strikes us as relevant to the question of the man's criminal responsibility—never mind the ludicrousness of her verbal protest possibly being used to support a defence of mistake of fact to the effect that he honestly and reasonably believed she was making him a gift. They are not relevant because they do not constitute violations of the norms of property and theft and so are not viable targets of intervention. Police *advice* is never to resist but always to hand over your property, and it does not matter if you are intoxicated and in your underwear. He is the norm violator in this case, not her. This is why—even though it may be true that, had she behaved differently, the outcome would have been different—we do not use these counterfactuals to select 'the cause' and explain what happened any more than we use them to allocate responsibility for what happened.

Contrast rape. Given the existence and influence of rape culture norms, introducing a woman's violation of any of them can serve to (implicitly or explicitly) focus our attention on these violations as causally salient and hence explanatory of what happened, and hence on her as the bearer of responsibility for what happened. In this regard, it is important to note that some violations of women-specific rape culture norms will be introduced into the court merely by recounting *the setting* for the crime—as women are not supposed to go to men's houses, or to bars, or to walk the streets alone at night—never mind if the defence deliberately employs so-called 'discrediting' information about the victim to this effect. What explains the rape? *She went to his house when she shouldn't have.* Who is responsible for the rape? *She is, because she went to his house when she shouldn't have.* Of course, the fact that we are prone to see her as responsible when we consider (implicitly or explicitly) these counterfactuals does not mean that we fail to see him as responsible *at all.* The fact she went to his house may be *partly* explanatory and correspondingly she can be *partly* responsible—responsibility can be shared.[62] But her partial responsibility is likely to be seen as *mitigating* his—on the assumption that sharing a burden reduces the amount that would otherwise be borne by each individual.[63] Hence, our tendency to allow ascriptions of responsibility to mirror

[62] Arguably, this can be understood to follow from the fact that causation can be shared. See Joseph Y Halpern and Christopher Hitchcock, 'Graded Causation and Defaults' (2014) 66(2) British Journal of Philosophy of Science 413.

[63] Gravelin, Biernet, and Bucher, 'Blaming the Victim of Acquaintance Rape' (n. 27). Somewhat extraordinarily, one study found that exposure to pornography (less than one hour per week over six weeks) led to participants recommending *half* the length of a prison sentence for a rape conviction, as compared to the recommendation of participants who had had no pornography exposure; Dolf Zillman and Jennings Bryant, 'Pornography, Sexual Callousness, and the Trivialization of Rape' (1982) 32 Journal of Communication 10. Given that use of pornography appears to increase endorsement of rape culture myths as well as interest in and perpetration of sexual violence (for a review see Lori Watson's part of her book authored alongside Andrew Altman, *Debating Pornography* (Oxford University Press 2019), one explanation of the reduction in recommended sentence is reduction of responsibility ascribed to the rapist, because of increase of responsibility ascribed to the victim; another

what look to us like good explanations can interact with rape culture norms to redistribute responsibility from him onto her. In this light, the grotesque and persistent failure of the courts to convict and appropriately sentence rapists—given the fact that rape culture norms are bound to (implicitly or explicitly) influence at least some judges and jurors—is all too predictable.

Lacey situates her analysis of criminal responsibility squarely within historically changing social, political, and economic contexts. In doing so, she displays a remarkably keen eye for descriptive detail. But deep down her project is, at least in part, aspirational. She hopes the analysis to reveal ways in which our ideas and practices of criminal responsibility could be better. Our co-authored work also embodies this hope: in arguing for *criminal responsibility without affective blame*, we have tried to construct an idea and corresponding set of practices of responsibility fit not only for the purpose of holding to account, but equally for rehabilitation, reparation, and the ideal of equal treatment and respect for all members of our community. To this end, we have focused on responsibility as capacity, precisely because of its potential to identify when practices that hold to account can also promote behavioural change and make a difference, thereby serving these forward-looking ends. As I said above, I believe it is possible to resist the temptation to allow our responsibility ascriptions to mirror our explanatory judgments, by keeping our eyes fixed firmly on the issue of the defendant's capacity, and nothing more. Possible, yes. But probable, perhaps not. The invitation that any idea of responsibility linked to explanation offers—an invitation to widen the scope of inquiry, and attribute responsibility to other agents who strike us as a salient part of the explanation of why the crime occurred— is psychologically real. It may also, alas, be especially tempting in relation to those ideas of responsibility that embody forward-looking interventionist aspirations. But, when the invitation is offered within a culture influenced by norms that enable and license subordination of, and violence towards, the group to which the victim belongs, it augurs a violation of justice.

I do not know what the solution is, apart from starting by acknowledging the problem. In her inaugural lecture, Lacey remarks that 'the most important conditions for sexual equality and integrity lie in cultural attitudes rather than coercive legal rules'.[64] Are cultural attitudes changing? The #metoo movement suggests yes, while the meteoric rise of ever-more violent and degrading pornography

is reduction in perceived wrongness of rape; these mechanisms may, of course, work in tandem. To my knowledge, this particular study has not been replicated; but, more generally, empirical studies of actual and mock juries suggest that jurors who endorse rape culture norms are more disposed to victim-blame and to acquit—as one would expect, given that jurors, like study participants, are ordinary people. For a review of this evidence, see Meagen M Hildebrand and Cynthia J Najdowski, 'The Potential Impact of Rape Culture on Juror Decision Making: Implications for Wrongful Acquittals in Sexual Assault Trials' (2015) 78 Albany Law Review 1059. Hildebrand and Najdowski suggest endorsement of rape culture affects juror decision-making via a number of psychological mechanisms distinct from the proposal put forward here, including schema theory, confirmation bias, and attribution theory.

[64] Lacey, *Unspeakable Subjects* (n. 2) 122.

suggests no.[65] But, until they do, even the most forgiving and forward-looking idea of criminal responsibility carries its own undoing within it. For those of us who have been convinced by Lacey's overall project, perhaps it should come as no surprise that, in legitimating and coordinating state power, our ideas and practices of criminal responsibility have proven to be so useful a tool for legitimating and coordinating male power.

Bibliography

Alicke, MD, Rose, D, and Bloom, D, 'Causation, Norm Violation, and Culpable Control' (2011) 108 The Journal of Philosophy 670

Anderson, K, Cooper, H, and Okamura, L, 'Individual Differences and Attitudes toward Rape: A Meta-analytic Review' (1997) 23 Personality and Social Psychology Bulletin 295

Basow, S and Minieri, A, 'You Owe Me": Effects of Date Cost, who Pays, Participant Gender, and Rape Myth Beliefs on Perceptions of Rape' (2011) 26 Journal of Interpersonal Violence 479

Björnsson, G and Persson, K 'A Unified Empirical Account of Responsibility Judgments' (2013) 87 Philosophy and Phenomenological Research 611

Björnsson, G and Persson, K, 'The Explanatory Component of Moral Responsibility' (2012) 46 Noûs 326Briere, J and Malamuth, N, 'Self-reported Likelihood of Sexually Aggressive Behavior: Attitudinal versus Sexual Explanations' (1983) 17 Journal of Research in Personality 315

Dretske, F, *Explaining Behavior: Reasons in a World of Causes* (MIT Press 1991)

Dworkin, A, *Our Blood: Prophecies and Discourses on Sexual Politics* (Perigree Books 1976)

Gravelin, CR, Biernet, M, and Bucher, CE, 'Blaming the Victim of Acquaintance Rape: Individual, Situational, and Sociocultural Factors' (2019) 9 Frontiers in Psychology Article 2422

Hagerty, B, 'An Epidemic of Disbelief' (2009) The Atlantic 72

Halpern, JY and Hitchcock, C, 'Graded Causation and Defaults' (2014) 66(2) British Journal of Philosophy of Science 413

Hart, HLA and Honoré, T *Causation in the Law* (Clarendon Press 1959)

Hildebrand, MM and Najdowski, CJ, 'The Potential Impact of Rape Culture on Juror Decision Making: Implications for Wrongful Acquittals in Sexual Assault Trials' (2015) 78 Albany Law Review 1059

Hitchcock, C and Knobe, J, 'Cause and Norm' (2009) 106 The Journal of Philosophy 587

Husak, DN and Thomas, GC, 'Date Rape, Social Convention, and Reasonable Mistakes' (1992) 11 Law and Philosophy 95

Koss, M, Gidycz, C, and Wisniewksi, N, 'The Scope of Rape: Incidence and Prevalence of Sexual Aggression and Victimization in a National Sample of Students in Higher Education' (1987) 55 Journal of Consulting and Clinical Psychology 162

Krahé, B, Temkin, J, and Steffen Bieneck, S, 'Schema-driven Information Processing in Judgements about Rape' (2007) 21 Applied Cognitive Psychology 602

Lacey, N, *In Search of Criminal Responsibility: Ideas, Interests, and Institutions* (Oxford University Press 2016)

65 See Andrew Altman, *Debating Pornography* (n. 63).

Lacey, N, 'Community, Culture, and Criminalization' in R Cruft, MH Kramer, and MR Reiff (eds), *Crime, Punishment and Responsibility: The Jurisprudence of Antony Duff* (Oxford University Press 2012) 292
Lacey, N, *Unspeakable Subjects: Feminist Essays in Legal and Social Theory* (Hart 1998)
Lacey, N and Pickard, H, 'A Dual Process Approach to Criminal Law: Victims and the Clinical Model of Responsibility without Blame' (2019) 27 The Journal of Political Philosophy 229
Lacey, N and Pickard, H, 'The Chimera of Proportionality: Institutionalising Limits on Punishment in Contemporary Social and Political Systems' (2015) 78 Modern Law Review 216
Lacey, N and Pickard, H, 'To Blame or to Forgive? Reconciling Punishment and Forgiveness in Criminal Justice' (2015) 35 Oxford Journal of Legal Studies 665
Lacey, N and Pickard, H, 'From the Consulting Room to the Court Room? Taking the Clinical Model of Responsibility without Blame into the Legal Realm' (2013) 33 Oxford Journal of Legal Studies 1
Lewis, DK, 'Causation' (1973) 70 The Journal of Philosophy 556
Mackinnon, C, *Toward a Feminist Theory of the State* (Harvard University Press 1989)
Mackinnon, C, *Feminism Unmodified: Discourses on Life and Law* (Harvard University Press 1987)
Manne, K, *Down Girl: The Logic of Misogyny* (Oxford University Press 2018)
Mill, JS, *A System of Logic, Volume I, Fourth Edition* (J.W. Parker and Son 1856)
Moore, M, 'Causation in the Law' in EN Zalta (ed.), *The Stanford Encyclopedia of Philosophy* (Winter 2019 Edition) <https://plato.stanford.edu/archives/win2019/entries/causation-law/>
Niemi, L and Young, L, 'When and Why we See Victims as Responsible: The Impact of Ideology on Attitudes towards Victims' (2016) 42 Personality and Social Psychology Bulletin 1227
Pickard, H, 'Responsibility without Blame: Philosophical Reflections on Clinical Practice' in KWM Fulford et al. (eds), *The Oxford Handbook of Philosophy and Psychiatry* (Oxford University Press 2013)
Pickard, H, 'Responsibility without Blame: Empathy and the Effective Treatment of Personality Disorder' (2011) 18 Philosophy, Psychiatry, Psychology 209
Scully, D, *Understanding Sexual Violence: A Study of Convicted Rapists* (HarperCollins 1990)
Tieger, T, 'Self-rated Likelihood of Raping and Social Perception of Rape' (1981) 15 Journal of Research in Personality 147
Vandervoort, L, 'Mistake of Law and Sexual Assault: Consent and *Mens Rea*' (1987–1988) 2 Canadian Journal of Women & the Law 233
Watson, L and Altman, A, *Debating Pornography* (Oxford University Press 2019)
Zillman, D and Bryant, J, 'Pornography, Sexual Callousness, and the Trivialization of Rape' (1982) 32 Journal of Communic ation 10

6

Taking Guilt Seriously

Towards a Mature Retributivism

Alan Norrie[1,2]

1. Sex, Love, and Guilt

Some years ago, Nicola Lacey considered how gendered sexual relations underpinned the law of rape, privileged men, and excluded women's experience.[3] Doing so opened the door to broader issues traversing criminal law. Lacey had suggested we rethink the ethical relations underlying sex and law by use of psychoanalytic argument. This involved 'rethinking ... the philosophical framework of criminal law' in order to reshape 'the law of sexual offences', but also, she suggested, to consider the 'non-sexual offences of violence'.[4] Her critique of sexual offences related to the ethical abstraction and seeming neutrality to which general categories of legal responsibility aspire, so that her critique of neutrality was an aspect of the bigger question of how legal forms of responsibility are generally configured. Her argument is accordingly an invitation to consider how a psychoanalytic approach might view the criminal law across the board.

In this chapter, I take up the invitation to think about the criminal law in relation to what seems an all too suitable case for treatment, the concept of guilt. The finding of guilt or its absence is a key moment in any criminal trial, and it is also central to psychoanalytic understanding. But when the two disciplines use the same term, they do not mean the same thing. If they diverge, what could a deeper, psychoanalytic, account of guilt contribute to our understanding of law?[5] Nothing

[1] This chapter was presented at seminars at Leicester Law School and at the Criminal Law and Criminal Justice Theory Forum at the London School of Economics in October and December 2019. Thanks to all those who gave comments on it at these events, from which I benefited immensely. Thanks also to Niki Lacey for many years of intellectual companionship. I would like to take this opportunity to note the convergence in this volume of John Gardner's idea of 'immature' blame and guilt with my account of their 'early' form. Though I cannot match the elegance of John's style, I would like to have been able to acknowledge this late finding of common ground in person.

[2] Warwick Law School.

[3] Nicola Lacey, *Unspeakable Subjects* (Hart 1998) ch. 4.

[4] Ibid., 122.

[5] This chapter is part of a larger investigation into the moral psychology underlying law. Such an approach entails linking both moral and psychological elements so that a psychoanalytic approach provides one part of an overall picture.

Alan Norrie, *Taking Guilt Seriously* In: *On Crime, Society, and Responsibility in the Work of Nicola Lacey.* Edited by: Iyiola Solanke, Oxford University Press (2021). © The several contributors. DOI: 10.1093/oso/9780198852681.003.0007

is straightforward here, for psychoanalysis also speaks with many different voices, some of which are discussed below.

a. From Sex to Guilt

In feminist critical legal thinking, the figure of the French poststructuralist psychoanalyst, Jacques Lacan, looms large, in a way that Lacey finds disconcerting. She writes of the 'complex and sometimes unpalatable cocktail of psychoanalysis and deconstruction'[6] that influences feminist thinking. In Lacan, the subject at the heart of critique 'is marked by its acceptance of the Law of the Father through its entry into ... language'. This means the phallus 'becomes encoded in the role of... "transcendental signifier" which underpins the construction of meaning',[7] the nature of language, and the deficient position of those who lack a phallus. Lacey's response is a fairly profound scepticism that this could be the basis on which to reconceive *women's* position in gender relations, and how it might change. Given Lacan's assumptions, one might not be surprised that even the reimagined woman fails to get beyond the existing gendered world. For Lacey, the feminist psychoanalytic critique looks a blind alley.[8] Perhaps in the area of gender, psychoanalysis will always be at its most vulnerable, but might it be more helpful about the issue of guilt in criminal law?

b. Love, Sex, and Guilt

We should remember that other forms of psychoanalytic theory are available, so that the invitation to explore law and the idea of guilt should not be cut short by criticism of one approach. The route I will take brings together two different approaches which, I shall argue, can form an overall perspective. The first is provided by the German emigré psychoanalyst to the United States, Hans Loewald,[9] whose work on Freud's later structural theory has been carried forward in brilliant fashion by the Aristotelian philosopher Jonathan Lear.[10] The second is provided by the British object relations school first developed by Melanie Klein.[11] Both approaches help us understand the nature of guilt as a category in moral psychology, and one that is engaged with the criminal law in a complex way. In that regard,

6 Ibid., 206.
7 Ibid., 207.
8 Ibid., ch. 7.
9 Hans Loewald, *Papers on Psychoanalysis* (Yale University Press 1980).
10 Jonathan Lear, *Love and Its Place in Nature* (Yale University Press 1998); *Open Minded* (Harvard University Press 1998); *Freud* (2nd edn, Routledge 2015); *Wisdom Won from Illness* (Harvard University Press 2017).
11 Melanie Klein, *Envy and Gratitude* (Vintage 1997); *Love, Guilt and Reparation* (Vintage 1998).

Loewaldian-Freudian and Kleinian forms of psychoanalysis may do for criminal law analysis what Lacanian psychoanalysis sought to do for feminism: to provide a deeper understanding of the embodied and enformed human psyche which helps us grasp the working of the criminal law. In different ways, these approaches understand *love* as a creative and developmental force in the human psyche and link this to an understanding of guilt. This may prove an appropriate starting point for thinking about what criminal law does, and how it may be critically understood.

To see this, let us return to Lacey's argument about what is wrong with the law of rape. Its categories lack an interest in the body and its affectivity, never asking 'what is valuable about sexual experience, sexual expression, lived sexuality'.[12] To that question, her answer is that it is ideas of 'self-expression, connection, intimacy, relationship', which 'underpin contemporary understandings of what is valuable about sexuality',[13] and these are missing from the legal analysis of autonomy and responsibility in the sexual offences. Note, however, that what underpins the value of sex is also what is important for human wellbeing generally. Many forms of violation exist alongside sexual violation, which it is the role of criminal law to suppress. To be seriously assaulted, robbed, or otherwise attacked, all impinge on a person's ability to express herself and to have confidence in her ability to relate and connect. Sexual love is one form of human love, and it is love, including love of self, and as it is appropriately engaged *mutatis mutandis* in different kinds of human relationship, which lies at the core of what we think valuable in human existence.[14]

It makes sense to think about how love comes about, how it lies at the heart of human metapsychology, and how this relates not only to the law controlling sexual relations but more generally in criminal law, where guilt, at least for serious offences involving interpersonal violence, is a central concept.[15] Lacey's argument about what is lacking from the law of sexual relations, extended to human relations

[12] Lacey, *Unspeakable Subjects* (n. 3) 103.

[13] Ibid., 106.

[14] Love, as Mario Lanza, and my father, used to sing, is a 'many splendoured thing'. Thus Roy Bhaskar: 'love is consistent with many different forms of action, and can be expressed in an infinity of number of ways. There are various conventional categorisations—which range from erotic, romantic, familial, civic, through to ethical and spiritual modalities' (Roy Bhaskar, *The Philosophy of Metareality* (Routledge 2012) 181). Compare Freud: 'The nucleus of what we mean by love naturally consists (and this is what is commonly called love, and what the poets sing of) in sexual love with sexual union as its aim. But we do not separate from this ... self-love ..., love for parents and children, friendship and love for humanity ..., and also devotion to concrete objects and to abstract ideas ... all these tendencies are an expression of the same instinctual impulses ... ' (Sigmund Freud, 'Group Psychology and the Analysis of the Ego' in *Civilization, Society and Religion* (Penguin 1985) 119.

[15] I accept the case Lindsay Farmer has made with regard to the administrative character of much modern criminal law, so that the distinction between *mala in se* and *mala prohibita* offences reflects real differences in uses to which the criminal law is put. I do not, however, think that an administrative perspective can account for the nature of the criminal law as a whole. Issues of responsibility and guilt remain central to the *mala in se* crimes, and, in the distorted way these are publicly mobilized, to the nature of political discourse. They also have real, first order, relevance to issues of moral responsibility. See Lindsay Farmer, *Making the Modern Criminal Law* (Oxford University Press 2016), discussed in Alan Norrie, 'Criminal Law and Ethics: Beyond Normative Assertion and Its Critique' (2017) 80 Modern Law Review 955.

more broadly, suggests a general interrogation of the criminal law. Guilt, with its broad range of references both within and beyond the law, is potentially a category with important diagnostic value. The door Lacey opens with regard to metapsychology and sexual relations becomes, in short, an invitation to understand criminal law more generally.

c. Towards a Mature Retributivism

I take up this invitation here by investigating the nature of guilt in criminal justice in terms of an underlying relationship between such justice and love, through a metapsychology drawing on Freud, Loewald, and Klein. The chapter has three main sections. In the first, I identify two forms of guilt in childhood identified by Freud, an 'early' and a 'mature' form. I argue the former is ethically regressive, the latter progressive. In the middle section, I take up Klein's account of infantile guilt in the 'paranoid-schizoid' and 'depressive' positions she identifies. I argue that these can also be characterized as early and mature forms, and that her and Freud's accounts dovetail to offer a coherent metapsychology of guilt at the infant and child stages of human development. Both writers, it should be noted, argue that what is developed in early mental life is relevant to and ongoing in the different setting of adult life. In the final section, I suggest that a critical understanding of criminal justice benefits from seeing how both early and mature guilt are deployed in the modern criminal justice system. At the end, I suggest that the different forms of guilt allow us to identify the basis for a new retributive theory of 'punishment',[16] a *mature* retributivism based on psychoanalytical understanding. This way of recasting retributive theory then brings me back to Lacey, for it is relevant to the work she and Hanna Pickard have done recently, on the idea of 'responsibility without blame'.[17]

2. Early and Mature Guilt

In this section, I identify two accounts of guilt in Freud, one that is there on its face, the other which can be developed from his later structural theory of the psyche following the line of development begun by Loewald and pursued by Lear. This generates a view of a mature guilt that is developmentally and ethically progressive, alongside an early form that is punitive, persecutory, and ethically regressive.

[16] The inverted commas indicate that the new theory places the relationship between retributivism and punishment under question.

[17] Nicola Lacey and Hanna Pickard, 'From the Consulting Room to the Court Room? Taking the Clinical Model of Responsibility Without Blame into the Legal Realm' (2013) 33 Oxford Journal of Legal Studies 1; Nicola Lacey and Hanna Pickard, 'To Blame or to Forgive? Reconciling Punishment and Forgiveness in Criminal Justice' (2015) 35 Oxford Journal of Legal Studies 665.

a. Two Freuds

Martha Nussbaum has recently written of how she gave up her previous commitment to the psychoanalytic view of guilt. She came to see it as self-centred, self-lacerating, and narcissistic, and as echoing a harsh, retributive, Kantian style of ethics.[18] This is a one-sided view of what psychoanalysis can offer, for it misses the progressive ethical view of guilt described below. However, some of Freud's statements on the subject suggest she has a point:

> The super-ego—the conscience at work in the ego—may then become harsh, cruel and inexorable against the ego which is in its charge. Kant's Categorical Imperative is thus the direct heir of the Oedipus complex.[19]

This is a prominent line in Freud, and is properly subject to Nussbaum's strictures. In *Civilization and Its Discontents*, it can be said to be the dominant approach. However, the case can also be made for the conflicted nature of Freud's thought, and for an alternative approach implicit in his metapsychology, especially as it evolved in his later structural writings. From this approach we find a different way of thinking about guilt, in what I shall call its 'mature' form. Here, guilt is creative, developmental, and ethically progressive, warranting the label 'eudaimonistic' for its future-oriented commitment to human betterment.[20] It is a love-related version of guilt which contrasts with the hate, anger, and fear-related version foregrounded in *Civilization and Its Discontents*. This different account is as consistent with Freud's metapsychology as the other, 'Kantian', account, though it is not well known, and needs to be developed.[21] If we call the first, dominant, persecutory, account Freud's 'Kantian' account of an 'early' form in psychic development, we can call the second his 'mature' account, which I shall argue is creative, reparative, and progressive and may be termed 'Aristotelian', for its eudaimonistic quality.

18 Martha Nussbaum, *Anger and Forgiveness* (Oxford University Press 2016) 127–35. Such a view may be taken of a Kantian ethics of punishment, but it is not the whole picture. See e.g. Jeffrie Murphy's account of the ambivalences in Kant, discussed below at text to n. 57; and Alan Norrie, *Law, Ideology and Punishment* (Kluwer 1991) ch. 3.

19 Sigmund Freud, 'The Economic Problem of Masochism' in *On Metapsychology* (Penguin 1984) 422.

20 This is the approach developed by Jonathan Lear (above, n. 10). Nussbaum also writes of eudaimonic anger (*Anger and Forgiveness* (n. 18) 16), which could be related to eudaimonic guilt, but she does not develop either such an account of anger or guilt. Guilt, she says, would be the 'wrong motive' while 'positive love and compassion' are the right ones (ibid., 131). I shall argue that there is a mature kind of eudaimonic guilt, and anger, which is necessarily embedded in love and compassion, and is of the 'right' kind.

21 A fuller version of this argument is found in Alan Norrie, 'Animals Who Think and Love: Law, Identification and the Moral Psychology of Guilt' (2019) 13 Criminal Law and Philosophy 553. There I identify the immanent account of mature guilt also to be found in *Civilization and Its Discontents*.

b. Early Guilt: 'Kantian' and Persecutory

'Kantian' persecutory guilt runs through Freud's *Civilization and Its Discontents.* Two quotations from that work will indicate the nature of the argument:

> Thus we know of two origins of the sense of guilt: one arising from fear of an authority, and the other, later on, arising from fear of the super-ego. The first insists upon a renunciation of instinctual satisfactions; the second, as well as doing this, presses for punishment, since the continuance of the forbidden wishes cannot be concealed from the super-ego. We have also learned how the severity of the super-ego—the demands of conscience—is to be understood. It is simply a continuation of the severity of the external authority, to which it has succeeded and which it has in part replaced.[22]

The second quote:

> The tension between the harsh super-ego and the ego that is subjected to it, is called by us the sense of guilt; it expresses itself as a need for punishment. Civilization, therefore, obtains mastery over the individual's dangerous desire for aggression ... by setting up an agency within him to watch over it, like a garrison in a conquered city.[23]

In this account, guilt emerges from fear of the anger of authority figures, and as these are brought back into the psyche, fear of the person's own superego. The latter acts like 'a garrison in a conquered city', while the demands of conscience represent a continuation of the anger of external authority, once it is introjected into the psyche. Overall, the need for the 'civilizatory' authority of the superego stems from the forcefulness and the danger of instinctual satisfactions, especially of an aggressive and sexual kind, so that civilization, external authority figures, and the strict superego are all things that keep basic instinctual demands in place.

We can see here why Freud might have compared the superego to the categorical imperative, since both could be said to involve an external command system, which is internally endorsed. We can also see why Nussbaum might have objected to its self-centred narcissism: there is no regard here for the other, it is all about the ego's self-absorption. Freud's model of human conduct, social life, and moral psychology in this account of fear, anger, guilt, and the superego is bleak, primitive, and persecutory. In this vision, the human condition is one of domination by base instincts and fears, where guilt's facial expression is a

22 Freud, 'Civilization and Its Discontents' in *Civilization, Society and Religion* (n. 14) 319.
23 Ibid., 316–17.

snarl. Freud describes man as a wolf in *Civilization and Its Discontents*,[24] and we can see why. There is no development of a consolidated ethical subjectivity in this account, but rather ethical states, or rather psychic states playing the role of ethical censors, emerge to control animal instincts. All that stands between humans and their viciousness is fear and its internal mental representative, the superego: the garrison in the conquered city, the categorical imperative imposed upon animal passions. Small wonder that Nussbaum should distance herself from this 'Kantian' Freud, with his primitive and persecutory account of guilt, but another Freudian view beckons.

c. Mature Guilt: 'Aristotelian' and Reparative

While Freud's main argument in *Civilization and Its Discontents* is as we have described it, another view is implicit, but needs developing. Loewald emphasized the importance of love and the life instinct (libido) in the later Freud's structural theory, and Lear has developed this view, linking it to Greek, particularly Aristotelian, philosophy. From this position, it is possible to create another account of guilt as complex, morally creative, and psychologically developmental, that is, following Lear, as eudaimonistic, and therefore 'Aristotelian', in its nature.

This approach comes from Freud's later, structural, metapsychology of ego and superego development, as the process whereby the human psyche becomes 'enformed'. In the earliest stage of human life, the infant operates in a state of primary narcissism or what can be called 'ideal egoism',[25] which is a protean and inchoate state of love for life—an undifferentiated life instinct that Freud called libido or Eros. The process of childhood psychic development is one in which the child interacts with parent figures to differentiate itself as an individual with an identity, by creating an ego and thereby demarcating its self. Later, the ego evolves by creating a further, self-reflective, element or 'precipitate', which Freud called the superego.[26] Out of this evolution, we get the development of possibilities for a sense of responsibility, a conscience, the possibility of feelings of guilt, and a desire to repair wrongs. Importantly, all these developments are relational, that is they are emergent from social situations of love and solidarity with other human beings—primarily, but not exclusively, parent figures. The process of individual self-development is always at the same time a relational and a social process. This begins in childhood and remains significant through life.

[24] Ibid., 302.

[25] To simplify, 'ideal egoism' refers to the earliest stage of the narcissistic libido, which is distinguished from the later situation where the ego has taken on ego ideals from parent and other figures: Loewald, *Papers on Psychoanalysis* (n. 9) 46–7, 268–9.

[26] Freud, 'The Ego and the Id' in *On Metapsychology* (n. 19) 367–79.

Elements for an account of mature guilt

Three elements from Loewald's elucidation of Freud's structural theory are important: the sense of responsibility, the sense of guilt, and the desire to repair.[27]

A sense of responsibility. This basic element of human moral psychology is located in the evolution of the self, as the child develops its sense of its autonomy as an ego and superego out of and away from parental relationships. It identifies through how a parent relates to it, and builds from this a sense of how it could be a self (an ego) and have self-agency, culminating in its development of a superego:

> Responsibility to oneself, within the context of authoritative norms consciously and unconsciously accepted or assimilated from parental and societal sources, is the essence of superego as internal agency . . . It involves appropriating or owning up to one's needs and impulses as one's own, impulses and desires we appear to have been born with or that seem to have taken shape in interaction with parents during infancy . . . [So doing] we begin to develop a sense of self-identity [which] means to experience ourselves as agents, notwithstanding the fact that we were born without our informed consent and did not pick our parents.[28]

If one can feel responsible for what one has done, this implies both an ego that acts and an element in it, a superego, reflecting on those actions, establishing an agent capable of self-reflexivity. This is the basis for a sense of self-responsibility.

The possibility of guilt. Out of this development, there comes the monitoring of potential tensions in the psyche between the things one does and the things one would do if acting according to the best, or ideal, commitments one has developed. Tension between the ego's acts (as ego) and the ego's ideals (as evolved from parental and other social models of conduct, and ultimately as elements collected in a self-reflexive superego) can leave one feeling bad or angry about what one has done. Such a tense, negative, anxious, feeling is guilt, a 'form of tension between ego and superego'.[29] For Loewald, we 'have a sense of guilt concerning past or present thoughts, feelings and deeds, but only inasmuch as they represent a nonfulfillment of the inner image of ourselves, of the internal ideal we have not reached'.[30] Pace Nussbaum, this is not a question of beating oneself up for the pleasure of it. Nor is it grounded in an unreflective fear of parent figures. Rather it is a concerned self-reflection and criticism that leads a developed subject capable of both in the direction of their ideals in relations with others. Against the 'Kantian' Freud, this is not the screaming anger of the superego keeping one in line; it is the evolving self, seeking to act well according to its achieved sense of its own best lights. Against

27 For a more developed account, see Norrie, 'Animals Who Think and Love' (n. 21).
28 Loewald, *Papers on Psychoanalysis* (n. 9) 392.
29 Ibid., 273.
30 Ibid., 273–4.

the primitive, anger, and fear-driven animal that acts in persecutory and self-persecutory ways, guilt is here constructive, related to one's ideals, aimed at addressing how one has acted towards others, with a view to putting things right.

A desire to repair. There are two aspects to this. First, responsibility and guilt are accompanied by a desire to restore or repair wrongs, that is, to act responsibly to lay to rest psychic conflicts arising from negative behaviours. This is the corollary of guilt anxiety, but it is supported by something else: a second, deep-seated, reaction of the superego to the process of its own formation.

The superego emerges out of resolution of the so-called Oedipal struggle,[31] with profound consequences for establishing the child's autonomy from its parents and its own coherent agency. The psychological control parents have of the pre-Oedipal child comes because psychologically they dwell inside and are a part of it. The Oedipal struggle is the effort by the child to take control away from them, to become a person with a much greater degree of control over its own psyche. A successful struggle, 'kicking out' or 'killing' the parent inside, generates the possibility of a more coherent and self-reliant superego. Yet this necessary achievement in a child's psychic life leaves it with residual bad feeling—guilt—about what it has done. It absolutely needed to wrest to itself control of its own psyche, but in so doing, it also rejected the internal loving parent that was part of it. Normally, of course, a new modus vivendi is established, but the rejection of the old emotional order leaves a deep sense that the child has betrayed those it loved, and who loved it, the most.

This is the basis for a deep-set, residual, sense that one has done wrong, and that reparation is required. According to Loewald, the emergent superego develops an inbuilt desire *to atone*:

> In an important sense, by evolving our own autonomy, our own superego … , we are killing our parents. We are usurping their power, their competence, their responsibility for us, and we are abnegating them, rejecting them as libidinal objects. In short we destroy them in regard to some of their qualities hitherto most vital to us … Without the guilty deed of parricide there is no autonomous self … no individual self worthy of that name, no advanced internal organisation of psychic life, [so that] guilt and atonement are crucial motivational elements of the self … Guilt then is not a troublesome affect that we might hope to eliminate in some fashion, but one of the driving forces in the organisation of the self The

[31] This is commonly understood to relate to issues of sexual identification, but it has a broader implication with regard to super-ego formation, which, like the ego formation that precedes it, 'implies an abandonment of sexual aims, a desexualisation' (Freud, 'The Ego and the Id' (n. 26) 369). More broadly, the complex can be generalized to a deeper level than that of sexual identity or family structure, as a 'childhood florescence of ambivalence towards the important people in one's life' (Lear, *Freud* (n. 10) 180), regardless of gender or sexual desire.

> self, in its autonomy, is an atonement structure, a structure of reconciliation, and as such a supreme achievement.[32]

'To atone' as an active verb means to make good, but in its original sense, it is to find a way once again to be whole, to be 'at one'.[33] This is what makes this mature, superego-based, form of guilt instinctively and residually reparative. The superego has an inbuilt tendency to wish things restored to wholeness, and this works alongside the desire to address tensions around its ego ideals.[34]

It should be clear that this eudaimonistic account of a guilt that repairs or restores is very different from the persecutory kind we identified previously. It is different in both its form and its substance. The 'Kantian' anger-and-guilt model operates with a simplistic account of instincts and their control. While the superego is invoked, it can only be a primitive, early, rudimentary, version of the mature superego that Loewald draws out of superego formation and resolution of the Oedipal complex. The 'Kantian' superego is the voice of angry authority figures, introjected, and with the volume turned up. Anger may also be present in the mature, reparative, model, but it takes the form of a tension within the psyche resulting from unhappiness at failing to live up to one's best ways of dealing with things. The child's mature, eudaimonistic, development establishes moral action as the outcome of a complex, structural, psychic evolution which takes a person from the earliest phase of the basic life drive (primary narcissism) to ego formation, the creation of ego ideals, and the Oedipal struggle to create the 'Aristotelian', self- and other-respecting, superego. All these are complex—individual, social, relational—processes out of which guilt and the desire to repair emerge as ethical possibilities. The resulting human being is able to think and act creatively in relation to wrongs it may have done, or that it observes in the world. Mature guilt and anger are both about ethically valid self-criticism and the desire to repair, and they lead to a sense of responsibility to address personal wrongdoing or wrongs in the world at large—this is precisely the eudaimonistic anger that Nussbaum identifies but does not pursue in her account.[35] The reparative model of guilt is complex, evolved, emergent, mature, and creative, contrasting in most ways with an earlier form of guilt in which the person is less complete, and subject to basic instincts and controls. If we turn now to consider Melanie Klein's account of guilt at the earlier infantile stage, we will see a remarkable parallel to the early and mature forms we have identified in Freud.

[32] Loewald, *Papers on Psychoanalysis* (n. 9) 390–4.

[33] Herbert Morris, *On Guilt and Innocence* (University of California Press 1976) 100.

[34] The wish to restore wholeness has both a backward and a forward aspect. The desire to get back to an early childhood state is present but regressive; the desire to look forwards and to find wholeness in mature relations takes a form of early ideal egoism and puts it to progressive uses. Thanks to Peter Ramsay for raising this point with me.

[35] Nussbaum, *Anger and Forgiveness* (n. 18) 16.

3. Persecutory and Reparative Guilt

Klein's work on object relations pioneered a move grounded in Freud's thinking, but pushing it in two directions. The first was to take psychoanalytic thinking to the earliest time in an infant's life, where Klein found, earlier than Freud, the rudiments of ego and superego formation. Where Freud 'discovered the child still dynamic in the adult', Klein 'discovered the infant in the child and the adult'.[36] The second was to identify two successive 'positions' in an infant's early development, evolving stages that remained part of the child and the adult throughout a life. An infant developed from the earlier 'paranoid-schizoid' position into the later 'depressive' position, but there could also be regression, and though these positions were most obvious in the behaviour of disturbed children and adults, they represented general forms of human psychology, which could be observed both in individual behaviour and in social practices. These two positions provide parallel accounts of early and mature guilt in Klein to those in Freud, at an earlier stage of development.

a. Klein's Two Positions[37]

A person's development involves a process of psychological integration that deals with basic human anxieties about being loved and having that love secured. In the 'paranoid-schizoid' phase, the infant has no clear sense of itself, or anything else, as whole. Profound emotions of fear, anger, and love jostle as the infant first experiences the world and reacts to an environment on which it depends. The first object it experiences is the breast,[38] which can be either giving (the so-called 'good breast') or withholding (the 'bad breast'). While the former is a source of nurture, warmth, and security, the latter generates perplexity, anxiety, and anger. Perceptions of the good and the bad remain unconnected in the infant mind, which deals only in 'part objects', and this is reflected in a psyche that perceives the world as split into either fearful and angry (bad) or loving and nurturing (good) forms. The world is seen as either all good or all bad: when good, it is very good, and when bad, very bad. Without any overall connection being made between good and bad parts, so that badness might be seen as a temporary experience in an overall good setting, anxiety

[36] Hanna Segal, 'Introduction' in Klein, *Love, Guilt and Reparation* (n. 11) ix.

[37] See Craig Reeves, 'What Punishment Expresses' (2019) 28 Social and Legal Studies 31 and Craig Reeves, Alan Norrie, and Henrique Carvalho, 'Criminal Law: Between Persecution and Reconciliation' in Emilios Christodoulidis, Ruth Dukes, and Marco Goldoni (eds), *Research Handbook on Critical Legal Theory* (Edward Elgar 2019) for fuller discussion of Klein's work and its implications for punishment and law. I am indebted to Craig Reeves for showing me the way into this work, and Freudian metapsychology more generally.

[38] Or an alternative source of nurture.

is overwhelming, and anger when it comes is all-consuming rage and aggression. Herein lies the root of a persecutory anger that responds instinctually in a destructive way to objects that are perceived as all bad. This is Klein's initial, paranoid-schizoid, position.

The 'depressive' position, which supervenes on this first position, also involves anxiety, but of a different kind. Gradually the infant sees that part objects it had perceived as all good or all bad are really one object that sometimes appears as good (e.g. gratifying) and sometimes bad (e.g. frustrating). It begins to see a whole object, and to understand, in a sufficiently reassuring environment, that the objects that surround it, the mother's body, the mother, the father, are all capable of acting in ways that gratify—while sometimes they may frustrate. As these objects come to be seen as whole objects, there is a growing sense in the infant that it too could be whole, and could love those who surround it in their own differentiated wholeness.

This position is an advance in developmental terms on the paranoid-schizoid position, but it brings its own emotional difficulties, which leads Klein to call it the 'depressive' position. It involves a new kind of anxiety related to the earlier persecutory forms of anger and rage against part objects. These now jostle in the infant with feelings of love for what it is coming to see as whole objects. Those whom the infant is coming to love as whole objects, and which give it a sense of its own wholeness, are the same objects at which it had directed its anger and rage. In a situation where the rageful wish to destroy is indistinguishable from the imagined outcome, the infant may imagine it has destroyed the whole object it is now coming to love. This generates a troubling anxiety about destroying what one loves, and in turn an anxious desire to repair the harm one thinks one has done. Related to this, developing and then becoming embedded in the infant's psyche, there emerges an urge to repair that which one loves and imagines to have harmed, and this becomes generalized in the infant's worldly interactions.

As with Freud, these two positions generate a sense of guilt, either of an 'early' or a more 'mature' form. I will now consider these, starting first with mature guilt and working back to its earlier form.

b. Mature Guilt: The Wish to Repair

From early infantile experiences, there comes an anxious desire to restore loved objects, and this is the basis for a sense of guilt and remorse:

> The feeling that the harm done to the loved object is caused by the subject's aggressive impulses I take to be the essence of guilt ... The urge to undo or repair this harm results from the feeling that the subject has caused it, i.e. from guilt. The

> reparative tendency can, therefore, be considered as a consequence of the sense of guilt.[39]

Love is developing, but there is also hate from the earlier paranoid-schizoid position, and the anxiety that the hate might have been efficacious against loved objects produces a reparative default position. This becomes a formative experience in the human psyche. Since the early emotional states are retained in later life, this reparative desire becomes an important aspect of the grown adult in social settings. The infant is parent to both the child and the adult as it comes to terms with its loving commitments and its fears for what it may have done. A wish to make things better, because one might have wished them to be worse, stems from the early depressive position, interacting with the paranoid-schizoid position it comes to supersede.

The anxiety operating within this tendency becomes what we know as moral states of guilt and remorse, and lies at the root of the development of a conscience. In the depressive position, the infant's primary aim is to make good the whole object, of which it now understands itself to be a part. While the child feels 'strong conflicts between aggressive impulses and feelings of love', the latter lead to 'feelings of guilt and . . . wishes to make good'.[40] The depressive position thus lies behind 'the urge to make people happy', a 'strong feeling of responsibility and concern for them', and a 'genuine sympathy with other people . . . as they are and as they feel'.[41] This generates a sense of 'conscience in the true sense of the word' and the means whereby 'a moral and ethical attitude are activated'.[42] It raises the interesting question as to how this early, but developed, instinct towards reparation through the emergence of a sense of conscience fits with Freud and Loewald's arguments in the previous section concerning responsibility, guilt, and atonement. We will return to that question below, once we have identified a second, more primitive, account of guilt in Klein.

c. Early Guilt: Persecutory Anger

If the later, depressive, position is the source of a more developed, rounded, orientation to loved objects, and thence of a mature ethical guilt with its desire to make

[39] Klein, *Envy and Gratitude* (n 11) 36; see also Klein, *Love, Guilt and Reparation* (n. 11) 270. 'The ego comes to a realization of its love for a good object, a whole object and in addition a real object. Together with an overwhelming feeling of guilt towards it. Full identification with the [loved] object . . . goes hand in hand with anxiety for it (of its disintegration), with guilt and remorse, with a sense of responsibility for preserving it intact against persecutors . . . These emotions, whether conscious or unconscious, are in my view among the essential and fundamental elements of the feelings we call love.'

[40] Klein, *Love, Guilt and Reparation* (n. 11) 310.

[41] Ibid., 311.

[42] Ibid., 252.

good, the earlier paranoid-schizoid position, which it seeks to overcome, leaves its trace on guilt through the forms of anger and rage that are its stock in trade. These direct their attention to what are seen as all-bad others, who are split off from any redeeming features, and are therefore only worthy of outright, and potentially ferocious, condemnation. In this position, the primary aim of the immature infantile ego is to defend itself by going on the attack. Through Manichean splitting, it angrily blames and persecutes an all-bad other, while preserving an absolute sense of its own goodness. The persecutory attitude in its hostility holds the all-bad other guilty and subject to recrimination, and this attitude is then turned back on the infant itself.

In her clinical work, Klein had noticed how fiercely punitive young children could be in their play, and how this attitude was turned on the child itself as a form of stringent guilt. Writing before she had identified the paranoid-schizoid position, Klein described an early feeling of guilt that was engendered by the nascent superego in what she called its 'sadistic' phase. In this phase, a sense of guilt emerges in the infant that stems from the prohibitions of parents and fear of them, but it is augmented many times over by the sadistic imagination of the infant itself. Such infants develop 'fantastic ideas of *what the parent might do to them*: kill them, cook them, castrate them and so on'.[43] In this way, early sadistic impulses in the infant ensure that a persecutory form of guilt emerges such that 'the Biblical precept "an eye for an eye" is at work' in the infant's psyche.[44] Thus an early 'sadistic' instinct, magnified inside the very young infant, becomes the basis for a rudimentary, but very aggressive, superego dishing out a persecutory sense of self- as well as other-guilt.

Effects of persecutory blame in the two positions

This theme of persecutory self- and other-guilt in what Klein initially called the sadistic phase reflects the logic of what she would later call the paranoid-schizoid position. Towards the end of her career, Klein returned to this idea of persecutory guilt, considering the effect of blaming a person who lives with paranoid-schizoid thinking. This may be relevant to thinking about persecutory punishment and its effects in adult social settings today.

Optimally, the later depressive position supercedes the earlier paranoid-schizoid position, but it does not abolish it, so that it may re-emerge, for example in situations of social disruption and heightened anxiety. Blame that is targeted on a mind in the paranoid-schizoid position does not trigger a desire to repair or a sense of responsibility, as in the depressive position, but the perception in the

[43] Ibid., 179.

[44] Ibid., 179. That the superego promotes an 'excessive violence in this early stage would thus be accounted for by the fact that it is an offshoot of very intense destructive instincts, and . . . very large quantities of aggressive ones' (*Love, Guilt and Reparation* 250). In this setting the limit form of the *lex talionis* might appear an ethical advance on a more general destruction!

paranoid-schizoid person that they are being further persecuted. This person cannot bear a guilt and blame that is 'premature'[45] in terms of his psychic state, and which cannot lead to a desire to restore wholeness. Instead, there is further disintegration in one who in the paranoid-schizoid state is essentially marked by its lack. While guilt for the person in whom depressive sentiments are strong represents an opportunity to do better in outward relation to others, for the paranoid-schizoid mind, it can only lead to further internal breakdown. The reason for this disparity in outcomes stems from the different kinds of anxiety in the two positions, and what they focus on. Directed at oneself, persecutory anxiety in the paranoid-schizoid position 'relates predominantly to the annihilation of the ego, while depressive anxiety is predominantly related to the harm done to internal and external loved objects by the subject's destructive impulses'.[46] Thus persecutory guilt is not only savage and Manichean, it will also be morally counter-productive for many on whom it is imposed. For the person experiencing paranoid-schizoid emotions, who is already inclined to self-persecution, it leads to further internal disintegration. Angry recrimination against the person who cannot handle it, because that person operates at the level of immature, angry reaction, simply undermines further their ability to develop a whole response to what they have done.

Persecutory guilt is outright, recriminatory, blame directed at an 'all bad' person. If it is destructive for the person who already feels persecuted, how would it affect the person who is able to think reparatively about their guilt? One response might be to shut down the desire to repair in the broadly depressive and reparative mind. If I am inclined to seek to do better in relation to the wrongs I do, but I experience blame as outright condemnation for my unchangeable badness, this is likely to undermine my sense of myself as a person who seeks to repair things in the world. I *thought* I was a person who could respond, as one capable of repairing harm I may have done. If I am addressed as an inherently bad person, for whom persecutory blame is the only valid response, I may come to think that is after all what I am. Alternately, persecutory blame may provoke resistance and indignation at the calumnies directed at me, so that I feel further and wholesale resentment against a world that could only see me in this way, pushing me to become the 'animal' 'they' always thought I was.[47]

Comparing reparative and persecutory guilt and blame, we can see how these have different ethical consequences and logics, and that they could lead to different reactions and outcomes. I make these points, albeit briefly, because they have

[45] Klein, *Envy and Gratitude* (n. 11) 194.

[46] Ibid., 34.

[47] Two great prisoner memoirs that came out of the Special Unit run at Glasgow's Barlinnie prison (1973–1994) depict life in a prison system that juxtaposed an overall persecutory environment with one pocket of reparative practice (the Unit). The nurturing effect of the Special Unit is remarkable, but so too is the impact of a persecutory environment on men who might be characterized as living on the borderline between Klein's paranoid-schizoid and depressive positions. See Jimmy Boyle, *A Sense of Freedom* (Ebury 2016) and Hugh Collins, *Autobiography of a Murderer* (MacMillan 1997).

implications for how punishment is utilized in society today. Klein's early and mature forms of guilt are not just infantile manoeuvres, they have effects for individuals throughout their lives, and in adult social settings. They matter when we think about how punishment and blame in the social world might take on a persecutory or a reparative form. For example, is a modern punitive response persecutory, that is, exclusionary, condemnatory, and lacking in a possibility of re-inclusion? Alternatively is it restorative, offering the opportunity for repair or retrieving wholeness in perpetrators and victims? It is all too easy to see the enclosed and overcrowded world of prisons together with the political rhetoric of 'lock them up and throw away the keys' as essentially persecutory. This is not to deny that pockets of restorative practice can be present. Perhaps one should see the prison system as persecutory in the major key, restorative in the minor, or that these two strands are contained in a system governed by an overall 'structure in dominance' that is persecutory.[48]

d. Klein and Freud-Loewald Compared

Comparing Klein and Freud on early and mature guilt, I will argue that Klein's two infantile forms can be seen as rudimentary forms that are essentially homologous to those found in childhood by Freud-Loewald.

Early persecutory guilt. In writing of early guilt, Klein starts from Freud's view in *Civilization and Its Discontents*. Her account is based on his understanding of an aggression deployed against aggressive instincts.[49] However, she pushes back the beginnings of this process to the very early period in life, where the aggression is all the infant's. Nonetheless, the idea of a persecutory guilt founded in aggression and anxiety is present in both thinkers.[50] Klein's paranoid-schizoid position with its account of persecutory anger and rage at all-bad, non-whole, others may be seen as an early fit with Freud's 'Kantian' side. As in Klein, the Freudian subject of introjected anger, dealing with fear of the father's wrath, and deploying this to control basic instinctual desires, is not really a whole person. It is a split subject with uncontrollable instincts, which need external controls to be internalized. In both accounts of early guilt, the subject is submitted to the rule of an anger which starts within, and which it never rises above.

Similarly, love is lacking from both positions. Klein's model of persecutory anger and guilt may be present at the earlier, infantile stage, but both she and Freud retain the sense of a split, anger- and fear-related, guilt superseded by a later, more

[48] On the idea of two keys, present in the history of the western penal system, see also Alan Norrie, 'Beyond Persecutory Impulse and Humanising Trace: on Didier Fassin's *The Will to Punish*' (2019) 13 Criminal Law and Philosophy 681.

[49] Klein, *Love, Guilt and Reparation* (n. 11) 250.

[50] See e.g. Klein, *Envy and Gratitude* (n. 11) 2.

complex, ethically progressive, holistic, form. Klein's persecutory guilt, based on infantile fantasy, might be seen as the early mapping of what becomes the more complex forms of persecution, incorporating the internalization of fear of the father, into Freud's harsh superego. Klein deals with the infant in the child, Freud with the child evolving towards adulthood. Both, however, develop an account of early persecutory anger and guilt in contrast to a later, more mature, love-based, form.

Mature reparative guilt. Klein develops her own account of the later, mature, reparative, guilt that she identifies in the depressive position. This again comes much earlier than it does in Freud. Is there a parallel between Klein's account of mature and reparative guilt in the depressive position and what we find in the Freud-Loewald interpretation? As we have seen, Loewald's account suggests that the way in which libido or the life instinct (Eros) develops and is enformed leads ultimately to feelings of guilt, responsibility, and the desire to atone. The ego develops a sense of its own autonomy and responsibility, incorporates ego ideals, and then, through resolution of the Oedipus complex, evolves a superego with an inbuilt tendency to restore wholeness after rejection of internalized love figures. This is a later phase in the child's life, but we can see a similar pattern evolving. Klein's account of a much earlier, more rudimentary, superego has less space for the enformed structure of id, ego, and superego in Freud. Emphasis is placed on the earlier stage at which an infant becomes able to perceive both others and itself as whole objects. Yet, in this infant period, love and anger *are* mediated by early psychic organization, hence Klein's argument that the foundation of the superego is found in this early stage.[51] We are talking here of developments that are relevant for the early phases of infancy, and not for a developing child, but it seems these rudimentary forms in Klein may be interpreted to form the basis for later, more sophisticated, yet essentially homologous, developments in Freud's structural theory.

That we might see the Kleinian and Freudian forms of guilt, either in persecutory or in reparative mode, as building on each other is supported by the view that, once experienced, a basic mental structure is seldom discarded. It is rather taken up and finds its place in a more advanced form of psychic organization. Klein thinks that the reparative tendency in the depressive position continues into adult life, while Loewald's argument makes the same claim for the superego as an atonement structure. These look like similar moves at different stages, with the earlier reparatory move being taken up and renewed in the later atonement structure. More broadly, one can see how Klein's reparative instinct aligns with Loewald's account of responsibility and atonement; how anxiety around doing harm to loved objects could be recast as anxiety around the conflict between ego action and ego ideals; and how the early Kleinian foundations of the ego and superego as a whole subject facing

[51] Ibid., 74.

whole objects could develop into Loewald's account of atonement as the superego emerges from the Oedipus conflict, as a holistic, restorative, 'at-one-ment'.

The upshot is that we might expect to see both persecutory and restorative trends in guilt and blame as a part of the human condition. But this general observation would need to be integrated with a sociological understanding of how such trends play out in particular social formations. I will now proceed to consider, albeit briefly, the relationship of law to these early and mature forms of guilt under modern societal conditions through analysis of the retributive theory of punishment.

4. Towards Mature Retributivism

It is permanently fashionable to be sceptical of the claims of Freud and Klein about guilt, to believe that what they had to say depends on imaginative projections that are scientifically ungrounded. Indeed scepticism extends to the entire psychoanalytical enterprise,[52] so it may seem unpromising to consider links between these accounts of guilt and the way that a society thinks about forms of penal practice. Yet, it is plain that modern punishment expresses forms of hostile affect which portray the offender as 'the other', an all-bad, evil, perpetrator who should be shunned and may be treated as a general enemy of humanity. The present Home Secretary in the United Kingdom recently stated that she wanted criminals 'to literally feel terror at the thought of committing offences', a view that is consistent with her past support for capital punishment.[53] These thoughts of terror and of the irredeemable offender might be cast in either Kleinian or Freudian terms, but whichever, it would be the persecutory, early, form of guilt that was reflected. It would be a person who is all-bad, who can only be restrained from base instincts by angry and fearful punishment.

Politicians come and go, and others take a more mature view, emphasizing for example the need to support young people to stop them offending, to deal with the conditions of crime, and so on. The overall point is how different social and political views express different affective perspectives. The degree of affect revealed in comments about fear and terror, and their ability to conjure a socially hostile

[52] For a helpful overview and defence against repetitive Freud-bashing, see Jonathan Lear 'Killing Freud (Again)' in Jonathan Lear, *Open Minded* (Harvard University Press 1998) 16.

[53] See Priti Patel, UK Home Secretary: 'I do actually think when we have a criminal justice system that continuously fails in this country and where we have seen murderers, rapists and people who have committed the most abhorrent crimes in society, go into prison and then are released from prison to go out into the community to then re-offend and do the types of crime they have committed again and again. I think that's appalling. And actually on that basis alone I would actually support the reintroduction of capital punishment to serve as a deterrent.' BBC, 3 August 2019 <https://www.bbc.co.uk/news/uk-49213743>. Last accessed 29 October 2020.

solidarity,[54] or the more supportive, holistic, views expressed elsewhere replicate at the political level the two approaches to guilt and punishment described by Klein and Freud. If some politicians, together with the sections of society they seek to represent, get caught up in persecutory fantasies, we have to eventually wonder why these are so compelling, and why they resonate within the human psyche. Every time someone feels *either* anger at, *or* compassion for, an offender, a question is raised about the psychological tripwires that have been engaged. Political ideologies work because they have psychological traction, so the investigation of the grounds of human affect is important, as is how these become integrated into punitive programmes.

a. Is Retributive Guilt Necessarily 'Early'?

The views of politicians inevitably feed into their policies, so early or mature thinking around guilt will shape criminal law and criminal justice. For example, sentencing strategies are an obvious target. There is, however, a deeper question as to the law's internal connection to psychological approaches to guilt. How does law itself reflect these different emotions which are part of the public imagination? Is law simply a neutral form which may be more or less coloured by social, political, and psychological emotion, or is it more directly implicated in early or mature kinds of affect?

My starting point is to note that law is a social form which proclaims itself ethically neutral, but this is only superficially so. The claim to neutrality derives from the nature of the abstract and universal legal subject, *homo juridicus*, who sits alongside *homo economicus* in modern political discourse. Legal abstraction or formalism possesses the structural tendency to hide, finesse, or manage substantive, morally and politically contested, issues which lurk behind the form. Abstract legal form endorses substantive ethical positions, though it does so by appearing to say nothing about them. Its substantive commitments are wrapped up in its formal appearance, revealed only in situations of disruption.[55] From this position, we could ask how abstract legal subjectivity operates in relation to the early, persecutory, and the mature, restorative, accounts of guilt we have examined here. I suggest that when it comes to justifying punishment in ethical terms, the legal form reflects early, persecutory, themes by virtue of its abstract character, but that the same

[54] Henrique Carvalho and Anastasia Chamberlen, 'Why Punishment Pleases: Punitive Feelings in a World of Hostile Solidarity' (2018) 20 Punishment and Society 217.

[55] Alan Norrie, *Crime, Reason and History* (3rd edn, Cambridge University Press 2014). The *leitmotif* of this work, which is a sustained critique of legal formalism across the criminal law's general part, is 'substance will out'. See also Alan Norrie, *Punishment Responsibility and Justice* (Oxford University Press 2000), which tracks the way in which abstract legal form informs different versions of orthodox criminal justice theory.

abstract character indicates the possibility of its opening up towards mature, restorative, approaches. The obvious place to examine this issue is the abstract theory of punishment known as retributivism, which grounds much that is done within the criminal justice system.

In thinking through the nature of retributive guilt as early or mature, Jeffrie Murphy is a helpful interlocutor.[56] Murphy's work from the 1970s onwards has reflected an ambivalence about retributivism as the central ethical rationale for justifying punishment. The defender of a theory of retributive hatred as a justified response to wrongdoing, Murphy has also argued for: the need to balance this against compassion for the perpetrator as a fellow human being; that we cannot know the depths of a person's character, and therefore cannot condemn that person as irretrievably bad; and that when we judge another, our own unpleasant resentments may come into play.[57]

If we take the third caution first, Murphy is fond of quoting Nietzsche's aphorism that in condemning others for their monstrosity, there is a danger that we become what we condemn.[58] There is a slippery psychological slope in condemnation which leads from the judging of a bad act to the judgment that the person is bad, and then to move on to further persecutory condemnation. From a legal finding of guilt, we move easily to persecutory judgements like ' "you have a vicious character" to "you have a hardened, abandoned, and malignant heart" to "you are evil and rotten to the core" to "you are scum" to "you deserve whatever cruel indignity I choose to inflict on you" '.[59] Murphy adds that while this is not 'a logical transition' he fears 'that the transition is psychologically a rather common and in some ways compelling one, one that may tempt us to endorse cruelty and inhumanity'.[60] This is precisely the kind of persecutory account of blame described by Klein in terms of the guilt of the all-bad person, who is worthy only of hatred and destruction. The question Murphy raises is whether the slide he describes is indeed non-compelling and without an immanent logic in law or legal theory. Is it caused only

56 See also Jean Hampton's probing essays on what she calls resentment-based and indignation-based retributivism in Jeffrie Murphy and Jean Hampton, *Forgiveness and Mercy* (Oxford University Press 1988). The former (see e.g. 144–5) resembles early, the latter (e.g. 146–7, 151) mature retributivism in my terms, though her emphasis is always on the nature of state responses to wrongdoing, rather than developing the moral psychology of subjects as here.

57 See Jeffrie Murphy, *Punishment and the Moral Emotions* (Oxford University Press 2012) 41. Murphy's work describes a parabola, moving from what I would call a more mature (in the 1970s) to a more early (in the 1980s) account of guilt, and then back to the more mature approach in the new millennium. Compare the essays in the 2012 collection with those in Jeffrie Murphy, *Retribution, Justice, and Therapy* (Reidel 1979) and in Murphy and Hampton, *Forgiveness and Mercy* (n. 56). It was an early, mature, essay by Murphy that triggered my first venture into academic writing: Alan Norrie, 'Marxism and the Critique of Criminal Justice' (1982) 6 Contemporary Crises 59.

58 'Whoever fights monsters should see to it that in the process he does not become a monster': Friedrich Nietzsche, *Beyond Good and Evil* epigram 146 (Walter Kaufmann, *Basic Writings of Nietzsche* (Random House 2000) 279).

59 Murphy, *Punishment and the Moral Emotions* (n .57) 88–9.

60 Ibid.

by unfortunate psychological side-commitments, or is there an intrinsic connection between persecutory punishment and the form retributive theory takes?

b. An Historical and Structural Logic

The missing link in Murphy's thinking is provided by the historical and structural logic that underpins modern legal form, and links it to the play of a persecutory psychological mind set. In an early essay, Murphy pointed to the need to align a Marxist analysis of the social conditions of crime and the philosophical justification of criminal justice.[61] In a social and economic world premised on class exploitation, violence is structural, and the role of law is, through its abstraction, to present a different image and practice, one premised on individual responsibility at a remove from the social forces which condition it. This works well enough most of the time to legitimate punishment, while calling attention to it presses the need for radical social reform. Without that, the law's abstract individualist conception of justice, expressed through the retributive theory of punishment, aligns with the underlying structural violence, obscures the underlying social explanation of that violence, and constitutes a form of injustice.

This leads to the following question. If the socially causative, structural, conditions of crime have been obscured, what explanation may be given why an individual did something that was very bad? Without the obvious social explanation, the compelling alternative would be that there was something intrinsically bad about *that person* that made her act in that way. Hence the attribution of individual badness may not be connected in formal logic to perpetrating an evil act, but in terms of a causal, functional, explanation, the linking of act to individual character is compelling if a social explanation has been excluded. Where else can one look? To condemn the act is logically *not* the same as condemning the actor, but the retributive attribution of responsibility for bad acts to individuals apart from their social context carries as its corollary the attribution of bad qualities to the actor. Hence, either a split, persecutory, sense of a person as all bad (early guilt in Klein), or a fear based, punitive, view that violent natural instincts in an individual must be deterred (early guilt in Freud), or both, is invoked by the abstract subject of law as this is reflected in the responsible subject of retributive philosophy. Murphy's slide follows an historical logic under modern social conditions. Abstract legal form comes to entail an early account of guilt despite its seeming neutrality where a structurally violent setting is excluded. This is not logical in formal terms, but it is logical in the historical context of modern Western capitalist societies.

[61] Murphy, 'Marxism and Retribution' in Murphy, *Retribution, Justice, and Therapy* (n. 57).

c. Could Retributive Guilt Find Maturity?

This then leaves the two other checks on Murphy's support for punishment. The first is that the perpetrator is also a human being, a view that Murphy links with an ethic of Christian love. The second is that we cannot access the deep moral character of any other person, so cannot judge it. This is a view Murphy takes from Kant, where this represents the underside of Kant's otherwise somewhat self-righteous stance on the justification of punishment.[62] The problem with both these objections is that they are reactive to the persecutory, punitive, impulse and do not go far enough. Yes, we are all human beings, and yes, we cannot know the inner workings of another's heart and mind. So these provide a caution against persecutory punishment, but they do not provide an alternative to it. Eventually, Murphy will say that he remains a retributivist, though reluctantly so, but this is having one's cake and eating it.[63]

Against this reluctant retributivism I would first reiterate the social critique of the structural conditions that generate the form of law, which are obscured by law's abstract individualism. It is also necessary to think about how modern society cultivates persecutory psychic positions which treat as all bad a variety of out groups in terms of race, sexuality, gender, ethnicity, poverty, and, of course, criminality. In this situation, even a reluctant retributivism looks parlous.

More than this, however, another route is missed. Regarding punishable subjects 'with compassion' overlooks the possibility that people who commit violative acts might be self-acting psychic subjects who could contemplate in mature ways the nature of the harms they have done, and how they might set out to make things right for their victims. Where compassion is paired with punishment, there is no conception yet of the potential for mature guilt as a psychic mechanism in actors who have done bad things. To think in these terms could lead us to a new, different, mature retributivism in which the abstract rebalancing of right and wrong took on a real, human, form. Under classical retributivism, punishment acts as the rational restoration of the moral order that has been undermined by the crime.[64] The abstract proportioning of punishment to crime through the *lex talionis*[65] or the exchange of equivalents[66] reflects this rebalancing of the moral order. It is carried out by the state, directed at the criminal, and, as the criminal's own act returning to him, it tends to ignore the victim. It easily becomes seen as the vindicated allocation of a just amount of pain on a criminal, without a further progressive outcome

[62] Murphy, *Punishment and the Moral Emotions* (n. 57) 41.

[63] Murphy disparages his own valid doubts when he describes them as leading to 'some sentimental orgy of love and self-doubt': ibid., 42.

[64] Georg Hegel, *Outlines of the Philosophy of Right* (Oxford University Press 2008) 96–108.

[65] Immanual Kant, *Political Writings* (Cambridge University Press 1991) 155.

[66] Hegel, *Outlines of the Philosophy of Right* (n. 64) 103–5.

either for the criminal, the victim, or society as a whole. It easily becomes seen, in other words, as punitive, persecutory, pain for its own sake.

d. Starting with Mature Guilt

Let us assume the position of a perpetrator who has committed a violent and angry act on a victim. What morally should she do about it? From her point of view, working through what she has done, there is a need to process the fact that she has violated another human being who is, in the ways that matter, just like her. As she works through her feelings, she comes to realize that this was a whole person worthy of dignity, and not the all bad, split, object she felt no need to respect. She moves from a persecutory to a depressive position in Klein's terms, and begins to think of what she might do to restore what she violated. Alternatively, she comes to realize that in violating another, she acted against the ego ideals she possesses but which had been submerged when she acted. She realizes that in violating another who is a human being just like herself, she placed herself at odds with a sense of the world in which she could herself be whole. She wants to be at one with herself and her world; she wants in Loewald's Freudian terms, to atone.

However we describe mature guilt and its working through, we can see how it begins with a subject who has to acknowledge a harm they have done, rather than a state that allocates a punishment. In the social context of punishment, persecutory guilt is 'top down'—from the state or blaming body to the perpetrator, while mature guilt is 'bottom up'—from within the individual towards the victim. State punishment taking a persecutory punitive form may be the last place to look for activating a process of self-grounded remorse, restoration, and atonement. But the kind of making amends that comes from the mature desire for these things could represent the real foundation for a different kind of retributive theory, one in which past and future action are fully combined through the medium of the mature, guilty, subject. That subject wishes to make amends for those past acts, and to make things better in the future. This would be the basis for a *mature* retributive response to violating another.

Of course, much more would need to be said about this, but the aim of this chapter has been only to identify a new and different starting point for thinking about crime and punishment. From this position, I think we might be able to renew our vocabulary, so that we speak not of crime and punishment at all, but of violation and of making amends, a process in which the state and law may or may not play a part. If they do, it could only be a limited one. And when we use old words like retribution, we give them a new, fuller, meaning, one in which the age old conflation of retribution (a severe, persecutory, punishment) and retributivism (a restorative giving back) is clarified and made untenable. Under a mature retributive theory, the violating actor comes to want to make amends in order to restore a sense of wholeness for himself and his victim, and this rests on a mature, moral, account of guilt. We can find the grounds for such an account in Kleinian and Freudian metapsychology.

I began this chapter with a discussion of the possible contribution psychoanalysis could make to an understanding of criminal law through investigating ideas of violation and guilt. I started with Nicola Lacey's discussion of Lacanian psychoanalysis and suggested that less of a blind alley could be found in revisiting the accounts of Klein, Freud, Loewald, and Lear. Now at the end, I finish with the observation that this different route might be seen as strongly linked to Lacey's recent work with Hanna Pickard on the possibility of a form of responsibility without blame, based on forgiveness, and against what they call affective blaming.[67] Broadly, it seems to me that the ideas of mature blame, guilt, and retributivism discussed here are in line with this project. Affective blaming looks similar to early, persecutory, blaming in my terms. The kind of responsibility Lacey and Pickard seek, with its close link to forgiveness, is surely connected to the acceptance of wrongdoing, from which forgiveness may flow, and acceptance of their wrongdoing is precisely what a mature, guilty, subject pushes towards.

Bibliography

Bhaskar, R, *The Philosophy of Metareality* (Routledge 2012)

Boyle, J, *A Sense of Freedom* (Ebury 2016)

Carvalho, H and Chamberlen, A, 'Why Punishment Pleases: Punitive Feelings in a World of Hostile Solidarity' (2018) 20 Punishment and Society 217

Collins, H, *Autobiography of a Murderer* (MacMillan 1997)

Farmer, L, *Making the Modern Criminal Law* (Oxford University Press 2016)

Fassin, D, 'The Will to Punish' (2019) 13 Criminal Law and Philosophy 681

Freud, S, 'Civilization and Its Discontents' in *Civilization, Society and Religion* (Penguin 1985)

Freud, S, 'Group Psychology and the Analysis of the Ego' in *Civilization, Society and Religion* (Penguin 1985)

Freud, S, 'The Economic Problem of Masochism' in *On Metapsychology* (Penguin 1984)

Hegel, G, *Outlines of the Philosophy of Right* (Oxford University Press 2008)

Kant, I, *Political Writings* (Cambridge University Press 1991)

Klein, M, *Love, Guilt and Reparation* (Vintage 1998)

Klein, M, *Envy and Gratitude* (Vintage 1997)

Lacey, N *Unspeakable Subjects* (Hart 1998)

Lacey N, and Pickard, H, 'To Blame or to Forgive? Reconciling Punishment and Forgiveness in Criminal Justice' (2015) 35 Oxford Journal of Legal Studies 665

[67] Nicola Lacey and Hanna Pickard, 'From the Consulting Room to the Court Room? Taking the Clinical Model of Responsibility Without Blame into the Legal Realm' (2013) 33 Oxford Journal of Legal Studies 1–29; Nicola Lacey and Hanna Pickard, 'To Blame or to Forgive? Reconciling Punishment and Forgiveness in Criminal Justice' (2015) 35 Oxford Journal of Legal Studies 665.

Lacey, N and Pickard, H, 'From the Consulting Room to the Court Room? Taking the Clinical Model of Responsibility Without Blame into the Legal Realm' (2013) 33 Oxford Journal of Legal Studies 1
Lear, J, *Wisdom Won from Illness* (Harvard University Press 2017)
Lear, J, *Freud* (2nd ed, Routledge 2015)
Lear, J, *Love and Its Place in Nature* (Yale University Press 1998)
Lear, J, *Open Minded* (Harvard University Press 1998)
Loewald, H, *Papers on Psychoanalysis* (Yale University Press 1980)
Morris, H, *On Guilt and Innocence* (University of California Press 1976)
Murphy, J, *Punishment and the Moral Emotions* (Oxford University Press 2012)
Murphy, J, *Retribution, Justice, and Therapy* (Reidel 1979)
Murphy, J and Hampton J, *Forgiveness and Mercy* (Oxford University Press 1988)
Nietzsche, F, *Beyond Good and Evil* epigram 146 (Walter Kaufmann, *Basic Writings of Nietzsche* (Random House 2000)
Norrie, A, 'Animals Who Think and Love: Law, Identification and the Moral Psychology of Guilt' (2019) 13 Criminal Law and Philosophy 553
Norrie, A, 'Criminal Law and Ethics: Beyond Normative Assertion and Its Critique' (2017) 80 Modern Law Review 955
Norrie, A, *Crime, Reason and History* (3rd edn, Cambridge University Press 2014)
Norrie, A, *Punishment Responsibility and Justice* (Oxford University Press 2000)
Norrie, A, *Law, Ideology and Punishment* (Kluwer 1991)
Norrie, A, 'Marxism and the Critique of Criminal Justice' (1982) 6 Contemporary Crises 59
Nussbaum, M, *Anger and Forgiveness* (Oxford University Press 2016)
Reeves, C, 'What Punishment Expresses' (2019) 28 Social and Legal Studies 31
Reeves, C, Norrie, A, and Carvalho, H, 'Criminal Law: Between Persecution and Reconciliation' in E Christodoulidis, R Dukes, and M Goldoni (eds), *Research Handbook on Critical Legal Theory* (Edward Elgar 2019)

PART III

CRIMINAL RESPONSIBILITY IN POLITICAL AND HISTORICAL CONTEXT

7

Re-Situating Criminal Responsibility

Introducing Interstitial Spaces

Arlie Loughnan[1]

Criminal responsibility—the basis on which individuals are held to account via the criminal law and the form or structure of the law—forms the subject matter of a vibrant strain of criminal law theory. Nicola Lacey's work on criminal responsibility is a salient part of this scholarship. Lacey has developed her analysis of criminal responsibility over a number of years and publications.[2] Her analysis is rich and nuanced: at its heart is the idea that criminal responsibility plays a distinctive symbolic and functional role in criminal law. For Lacey, criminal responsibility is the key to the criminal law understood as a system of regulation which governs individual and group behaviour and structures the interaction of people and systems.[3] She argues that criminal responsibility serves both coordinating and legitimating functions, providing a symbolic resource for the criminal legal system and enabling it to be regarded as a system of justice, rather than one of sheer force.[4] According to Lacey, criminal responsibility, which is usually thought of solely as a legitimating concept, must be understood in its context, and, specifically, in the context of criminalization, which is usually thought of as a positive concept shaped by power and interests.[5] This sophisticated analysis demonstrates that criminal responsibility must be understood in a 'situated' way—taking into account not just

[1] Professor of Criminal Law and Criminal Law Theory, University of Sydney. My research on criminal responsibility is supported by Australian Research Council Grant, *Responsibility in Criminal Law* (DE130100418). I would like to thank Sabine Selchow and Iyiola Solanke for comments, and Hae Soo Park for assistance in preparing this chapter for publication. I would also like to thank Niki for nurturing and inspiring my own work in so many ways, and for her warm friendship over many years.

[2] See Nicola Lacey, *In Search of Criminal Responsibility: Ideas, Interests, and Institutions* (Oxford University Press 2016); Nicola Lacey, 'Jurisprudence, History and the Institutional Quality of Law' (2015) 101 Virginia Law Review 919; Nicola Lacey, 'Institutionalising Responsibility: Implications for Jurisprudence' (2013) 4 Jurisprudence 1; Nicola Lacey, 'The Resurgence of Character: Responsibility in the Context of Criminalization' in R Antony Duff and Stuart P Green (eds), *Philosophical Foundations of Criminal Law* (Oxford University Press 2011); Nicola Lacey, 'Space, Time and Function: Intersecting Principles of Responsibility Across the Terrain of Criminal Justice' (2007) 1 Criminal Law and Philosophy 233; Nicola Lacey, 'In Search of the Responsible Subject: History, Philosophy and Social Sciences in Criminal Law Theory' (2001) 64 Modern Law Review 350; Nicola Lacey, 'Responsibility and Modernity in Criminal Law' (2001) 9 Journal of Political Philosophy 249.

[3] See Lacey, *In Search of Criminal Responsibility* (n. 2) 178–9, and 178–85 more generally.

[4] Ibid., 19–20, 137.

[5] Ibid., 15.

Arlie Loughnan, *Re-Situating Criminal Responsibility* In: *On Crime, Society, and Responsibility in the Work of Nicola Lacey.* Edited by: Iyiola Solanke, Oxford University Press (2021). © The several contributors.
DOI: 10.1093/oso/9780198852681.003.0008

ideas about accountability and blame, for instance, but the traditions and practices of systems of criminal law in which such ideas operate.

The pioneering analysis of responsibility in criminal law developed by Lacey spearheads the growing body of what Lacey herself calls critical criminal responsibility scholarship.[6] Critical studies of criminal responsibility share a conviction that normative concepts like responsibility are shaped by their given social, political, and institutional context. Approaching criminal responsibility in this way extends the scholarly lens beyond conceptions of criminal responsibility—the 'nature' of criminal responsibility—to include responsibility principles and practices and the wider processes relating to the organization of the criminal law around criminal responsibility. As Lacey puts it, scholars must examine not just what criminal responsibility 'is', but what it is 'for'.[7] In dialogue with scholars working in the legal-philosophical tradition, discussed below, critical scholars have developed fascinating and provocative accounts of responsibility in criminal law. They chart the dynamic relationship between ideas about criminal responsibility and criminal law more generally, and reveal the complex processes by which individual responsibility for crime has come to act as a lynchpin in criminal law in the late modern era.[8] This work testifies to the significance of criminal responsibility in the legal order and the wider social order of which it is a part.

A hallmark of the critical criminal responsibility scholarship is an appreciation of the significance of space and time in responsibility principles and practices. In critical studies of criminal responsibility, space and time are recognized as variables. This means that responsibility principles and practices must be assessed *within* the particular traditions of criminal justice systems as they exist at particular junctures. And this opens the way for recognition of variation across different systems, and change in principles and practices of criminal responsibility over time. This commitment to space and time has been taken up in different ways within critical criminal responsibility studies. Some analyses of space and time have been specific, focusing, for instance, on the distinctive time frames applying to adjudication of non-responsibility.[9] Others have been more wide-ranging, taking into account the way in which criminal offences encode particular temporal and spatial logics, which themselves construct social and political hierarchies.[10] Studies such as these highlight the value of taking space and time into account in developing a deep understanding of criminal responsibility.

[6] See ibid., 176.

[7] See ibid., 178–9.

[8] See e.g. Markus D Dubber, *The Police Power: Patriarchy and the Foundations of American Government* (Columbia University Press 2005); Alan Norrie, *Crime, Reason and History: A Critical Introduction to Criminal Law* (2nd edn Butterworths 2001).

[9] See e.g. Arlie Loughnan, 'Asking (Different) Responsibility Questions: Responsibility and Non-Responsibility in Criminal Law' (2016) 4 Bergen Journal of Criminal Law and Criminal Justice 25.

[10] See e.g. Lacey, 'Space, Time and Function' (n. 2); see also Lindsay Farmer, 'Time and Space in Criminal Law' (2010) 13 New Criminal Law Review 333.

Following in the tradition of critical criminal responsibility scholarship, in this chapter, I extend some of the ideas about the space and time and criminal responsibility that I introduce in my recent monograph.[11] In my book, I adopt a delimited scholarly frame that enables me to present a located or grounded analysis of criminal responsibility. My study focuses on the twentieth-century development of responsibility principles and practices in Australian criminal laws. In this context, I reassess the general story of the rise to prominence of criminal responsibility over this period, paying close and careful attention to the intricacies of developments in criminal responsibility, and reconsider the role and significance of criminal responsibility in criminal law. I argue that criminal responsibility is significant as it organizes keys sets of relations—between self, others, and the state—as relations of responsibility. Recognizing this role for criminal responsibility shows that it is the means by which matters of subjectivity, relationality, and power make themselves felt in the criminal law in particular ways. My analysis reveals the gradual and distinctive way in which criminal law came to be organized around criminal responsibility, and exposes the complexity and dynamism of the relations of responsibility that subtend criminal responsibility principles and practices. In addition, and as I discuss below, my study demonstrates the relevance of what I call interstitial spaces and moments—spaces existing within or between, or in advance of, standard or orthodox legal spaces—for the development of criminal responsibility in Australian criminal laws.

Building on this work, in this chapter, I take up the notion of interstitial spaces and moments to offer a reflection on critical criminal responsibility thinking about time and space. I suggest that the next step for critical criminal responsibility scholarship is to move beyond the frame of the nation state and acknowledge the relevance of interstitial spaces in the development of responsibility principles and practices. To date, there has been a tendency to treat space as national, and this has meant that some dimensions of criminal responsibility have been overlooked. The notion of interstitial space is a useful analytical device to assist in pushing the scholarship forward because it exposes previously obscured aspects of criminal responsibility. In this chapter, I introduce an historical example of an interstitial space—the intellectual sphere of comparative jurisprudence as it crystallized at the turn of the twentieth century. As I discuss, as a hybrid scholarly-practice, comparative jurisprudence examined national laws from a transnational vantage point, meaning legal analysis was simultaneously embedded *and* disembedded, both tied to territorial space and free-floating. As part of a wider discussion about crime, criminal justice, and punishment, a number of dimensions of responsibility for crime were canvassed within the sphere of comparative jurisprudence. In the light of comparative jurisprudence, the connection between criminal responsibility

[11] Arlie Loughnan, *Self, Others and the State: Relations of Criminal Responsibility* (Cambridge University Press 2020).

principles and practices and broader ideas about 'civilization' and 'progress'—the ideological resources of imperialism and colonialism which were themselves markers of the power relations between states—are unveiled.

In my analysis, I draw on one of the key institutional texts of comparative jurisprudence as it developed at the turn of the twentieth century, the *Journal of the Society of Comparative Legislation* (the *Journal*).[12] Published by the *Society of Comparative Legislation*, which was founded in London in 1894, the *Journal* was a prominent English language text of comparative jurisprudence. Based on a study of the discussion of criminal responsibility presented in the *Journal* over its first two decades, I illustrate the value for responsibility scholars of comparative jurisprudence, interpreted through the frame of interstitial space.

1. Space and Time in Criminal Responsibility

Critical criminal responsibility scholarship recognizes the role of time and space in framing responsibility for crime.[13] To advance this work, critical scholars must move beyond the frame of the nation state, to take into account the part played by interstitial spaces and moments in the development of responsibility principles and practices.

In taking time and space seriously, critical criminal responsibility scholars are responding to their relative neglect in the mainstream of work on responsibility for crime. In the dominant legal-philosophical scholarly tradition—broadly, the type of criminal law scholarship inspired by normative philosophical thinking—the spatial and temporal setting of criminal responsibility is outlined only in the faintest brush strokes. In this tradition, criminal responsibility is regarded as the 'grammar' of the criminal law, the common basis of different systems of positive law.[14] With the emphasis on the conception of responsibility, rather than its contextual or purposive aspects, accounts are not genuinely 'set' in any particular space or time.[15] As a result, some of this scholarship has, in effect, an a-jurisdictional and a-temporal character. As Ngaire Naffine writes, this scholarly tradition is marked by 'the search for enduring universal principles', and the pursuit of correspondence between the

[12] The journal had this title from 1896 until 1916; from 1918, the journal was published as the *Journal of the Society of Comparative Legislation and International Law*, and from 1952, when the journal merged with the *International Law Quarterly* it became the *International & Comparative Law Quarterly*, and was published by the *British Institute of International and Comparative Law* in London from 1958: see A T Denning, 'Foreword' (1952) 1 The International and Comparative Law Quarterly 1.

[13] This section of this chapter draws on Loughnan, *Self, Others and the State* (n. 11).

[14] See George P Fletcher, *The Grammar of Criminal Law: American, Comparative, and International* (Oxford University Press 2007) ch. 1.

[15] Lacey, 'Jurisprudence, History and the Institutional Quality of Law' (n. 2) 939; Nicola Lacey, 'Legal Constructions of Crime' in Mike Maguire, Rod Morgan, and Robert Reiner (eds), *The Oxford Handbook of Criminology* (4th edn, Oxford University Press 2007) 190.

criminal law, and moral notions of harm and wrong.[16] And, as Lacey argues, this sort of approach assumes that a core idea of responsibility exists through time and space, transcending major changes in criminal law, and social and other discourses about responsibility.[17] As this suggests, philosophical accounts are not 'located' in a set of institutions or a body of laws as they exist at a particular juncture or in a particular jurisdiction.

In critical studies of criminal responsibility, the influence of disciplines such as history, criminology, and sociology on the field means that scholars are more attuned to the context in which the legal principles operate and to variation in practices over time.[18] Thus in her work, Lacey is attentive to the ways in which criminal responsibility is operationalized, and the way that responsibility principles and practices develop over time. In her monograph on responsibility in criminal law, Lacey assesses the coordinating and legitimating functions of criminal responsibility under a tripartite frame—of ideas, interests, and institutions—where these are aspects of the environment that have shaped the changing 'conceptual contours' and roles of criminal responsibility in criminal law over time.[19] Lacey argues that there are four main concepts or principles of responsibility attribution operative across criminal law—capacity, character, outcome, and risk—which compete for dominance as the basis on which individuals are held to account for crimes via the criminal law.[20] Taking into account the influence of interests and institutions, Lacey tracks changes in ideas about criminal responsibility over time, connecting the ascendance and descendance of the different bases on which individuals are held responsible to broader changes in the political, social, and economic order. As this suggests, Lacey's analysis of the role of criminal responsibility operates on two levels—as legal history and legal theory.[21]

Other critical scholars are also sensitive to the role of time and space in criminal responsibility. Lindsay Farmer assesses criminal responsibility as part of a larger analysis of criminalization or the 'making the modern criminal law'.[22] In his analysis, Farmer argues that criminal responsibility is significant because, along with jurisdiction and codification, it has come to be 'central' to 'the modality or form of criminal law'—which is, for Farmer, 'facilitating relative peace and mutual trust

16 See Ngaire Naffine, 'Criminal Conversations: Farmer, Lacey and the New Social Scholarship' (2016) 38 Sydney Law Review 505, 506.

17 Lacey, *In Search of Criminal Responsibility* (n. 2) 8–9.

18 See e.g. Lacey, 'Space, Time and Function' (n. 2); Farmer, 'Time and Space in Criminal Law' (n. 10).

19 Lacey, *In Search of Criminal Responsibility* (n. 2) 2–3, and, more generally, ch. 1.

20 See ibid., ch. 1; see also Lacey, 'Space, Time and Function' (n. 2); Lacey, 'The Resurgence of Character' (n. 2) 153–5.

21 Lacey's account of the development of criminal responsibility principles and practices is connected to a wider methodological project, addressing the role that history and social science play in theorizing law: see Lacey, 'Jurisprudence, History and the Institutional Quality of Law' (n. 2); Lacey, 'Institutionalising Responsibility' (n. 2).

22 See Lindsay Farmer, *Making the Modern Criminal Law: Criminalization and Civil Order* (Oxford University Press 2016).

between strangers' in complex modern societies, under 'the broad aim of securing civil order'.[23] Farmer suggests that criminal responsibility should not be thought of as external, or prior, to the criminal law: rather, he argues that criminal responsibility is primarily 'a legal artefact', that is, a creature of the criminal law that is linked to 'the particular nature of civil order in modernity'.[24] This approach renders criminal responsibility less time-less—because it is connected to unchanging moral norms, as per legal-philosophical approaches—and more time-sensitive, varying over time and space according to the particular emphases of civil order.

Yet, even within the body of work self-consciously responding to scholarship in the legal-philosophical tradition, space and time may not be accorded sufficient attention. Here, the spatial units of analysis adopted by scholars may be supra- or transnational, and consideration of the temporal dimension of criminal responsibility may be minimal or absent. For instance, one popular spatial unit of analysis in such scholarship is 'liberal democracies', which, as Claes Lernestedt comments, brings jurisdictions as diverse as the United States, Scotland, and Sweden 'under the same theoretical umbrella', something Lernestedt describes as 'downright wrong'.[25] Another collective term in use is 'Anglian' legal systems—referring to those systems that derive their conceptual structure from that of English law—which features in Peter Cane's examination of moral and legal responsibility.[26] For Cane, it is appropriate to frame his analysis in this transnational way because his concern is with concepts, and 'differences from one jurisdiction to another in the detailed application and outworking of those concepts are not relevant to the analysis'.[27] This is the case although Cane is concerned to foreground the law and legal systems in his work, contra-distinguishing his approach from legal-philosophical accounts on that basis.[28]

Taken as a whole, the critical criminal responsibility scholarship tends to reflect what I call a 'default northern orientation'. By this I mean that, where a system of positive law is considered in the critical study of criminal responsibility, it tends to be the system of England and Wales or those of North America. Within this restricted jurisdictional range, the specificities of these particular jurisdictions disappear from the scholarly radar. Of course, the high profile of these legal systems in criminal law scholarship partly reflects the impact of English common law on the development of criminal laws (and laws more generally) around the world, and the influence of the intellectual traditions—most notably, the legal-philosophical tradition—that have grown up in those parts of the world. In addition, this default

[23] Ibid., 165, 299.
[24] Ibid., 165.
[25] See Claes Lernestedt, 'Vertical, Horizontal, Backwards, Forwards' (2017) 4 Critical Analysis of Law 22, 22.
[26] Peter Cane, *Responsibility in Law and Morality* (Hart Publishing 2002) 7.
[27] Ibid., 10.
[28] Ibid., 2–3.

northern orientation reflects the size of these jurisdictions, and their respective legal academies, as well as, in some instances, the assumed significance, in the modern era, of criminal laws that are coextensive with nation-state boundaries.

While the reasons for the default northern orientation of critical criminal responsibility studies are understandable, it has at least three negative effects. First, it operates to homogenize aspects of those 'northern' legal systems most commonly studied by scholars, and obscure differences in the social and political contexts in which those legal systems are embedded. Second, where critical accounts are without express time frames, they may be somewhat present-ist, drawing out the current era to begin in, for example, the mid-century, when legal-philosophical approaches first rose to prominence with the work of HLA Hart at Oxford, without sufficient attention to change over time.[29] Third, and crucially, the default northern orientation carries with it the implication that it is possible to fully grasp the development of criminal responsibility within this circumscribed frame—which is typically centred on English law—on the basis that other legal systems have a lesser or merely derivative place.

Subverting the default northern orientation of existing scholarship, and pitching a critical account of criminal responsibility 'close the ground' in Australian criminal laws, my monograph explores the topic of responsibility in criminal law in new light. In accounting for the book's spatial and temporal frame—Australian criminal laws as they develop over the twentieth century—I make a case for the relevance of spaces and moments that are 'in between' or interstitial—spaces existing within or between, or in advance of, standard or orthodox legal spaces—in the study of criminal responsibility. In particular, I suggest that the spaces created by the broad and multifaceted changes in identities, and social, legal and political arrangements, that are gathered together under the labels of Empire and colonialism, and the intellectual sphere formed by comparative jurisprudence at the turn of the century, constitute a neglected dimension of the analyses of criminal responsibility offered by critical scholars. As I aim to show in the book, with the borrowings and lendings that feature in the development of responsibility for crime, and the distinctive way in which a meaningfully *Australian* criminal law took shape, interstitial spaces and moments are vital ingredients of an appreciation of responsibility principles and practices in Australian criminal laws.

The relevance of interstitial spaces and moments to the Australian criminal law story suggests that critical scholarship on criminal responsibility should not be limited to the temporal and spatial frame of the nation state. That is, the story of the development of criminal responsibility principles and practices is not solely a national story. Recognizing what I call interstitial spaces and moments permits

[29] See HLA Hart, *The Concept of Law* (3rd edn, Oxford University Press 2012 (first published 1961); on the dangers of collapsing different historical and jurisprudential periods, see Farmer, *Making the Modern Criminal Law* (n. 22) 2–3, 102–3.

scholars to move beyond this frame. And this opens the way for scholars to track movement in criminal responsibility principles and practices *across* as well as within legal spaces. Tracking movement in criminal responsibility exposes the dynamic nature of responsibility in criminal law, and adds another dimension to the context in which critical scholars assess responsibility for crime, enhancing the practice of 'situating' criminal responsibility. In particular, and as I discuss below, it ensures that states themselves are viewed in context, as part of an international order which reflects power relations between them as well as their own exercise of power. Consideration of interstitial spaces and moments permits scholars to think 'in more complex ways' about responsibility, and, as Farmer suggests, to think across boundaries—such as those between one jurisdiction and another—in order to develop deep accounts of legal subject matter.[30]

Proceeding on the basis that a deep understanding of criminal responsibility requires that critical scholars recognize the relevance of interstitial spaces and moments in the development of responsibility principles and practices, I now focus my attention on the intellectual sphere of comparative jurisprudence, which I suggest is an historical example of an interstitial space. Reversing the lens that I utilized in my monograph, that is, rather than examining the use of ideas about responsibility for crime in domestic or national criminal law, here, I explore the circulation of such ideas within comparative jurisprudence. My interest is concentrated on the period around the turn of the twentieth century, when, as I discuss in the next section, comparative jurisprudence was revitalized, taking institutional form and laying the foundation of the modern scholarly field of comparative law.

2. Comparative Jurisprudence as Interstitial Space

> . . . like rays of light diffused from a central focus, the experience of each country will be made known to the rest.[31]

Comparative jurisprudence—broadly, the comparison of two or more sets of laws or legal traditions—is an intellectual sphere that represents an interstitial space, understood as a space that exists within or between, or in advance of, standard or orthodox legal spaces. As a hybrid scholarly-practice, and with its focus on national laws viewed from a transnational vantage point, comparative jurisprudence

[30] Farmer, 'Time and Space in Criminal Law' (n. 10) 354; see also Markus D Dubber, 'Colonial Criminal Law and Other Modernities: European Criminal Law in the Nineteenth and Twentieth Century' in Heikki Pihlajamäki, Markus D Dubber, and Mark Godfrey (eds), *The Oxford Handbook of European Legal History* (Oxford University Press 2018) 1052.

[31] 'International Commission on Sentences' (1901) 3 Journal of the Society of Comparative Legislation 238, 238.

formed a domain in which legal analysis was simultaneously embedded *and* disembedded, both tied to territorial space and free-floating.

Comparative jurisprudence is part of a long tradition of analysis. In the modern era, comparative methods were employed in the study of politics and the social sciences from the eighteenth century.[32] These methods were carried over into law: from around this time, law was coming to be thought of as *national* rather than universal,[33] and the study of different laws and legal systems generated new opportunities for legal analysis. Employing a variety of methods of analysis in the comparison of laws and legal systems, comparative scholars trained their focus on what might be learnt about systems other than their own. The aim was to avoid situations in which 'one English-speaking community proposing and adopting enactments [is] in entire ignorance of the fact that similar measures have after trial been abandoned or modified in another'.[34] Against the backdrop of the rise of legal science in the nineteenth century, comparative scholars made claims about the truth and objectivity of their research, and the emphasis within comparative jurisprudence was on developing accurate and detailed description of subject matter.[35] As Frederick Pollock stated in the pages of the *Journal*, because it concerned the evolution of moral science (rather than natural science), comparative scholarship was 'one and same' with Charles Darwin's theory of natural selection.[36]

The comparative study of law and legal systems was closely connected to what is now recognized as the field of historical jurisprudence.[37] Each of these fields demanded that law be studied in context. Historical jurisprudence developed over the nineteenth century as a reaction against both natural law and analytical jurisprudence, in which law was regarded either as a timeless and logical system or as the command of the sovereign.[38] In general terms, scholars working in historical jurisprudence focused on the doctrinal and institutional aspects of law, rather than its social and political aspects, with the main aim of developing a deep understanding of law through a study of its growth from the past to the present.[39] For

[32] See Melvin Richter, 'The Comparative Study of Regimes and Societies' in Mark Goldie and Robert Wokler (eds), *The Cambridge History of Eighteenth-Century Political Thought* (Cambridge University Press 2006).

[33] See John W Cairns, 'Development of Comparative Law in Great Britain' in Mathias Reimann and Reinhard Zimmermann (eds), *The Oxford Handbook of Comparative Law* (Oxford University Press 2006).

[34] 'Notes' (1899) 1(1) Journal of the Society of Comparative Legislation 193, 193.

[35] See Günter Frankenberg, 'Critical Histories of Comparative Law' in Markus D Dubber and Christopher Tomlins (eds), *The Oxford Handbook of Legal History* (Oxford University Press 2018).

[36] Frederick Pollock, 'The History of Comparative Jurisprudence' (1903) 5 Journal of the Society of Comparative Legislation 74, 79.

[37] John W Cairns refers to two forms of comparative jurisprudence, one historical and one contemporary: see Cairns, 'Development of Comparative Law in Great Britain' (n. 33) 133–4.

[38] See Mathias Reimann, 'Historical Jurisprudence' in Markus D Dubber and Christopher Tomlins (eds), *The Oxford Handbook of Legal History* (Oxford University Press 2018) 397–8. The first appearance of historical jurisprudence was in Germany, and it developed later in England: see Mathias Reimann, 'Nineteenth Century German Legal Science' (1990) 31 Boston College Law Review 837

[39] Reimann, 'Historical Jurisprudence' (n. 38) 404–5.

example, Sir Henry Sumner Maine, who spearheaded the development of historical jurisprudence in England, held that 'a proper explanation of a legal system' required not the elucidation of general legal concepts, but 'an examination of the history of the society living under that system'.[40] Historical jurisprudence claimed to be a modern science, looking for 'data in the law's past'.[41] Similarly, comparative jurisprudence encompassed historical exploration of law and legal systems. As discussed in the *Journal*, this entailed bringing legal scholars and practitioners together with 'brethren of History and of Arts', in order 'to understand what it is that we inherit, and what has been the part of the law and of its ideas in the life of the nation'.[42]

Comparative jurisprudence underwent a revitalization as a result of the imperial reach of Britain, France, and other European countries. In relation to English language scholarship, the British Empire inspired what has been called a 'second renaissance' of comparative law.[43] The complex power structures of domination and subordination that characterized Empire—territorially extended rule—brought peoples and systems into contact in unprecedented ways. Under Empire, law and legal systems were harnessed to the task of ordering legal and social relations in new contexts. The trading, commercial, and other interactions of people and laws across Empire stimulated interest in and study of comparative jurisprudence.[44] As a member of the Privy Council, Arthur Cohen KC, commented in a piece in the *Journal* advocating that English lawyers study Roman-Dutch law, '[w]hat we must expect is this: there will in all probability gradually grow up a system compounded of Roman-Dutch law and English law and perhaps Scotch law'.[45] The reality of Empire meant that the experience of commentators and reformers in the colonies came to inform understandings of English law, and its critique and reform, and 'English law was perforce thrown into juxtaposition with many other legal systems'.[46] In relation to criminal law and justice, for instance, comparison between England and other jurisdictions was taken to indicate a need to simplify criminal procedure, and to reassess the value of the evidence of the accused.[47]

Comparison of the laws and legal systems that could be found across the British Empire and the United States was considered to be particularly valuable within

[40] See Neil Duxbury, 'English Jurisprudence Between Austin and Hart' (2005) 91 Virginia Law Review 1, 22.

[41] See Reimann, 'Historical Jurisprudence' (n. 38) 397–8.

[42] Pollock, 'The History of Comparative Jurisprudence' (n. 36) 88.

[43] See L Neville Brown, 'A Century of Comparative Law in England: 1869–1969' (1971) 19 The American Journal of Comparative Law 232, 233.

[44] See generally Cairns, 'Development of Comparative Law in Great Britain' (n. 33) 132–73.

[45] Extracted in 'The Fate of the Roman-Dutch Law in the British Colonies' (1906) 7(2) Journal of the Society of Comparative Legislation 356, 357.

[46] Neville Brown, 'A Century of Comparative Law in England' (n. 43) 236.

[47] See Courtney Kenny, 'Abbreviation of Indictments in India' (1899) 1 Journal of the Society of Comparative Legislation 390; and A Taylor Innes, 'The Evidence of the Accused in the Criminal Law of Scotland' (1899) 1 Journal of the Society of Comparative Legislation 18, respectively.

English language comparative jurisprudence, and developments in one jurisdiction informed those elsewhere. Empire was thought to provide the possibility of 'systematic exchange of ideas between persons at a distance'.[48] While as a matter of 'strict legal theory', 'the mother country and the Colonies' were 'all one',[49] the degree of autonomy some of the colonies exercised in their internal affairs meant that, across the span of Empire, there was a great sense of legal experimentation. Noting that the British Empire comprised 'some sixty legislatures', and that the United States of America included 'nearly fifty', the individuals who founded the *Society of Comparative Legislation*, mentioned above, observed that 'experiments as to similar subjects are being made by more than a hundred legislatures in English-speaking countries'.[50] These 'experiments' played out in different ways in different contexts. For example, the English attempts at codification of criminal law from the 1830s, including the English draft criminal code prepared by James Fitzjames Stephen, influenced the development and the content of the *Criminal Code of Canada 1892*,[51] and the codification of the criminal law in Queensland, and its consolidation in New South Wales.[52]

At around the turn of the twentieth century, comparative jurisprudence took durable institutional form and crystallized as a hybrid scholarly-practice. At this time, several institutions for the study of comparative jurisprudence formed around the world.[53] These learned societies focused on exchange of knowledge and ideas about law and legal systems across jurisdictional boundaries. It was around this time that the *Society for Comparative Legislation* was founded in London.[54] The *Society* acted as a hub for the development of comparative jurisprudence in the English language. Its objects included 'promoting knowledge of the course of legislation in different countries, more particularly in the several parts of her Majesty's Dominions, and in the United States'.[55] The *Society* regarded itself as both 'practical and scientific', and aimed 'to be of service to legislative bodies, practising lawyers, jurists and students of sociology'.[56] As these objects and aims suggest, at this time,

[48] Richard B Haldane, 'The Constitution of the Empire and the Development of its Councils' (1902) 4 Journal of the Society of Comparative Legislation 11, 16.

[49] Frederick Pollock, 'Imperial Organisation' (1905) 6 Journal of the Society of Comparative Legislation 237, 239–40.

[50] 'Statement of the Objects of the Society' (1896–97) 1 Journal of the Society of Comparative Legislation vi, vii.

[51] See Desmond H Brown, *The Genesis of the Canadian Criminal Code of 1892* (University of Toronto Press 1989) 132.

[52] See further Loughnan, *Self, Others and the State* (n. 11) ch. 3.

[53] Cairns, 'Development of Comparative Law in Great Britain' (n. 33) 142; see also Mathias Reimann, 'The Progress and Failure of Comparative Law in the Second Half of the Twentieth Century' (2002) 50 The American Journal of Comparative Law 671.

[54] The *Society* was founded in 1894 by Sir Courtenay Ilbert, then the parliamentary draftsman in England and later clerk to the House of Commons. Its first president was the Lord Chancellor, Farrer Herschell.

[55] 'Statement of the Objects of the Society' (n. 50) vi.

[56] Ibid., vi; see also CEA Bedwell, 'An Imperial Legislative Reference Bureau' (1915) 15(1) Journal of the Society of Comparative Legislation 104.

there was broad interest in comparative jurisprudence. By this time, English language comparative jurisprudence had morphed from 'a few individuals of great learning',[57] to a wider group comprising scholars, practitioners, and civil servants who were located both 'at home', in England, and abroad. Comparative lawyers saw themselves as part of a shared enterprise, and comparative law took on the qualities of a scholarly discipline, with its own theories and projects.[58] This period was marked by several major international congresses on comparative law which attracted participants from all over the world.[59] By this time, comparative jurisprudence was recognized as a 'new branch of legal science'.[60]

The institutionalization of comparative jurisprudence in learned societies was associated with the publication of some key institutional texts which were aimed at scholars and practitioners. As mentioned above, the *Journal of the Society of Comparative Legislation* was published from 1896. The *Journal* provided 'reliable information concerning legislation in the different parts of the Empire and, as far as possible, in foreign countries' to 'persons interested in legal, economic and social questions'.[61] It published summaries of legislative developments in numerous jurisdictions, scholarly articles of historical jurisprudence, and surveys of 'foreign' law. In its first decades, some of the most well-known lawyers and scholars of the time—including Courtney Kenny and Frederick Pollock—contributed speeches, articles, and other commentary to the *Journal*. In addition, contributions to the *Journal* were made by less well-known individuals from Britain and around the world.[62] With the aim of producing reliable information and gaining knowledge, the publication of materials 'in a concise and intelligible form'[63] in the *Journal* reflected its goal to provide a practical resource for lawyers and other professionals. Gathering together 'materials now scattered through many periodicals' for the consideration of members of the *Society* and others,[64] the *Journal* provided a popular and readily accessible reference, and colonial governments such as Victoria in Australia subscribed to the *Journal*.[65]

[57] George Winterton, 'Comparative Law Teaching' (1975) 23 The American Journal of Comparative Law 69, 90–91.

[58] See Frankenberg, 'Critical Histories of Comparative Law' (n. 35) 44.

[59] See David S Clark, 'Nothing New in 2000? Comparative Law in 1900 and Today' (2001) 75 Tulane Law Review 871.

[60] Pollock, 'The History of Comparative Jurisprudence' (n. 36) 86.

[61] Columbia Law Review Association, 'Journal of the Society of Comparative Legislation' (Book Review) (1916) 16 Columbia Law Review 365.

[62] For example, a number of Australian practitioners, judges, and others wrote a number of articles that were published in the journal. These articles covered topics such as the 'mode of legislation' in the Australian colonies, developments in criminal procedure and punishment, and the Australian constitution.

[63] 'Statement of the Objects of the Society' (n. 50) x.

[64] Ibid., vii.

[65] Harrison Moore, 'The Legal Relations of the Several States of the Empire' (1908) 9 Journal of the Society of Comparative Legislation 113, 120.

As indicated in its title, the *Journal* focused on legislation, and, in its focus on national laws, comparative jurisprudence was particularly trained on parliamentary law-making activity. Around the turn of the twentieth century, increasingly ambitious national governments were seeking to 'raise and fortify the new structure of society', and utilizing law as a means of doing so.[66] In this context, it seemed that 'the modern legislator tries to do more than his predecessor', and was not content to leave matters to 'the good sense of the jury and the judge'.[67] With the role of countries in the British Empire to bring wealth to Britain, and against a background of the general absence of legislation in private law until the twentieth century,[68] the growing number of statutes—'superabundant legislation'[69]—being passed by parliaments within and beyond the British Empire attracted particular concern.[70] Juristic interest in the growing number of new statutes is reflected in the publication of surveys of legislation in the *Journal*, which were developed by circulating a 'carefully framed series of questions' via the Colonial Office, and publishing the responses received from governments around the world.[71] Questions asked of governments related to the application of the English common law, and the methods by which legislation was generated.[72] The published responses provided 'a very full summary of current legislation' across the British Empire and beyond.[73] Interest in statutes was also reflected in demands for greater uniformity of legislation across Empire.[74] In this context, the absence of indexes of statutes in jurisdictions such as Victoria in Australia was considered to be a cause for concern,[75] mirroring domestic concerns about the lack of 'clear and orderly presentation' of statutory law in that state.[76]

[66] Earl of Rosebery, 'Speech by the Earl of Rosebery' (1908) 9 Journal of the Society of Comparative Legislation 10, 11.

[67] 'Classification of Crimes in Modern Codes' (1900) 2 Journal of the Society of Comparative Legislation 348, 349.

[68] See Mark Van Hoecke, 'Legal Culture and Legal Transplants' in Richard Nobles and David Schiff (eds), *Law, Society and Community: Socio-Legal Essays in Honour of Roger Cotterrell* (Ashgate 2014) 278–9.

[69] Earl of Rosebery, 'Speech by the Earl of Rosebery' (n. 66) 10.

[70] As Mathias Reimann argues in the context of historical jurisprudence, concern about legislative law-making arose in part from beliefs held by scholars that law was 'essentially a form of custom', and from the professional interest scholars and practitioners had as 'legal scientists' in leading legal change: see Reimann, 'Historical Jurisprudence' (n. 39) 413–14.

[71] Munroe Smith, 'Review of the Journal of the Society of Comparative Legislation' (1897) 12 Political Science Quarterly 537, 539.

[72] See 'Modes of Legislation in the British Colonies' (1896–97) 1 Journal of the Society of Comparative Legislation 134.

[73] Moore, 'The Legal Relations of the Several States of the Empire' (n. 65) 120. For some years after the *Journal* ceased to publish surveys of commonwealth legislation, a separate *Annual Survey of Commonwealth Law* was published between 1965 and 1977.

[74] 'Review of The Oxford Survey of the British Empire by Andrew J Herbertson and Osbert John R Howarth' (1915) 15(1) Journal of the Society of Comparative Legislation 39.

[75] Moore, 'The Legal Relations of the Several States of the Empire' (n. 65) 120–1; see also Bedwell, 'An Imperial Legislative Reference Bureau' (n. 56).

[76] Donald MacKinnon, 'The Consolidation of the Statute Law of Victoria' (1916) 16(2) Journal of the Society of Comparative Legislation 220.

Comparative jurisprudence cast national laws and legal systems in a new light: it offered analysis of these laws from a transnational vantage point. In comparative jurisprudence, legal analysis was simultaneously embedded *and* disembedded, both tied to territorial space and free-floating. On the one hand, laws were understood as the products of particular national contexts as they developed at particular times, and, on the other hand, those same laws were thought to be able to be transplanted from one context to another, and from one time period to another. By the turn of the twentieth century, against the backdrop of Empire, legal space had come to be thought of as territorial space. As Farmer argues in relation to criminal law, the key feature of modern law is the idea that it is a 'body of norms which applies consistently and seamlessly within a given legal space'.[77] In comparing laws across jurisdictions, comparative jurisprudence transcended territorial space, and, in its inter-relation to historical jurisprudence, it involved looking back in time as well as across in time. Evaluating laws from this new transnational perspective revealed contingencies in local laws, and held out the promise that different systems might offer novel and useful alternatives. The hybrid scholarly-practice character of comparative jurisprudence meant that nations stood to benefit, because '. . . like rays of light diffused from a central focus, the experience of each country will be made known to the rest'.[78]

3. Criminal Responsibility in Comparative Jurisprudence

Comparative jurisprudence offered an informative discussion of criminal responsibility. As part of a wider discussion about crime, criminal justice, and punishment, a number of dimensions of responsibility for crime were canvassed in the *Journal of the Society of Comparative Legislation*. The new light of comparative jurisprudence revealed the connection between criminal responsibility principles and practices and broader ideas about 'civilization' and 'progress' which were the ideological resources of imperialism and colonialism and which marked power relations between states.[79]

One of the dimensions of criminal responsibility to receive coverage in the *Journal* was individual fault, a central tenet of responsibility for crime. At around the turn of the twentieth century, individual fault came to be seen as increasingly significant in criminal law. At this time, consideration of individual fault was in

[77] See Lindsay Farmer, 'Territorial Jurisdiction and Criminalization' (2013) 63 University of Toronto Law Journal 225, 230.

[78] 'International Commission on Sentences' (1901) 3 Journal of the Society of Comparative Legislation 238, 238.

[79] See generally Lauren A Benton, *Law and Colonial Cultures: Legal Regimes in World History, 1400–1900* (Cambridge University Press 2002) ch. 5.

ascendance in systems such that of England; as Lacey argues, over the nineteenth century, reliance on character as a basis for responsibility ascription was on the wane, and capacity responsibility—which was concerned with agency, choice, and individual autonomy—was becoming more central to criminal law.[80] This was thought to mark progress as it indicated the centrality of the individual in law and politics. And, as is apparent in the light of comparative jurisprudence, the significance of individual fault was throught to provide a guide to the relative state of development of legal systems. As Maitland put it in the *Journal*, because taking fault into account in criminal law was 'a good index of the general level of civilisation',[81] its role in criminal law was regarded as a measure of the comparative advancement of legal systems. According to some *Journal* commentators, on this basis, both English and Roman criminal law could claim advanced status.[82] But, what was referred to as 'Mohammedan' law (Islamic law), had yet to progress beyond the consideration of 'irrelevancies' to a 'rational method' for the determination of guilt.[83] As this suggests, criminal responsibility was tied up with notions of 'civilization' and 'progress', which were used as markers of the modernity of Europe (and the United States) and the primitiveness or barbarity of states in other parts of the world.[84]

At the same time as individual fault was coming to be recognized as increasingly significant, it was subject to a fundamental challenge by the application of psychology to individual responsibility for crime. The period around the turn of the twentieth century was marked by a flowering of expert knowledges—including psychiatry, psychology, and related fields—that reconstructed understanding of the relationship between the mind and the body. As is well known, these expert knowledges were the basis for the wholesale transformation of criminal justice systems in a number of countries.[85] The ideas advanced within these new categories of expertise challenged individual responsibility for crime because, as one *Journal* contributor put it, they cast doubt on the extent to which 'all men are equally responsible for their actions'.[86] As was explained in the *Journal*, according to these ideas, an individual who is 'actuated by malice, is now believed to be the creature of circumstance', and that 'the criminal, even if completely sane, is generally not

[80] See Lacey, *In Search of Criminal Responsibility* (n. 2) ch. 5.

[81] FW Maitland, 'The Oldest Code of Laws' (1903) 5 Journal of the Society of Comparative Legislation 11, 13.

[82] See WD Aston, 'Problems of Roman Criminal Law' (1913) 13 Journal of the Society of Comparative Legislation 213.

[83] Raymond West, 'Modern Developments of Mohammedan Law' (1900) 2 Journal of the Society of Comparative Legislation 271, 272.

[84] See Karuna Mantena, *Alibis of Empire: Henry Maine and the Ends of Liberal Imperialism* (Princeton University Press 2010).

[85] See further Harry Oosterhuis and Arlie Loughnan, 'Introduction—Madness and Crime: Historical Perspectives on Forensic Psychiatry' (2014) 37 International Journal of Law and Psychiatry 1.

[86] Montague Crackanthorpe, 'Crime and Punishment from the Comparative Point of View' (1901) 3 Journal of the Society of Comparative Legislation 17–18, 19.

his own master; is not self-sufficient for guidance of his own conduct'.[87] From this perspective, fault came to be seen as beside the point, with the 'sense of guilt as to crime disappearing' in light of 'a sense of pity, partly from indifference' which generated 'toleration towards offenders'.[88]

These 'new theories as to responsibility' fostered the greater differentiation of 'degrees and forms of guilt'.[89] Expert knowledges suggested that individual responsibility for crime varied and that responsibility may be impaired but not abrogated, meaning that there was a 'limited responsibility' located 'half-way between plenary free will and complete mental alienation'.[90] Accordingly, 'there are those whose mental taint, though often innate, does not amount to insanity: the epileptic, the neurasthenic, the weak-minded', and that individual will may be 'paralysed wholly or partly'.[91] A prominent example of the greater differentiation prompted by the development of psychological knowledges is what would come to be known as the offence of infanticide. As discussed in the *Journal*, by the early twentieth century, a woman's act of killing her newborn child had come to be regarded as distinct from other forms of homicide, on the basis of the woman's 'solitude, misery, and shame', and popular sentiment that ran counter to the severity of the law of murder in such cases.[92] In England and in legal systems of the British Empire such as the Australian criminal jurisdictions of New South Wales and Victoria, these sentiments impacted on jury decision-making, and generated momentum for the creation of special offence provisions under which women could be charged with, or plead guilty to, infanticide rather than murder (and avoid the death penalty that typically applied to murder).[93]

'New theories as to responsibility' were also connected to the rise of the new science of criminology, which was transforming understandings of crime and criminals. The appearance of criminology ushered in an era of 'penal modernism', in which crime was regarded as a social problem which could be addressed via a range of different regulatory responses.[94] As explained in the *Journal*, the 'great principle' of this new science was to study, 'not the offence, but the offender'.[95]

[87] John Macdonell, 'The Foundations of Criminal Law' (1912) 13 Journal of the Society of Comparative Legislation 108, 112, and 110, respectively.

[88] Ibid., 113.

[89] 'Classification of Crimes in Modern Codes' (n. 67) 348–9.

[90] Crackanthorpe, 'Crime and Punishment from the Comparative Point of View' (n. 86) 19.

[91] Courtney Kenny, 'The Death of Lombroso' (1909) 10 Journal of the Society of Comparative Legislation 220, 223; and Macdonell, 'The Foundations of Criminal Law' (n. 87) 115, respectively.

[92] See 'Classification of Crimes in Modern Codes' (n. 67) 350; and Macdonell, 'The Foundations of Criminal Law' (n. 87) 108, respectively.

[93] On infanticide generally, see further Arlie Loughnan, 'The "Strange" Case of the Infanticide Doctrine' (2012) 32 Oxford Journal of Legal Studies 685; on infanticide in Australia, see Arlie Loughnan, 'Women's Responsibility for Crime: Dynamics of Change in Australia since the Turn of the Twentieth Century' (2018) 5(2) Law & History 137.

[94] See David Garland, 'Penal Modernism and Postmodernism' in Thomas G Blomberg and Stanley Cohen (eds), *Punishment and Social Control* (Walter de Gruyter 2003).

[95] Kenny, 'The Death of Lombroso' (n. 91) 223.

The offender—a person who could be assessed and made known to an emerging body of experts—was regarded as unique, and the object of criminal justice was 'not to punish the criminal but to reform him'.[96] The science of criminology demanded that criminal justice institutions and practices embrace 'the necessity of individualising' matters such as punishment.[97] This resulted in moves to individualize sentences—to ensure that 'the shoe shall always fit the foot'[98]—with, for example, the introduction of indeterminate and future-oriented sentencing, in which any given sentence was informed by specialist criminological knowledge and took into account the dangerousness of the individual.[99] The growth of the new science of penology enhanced interest in criminal justice, and the institutions and practices in place in other legal systems, and generated new societies for exchange on criminology.[100]

Another dimension of criminal responsibility examined within comparative jurisprudence concerned mental incapacity in criminal law. The laws governing insanity and the treatment of 'lunatics' attracted significant attention at the turn of the century, and 'some of the tests of criminal responsibility in mental disease that have been adopted in different countries' were canvassed in the *Journal*.[101] Here, again, criminal responsibility was thought to be connected to the relative state of development of different legal systems. In noting the similarity of laws on 'lunacy' across Europe and the United States, one commentator stated that '[t]his similarity is partly due, no doubt, to the fact that civilised nations brought face to face with the same administrative problems will naturally light upon similar solutions of them'.[102] Nonetheless, it was suggested that surveys of practices adopted 'on the Continent and in America' revealed the need for 'practical reforms in lunacy legislation' in England.[103] This commentator noted that 'the modern trend of American judicial opinion is distinctly adverse to the [M'Naghten] rules' (providing the test for insanity), and observed that, in England, the trend was to 'manipulate' the rules so as to 'afford protection in the more marked cases of moral insanity',[104] while another commentator concluded that 'the old tests of insanity' were in need of 'revision or modification'.[105] Such modification was undertaken in Queensland, and,

[96] Macdonell, 'The Foundations of Criminal Law' (n. 87) 113.
[97] Kenny, 'The Death of Lombroso' (n. 91) 228.
[98] Kenny, 'The Death of Lombroso' (n. 91) 221.
[99] See generally Michele Pifferi, *Reinventing Punishment: A Comparative History of Criminology and Penology in the Nineteenth and Twentieth Centuries* (Oxford University Press 2016).
[100] See ibid.
[101] A Wood Renton, 'Criminal Responsibility in Mental Disease' (1901) 3(1) Journal of the Society of Comparative Legislation 76, 76.
[102] A Wood Renton, 'Comparative Lunacy Law' (1899) 1(2) Journal of the Society of Comparative Legislation 253, 272.
[103] Ibid., 253.
[104] Ibid., 275.
[105] Macdonell, 'The Foundations of Criminal Law' (n. 87) 115.

on the tacit assumption that the new approach could be adopted elsewhere, the change was canvassed in the *Journal*.[106]

Along with modification of the law of insanity, laws applying to an allied condition—intoxication or inebriation—were also subject to analysis within comparative jurisprudence. Like insanity, at around the turn of the twentieth century, intoxication had become the object of public and political concern, and intoxicated offending raised questions about the appropriateness of criminal sanction, and the boundary between punishment and treatment. As it was put in the *Journal*, the laws governing intoxicated offenders struck 'very deep' into the theory of the 'responsibility of the individual for his own actions'.[107] At this time, drunkenness was coming to be thought about as a disease rather than a vice,[108] and this resulted in changed attitudes to intoxicated offending. Colonies such as New South Wales and New Zealand were considered to have made more progress than England in dealing with drunkards, with laws that acknowledged that there is 'a point at which a man ceases to be a free agent'.[109] On the basis that this sort of approach reflected contemporary expert knowledges about intoxication, it was regarded as progressive, and held up as a model for adoption by others.

The discussion about the treatment of drunkards and the laws applying to insanity articulated into a wider debate about criminal punishment. At this time, in the context of changing social attitudes to physical punishments and capital punishment, sentencing and punishment attracted strong public and political interest. Some of the debate in the *Journal* addressed the value of moderation and certainty in punishment, claiming that England might learn from moderate practices adopted in other countries.[110] This comparison raised the question of the purposes of punishment—in deterrence or reform—which were then hotly contested issues among reformers and commentators. Debate about criminal punishment within the sphere of comparative jurisprudence also considered the efficacy of punishment ('the influence of punishment as a deterrent from crime was enormously exaggerated').[111] Given doubts about the existence of free will then being raised, the appropriateness of lesser punishments for minor offences was called into question ('what reason for retaining the distinction between great and small offences since the anti-social feeling may be revealed in both alike?').[112] Debate about criminal

[106] See Henry E Gurner et al., 'Australasia' (1900) 2 Journal of the Society of Comparative Legislation 551: see further Loughnan, *Self, Others and the State* (n. 11) ch. 3.

[107] E Pollock and A Latter, 'Recent Legislation on Inebriates in England and the Colonies' (1900) 2(2) Journal of the Society of Comparative Legislation, 289, 289.

[108] See R Lee, 'Comparative Legislation as to Habitual Drunkards' (1901) 3(2) Journal of the Society of Comparative Legislation 241.

[109] Pollock and Latter, 'Recent Legislation on Inebriates in England and the Colonies' (n. 107) 292.

[110] JS Mosely, 'Foreign Criminal Codes' (1900) 2 Journal of the Society of Comparative Legislation 481.

[111] See Macdonell, 'The Foundations of Criminal Law' (n. 87) 111.

[112] See ibid., 116.

punishment was itself connected to the topic of prisons, and prison modernization was on the agenda in a number of jurisdictions at around this time.[113]

As this discussion suggests, debate about the dimensions of criminal responsibility was part of wider discussion about crime, criminal justice, and punishment. Based on a conviction that, in the words of one contributor to the *Journal*, 'splendid isolation is as foolish in criminology as in the conduct of foreign affairs', and with 'the same questions as to criminal law and the administration of justice' being asked by parliaments within and beyond the British Empire, developments in crime and justice were debated within the sphere of comparative jurisprudence.[114] In this context, the use of the criminal law for 'the special forms of evil with which different communities have to contend' attracted coverage in the *Journal*.[115] Innovative practices in different jurisdictions, such as the Children's Courts in South Australia, and the codification of the criminal law in Queensland, were outlined in the pages of the *Journal*.[116] On the assumption that such innovations could be transplanted to other jurisdictions, they were held out to reflect on practices 'at home', in England, as well as in other countries. Thus, in relation to the availability of defence counsel in criminal trials, it appeared to one contributor to the *Journal* that England was far behind 'both Scotland and her colonies and many foreign countries'.[117] Similarly, in relation to the codification of laws, successful codification projects in the colonies of the British Empire and elsewhere were seen to provide an example to England.[118] As the author of the Jamaican criminal code, HL Stephen, cautioned in the *Journal*, the colonies were getting ahead of England,[119] and, in the words of another commentator, codifications of criminal law in the colonies provided a 'lesson which might well be taken to heart by the Parliament at Westminster'.[120]

***

Inspired by the work of Nicola Lacey and other critical criminal responsibility scholars, in this chapter, I offered a reflection on time and space and criminal

113 The Colonial Office commissioned a report on colonial prisons, prepared by RS Wright, and published in 1867: see Martin L Friedland, 'R S Wright's Model Criminal Code: A Forgotten Chapter in the History of the Criminal Law' (1981) 1 Oxford Journal of Legal Studies 307, 309–11.

114 Crackanthorpe, 'Crime and Punishment from the Comparative Point of View' (n. 86) 17.

115 Courtenay Ilbert, 'Introduction to the Review of the Legislation of the Empire' (1899) 1 Journal of the Society of Comparative Legislation xiii, xiv (referring to South Australian laws against betting and gambling).

116 See Gurner et al., 'Australasia' (n. 106).

117 TR Bridgwater, 'The Defence of Prisoners' (1899) 1 Journal of the Society of Comparative Legislation 302, 308.

118 See e.g. WF Craies, 'The Proposed Penal Code for Japan' (1899) 1 Journal of the Society of Comparative Legislation 322.

119 See HL Stephen, 'A Model Criminal Code for the Colonies' (1899) 1 Journal for the Society of Comparative Legislation 439.

120 Ilbert, 'Introduction to the Review of the Legislation of the Empire' (n. 115) xii.

responsibility. I introduced the notion of interstitial space as a useful analytical device to advance critical scholarship. This chapter examined the discussion of responsibility in criminal law that emerged within the intellectual sphere of comparative jurisprudence around the turn of the twentieth century, which I suggested was an historical example of an interstitial space. Although not subject to attention by critical criminal responsibility scholars, the revitalization of comparative jurisprudence forms part of the story of the development of ideas of responsibility for crime in this period and subsequent decades. In comparative jurisprudence, national laws and legal systems were viewed from a transnational vantage point, and, as such, legal analysis was simultaneously embedded and disembedded, both tied to territorial space and free-floating. My examination of the first decades of the life of a key institutional text of comparative jurisprudence, the *Journal of the Society of Comparative Legislation*, showed that the 'free interchange of international ideas'[121] on crime, punishment, and criminal justice encompassed an informative discussion of responsibility for crime, with the new light of comparative jurisprudence revealing the connection between criminal responsibility and broader ideas about 'civilization' and 'progress', which themselves reflected power relations between states.

Bibliography

Aston, WD, 'Problems of Roman Criminal Law' (1913) 13 Journal of the Society of Comparative Legislation 213

Bedwell, CEA, 'An Imperial Legislative Reference Bureau' (1915) 15(1) Journal of the Society of Comparative Legislation 104

Benton, LA, *Law and Colonial Cultures: Legal Regimes in World History, 1400–1900* (Cambridge University Press 2002)

Blomberg, TG and Cohen, S (eds), *Punishment and Social Control* (Walter de Gruyter 2003)

Bridgwater, TR, 'The Defence of Prisoners' (1899) 1 Journal of the Society of Comparative Legislation 302

Brown, DH, *The Genesis of the Canadian Criminal Code of 1892* (University of Toronto Press 1989) 132

Brown, NL, 'A Century of Comparative Law in England: 1869-1969' (1971) 19 The American Journal of Comparative Law 232

Cairns, JW, 'Development of Comparative Law in Great Britain' in M Reimann and R Zimmermann (eds), *The Oxford Handbook of Comparative Law* (Oxford University Press 2006)

Cane, P, *Responsibility in Law and Morality* (Hart Publishing 2002)

Clark, DS, 'Nothing New in 2000? Comparative Law in 1900 and Today' (2001) 75 Tulane Law Review 871

Crackanthorpe, M, 'Crime and Punishment from the Comparative Point of View' (1901) 3 Journal of the Society of Comparative Legislation 17

[121] Crackanthorpe, 'Crime and Punishment from the Comparative Point of View' (n. 86) 30.

Craies, WF, 'The Proposed Penal Code for Japan' (1899) 1 Journal of the Society of Comparative Legislation 322

Denning, AT, 'Foreword' (1952) 1 The International and Comparative Law Quarterly 1

Dubber, MD, 'Colonial Criminal Law and Other Modernities: European Criminal Law in the Nineteenth and Twentieth Century' in H Pihlajamäki, MD Dubber, and M Godfrey (eds), *The Oxford Handbook of European Legal History* (Oxford University Press 2018)

Dubber, MD, *The Police Power: Patriarchy and the Foundations of American Government* (Columbia University Press 2005)

Duxbury, N, 'English Jurisprudence Between Austin and Hart' (2005) 91 Virginia Law Review 1

Earl of Rosebery, 'Speech by the Earl of Rosebery' (1908) 9 Journal of the Society of Comparative Legislation 10

Farmer, L, *Making the Modern Criminal Law: Criminalization and Civil Order* (Oxford University Press 2016)

Farmer, L, 'Territorial Jurisdiction and Criminalization' (2013) 63 University of Toronto Law Journal 225

Farmer, L, 'Time and Space in Criminal Law' (2010) 13 New Criminal Law Review 333Fletcher, GP, *The Grammar of Criminal Law: American, Comparative, and International* (Oxford University Press 2007)

Frankenberg, G, 'Critical Histories of Comparative Law' in MD Dubber and C Tomlins (eds), *The Oxford Handbook of Legal History* (Oxford University Press 2018)

Friedland, ML, 'R S Wright's Model Criminal Code: A Forgotten Chapter in the History of the Criminal Law' (1981) 1 Oxford Journal of Legal Studies 307

Garland, D, 'Penal Modernism and Postmodernism' in TG Blomberg. and S Cohen (eds), *Punishment and Social Control* (Walter de Gruyter 2003)

Gurner, HE et al., 'Australasia' (1900) 2 Journal of the Society of Comparative Legislation 551

Haldane, RB, 'The Constitution of the Empire and the Development of its Councils' (1902) 4 Journal of the Society of Comparative Legislation 11

Hart, HLA, *The Concept of Law* (3rd edn, Oxford University Press 2012) (first published 1961)

Hoecke, MV, 'Legal Culture and Legal Transplants' in R Nobles and D Schiff (eds), *Law, Society and Community: Socio-Legal Essays in Honour of Roger Cotterrell* (Ashgate 2014)

Ilbert, C, 'Introduction to the Review of the Legislation of the Empire' (1899) 1 Journal of the Society of Comparative Legislation xiii

Innes, AT, 'The Evidence of the Accused in the Criminal Law of Scotland' (1899) 1 Journal of the Society of Comparative Legislation 18

Kenny, C, 'The Death of Lombroso' (1909) 10 Journal of the Society of Comparative Legislation 220

Kenny, C, 'Abbreviation of Indictments in India' (1899) 1 Journal of the Society of Comparative Legislation 390

Lacey, N, *In Search of Criminal Responsibility: Ideas, Interests, and Institutions* (Oxford University Press 2016)

Lacey, N, 'Jurisprudence, History and the Institutional Quality of Law' (2015) 101 Virginia Law Review 919

Lacey, N, 'Institutionalising Responsibility: Implications for Jurisprudence' (2013) 4 Jurisprudence 1

Lacey, N, 'The Resurgence of Character: Responsibility in the Context of Criminalization' in Duff, RA and Green, SP, (eds), *Philosophical Foundations of Criminal Law* (Oxford University Press 2011)

Lacey, N, 'Space, Time and Function: Intersecting Principles of Responsibility Across the Terrain of Criminal Justice' (2007) 1 Criminal Law and Philosophy 233

Lacey, N, 'Legal Constructions of Crime' in Maguire, M., Morgan R. and Reiner, R, (eds), *The Oxford Handbook of Criminology* (4th edn, Oxford University Press 2007)

Lacey, N, 'In Search of the Responsible Subject: History, Philosophy and Social Sciences in Criminal Law Theory' (2001) 64 Modern Law Review 350Lacey, N, 'Responsibility and Modernity in Criminal Law' (2001) 9 Journal of Political Philosophy 249

Lee, R, 'Comparative Legislation as to Habitual Drunkards' (1901) 3(2) Journal of the Society of Comparative Legislation 241

Lernestedt, C, 'Vertical, Horizontal, Backwards, Forwards' (2017) 4 Critical Analysis of Law 22

Loughnan, A, *Self, Others and the State: Relations of Criminal Responsibility* (Cambridge University Press 2020)

Loughnan, A, 'Women's Responsibility for Crime: Dynamics of Change in Australia since the Turn of the Twentieth Century' (2018) 5(2) Law & History 137

Loughnan, A, 'Asking (Different) Responsibility Questions: Responsibility and Non-Responsibility in Criminal Law' (2016) 4 Bergen Journal of Criminal Law and Criminal Justice 25

Loughnan, A, 'The "Strange" Case of the Infanticide Doctrine' (2012) 32 Oxford Journal of Legal Studies 685

Macdonell, J, 'The Foundations of Criminal Law' (1912) 13 Journal of the Society of Comparative Legislation 108

MacKinnon, D, 'The Consolidation of the Statute Law of Victoria' (1916) 16(2) Journal of the Society of Comparative Legislation 220.

Maitland, FW, 'The Oldest Code of Laws' (1903) 5 Journal of the Society of Comparative Legislation 11

Mantena, K, *Alibis of Empire: Henry Maine and the Ends of Liberal Imperialism* (Princeton University Press, 2010)

Moore, H, 'The Legal Relations of the Several States of the Empire' (1908) 9 Journal of the Society of Comparative Legislation 113

Mosely, JS, 'Foreign Criminal Codes' (1900) 2 Journal of the Society of Comparative Legislation 481.

Naffine, N, 'Criminal Conversations: Farmer, Lacey and the New Social Scholarship' (2016) 38 Sydney Law Review 505

Norrie, A, *Crime, Reason and History: A Critical Introduction to Criminal Law* (2nd edn, Butterworths 2001)

Oosterhuis, H and Loughnan, A, 'Introduction—Madness and Crime: Historical Perspectives on Forensic Psychiatry' (2014) 37 International Journal of Law and Psychiatry 1

Pifferi, M, *Reinventing Punishment: A Comparative History of Criminology and Penology in the Nineteenth and Twentieth Centuries* (Oxford University Press 2016)

Pollock, F, 'Imperial Organisation' (1905) 6 Journal of the Society of Comparative Legislation 237

Pollock, F, 'The History of Comparative Jurisprudence' (1903) 5 Journal of the Society of Comparative Legislation 74

Pollock, E and Latter, A, 'Recent Legislation on Inebriates in England and the Colonies' (1900) 2(2) Journal of the Society of Comparative Legislation 289

Pollock, F, 'The History of Comparative Jurisprudence' (1903) 5 Journal of the Society of Comparative Legislation 74

Reimann, M, 'Historical Jurisprudence' in Dubber, MD and Tomlins, C, (eds), *The Oxford Handbook of Legal History* (Oxford University Press 2018)

Reimann, M, 'The Progress and Failure of Comparative Law in the Second Half of the Twentieth Century' (2002) 50 The American Journal of Comparative Law 671
Reimann, M, 'Nineteenth Century German Legal Science' (1990) 31 Boston College Law Review 837
Richter, M, 'The Comparative Study of Regimes and Societies' in M Goldie and R Wokler (eds), *The Cambridge History of Eighteenth-Century Political Thought* (Cambridge University Press 2006)
Smith, M, 'Review of the Journal of the Society of Comparative Legislation' (1897) 12 Political Science Quarterly 537
Stephen, HL, 'A Model Criminal Code for the Colonies' (1899) 1 Journal for the Society of Comparative Legislation 439
West, R, 'Modern Developments of Mohammedan Law' (1900) 2 Journal of the Society of Comparative Legislation 271
Winterton, G, 'Comparative Law Teaching' (1975) 23 The American Journal of Comparative Law 69
Wood Renton, A, 'Criminal Responsibility in Mental Disease' (1901) 3(1) Journal of the Society of Comparative Legislation 76
Wood Renton, A, 'Comparative Lunacy Law' (1899) 1(2) Journal of the Society of Comparative Legislation 253

8

In Whose Interests?

The Prohibition of Assisted Suicide in the United Kingdom

Emily Jackson[1]

1. Introduction

In the third chapter of *In Search of Criminal Responsibility*, Nicola Lacey draws attention to the 'significant over-reaction' to some of the 'real difficulties with interest analyses of law'.[2] Monolithic class-based theories of law may be too simplistic, but in 'more or less evacuating the analysis of interests for the study of law and legal development',[3] we risk diverting attention from the reality that 'criminal law is generally shaped by powerful interests: it is made by elites, while it is disproportionately enforced against non-elites'.[4] In this chapter, in the context of a discussion of the United Kingdom's prohibition of assisted suicide, I will take up Nicola Lacey's suggestion that 'we need to reinsert a concern with interests into criminal law scholarship'.[5] In particular, I will argue that the core justification for the United Kingdom's 'blanket ban' on assisted suicide—namely that it is necessary in order to protect 'the vulnerable'—has tended to obscure two other important sets of interests.

Who are 'the vulnerable' whose interests can be protected only by the absolute prohibition of assisted suicide? The UK courts commonly refer back to *R. v. Pretty*, in which the European Court of Human Rights explained that the ban was designed, in particular, to protect the subset of the dying who are less able to resist pressure from others:

> The law in issue in this case, section 2 of the 1961 Act, was designed to safeguard life by protecting the weak and vulnerable and especially those who are not in a condition to take informed decisions against acts intended to end life or to assist in ending life. Doubtless the condition of terminally ill individuals will vary. But

[1] London School of Economics and Political Science

[2] Nicola Lacey, *In Search of Criminal Responsibility: Ideas, Interests and Institutions* (Oxford University Press 2016) 81.

[3] Ibid.

[4] Ibid., 79.

[5] Ibid., 81.

Emily Jackson, *In Whose Interests?* In: *On Crime, Society, and Responsibility in the Work of Nicola Lacey.* Edited by: Iyiola Solanke, Oxford University Press (2021). © The several contributors. DOI: 10.1093/oso/9780198852681.003.0009

> many will be vulnerable and it is the vulnerability of the class which provides the rationale for the law in question.[6]

The core claim, therefore is that while not everyone who is terminally ill is vulnerable,[7] many are, and that without the 'blanket ban' on assisted suicide, it would be impossible to prevent them from ending their lives prematurely. This, I will argue, not only marginalizes the interests of patients who are not vulnerable, but it also serves to disguise the interests of the medical profession and the extent to which its opposition to assisted suicide may be the most important obstacle to legalization in the United Kingdom.

It could be argued that the claim that it is possible to protect the vulnerable only through an exceptionless ban treats the interests of non-vulnerable patients as a means to an end. Evidence from countries where assisted dying is lawful suggests that the group of patients who are most likely to take comfort in the availability of assisted dying are those for whom control has been particularly important throughout their lives. For these patients, taking 'informed decisions' at the end of their lives is not only possible, it is of vital importance.

More significantly, for an interest-based analysis of the prohibition of assisted suicide, the core justification for the 'blanket ban' deflects attention away from the interests of the medical profession itself, which in the United Kingdom has a long tradition of organized and powerful opposition to assisted suicide. Although doctors' organizations often emphasize the risk assisted dying poses to frail and elderly patients, the medical profession itself may be challenged by a medicalized assisted dying regime. For understandable reasons, the prospect of helping a patient to die is difficult for some doctors,[8] who may worry that facilitating a suicide is not a proper use of their medical skills.[9] Even in countries where assisted dying is lawful, there appears to be a growing divide between the circumstances in which doctors are willing to help patients to die, and the circumstances in which patients may want to be helped to bring their lives to an end.

The latest challenges to the prohibition of assisted suicide in s. 2(1) of the Suicide Act 1961[10] paid surprisingly little attention to evidence from countries

[6] (2002) 35 EHRR 1, [74].

[7] For discussion of universal vulnerability, see further Martha Albertson Fineman, 'The Vulnerable Subject: Anchoring Equality in the Human Condition' in MA Fineman (ed.), *Transcending the Boundaries of Law: Generations of Feminism and Legal Theory* (Routledge-Cavendish 2010) 177–91.

[8] It would be possible for doctors to claim that helping a patient to die would be a breach of the Hippocratic Oath, but then so would carrying out an abortion.

[9] Søren Holm, 'The Debate about Physician Assistance in dying: 40 Years of Unrivalled Progress in Medical Ethics?' (2015) 41 Journal of Medical Ethics 40; Benny Chan and Margaret Somerville, 'Converting the "Right to Life" to the "Right to Physician Assisted Suicide and Euthanasia": An Analysis of *Carter v Canada (Attorney General), Supreme Court of* Canada' (2016) 24 Medical Law Review 143.

[10] Section 2(1) provides that 'A person ("D") commits an offence if—

(a) D does an act capable of encouraging or assisting the suicide or attempted suicide of another person, and

(b) D's act was intended to encourage or assist suicide or an attempt at suicide.'

which have legalized assisted dying.[11] I will suggest that this now rich body of evidence points first to a distinct lack of vulnerability among patients seeking access to assisted dying, and, second, to the existence of some considerable discomfort among doctors about assisted dying as a response to non-medical suffering. Taking seriously the interests of non-vulnerable patients, and of doctors, will be important in any further attempts to change the law. It is, however, important to admit that these interests are not only in tension with each other, but may point in entirely different directions. My claim is not that law reform will be easy. Rather it is that we need to move away from the platitude that the prohibition on assisted suicide is necessary in order to protect the vulnerable in order to reveal the existence of other important interests which undermine the justification for the prohibition of assisted suicide, on the one hand, and are disguised by it on the other.

2. A 'Blanket Ban' to Protect the Vulnerable?

Over the past few decades, in addition to those jurisdictions in which assisted dying has been legalized (the Netherlands, Belgium, Luxembourg, Canada, Victoria (Australia), and the US states of Oregon, Washington, Vermont, Hawaii, California, Colorado, Washington DC, Maine, and New Jersey),[12] other countries have employed existing legal provisions in order to give patients more control over how and when they die. In Switzerland, assisting someone to commit suicide is a criminal offence only if the assister's motive is selfish. Although there is a ban on the 'commercial promotion of suicide' in Germany, the Federal Administrative Court has held that the Basic Law right of self-determination 'includes the right of a seriously and incurably ill person to decide how and at what time his life should end, provided that he is free to form his will and act accordingly'.[13] French terminally ill patients can ask for continuous deep sedation,[14] that is, being sedated into unconsciousness, when it will be lawful for life-prolonging treatment to be withdrawn.

In the United Kingdom, if the person whose death was assisted had reached a settled and voluntary decision to die, and the person who assisted her was wholly motivated by compassion, the assister is unlikely to be prosecuted, although she

[11] Assisted dying is an umbrella term that covers both euthanasia, when the doctor injects the patient with a lethal dose, and assisted suicide, when the patient is helped to end her own life, for example by being given a drink containing lethal medication.

[12] During the production of this book, New Zealand and Western Australia have also passed legislation which legalises assisted dying.

[13] BVerwG 3 C 19.15ECLI: DE: BVerwG: 2017: 020317U3C19.15.0

[14] Ruth Horn, 'The "French Exception": The Right to Continuous Deep Sedation at the End of Life' (2018) 44 Journal of Medical Ethics 204.

may face a police investigation and be interviewed under caution.[15] In response to *R. (on the application of Purdy) v. Director of Public Prosecutions (Purdy)*,[16] the Director of Public Prosecutions set out the factors which make prosecution for assisting a suicide more or less likely, but despite this flexibility at the level of prosecutorial discretion, it has proved to be impossible to set out an exception on the face of the statute.

Since *R. v. Pretty*, the UK courts had appeared to move some considerable distance towards acknowledging the hardship caused by this 'blanket ban'. In *Purdy* and again in *R. (Nicklinson and Another) v. Ministry of Justice* (*Nicklinson*),[17] the House of Lords and then the UK Supreme Court expressed considerable sympathy for those who are prevented by s. 2(1) of the Suicide Act 1961 from being helped to end their lives, once their suffering has become unbearable. In *Purdy*, for example, Lord Brown described a hypothetical scenario in which helping a loved one to end her life might even be 'commended':

> ... suppose, say, a loved one, in desperate and deteriorating circumstances, who regards the future with dread and has made a fully informed, voluntary and fixed decision to die, needing another's compassionate help and support to accomplish that end (or at any rate to achieve it in the least distressing way), is assistance in those circumstances necessarily to be deprecated? Are there not cases in which (although no actual defence of necessity could ever arise) many might regard such conduct as if anything to be commended rather than condemned? In short, as it seems to me, there will on occasion be situations where, contrary to the assumptions underlying the Code, it would be possible to regard the conduct of the aider and abettor as altruistic rather than criminal ...[18]

Lord Brown is not confining himself here to the narrow question at issue in this case, namely the clarity, or otherwise, of the Code for Crown Prosecutors, rather he suggests that the 'blanket ban' captures some individuals whose apparently criminal behaviour should be regarded as altruistic.

Five years later, in *Nicklinson*, by a seven to two majority, the UK Supreme Court was not prepared to issue a declaration of incompatibility between the failure to provide for any exceptions to the prohibition of assisted suicide in s. 2(1) of the Suicide Act 1961 and Tony Nicklinson's Article 8 rights. Nevertheless, in *obiter* comments, three of the Justices who were not prepared to issue a declaration of incompatibility now said that they might be prepared to intervene in the future,[19] if

[15] Amy Walker, 'Assisted Dying: Couple Tell of Anguish over Police Inquiry' *The Guardian* 7 February 2019.
[16] [2009] UKHL 45.
[17] [2014] UKSC 38.
[18] Ibid., [83].
[19] [2014] UKSC 38, [118] and [202]. See also Lord Mance, [190].

Parliament failed 'satisfactorily' to address this issue. Lords Neuberger and Wilson indicated that a further application might have a 'real prospect' of success,[20] and Lord Neuberger even suggested that a system of prior approval might provide more robust protection for the vulnerable than the status quo:

> A system whereby a judge or other independent assessor is satisfied in advance that someone has a voluntary, clear, settled, and informed wish to die and for his suicide then to be organised in an open and professional way, would, at least in my current view, provide greater and more satisfactory protection for the weak and vulnerable, than a system which involves a lawyer from the DPP's office inquiring, after the event, whether the person who had killed himself had such a wish.[21]

Parliament had the opportunity to 'address the issue' a year later, when, by 330 votes to 118, the House of Commons rejected Rob Marris MP's Assisted Dying Bill.[22] In introducing his Bill to the House of Commons, Marris said that 'coercion of the vulnerable is the most difficult issue, for me and many people in the House and outside'.[23] The need to protect the vulnerable was a repeated theme throughout the debate that followed: for example, Lyn Brown MP was concerned the Bill would 'fundamentally change the way that our society thinks about and deals with the terminally ill, severely disabled people and the vulnerable, troubled and elderly'.[24]

The question that was therefore left to be resolved in a future case was whether, by debating and voting on an Assisted Dying Bill, Parliament had addressed the issue satisfactorily, or whether, by rejecting the Bill and leaving the 'blanket ban' intact, Parliament had addressed the issue, but not satisfactorily. Noel Conway's case gave the courts the opportunity to answer this question, but the approaches adopted in the lower courts, and in the UK Supreme Court, were surprisingly cautious, and represented a significant retreat from the sympathetic depiction of assisted suicide evident in both *Nicklinson* and *Purdy*.

In *R. (Conway) v. Secretary of State for Justice* (*Conway*)[25] Noel Conway argued once again that the 'blanket ban' in s. 2 was incompatible with his Article 8 rights, but this time he proposed 'an alternative statutory scheme' in order to 'sufficiently protect the weak and vulnerable'.[26] Although it was accepted that 'the right of an

[20] Ibid., [118] and [202].

[21] Ibid., [108].

[22] Hansard, 11 September 2015. Since then, the Assisted Dying Bill has been introduced in the House of Lords on two occasions, but there has not been sufficient time for it to be debated. It should be noted that in a debate on 4 July 2019, the House of Commons 'considered the functioning of the existing law relating to assisted dying' Hansard 4 July 2019 vol. 662, col. 1412. Several MPs suggested that they had changed their minds in response to meeting with constituents and following the case of Ann and Geoff Whaley, who had been interviewed by the police under caution before making the journey to Switzerland.

[23] Hansard 11 September 2015 col. 661.

[24] Hansard 11 September 2015 col. 669.

[25] [2018] EWCA Civ 1431.

[26] Ibid., [51].

individual to decide how and when to end his or her life is an aspect of the right to respect for private life protected by Article 8 of the Convention',[27] Mr Conway's claim was rejected in the Divisional Court on the grounds that there is 'a rational connection between the prohibition in section 2 and the protection of the weak and vulnerable'.[28] The court further maintained that 'the prohibition serves to reinforce a moral view regarding the sanctity of life', and that it 'also serves to promote relations of full trust and confidence between doctors and their patients, and hence to promote the provision and acceptance of high quality medical advice to patients, particularly those who might be in a vulnerable position'.[29] The Court of Appeal accepted these conclusions,[30] and Mr Conway was refused permission to appeal by the Supreme Court, on the grounds that the prospects of success were 'not sufficient to justify giving permission to appeal'.[31]

In short, it was accepted in *Conway* that the 'blanket ban' on assisted suicide is necessary in order to protect (a) the vulnerable; (b) trust in the medical profession; and (c) the sanctity of human life.[32] In reaching these conclusions, the Divisional Court paid scant attention to the now significant body of evidence of how assisted dying works in practice in several US states and in Belgium and the Netherlands, and instead placed considerable weight on evidence from UK healthcare professionals and medical organizations, known to be opposed to a change in the law

In relation to the 'rational connection' between 'the prohibition in s. 2 and the protection of the weak and vulnerable', the Divisional Court said that it agreed 'in that regard with [183]–[185] in the judgment of Lord Mance in Nicklinson'.[33] The evidence Lord Mance points to in these passages is the fact that the cases of '*R (Pretty)* and *Pretty v United Kingdom* proceed on that basis',[34] as did the US Supreme Court's majority judgment in *Washington v. Glucksberg*. The fact that two cases decided twelve and seventeen years ago 'proceeded on the basis' of a connection between the prohibition in s. 2 and protection of the vulnerable does not establish

[27] Ibid., [120].

[28] [2017] EWHC 2447 (Admin), [96].

[29] Ibid., [97].

[30] [2018] EWCA Civ 1431, [204].

[31] *per* Lady Hale, Lord Reed, and Lord Kerr at < www.supremecourt.uk/docs/r-on-the-application-of-conway-v-secretary-of-state-for-justice-court-order.pdf>

[32] I will not discuss the Divisional Court's discussion of the sanctity of life, but it is worth noting that it had simply said that 'Many people would regard considerations of the sanctity of life to be at the heart of the issues in this case', and that, as a result, it 'seems unreal to discount this as a relevant consideration' (ibid., [93]). In *Nicklinson*, Lord Sumption had considered whether the prohibition might also be justifiable under Article 8.2 for the protection of morals, and said that he 'would certainly not rule it out' (*Nicklinson*, [235]), while in the same case, Lady Hale said that 'Respect for individual autonomy and human dignity are also important moral principles. The very complexity of the moral argument, amply demonstrated in the material before this court, tells against relying upon this as the legitimate aim of the legislation' (*Nicklinson*, [311]).

[33] [2017] EWHC 2447 (Admin), [96].

[34] *R. (on the application of Pretty) v. Director of Public Prosecutions* [2001] UKHL 61; *Pretty v. United Kingdom* (2002) 35 EHRR 1.

that such a connection exists today.[35] The Divisional Court went on to say that 'The further evidence from Baroness Finlay, the BGS [British Geriatrics Society], Scope and Baroness Campbell in the present proceedings strongly supports Lord Mance's analysis.' Baroness Finlay (a palliative care consultant) and Baroness Campbell are vocal opponents of assisted dying, and the BGS and Scope are also opposed to a change in the law. Of course, the views of opponents of legalization are relevant and important, but they do not necessarily tell the whole story, or represent the range of views among healthcare professionals and people living with disability.

The Divisional Court also referred to a British Medical Association report on assisted dying (the BMA is also opposed to a change in the law), which cited evidence from Switzerland:

> It referred to a study of over 1,000 assisted suicides in Switzerland across a five year period which found that 'although assisted suicide was associated with people with higher educational attainment and higher socio-economic status, it was also more likely amongst women and amongst groups with particular vulnerabilities, such as those who live alone, and *perhaps* experiencing social isolation and loneliness'.[36] (my emphasis).

Well-educated and relatively wealthy people who live alone are not necessarily lonely, isolated, and vulnerable. Nor does one Swiss study establish that assisted suicide is more common among women, when the weight of evidence from other jurisdictions is that, in countries where assisted dying is lawful, men access it more frequently than women. In Oregon, between 1998 and 2016, 51.7 per cent of those who died assisted deaths were men.[37] In the Netherlands and Belgium too, where assisted dying has been lawful for forty-seven and eighteen years respectively, men represent the majority of those accessing assisted deaths.[38]

On the evidence that an exception to the 'blanket ban' would have a negative impact upon the doctor–patient relationship, the Divisional Court said:

> The evidence before us shows that there is a real concern amongst doctors *and a real risk* that if the prohibition against assistance for suicide were relaxed, patients (particularly vulnerable and elderly patients) would have less confidence in their

[35] The rest of the evidence cited in paragraphs [183]–[185] by Lord Mance was concerned only with the risk to the vulnerable if assisted dying were to be extended to people who are not terminally ill. This is not relevant to Mr Conway's case, because he is terminally ill, and his claim was confined to the impact of the blanket ban on the terminally ill.

[36] [2017] EWHC 2447 (Admin), [63].

[37] Oregon Health Authority, *Oregon's Death with Dignity Act: 2017 Data Summary* (Oregon Health Authority 2018).

[38] Regional Review Committees *Annual Report 2017* (RTE 2018); ML Rurup et al., 'The First Five Years of Euthanasia Legislation in Belgium and the Netherlands: Description and Comparison of Cases' (2012) 26 Palliative Medicine 43.

> doctors and the advice they might give. This *could well have deleterious consequences* on the extent to which patients are willing to share information about their conditions freely with their doctors and the extent to which patients would be willing to accept and act upon medical advice given to them. Both these things would tend to undermine the quality and efficacy of medical treatment made available to them.[39] (my emphasis)

With respect, this looks like speculation about the impact legalization would have on patient care rather than evidence that the quality and efficacy of medical treatment would be undermined if the 'blanket ban' were to be relaxed.

The Divisional Court had also heard evidence from witnesses called by Mr Conway, which included a number of distinguished experts in intensive care, palliative medicine, and geriatric psychiatry. One of Mr Conway's witnesses was Professor Linda Ganzini, a geriatrician at Oregon Health and Science University, who has more than twenty years' experience of carrying out empirical research into the practice of physician-assisted suicide in Oregon. As the author of nearly 100 peer-reviewed publications on the issue,[40] Professor Ganzini would have been well placed to give the court evidence-based information about the impact of assisted suicide on patient trust, but none of the evidence provided by Mr Conway's witnesses was cited or summarized in the Divisional Court's judgment. Rather, the Divisional Court referred to Baroness Finlay's interpretation of the data from Oregon,[41] in preference to Professor Ganzini's empirical research. On appeal, the Court of Appeal confirmed that it did 'not consider that the Divisional Court was under an obligation to set out in meticulous detail all the evidence before them'.[42]

In addition to making no reference to Mr Conway's expert witnesses' evidence, the Divisional Court was also not assisted by reference to the recent change in the law in Canada:

> Mr Gordon also referred to the decision of the Supreme Court of Canada in *Carter v Canada*, in which the court held that the ban on assisted dying in Canada was

39 [2017] EWHC 2447 (Admin), [94].

40 See e.g. Linda Ganzini, Steven K Dobscha, Ronald T Heintz, and Nancy Press, 'Oregon Physicians' Perceptions of Patients who Request Assisted Suicide and their Families' (2003) 6 Journal of Palliative Medicine 381; Linda Ganzini, Maria J Silveira, and Wendy S Johnston, 'Predictors and Correlates of Interest in Assisted Suicide in the Final Month of Life among ALS Patients in Oregon and Washington' (2002) 24 Journal of Pain and Symptom Management 312; Linda Ganzini, Gregory B Leong, Darien S Fenn, J Arturo Silva, and Robert Weinstock, 'Evaluation of Competence to Consent to Assisted Suicide: Views of Forensic Psychiatrists' (2000) 157 American Journal of Psychiatry 595; Linda Ganzini, Elizabeth R Goy, and Steven K Dobscha, 'Why Oregon Patients Request Assisted Death: Family Members' Views' (2008) 23 Journal of General Internal Medicine 154; Kathryn A Smith, Theresa A Harvath, Elizabeth R Goy, and Linda Ganzini, 'Predictors of Pursuit of Physician-assisted Death' (2015) 49 Journal of Pain and Symptom Management 555; Linda Ganzini and Anthony L Back, 'The Challenge of New Legislation on Physician-assisted Death' (2016) JAMA Internal Medicine 427.

41 [2017] EWHC 2447 (Admin), [75].

42 [2018] EWCA Civ 1431, [204].

> invalid under the Canadian Charter of Rights and Freedoms. He relied in particular on [114]–[115], in which the court referred to concerns about decisional capacity and vulnerability and observed that these concerns already arise in all end-of-life medical decision-making, including in relation to refusal by an individual of life support treatment. We did not find the decision in Carter to be of assistance. It turned critically on provisions of the Canadian Charter which are in different terms from Article 8 of the ECHR and which engage a different analysis.[43]

Of course, it is true that the Canadian Charter is different from the European Convention on Human Rights, but it seems improbable that concerns about vulnerability are so different in Canada as to be entirely irrelevant in the United Kingdom.

3. Who Is Vulnerable?

It seems so obvious as to barely need stating that people who are dying are a potentially vulnerable group: all of them are ill, and most of them are elderly. In countries where assisted dying is lawful, however, it seems clear that patients who request assisted dying have something in common other than their vulnerability. Data from the Netherlands and Oregon suggest that people who access assisted dying are 'more likely to be members of groups enjoying comparative social, economic, educational, professional and other privileges'.[44] In Switzerland, patients who request assisted suicide are more likely to have no religious affiliation, to be well educated, and to live in urban rather than rural areas and in more affluent neighbourhoods.[45] In Belgium, 'the prevalence of euthanasia remains highest in patients ... with a college or university education'.[46] In Oregon and Washington state, typical patients who request assisted death are 'older, white and well-educated',[47] leading Emanuel et al. to conclude that:

43 [2017] EWHC 2447 (Admin), [122] and [123].

44 Margaret P Battin, Agnes Van der Heide, Linda Ganzini, Gerrit Van der Wal, and Bregje D Onwuteaka-Philipsen, 'Legal Physician-assisted Dying in Oregon and the Netherlands: Evidence Concerning the Impact on Patients in "Vulnerable" Groups' (2007) 33 Journal of Medical Ethics 591.

45 Nicole Steck et al. and Swiss National Cohort, 'Suicide Assisted by Right-to-Die Associations: A Population Based Cohort Study' (2014) 43 International Journal of Epidemiology 614.

46 Sigrid Dierickx, Luc Deliens, Joachim Cohen, and Kenneth Chambaere, 'Comparison of the Expression and Granting of Requests for Euthanasia in Belgium in 2007 vs 2013' (2015) 10 JAMA Internal Medicine 1703.

47 Ezekiel J Emanuel, Bregje D Onwuteaka-Philipsen, John W Urwin, and Joachim Cohen, 'Attitudes and Practices of Euthanasia and Physician-assisted Suicide in the United States, Canada, and Europe' (2016) 316 JAMA 79.

> the concern that minorities, the disabled, the poor, or other socioeconomically marginalized groups might be pressured to accept PAS [physician assisted suicide] does not seem to be borne out. The demographic profile of patients in the United States who have received these interventions is white, well-educated, and well-insured.[48]

Smith et al. found that requesters of assisted dying have what they describe as 'dismissive styles of attachment', that is, they prioritize 'self-reliance, autonomy and independence', and are interested in assisted dying in order to 'maintain an ultimate sense of control and autonomy within a process that allows very little opportunity for either'.[49] These characteristics are reproduced among those who are in favour of assisted dying for older people who are 'tired of life', whom Raijmakers et al. found 'were more likely than opponents to be highly educated, to be non-religious, to have little trust in physicians, and to prefer to make their own healthcare decisions'.[50]

Systematic reviews of attitudes towards assisted dying have consistently found support is strongest among the irreligious,[51] the middle classes,[52] and the 'highly educated',[53] and lowest among people with strong religious or spiritual beliefs.[54] People want to be able to access assisted dying because they want to be able to exert control over the dying process: 'a shared theme seems to be that those who support assistance in dying value control'.[55] They are 'not prepared to accept paternalistic attitudes on the part of health staff', and see access to assisted dying 'as a way of rising above one's circumstances'.[56] Interviews with British patients who have started the process of seeking an assisted death with Dignitas in Switzerland have found that 'getting the green light' from Dignitas becomes 'a different object towards which they could direct their hope'.[57] It becomes a goal to aim for, and 'a hedging strategy for maximising control'.[58]

48 Ibid.

49 Kathryn A Smith, Theresa A Harvath, Elizabeth R Goy, and Linda Ganzini, 'Predictors of Pursuit of Physician-assisted Death' (2015) 49 Journal of Pain and Symptom Management 555.

50 Natasja J H Raijmakers et al., 'Assistance in Dying for Older People without a Serious Medical Condition who Have a Wish to Die: A National Cross-sectional Survey' (2015) 41 Journal of Medical Ethics 145.

51 Smith et al., 'Predictors of Pursuit of Physician-assisted Death' (n. 49).

52 Sandy Macleod, 'Assisted Dying in Liberalised Jurisdictions and the Role of Psychiatry: A Clinician's View' (2012) 46 Australian & New Zealand Journal of Psychiatry 936.

53 Maggie Hendry et al., 'Why Do we Want the Right to Die? A Systematic Review of the International Literature on the Views of Patients, Carers and the Public on Assisted Dying' (2012) 27 Palliative Medicine 13–26.

54 Macleod, 'Assisted Dying in Liberalised Jurisdictions' (n. 52); Ruaidhri McCormack, Margaret Clifford, and Marian Conroy, 'Attitudes of UK Doctors towards Euthanasia and Physician-assisted Suicide: A Systematic Literature Review' (2011) 26 Palliative Medicine 23.

55 Natasja JH Raijmakers et al., 'Assistance in Dying for Older People' (n. 50).

56 Ibid.

57 Naomi Richards and Rebecca Rotter, 'Desperately Seeking Certainty? The Case of Asylum Applicants and People Planning an Assisted Suicide in Switzerland' (2013) 18 Sociological Research Online 26.

58 Ibid.

Interest in assisted dying therefore appears to be associated most strongly with patients who are accustomed to being able to exercise choice and control over their lives and who wish to continue to do so over their deaths. For these patients, an assisted death represents 'liberation from a situation that [is] perceived as an affront'.[59]

Some commentators have attempted to argue that social groups whom we normally think of as privileged, such as rich, educated, white males,[60] are, in fact, particularly vulnerable in the context of assisted suicide. Ilora Finlay and Rob George, for example, discuss 'the vulnerabilities that wealth may bring', and ask whether 'the better educated [are] more vulnerable, in the context of PAS [physician assisted suicide], because illness and potential dependence are more frightening to them or because they have fewer psychosocial supports'.[61]

Evidence of the characteristics shared by those who request assisted dying has significance beyond the question of whether or not they are vulnerable. The principal predictor of the desire to access an assisted death seems to be the patient's beliefs, characteristics, and priorities, rather than their illness or symptoms. Patients' interest in assisted dying stems not from objectively inadequate symptom control, which might be alleviated through access to better palliative care, but from their subjective perception of what makes life tolerable. Smith et al. explain that, for some patients, 'the anticipated dependency of terminal illness ... may have been more unbearable than the physical symptoms themselves'.[62] According to al-Awamer, 'these are rational capable patients who are not depressed and who want to die early based on their personal values and views of suffering and life. These wishes are not driven by a failure of palliative care but by a desire to live and die "on their own terms." "[63]

Opponents of assisted dying often argue that high quality palliative care can eliminate the desire for assisted dying,[64] but if it is the intrinsic characteristics of an individual—such as her lack of spirituality and her desire for control and independence—that trigger the desire for an assisted death, it is not clear that palliative care can, or should, be able to eliminate these.

[59] Kathrin Ohnsorge, Heike Gudat, and Christoph Rehmann-Sutter, 'What a Wish to Die Can Mean: Reasons, Meanings and Functions of Wishes to Die, Reported from 30 Qualitative Case Studies of Terminally Ill Cancer Patients in Palliative Care' (2014) 13 BMC Palliative Care 38.

[60] Erik Krag, 'Rich, White, and Vulnerable: Rethinking Oppressive Socialization in the Euthanasia Debate' (2014) 39 Journal of Medicine and Philosophy 406.

[61] Ilora Finlay and Rob George 'Legal Physician-assisted Suicide in Oregon and the Netherlands: Evidence Concerning the Impact on Patients in Vulnerable Groups—Another Perspective on Oregon's Data' (2011) 37 Journal of Medical Ethics 171.

[62] Smith et al., 'Predictors of Pursuit of Physician-assisted Death' (n. 49).

[63] Ahmed al-Awamer, 'Physician-assisted Suicide is not a Failure of Palliative Care' (2015) 61 Canadian Family Physician 1039.

[64] YY Mak, G Elwyn, and IG Finlay, 'Patients' Voices Are Needed in Debates on Euthanasia' (2003) 327 British Medical Journal 213.

Of course, I do not mean to suggest that concern for the vulnerable is entirely misplaced. On the contrary, it is clearly important that any law which permits assisted dying contains safeguards which enable the identification and rejection of requests that are prompted not by someone's desire to die, but by other people exerting pressure upon them. This could be done through a mandatory psychiatric assessment; a requirement for a second opinion from an independent medical professional; or, in the scheme put forward in the Assisted Dying Bill and by Noel Conway, by requiring the permission of a High Court judge.

Contrary to the assumptions made in *Conway*, however, there is now a considerable body of evidence that, in countries where assisted dying is lawful, requests are driven most commonly by the non-vulnerable patient's desire for control, rather than the vulnerable patient's susceptibility to pressure. Vulnerable patients seldom make requests for assisted dying, and if they do, robust mechanisms are in place to turn them down. Yet in parliamentary debates and in the courts, the interests of these vulnerable patients have operated as a trump card, overruling and eclipsing the interests of other subsets of patients. Ironically, it is those patients whose interests have been trumped who are, in practice, the ones who are more likely to take comfort in the availability of assisted dying. We thus seem to be more concerned about the hypothetical interests of the weak and vulnerable than we are in the real interests of patients, like Tony Nicklinson, Noel Conway, and Phil Newby,[65] whom no-one considers vulnerable, and who have clearly and unambiguously expressed their desire to control the timing of their death.

4. The Impact of Legalization on the Doctor–Patient Relationship?

The Divisional Court in *Conway* was concerned that, if assisted suicide were to be legalized, patients would trust their doctors less and this would result in poorer medical care.[66] There is, however, no evidence that patients trust their doctors less in countries where assisted dying is lawful; if anything, levels of trust among patients appear to be higher.[67] Nor is there any evidence of a negative impact upon the quality of patient care; on the contrary, the standard of palliative care appears to have improved in Belgium and Oregon since legalization.[68]

65 Katie Gibbons, 'Father's Plea to Die Legally and with Dignity' *The Times* 2 July 2019.

66 [2017] EWHC 2447 (Admin), [96] and [97].

67 Mark Hall, F Trachtenberg, and Elizabeth Dugan, 'The Impact on Patient Trust of Legalising Physician Aid in Dying' (2005) 31 Journal of Medical Ethics 693.

68 Linda Ganzini et al., 'Oregon Physician Attitudes about and Experiences with End of Life Care since the Passage of the Death with Dignity Act' (2001) 285 Journal of the American Medical Association 2363; E Dahl and N Levy, 'The Case for Physician Assisted Suicide: How Can it Possibly be Proven?' (2006) 32 Journal of Medical Ethics 335.

Rather than legalization having a negative impact upon patients, there is interesting and complex evidence about the impact of legalization on *doctors*. Although there is obviously a range of views among medical practitioners, some doctors undoubtedly find assisted dying difficult.[69] Given that people enter the medical profession in order to save and prolong lives, it should not be surprising that many doctors find the prospect of killing their patients, or helping them to commit suicide, challenging. A 2011 survey of Dutch doctors found that 86 per cent 'dread' the 'emotional burden of performing euthanasia'.[70] Opinion surveys consistently find that levels of support for assisted dying are higher among the public than they are among medical practitioners.[71]

Furthermore, there is evidence from the Netherlands and Belgium that doctors find involvement in assisted dying more difficult when the patient's reason for wanting to die is the result of either mental or psychosocial suffering.[72] Assisted dying in cases of mental disorder is lawful in both Belgium and the Netherlands, but, although the numbers have increased in recent years,[73] it continues to be rare in practice.[74] It may be difficult to judge whether a patient's mental suffering is objectively intolerable, and doctors may be wary of relying upon the patient's self-reporting.[75] While Dutch guidelines exist to help doctors respond to requests in cases of psychiatric disorders,[76] Bolt et al. found that a minority of Dutch physicians thought it conceivable that they would grant a euthanasia request in the case of a psychiatric disorder (34 per cent) or early-stage dementia (40 per cent), compared with 85 per cent for patients with cancer.[77]

Assisted dying may be most straightforward, from a doctor's point of view, for patients in the final stages of cancer, when it is possible to be confident about the patient's diagnosis and prognosis, and when the patient is usually able to confirm that her suffering is unbearable, and that she wants to die now. Interest in assisted

[69] Emanuel et al., 'Attitudes and Practices of Euthanasia' (n. 47).

[70] ALJ Van der Heide et al., *Second Evaluation of the Euthanasia Law* (ZonMw 2012), quoted in Emanuel et al., 'Attitudes and Practices of Euthanasia' (n. 47).

[71] Ibid.; McCormack et al., 'Attitudes of UK Doctors towards Euthanasia' (n. 54); Emily Tomlinson and Joshua Stott, 'Assisted Dying in Dementia: A Systematic Review of the International Literature on the Attitudes of Health Professionals, Patients, Carers and the Public, and the Factors Associated with these' (2015) 30 International Journal of Geriatric Psychiatry 310.

[72] Judith AC Rietjens et al., 'Judgement of Suffering in the Case of a Euthanasia Request in The Netherlands' (2009) 35 Journal of Medical Ethics 502.

[73] Sigrid Dierickx et al., 'Euthanasia for People with Psychiatric Disorders or Dementia in Belgium: Analysis of Officially Reported Cases' (2017) 17 BMC Psychiatry 203.

[74] Catherine S Shaffer, Alana N Cook, and Deborah A Connolly, 'A Conceptual Framework for Thinking about Physician-assisted Death for Persons with a Mental Disorder' (2016) 22 Psychology, Public Policy, and Law 141.

[75] Ibid.

[76] A Tholen et al., *Guideline dealing with the request for assisted suicide by patients with a psychiatric disorder* [Richtlijn omgaan met het verzoek om hulp bij zelfdoding door patiënten met een psychiatrische stoornis] (Dutch Psychiatric Association 2009).

[77] Eva Elizabeth Bolt et al., 'Can Physicians Conceive of Performing Euthanasia in Case of Psychiatric Disease, Dementia or Being Tired of Living?' (2015) 41 Journal of Medical Ethics 592.

dying is not limited to patients with cancer, however. And the reasons patients commonly give for wishing to end their lives are, unlike cancer, more difficult for doctors to diagnose and verify: namely, a loss of meaning, a loss of connectedness, a loss of control, or a belief that their life is now 'completed', and no longer worth living.[78] Van Wijnjgaarden et al.'s study of people who have developed a wish to die explain that this is often a result of them experiencing multiple losses, ranging from physical decline and its associated loss of privacy, to the shrinking of their social circle through successive bereavements.[79]

It appears that doctors in both the Netherlands and Belgium are increasingly confronted with requests for assisted dying that do not fit a standard medicalized model. The Dutch medical association (KNMG), for example, has reported a growth in requests from people with 'an accumulation of non-life-threatening geriatric afflictions, including loss of physical function and mental vitality, loneliness and loss of autonomy'.[80] In Snijdewind et al.'s interviews with physicians in the Netherlands, the majority reported that requests for euthanasia and assisted suicide (EAS) 'where there was no medical condition underlying the request', had become more frequent in recent years, and most found these requests problematic:

> Most physicians expressed the view that these requests based on non-medical reasons stemmed from loneliness and that this was not a medical problem but a societal one, not something for which EAS was the right solution. Most physicians also mentioned not feeling competent to make a decision about EAS in these cases where suffering was mostly existential, not motivated by a medical condition; they felt it did not belong to the domain of medical professionals.[81]

As a result, while medicalized assisted dying in the Netherlands and Belgium undoubtedly provides reassurance to some patients, there is evidence that it does not help everyone. For example, the number of patients in the Netherlands who choose to end their lives through voluntarily stopping eating and drinking (VSED) is much higher than one might expect in a country in which both euthanasia and assisted suicide have been lawful for more than four decades. VSED is the primary cause of death in between 0.4 and 2.1 per cent of all deaths (euthanasia is the primary cause in 4.5 per cent of deaths, and assisted suicide 0.1 per cent).[82] Bolt et al.

[78] Els van Wijngaarden, Carlo Leget, and Anne Goossensen, 'Experiences and Motivations Underlying Wishes to Die in Older People Who Are Tired of Living: A Research Area in its Infancy' (2014) 69 OMEGA—Journal of Death and Dying 191.

[79] Ibid.

[80] Claudia Grosse and Alexandra Grosse, 'Assisted Suicide: Models of Legal Regulation in Selected European Countries and the Case Law of the European Court of Human Rights' (2015) 55 Medicine, Science and the Law 246.

[81] Marianne C Snijdewind, Donald G van Tol, Bregje D Onwuteaka-Philipsen, and Dick L Willems, 'Developments in the Practice of Physician-assisted Dying: Perceptions of Physicians who Had Experience with Complex Cases' (2018) 44 Journal of Medical Ethics 292.

[82] *Deaths by Medical End-of-Life Decision; Age, Cause of Death* (Statistics Netherlands 2017).

found that nearly half (46 per cent) of all primary care physicians 'had cared for a patient who had hastened death by VSED'.[83] About a fifth of those who had died following VSED had previously requested an assisted death, but most had not.[84] Some opted for VSED in order not to have to rely upon their physician, and 77 per cent had 'existential' motives for hastening death.[85] Most were older than patients requesting an assisted death (median age 84), and a minority (27 per cent) suffered from cancer.[86]

Davis has explained that euthanasia in the Netherlands 'is not nearly as common as one might imagine', and 'is not at all easy to get':[87] doctors turn down 'two-thirds of the requests for euthanasia' that they receive.[88] Assisted dying is not available as of right, but is a matter of medical discretion.[89] As Vink points out, 'the physician's autonomy is decisive',[90] not the patient's. In recent years, the End of Life Clinic (levenseindekliniek) has been set up in order to offer the option of euthanasia to individuals whose lawful requests are turned down by their treating doctors. Although the numbers are relatively small, demand has increased significantly between 2013 and 2017, from 134 to more than 500 cases.[91]

Evidence that the legalization of assisted dying is difficult for some or even for most doctors does not establish that the 'blanket ban' in s. 2 of the Suicide Act is 'necessary', however. If assisted suicide were to be legalized, there would have to be a conscientious objection clause so that doctors were not obliged to participate. Some doctors would be willing to help patients to die, and hence it is not possible to conclude that a complete ban is necessary in order to protect the rights of those doctors who are not prepared to do so.

More importantly, it could be argued that there is a tension at the heart of the medicalization of assisted dying, given what we know about the reasons which prompt a growing number of requests. Patients are increasingly interested in being helped to die when their lives have lost meaning to them, while many doctors struggle to regard relief of this sort of suffering as a proper use of their medical training. If medicalized assisted dying gives doctors considerable discretion over

[83] Eva E Bolt, Martijn Hagens, Dick Willems, and Bregje D Onwuteaka-Philipsen, 'Primary Care Patients Hastening Death by Voluntarily Stopping Eating and Drinking' (2015) 13 The Annals of Family Medicine 421.

[84] Ibid.

[85] Ibid.

[86] Ibid.

[87] Kathy Davis, 'Dying, Self-determination, and the (Im)possibilities of a "Good Death"' (2015) 25 Feminism & Psychology 143.

[88] Ibid.

[89] A comparison could be drawn with the Abortion Act 1967, which did not give women the right to an abortion, but rather gave doctors broad discretion over women's access to abortion. I return to this point in the conclusion.

[90] Ton Vink, 'Self-Euthanasia, the Dutch Experience: In Search for the Meaning of a Good Death or Eu Thanatos' (2016) 30 Bioethics 681.

[91] Janene Pieters, 'Euthanasia Clinic Needs 50 more Doctors to Keep up with Demand' *NL Times* 27 October 2017.

when patients can be helped to die, it may provide a solution only for a subset of those patients who want to be able to exercise more control over their deaths.

Evidence from countries which have legalized assisted dying poses difficult questions about the limits of legalization, within a medicalized approval system, and raises the interesting question of whether *de*medicalized assisted dying might have advantages for both patients and doctors.[92] What it does not establish, however, is that a 'blanket ban' on assisted suicide is necessary in order to protect patient trust in the medical profession.[93]

5. Conclusion

It could be argued that the United Kingdom's 'blanket ban' on assisted suicide is a case study in the importance of professional interests to the shape and scope of the criminal law. The absolute prohibition on assisted suicide persists despite being at odds with an overwhelming majority of public opinion,[94] and with the reality that each week, one UK citizen travels to Switzerland for an assisted suicide.[95] Almost everyone who travels to Switzerland will have been helped to do so, and although the DPP invariably exercises his discretion not to prosecute, distressing police investigations are not uncommon. In his 2019 Reith Lectures, Lord Sumption expressed support for this 'untidy compromise':

> I think that the law should continue to criminalise assistance in suicide and I think that the law should be broken. I think that it should be broken from time to time. We need to have a law against it in order to prevent abuse but it has always been the case that this has been criminal and it has always been the case that courageous relatives and friends have helped people to die.[96]

While exercising compassion in an individual case may be simpler than devising a 'generalized response' to assisted dying, capable of anticipating and accommodating all of the difficult scenarios which might arise in the future,[97] the

[92] Ronald Kipke, 'Why not Commercial Assistance for Suicide? On the Question of Argumentative Coherence of Endorsing Assisted Suicide' (2014) 29 Bioethics 516.
[93] *R v Conway* [2017] EWHC 2447 (Admin), [94].
[94] Owen Bowcott, 'Legalise Assisted Dying for Terminally Ill, Say 90% of People in UK' *The Guardian* 3 March 2019.
[95] On average, each Swiss assisted death costs £10,000. Assisted Dying Coalition, *Briefing: Number of UK Citizens Going to Switzerland to Seek an Assisted Death* (Humanists UK 2019).
[96] The Reith Lectures 2019: Law and the Decline of Politics, 21 May 2019 (transcript available at <http://downloads.bbc.co.uk/radio4/reith2019/Reith_2019_Sumption_lecture_1.pdf>)
[97] Jonathan Herring, 'Escaping the Shackles of Law at the End of Life: *R(Nicklinson) v Ministry of Justice*' (2013) 21 Medical Law Review 487

consequence is an increase in the discretionary power of the police and prosecutorial authorities.[98]

In the United Kingdom, the trope of the vulnerable patient has been mobilized effectively in order to persuade Parliament and the courts that it is impossible to specify, in advance, when it could be legitimate for a doctor to help someone to end her life. In the most recent assisted suicide case, the courts speculated about the impact an exception to the blanket ban on assisted suicide might have on vulnerable patients and on the doctor–patient relationship. In doing so, it disregarded evidence from countries which have legalized assisted dying, which shows instead that patients request assisted dying because they want to maintain control over their deaths, in the same way as they have been able to exercise control over their lives. Nor does there appear to be evidence that assisted dying interferes with patients' trust in their doctors. Rather the picture that emerges from countries with experience of legalization is that assisted dying can be difficult for doctors, especially if patients seek assisted deaths in order to relieve their psychosocial or mental suffering, or if they want to make binding advance decisions for euthanasia.

For understandable reasons, campaigners for the legalization of assisted dying have focused their energies on human rights challenges to s. 2 of the Suicide Act's failure to provide any exceptions to the prohibition of assisted suicide. Further challenges are planned, with lawyers intending to argue next that s. 2 breaches Article 14 (the right not to be discriminated against in the exercise of one's Convention rights) read with Article 8.[99] At the same time as pursuing a declaration of incompatibility, it is also important for campaigners to engage thoroughly with doctors' representative bodies, on the grounds that their support, or perhaps more realistically, their lack of opposition is likely to make a difference in practice.

Before the final decision in *Carter v. Canada*, the Canadian Medical Association adopted a position of neutrality in order to be able to support all of its members, including ensuring that those who were opposed to assisted dying had their right not to participate protected in law.[100] Under the new law, responsibility for patients' ability to access medical assistance in dying (MAID) does not lie with individual physicians, but with society, and access programmes enable a patient to be put in touch with a healthcare professional who does provide MAID, even if their family doctor does not.[101] In Victoria, Australia, despite the Australian Medical Association's opposition to legalization, its Victoria branch adopted a neutral position and was involved actively with the design of the new law. Doctors' perspectives

[98] Lacey, *In Search of Criminal Responsibility* (n. 2) 99.

[99] Humanists UK, 'Paul Lamb to Bring New Legal Case for the Right to Die' 7 May 2019, and BBC News, 'Assisted suicide: Paul Lamb Renews Bid for Right to Die' 7 May 2019; 'Terminally Ill Man Phil Newby Launches New Assisted Dying Case' PoliticsHome.com, 2 July 2019.

[100] Jeff Blackmer, 'Commentary: How the Canadian Medical Association Found a Third Way to Support All its Members on Assisted Dying' (2019) 364 British Medical Journal 415.

[101] Diane Kelsall, 'Physicians Are not Solely Responsible for Ensuring Access to Medical Assistance in Dying' (2018) 190 Canadian Medical Association Journal E181.

were a central concern in the parliamentary debates (indeed, there were 348 references to doctors, compared with 68 references to religion and God).[102]

As a result, it would be difficult to overstate the significance of recent moves by UK healthcare professionals' representative bodies to canvas their members on whether to move their position on assisted dying from opposition to neutrality. The Royal College of Nursing adopted a position of neutrality in 2017,[103] and the first doctors' organization to do so was the Royal College of Physicians (RCP) in 2019.[104] In 2020 the Royal College of General Practitioners and the BMA surveyed their members, and at the time of writing, both remain opposed to a change in the law.[105]

In the RCP poll of fellows and members, 43.4 per cent had favoured continued opposition, 31.6 per cent were in favour of a change in the law, and 25 per cent wanted the College to be neutral. An application for judicial review of the RCP's decision to require a 'supermajority' of 60 per cent in order to adopt either a 'for' or 'against' position was unsuccessful.[106] Laing J held that it was not irrational to require a supermajority, and that, in any event, 'even if a simple majority had been required, there was not a simple majority in favour of the proposition that the [RCP's] public position should be to oppose a change in the law'.[107] Following a complaint, the Charity Commission investigated 'concerns with regard to how the charity dealt with and managed such a sensitive and high-profile subject matter',[108] but it too declined to challenge the RCP's decision.

It is hard to imagine assisted suicide being legalized in the United Kingdom in the face of universal opposition from doctors' representative bodies. At the same time, if doctors' organizations were to support a change in the law, the case for reform might become overwhelming. An obvious parallel could be drawn with the Abortion Act 1967, which provides statutory defences to the crimes of procuring a miscarriage set out in ss 58 and 59 of the Offences Against the Person

[102] Jodhi Rutherford, 'The Role of the Medical Profession in Victorian Assisted Dying Law Reform' (2018) 26 Journal of Law and Medicine 246.

[103] Royal College of Nursing Position statement on assisted dying March 2017 at <https://www.rcn.org.uk/about-us/policy-briefings/pol-2314>.

[104] Royal College of Physicians, *Press Release No Majority View on Assisted Dying Moves RCP Position to Neutral* 21 March 2019

[105] Royal College of General Practitioners, *Press Release Royal College of GPs remains opposed to change in the law on assisted dying* 21st February 2020 https://www.rcgp.org.uk/about-us/news/2020/february/royal-college-of-gps-remains-opposed-to-change-in-the-law-on-assisted-dying.aspx; British Medical Association, *Physician-assisted dying survey* 8 October 2020 https://www.bma.org.uk/advice-and-support/ethics/end-of-life/physician-assisted-dying-survey.

[106] Gareth Iacobucci, 'RCP Adopts Neutral Stance on Assisted Dying after Poll of Members' (2019) 364 British Medical Journal l1340.

[107] Unreported, 20 March 2019. Andrew Goddard, 'As RCP President I Stand by the College's Recent Survey on Assisted Dying and Wish to Set the Record Straight' BMJ Blog 3 July 2019 at <https://blogs.bmj.com/bmj/2019/07/03/andrew-goddard-as-rcp-president-i-stand-by-colleges-recent-survey-on-assisted-dying-and-wish-to-set-the-record-straight/>.

[108] Andrew Gilligan, 'Royal College of Physicians Questioned over Policy Change on Assisted Dying' *The Times* 12 May 2019.

Act 1961. The Abortion Act was passed not because Parliament had determined that women should have the right to end their unwanted pregnancies, but, rather, because 'abortion law reform campaigners were finally able to persuade the medical establishment of the need for a statute in order to accommodate abortion for reasons of foetal abnormality and protect doctors from prosecution for providing such procedures'.[109] Professional interests were therefore central to the creation of a statutory defence to the crime of procuring a miscarriage.

As Nicola Lacey has explained 'the growing power and organization' of professions, 'including the medical profession', has created 'new interests shaping the design and implementation of the criminal process'.[110] The role of professional interests in the design of the Abortion Act 1967 is often assumed to be an historical oddity which offers an explanation of how in 1967 Parliament was persuaded to accept that, in certain circumstances, termination of pregnancy would cause a pregnant woman less harm than continuing the pregnancy.[111] If the medical profession were to accept that, in certain circumstances, assisting a suicide could be less harmful to a dying patient than the death she would otherwise have to fear and endure, this might have more political traction than the claim that assisted suicide should be available as of right.

Just as with abortion over five decades ago, medicalizing assisted suicide—rather than framing it in terms of rights—might have considerable political advantages. At the same time, and in common with abortion, there are dangers in relying upon a medicalized regime, namely that it turns patients into supplicants, dependent upon the benign exercise of medical discretion. In short, in relation to both assisted suicide and abortion, the mobilization of professional interests has considerable political power, but it comes with the cost of allowing those interests to determine when someone should be permitted to terminate her pregnancy or her life.

Bibliography

al-Awamer, A, 'Physician-assisted Suicide is not a Failure of Palliative Care' (2015) 61 Canadian Family Physician 1039

Battin, MP, Van der Heide, A, Ganzini, L, Van der Wal G, and Onwuteaka-Philipsen, BD, 'Legal Physician-assisted Dying in Oregon and the Netherlands: Evidence Concerning the Impact on Patients in "Vulnerable" Groups' (2007) 33 Journal of Medical Ethics 591

Blackmer, J, 'Commentary: How the Canadian Medical Association Found a Third Way to Support all Its Members on Assisted Dying' (2019) 364 British Medical Journal 415

[109] Sheelagh McGuinness and Michael Thomson, 'Medicine and Abortion Law: Complicating the Reforming Profession' (2015) 23 Medical Law Review 177.

[110] Lacey, *In Search of Criminal Responsibility* (n. 2) 83–4.

[111] Sally Sheldon, *Beyond Control: Medical Power and Abortion Law* (Pluto Press 1997).

Bolt, EE et al., 'Can Physicians Conceive of Performing Euthanasia in Case of Psychiatric Disease, Dementia or Being Tired of Living?' (2015) 41 Journal of Medical Ethics 592

Bolt, EE, Hagens, M, Willems, D, and Onwuteaka-Philipsen, BD, 'Primary Care Patients Hastening Death by Voluntarily Stopping Eating and Drinking' (2015) 13 The Annals of Family Medicine 421

Bowcott, O, 'Legalise Assisted Dying for Terminally Ill, Say 90% of People in UK' *The Guardian* 3 March 2019

British Medical Association, *Physician-assisted dying survey* 8 October 2020 https://www.bma.org.uk/advice-and-support/ethics/end-of-life/physician-assisted-dying-survey.

Chan, B and Somerville, M, 'Converting the "Right to Life" to the "Right to Physician Assisted Suicide and Euthanasia": An Analysis of *Carter v Canada (Attorney General), Supreme Court of* Canada' (2016) 24 Medical Law Review 143

Dahl, E and Levy, N, 'The Case for Physician Assisted Suicide: How Can it Possibly Be Proven?' (2006) 32 Journal of Medical Ethics 335

Davis, K, 'Dying, Self-determination, and the (Im)possibilities of a "Good Death"' (2015) 25 Feminism & Psychology 143

Dierickx, S et al., 'Euthanasia for People with Psychiatric Disorders or Dementia in Belgium: Analysis of Officially Reported Cases' (2017) 17 BMC Psychiatry 203

Emanuel, EJ, Onwuteaka-Philipsen, BD, Urwin, JW, and Cohen, J, 'Attitudes and Practices of Euthanasia and Physician-assisted Suicide in the United States, Canada, and Europe' (2016) 316 Journal of the American Medical Association (JAMA) 79

Fineman, MA, 'The Vulnerable Subject: Anchoring Equality in the Human Condition' in MA Fineman (ed.), *Transcending the Boundaries of Law: Generations of Feminism and Legal Theory* (Routledge-Cavendish, 2010)

Finlay, IG and George, R, 'Legal Physician-assisted Suicide in Oregon and the Netherlands: Evidence Concerning the Impact on Patients in Vulnerable Groups—Another Perspective on Oregon's Data' (2011) 37 Journal of Medical Ethics 171

Ganzini L and Back, AL, 'The Challenge of New Legislation on Physician-assisted Death' (2016) JAMA Internal Medicine 427

Ganzini, L et al., 'Oregon Physician Attitudes about and Experiences with End of Life Care since the Passage of the Death with Dignity Act' (2001) 285 Journal of the American Medical Association 2363

Ganzini, L, Dobscha, SK, Heintz, RT, and Press, N, 'Oregon Physicians' Perceptions of Patients who Request Assisted Suicide and their Families' (2003) 6 Journal of Palliative Medicine 381

Ganzini, L, Goy, ER, and Dobscha, S K, 'Why Oregon Patients Request Assisted Death: Family Members' Views' (2008) 23 Journal of General Internal Medicine 154

Ganzini, L, Leong, GB, Fenn, DS, Silva, JA, and Weinstock, R, 'Evaluation of Competence to Consent to Assisted Suicide: Views of Forensic Psychiatrists' (2000) 157 American Journal of Psychiatry 595

Ganzini, L, Silveira, MJ, and Johnston, WS, 'Predictors and Correlates of Interest in Assisted Suicide in the Final Month of Life among ALS Patients in Oregon and Washington' (2002) 24 Journal of Pain and Symptom Management 312

Gibbons, K, 'Father's Plea to Die Legally and with Dignity' *The Times* 2 July 2019

Gilligan, A, 'Royal College of Physicians Questioned over Policy Change on Assisted Dying' *The Times* 12 May 2019

Grosse, C and Grosse, A, 'Assisted Suicide: Models of Legal Regulation in Selected European Countries and the Case Law of the European Court of Human Rights' (2015) 55 Medicine, Science and the Law 246

Hall, M, Trachtenberg, F, and Dugan, E, 'The Impact on Patient Trust of Legalising Physician Aid in Dying' (2005) 31 Journal of Medical Ethics 693

Hendry, M et al., 'Why Do we Want the Right to Die? A Systematic Review of the International Literature on the Views of Patients, Carers and The Public on Assisted Dying' (2012) 27 Palliative Medicine 13

Herring, J, 'Escaping the Shackles of Law at the End of Life: *R(Nicklinson) v Ministry of Justice*' (2013) 21 Medical Law Review 487

Holm, S., 'The Debate about Physician Assistance in Dying: 40 Years of Unrivalled Progress in Medical Ethics?' (2015) 41 Journal of Medical Ethics 40

Horn, R, 'The "French Exception": The Right to Continuous Deep Sedation at the End of Life' (2018) 44 Journal of Medical Ethics 204

Iacobucci, G, 'RCP Adopts Neutral Stance on Assisted Dying after Poll of Members' (2019) 364 British Medical Journal l1340.

Kelsall, D, 'Physicians Are not Solely Responsible for Ensuring Access to Medical Assistance in Dying' (2018) 190 Canadian Medical Association Journal E181

Kipke, R, 'Why not Commercial Assistance for Suicide? On the Question of Argumentative Coherence of Endorsing Assisted Suicide' (2014) 29 Bioethics 516

Krag, E, 'Rich, White, and Vulnerable: Rethinking Oppressive Socialization in the Euthanasia Debate' (2014) 39 Journal of Medicine and Philosophy 406

Lacey, N, *In Search of Criminal Responsibility: Ideas, Interests and Institutions* (Oxford University Press 2016)

Luc Deliens, SD, Cohen, J, and Chambaere, K, 'Comparison of the Expression and Granting of Requests for Euthanasia in Belgium in 2007 vs 2013' (2015) 10 JAMA Internal Medicine 1703

Macleod, S, 'Assisted Dying in Liberalised Jurisdictions and the Role of Psychiatry: A Clinician's View' (2012) 46 Australian & New Zealand Journal of Psychiatry 936

Mak, YY, Elwyn, G, and Finlay, IG, 'Patients' Voices Are Needed in Debates on Euthanasia' (2003) 327 British Medical Journal 213

McCormack, R, Clifford, M, and Conroy, M, 'Attitudes of UK Doctors towards Euthanasia and Physician-assisted Suicide: A Systematic Literature Review' (2011) 26 Palliative Medicine 23

McGuinness, S and Thomson, M, 'Medicine and Abortion Law: Complicating the Reforming Profession' (2015) 23 Medical Law Review 177

Ohnsorge, K, Gudat, H, and Rehmann-Sutter, C, 'What a Wish to Die Can Mean: Reasons, Meanings and Functions of Wishes to Die, Reported from 30 Qualitative Case Studies of Terminally Ill Cancer Patients in Palliative Care' (2014) 13 BMC Palliative Care 38.

Pieters, J, 'Euthanasia Clinic Needs 50 more Doctors to Keep up with Demand' *NL Times* 27 October 2017

Raijmakers, NJH et al., 'Assistance in Dying for Older People without a Serious Medical Condition who Have a Wish to Die: A National Cross-sectional Survey' (2015) 41 Journal of Medical Ethics 145

Richards, N and Rotter, R, 'Desperately Seeking Certainty? The Case of Asylum Applicants and People Planning an Assisted Suicide in Switzerland' (2013) 18 Sociological Research Online 26.

Rietjens, JAC, et al., 'Judgement of Suffering in the Case of a Euthanasia Request in The Netherlands' (2009) 35 Journal of Medical Ethics 502

Royal College of General Practitioners, Press Release Royal College of GPs remains opposed to change in the law on assisted dying 21st February 2020 https://www.rcgp.org.uk/about-us/news/2020/february/royal-college-of-gps-remains-opposed-to-change-in-the-law-on-assisted-dying.aspx.

Royal College of Nursing Position statement on assisted dying March 2017 <https://www.rcn.org.uk/about-us/policy-briefings/pol-2314>
Royal College of Physicians, *Press Release No Majority View on Assisted Dying Moves RCP Position to Neutral* 21 March 2019
Rurup ML, et al., 'The First Five Years of Euthanasia Legislation in Belgium and the Netherlands: Description and Comparison of Cases' (2012) 26 Palliative Medicine 43
Rutherford, J, 'The Role of the Medical Profession in Victorian Assisted Dying Law Reform' (2018) 26 Journal of Law and Medicine 246
Shaffer, CS, Cook, AN, and Connolly, DA, 'A Conceptual Framework for Thinking about Physician-assisted Death for Persons with a Mental Disorder' (2016) 22 Psychology, Public Policy, and Law 141
Sheldon, S, *Beyond Control: Medical Power and Abortion Law* (Pluto Press 1997)
Smith, KA, Harvath, TA, Goy, ER, and Ganzini, L, 'Predictors of Pursuit of Physician-assisted Death' (2015) 49 Journal of Pain and Symptom Management 555
Snijdewind, MC, van Tol, DG, Onwuteaka-Philipsen, BD, and Willems, DL, 'Developments in the Practice of Physician-assisted Dying: Perceptions of Physicians who Had Experience with Complex Cases' (2018) 44 Journal of Medical Ethics 292
Steck, N et al. and Swiss National Cohort, 'Suicide Assisted by Right-to-Die Associations: A Population Based Cohort Study' (2014) 43 International Journal of Epidemiology 614
Tholen, A et al., *Guideline dealing with the request for assisted suicide by patients with a psychiatric disorder* [Richtlijn omgaan met het verzoek om hulp bij zelfdoding door patiënten met een psychiatrische stoornis] (Dutch Psychiatric Association 2009)
Tomlinson, E and Stott, J, 'Assisted Dying in Dementia: A Systematic Review of the International Literature on the Attitudes of Health Professionals, Patients, Carers and the Public, and the Factors Associated with These' (2015) 30 International Journal of Geriatric Psychiatry 310
Van der Heide, ALJ et al., *Second Evaluation of the Euthanasia Law* (ZonMw 2012)
Vink, T, 'Self-Euthanasia, the Dutch Experience: In Search for the Meaning of a Good Death or Eu Thanatos' (2016) 30 Bioethics 681
Walker, A, 'Assisted Dying: Couple Tell of Anguish over Police Inquiry' *The Guardian* 7 February 2019
Wijngaarden, E, Leget, C, and Goossensen, A, 'Experiences and Motivations Underlying Wishes to Die in Older People Who Are Tired of Living: A Research Area in its Infancy' (2014) 69 OMEGA—Journal of Death and Dying 191

9
Responsibility, Criminalization, and Political Economy

Lindsay Farmer[1]

1. Introduction

Nicola Lacey has made important and distinctive contributions across such an impressively diverse range of areas—from criminal law theory, to the history of criminal responsibility to feminist legal theory to her biography of HLA Hart—that it is impossible to do justice to the depth and range of her contribution in a short piece such as this. My own engagement with her work, and with Lacey as a colleague and friend, over a period of some thirty years has been in the area of criminal law, where we have shared interests in the project of developing critical criminal law theory, and in particular in the use of history as a means of developing this critical jurisprudence. I have been extremely fortunate to have had Lacey leading the way in this area, and for her support and encouragement in developing my own projects and, in this chapter, I want both to pay tribute to her ground-breaking work and to explore new ways in which it might be developed.

One of the most important and distinctive themes of Lacey's recent work has been the analysis of penal practices from the perspective of political economy. This is most prominent in her book, *The Prisoners' Dilemma* (2008), which analyses variations in penal practices across a range of modern liberal democratic states according to the type of economy and state organization.[2] It is also a central theme in her work on the development of criminal responsibility which links responsibility practices in modern criminal law to the interests and institutions central to the development of modern western capitalism.[3] In this chapter I want to explore the meaning and critical potential of the concept of political economy—how it is used by Lacey, the different traditions that she draws on—and what the perspective

[1] University of Glasgow. I am grateful to Sarah Armstrong, Emilios Christodoulidis, Chloe Kennedy, David Lieberman, Scott Veitch, and, above all, Nicola Lacey for their comments on an earlier draft. Funding for this research was generously provided by the Leverhulme Trust (Grant No. MRF 2018-075).

[2] Nicola Lacey, *The Prisoners' Dilemma. Political Economy and Punishment in Contemporary Democracies* (Cambridge University Press 2008); Nicola Lacey, 'The Rule of Law and the Political Economy of Criminalisation: An Agenda for Research' (2013) 15 Punishment & Society 349.

[3] See primarily, Nicola Lacey, *In Search of Responsibility. Ideas, Interests and Institutions* (Oxford University Press 2016).

Lindsay Farmer, *Responsibility, Criminalization, and Political Economy* In: *On Crime, Society, and Responsibility in the Work of Nicola Lacey.* Edited by: Iyiola Solanke, Oxford University Press (2021). © The several contributors.
DOI: 10.1093/oso/9780198852681.003.0010

and theory of political economy contributes to our understanding of criminal law. However, in doing this I will also seek to deepen the relevance of political economy to the analysis of criminal responsibility by exploring how the development of the modern conception of English criminal law in the early nineteenth century was itself shaped by contemporary understandings of political economy. Most historical work on the development of the modern criminal law has focused on the impact of utilitarianism, and in particular the ideas of Jeremy Bentham, to show how changes in penal laws and institutions were linked to new efforts to shape individual conduct in society.[4] However, equally important to the intellectual and political culture of the early nineteenth century were understandings of the new 'science' of political economy—often alongside and closely intertwined with utilitarian thought.[5] The aim of this chapter, then, is to begin to explore the ways in which theories of political economy shaped the modern criminal law in this period and thereby to open up new possibilities for exploring connections between criminal law, criminal responsibility, and political economy—and thus for critical criminal law theory.

2. Political Economy in Lacey's Work

While the concept of political economy has been central to Lacey's work over a number of years, I am going to focus here on two books in particular, as illustrating the way in which Lacey has deployed the concept.

a. The Prisoners' Dilemma

In this book, based on her 2007 Hamlyn Lectures, Lacey explores the relationship between criminal justice and democracy, focusing in particular on the emergence of penal populism and its impact on rates of imprisonment. As is characteristic of Lacey's work, the argument combines a focus on the normative—a commitment to democratic values and social inclusion and reintegration—with analysis of the social and political context in which such values are shaped and given meaning. Her specific argument is 'that the varying institutional structures of contemporary democracies make a significant difference to their practical capacity to meet the

[4] See e.g. Lindsay Farmer, *Making the Modern Criminal Law. Criminalization and Civil Order* (Oxford University Press 2016); Keith JM Smith, *Lawyers, Legislators and Theorists. Developments in English Criminal Jurisprudence, 1800–1957* (Oxford University Press 1998); Martin Wiener, *Reconstructing the Criminal. Culture, Law and Policy in England, 1830–1914* (Cambridge University Press 1990).

[5] It is noteworthy, e.g. that both Bentham and John Stuart Mill wrote not only on utilitarianism but on political economy. See Jeremy Bentham, *Writings on Political Economy* (2 vols) (ed. Michael Quinn) (Oxford University Press 2016 and 2019); John Stuart Mill, *Principles of Political Economy* (John W Parker 1848).

normative demand of reintegrative inclusion which seems a natural corollary of liberal democratic aspirations'.[6] So, the aim is to explore the 'institutional preconditions for the realisation of values such as penal moderation or inclusionary practices in criminal justice'.[7] Moreover, she goes on to argue, this is not merely a matter of institutional design, as institutions operate 'within a broad socio-economic and political context which in turn shapes social actors' capacities'.[8] This institutional environment is understood in terms of political economy—which provides both the framework for analysis and for thinking about normative responses.

Her account of political economy draws on the work of political scientists Peter Hall and David Soskice which argues that 'political-economic forces at the macro-level are mediated not only by cultural filters, but also by economic, political and social institutions'.[9] This approach, in short, argues that it is not enough to talk about a neo liberal economy or state, but that it is necessary to explore further the role that political and social institutions play in mediating between the economy and developments in particular social spheres—including institutions and practices of punishment. This approach is, in part, a critique of some Marxist and neo-Marxist accounts which have used the idea of political economy to identify a particular form of neo-liberal penality.[10] Here Lacey argues that such approaches have tended to point to an inevitable emergence of 'cultures of control' (almost inevitably modelled on developments in the United States) because they are insufficiently sensitive to the kinds of legal, political, and social institutional arrangements that act as a buffer between macro-economic and social changes and particular national penal practices. The political and penal culture of states such as Germany or the Netherlands or Sweden is very different from the United States, because:

> the interlocking and diffused institutions of co-ordination of the corporatist and social-democratic systems ... conduce to an environment of relatively extensive informal social controls, and this in turn supports the cultural attitudes which underpin and help to stabilise a moderated approach to formal punishment.[11]

She thus argues that evidence of rising imprisonment rates is not necessarily evidence of an inevitable shift towards dystopia, shaped by a media-driven fear of

[6] Lacey, *The Prisoners' Dilemma* (n. 2) 8.
[7] Ibid., 13.
[8] Ibid., 15.
[9] Lacey, *The Prisoners' Dilemma* (n. 2) 56–7 drawing on Peter A Hall and David Soskice, *Varieties of Capitalism: The Institutional Foundations of Comparative Advantage* (Oxford University Press 2001).
[10] Discussing David Garland, *The Culture of Control. Crime and Social Order in Contemporary Society* (Oxford University Press 2001): Alessandro de Giorgi, *Re-Thinking the Political Economy of Punishment. Perspectives on Post-Fordism and Penal Politics* (Routledge 2006); Jock Young, *The Exclusive Society. Social Exclusion, Crime and Difference in Late Modernity* (Sage 1999); Loic Wacquant, 'Deadly Symbiosis: When Ghetto and Prison Meet and Mesh' in David Garland (ed.), *Mass Imprisonment in the United States: Social Causes and Consequences* (Sage 2001).
[11] Lacey, *The Prisoners' Dilemma* (n. 2) 61.

crime and insecurity, because they need to be analysed in terms of these more specific institutional and cultural factors. What is important then, on her account is the institutional organization of the political economy. She thus draws on a basic distinction between liberal market economies and coordinated market economies, but then goes on to explore the 'comparative institutional advantage and ... the capacities for strategic co-ordination inherent in differently ordered political-economic systems'.[12] So on this account, political economy must be seen as (loosely) a combination of the mode of production and forms of democratic and institutional organization, which are explored for their impact on criminal justice.[13]

b. In Search of Criminal Responsibility

This approach is further developed in her book *In Search of Criminal Responsibility* (2016) which, amongst many other things, seeks to develop a 'political economy of responsibility in English criminal law'.[14] The book is a wide-ranging exploration of the development of concepts of criminal responsibility since the late eighteenth century in which Lacey investigates the relations between ideas, or concepts, of criminal responsibility; the social interests that they serve; and legal, political, and economic institutions.[15] Her starting point is that responsibility cannot be viewed, as it is in much normative theory, as a purely moral concept, but that it has a history which has been shaped by:

> an interlocking set of conditions that change over time and place in tandem with factors such as the human situation, prevailing ideas, institutions, and the distribution of power.[16]

[12] Ibid., 56–7.

[13] See also Nicola Lacey and David Soskice, 'Crime Punishment and Segregation in the United States: The Paradox of Local Democracy' (2015) 17 Punishment & Society 454; Nicola Lacey, 'American Imprisonment in Comparative Perspective' (2010) 139 Daedalus 102; Zelia Gallo, 'Punishment, Authority and Political Economy: Italian Challenges to Western Punitiveness' (2015) 17 Punishment & Society 598.

[14] Lacey, *In Search of Responsibility* (n. 3) ch. 5. For other work on criminal responsibility see, in particular, 'Responsibility and Modernity in Criminal Law' (2001) 9 Journal of Political Philosophy 249; 'In Search of the Responsible Subject: History, Philosophy and the Social Sciences in Criminal Law Theory' (2001) 64 Modern Law Review 350; *Women, Crime and Character: From Moll Flanders to Tess of the D'Urbevilles* (Oxford University Press 2008); 'Psychologising Jekyll, Demonising Hyde: The Strange Case of Criminal Responsibility' (2010) 4 Criminal Law & Philosophy 109

[15] Cf. DFID, *Political Economy. How to Note* (July 2009) setting out a similar understanding of political economy as ideas, institutions, and interests for the purposes of distribution of foreign aid at <https://www.odi.org/sites/odi.org.uk/files/odi-assets/events-documents/3501.pdf>.

[16] Lacey, *In Search of Responsibility* (n. 2) 3.

As such, concepts of responsibility play a key role in both coordinating patterns of criminalization (by, e.g. standardizing tests for the attribution of liability) and in legitimating the social functions of the criminal law. Methodologically this approach thus challenges the dominant approach to analysing criminal responsibility which is normative and ahistorical.[17] In its place Lacey sets out an institutional approach, which argues that the reception of particular concepts of responsibility into the criminal law is always mediated through particular institutional frameworks (the 'institutional conditions of existence') and the practical and normative tasks which are performed by concepts of responsibility.[18]

While this is an inevitable simplification of a complex and sophisticated argument, rather than setting out more of the substance of that argument here, I want to focus on how Lacey deploys the concept of political economy. Broadly speaking, political economy is the theoretical framework which is used to show how *ideas* about responsibility were shaped by (and shaped) *interests* and *institutions*.[19] In the chapter on ideas, Lacey shows how different 'ideational frameworks' have coexisted in moral and legal thought for understanding criminal responsibility.[20] These different conceptions—capacity, character, outcome, and risk, respectively—each imply (to a greater or lesser degree) different understandings of the relationship between the individual and the state and are shaped by broader intellectual and cultural contexts. They are, moreover, not mutually exclusive, but can be shown to have coexisted, in different combinations, in English criminal law. These are, then, in a sense, 'ideal types', reconstructed from a close reading of patterns of responsibility attribution in English criminal law over the period since the eighteenth century. While one of Lacey's aims here is simply to demonstrate that the concept of criminal responsibility has a history, the larger aim is to show how the emergence and salience of particular conceptions (or combinations) of criminal responsibility are shaped by interests and institutions. Interests are understood in terms of the impact of political, social, and economic groups on the shaping of the law and the structure of the patterns of interest and power over time. Institutions explores features of the criminal justice process such as the development of the criminal trial, the formalization of the law of evidence, professional education and training of lawyers and judges, and the introduction of law reporting, arguing that these were necessary conditions to the adoption of a general conception of capacity responsibility.[21] The overall argument thus aims to link developments in doctrine to institutions, and to broader social, political, and economic transformations. She argues

[17] See e.g. Victor Tadros, *Criminal Responsibility* (Oxford University Press 2005).

[18] Lacey, 'Institutionalizing Responsibility' (2013) Jurisprudence 1, 3. See also Lacey, *In Search of Responsibility* (n. 3) 12–13 and Farmer, *Making the Modern Criminal Law* (n. 4) ch. 1.

[19] See e.g. Lacey, *In Search of Responsibility* (n. 3) 135: 'Legal doctrines and ideas may have a certain independent force . . . but the larger intellectual, institutional and interest-based environment has a decisive bearing on the changing shape of legal concepts over time.'

[20] Lacey, *In Search of Responsibility* (n. 3) ch. 3, at 25.

[21] Lacey, *In Search of Responsibility* (n. 3) chs 3 and 4.

that there was a broad movement from character to capacity responsibility over the course of the nineteenth century which was a consequence of a combination of changed beliefs about agency and changes in the institutional structure of the criminal justice system, while also being linked to an emerging democratic culture which placed a new value on democracy and equal citizenship.[22] Political economy on this account goes beyond identifying a 'particular form of capitalism' (such as liberal or neo-liberal capitalism) and requires further attention to the legal institutions, the social structure (more or less horizontal or coordinated) and political systems and the role that criminal law then plays in stabilizing, coordinating, and legitimizing structures of power in those societies.[23]

***

We can now note some of the key features of Lacey's approach. In general, it is a highly nuanced approach that builds on the work of institutional economists and applies their analysis of the different varieties of capitalism to the area of criminal law, by seeking to show specific linkages (or combinations of linkages) between legal doctrines and institutions and forms of social, political, and economic organization. It is also an explicitly comparative methodology, both historically and between jurisdictions, that aims to systematize while simultaneously recognizing difference. As noted above, one of Lacey's targets is thus the kind of generalizing claims made by some criminologists about 'neo-liberal penality' or the 'penal state' to analyse particular institutional configurations and their relationships with penal practices.[24] However, her approach is also critical of claims which are often made in normative criminal law theory which proceed on the assumption of an ideal 'liberal democratic state'.[25] Lacey argues that there can be no such thing: it is necessary to ask which kind of state, as there is a huge difference between the coordinated market economies of northern Europe and the liberal market economy of the United States, or indeed between liberal market economies in the United States and the United Kingdom.[26] And not only is it important to distinguish between different kinds of state, but also to explore the different kinds of institutional constraints on policy-making and the ways that different kinds of political institution can shape the political process. In a coordinated market economy greater

[22] Ibid., ch. 5 esp, at 138–45 and 162–6. See also 'The Resurgence of Character' in Antony Duff and Stuart Green, *Philosophical Foundations of Criminal Law* (Oxford University Press 2011); 'What Constitutes Criminal Law?' in Antony Duff et al. (eds), *The Constitution of the Criminal Law* (Oxford University Press 2013).

[23] Lacey, *In Search of Responsibility* (n. 3) 169.

[24] See e.g. the agenda for research comparing Germany, the United States, and the United Kingdom set out in Lacey, 'Rule of Law and the Political Economy of Criminalisation' (n. 2) 359.

[25] See e.g. Antony Duff, *The Realm of the Criminal Law* (Oxford University Press 2018) ch. 1.

[26] Lacey, 'Rule of Law and the Political Economy of Criminalisation' (n. 2). See also Arlie Loughnan, *Self, Others and the State. Relations of Criminal Responsibility* (Cambridge University Press 2020) ch. 1.

institutional and economic resources are devoted to building consensus, and the political process is less 'winner takes all'. It is thus central to Lacey's argument that a theory of criminal law is not merely a matter of creating an 'ideal' theory, but of theorizing criminal law as it actually functions in different kinds of liberal states, identifying its distinctive features and exploring the political, social, and economic factors which have shaped these.

This approach also puts the question of power at the heart of its analysis, by asking whose interests the criminal law serves. This is primarily understood in terms of economic power, but the focus on interests means that this can also be understood more broadly. This can be seen, for example, in the so-called 'resurgence of character', where recent developments in 'character responsibility' are persuasively linked to the political manipulation of new insecurities about migration and race, on the one hand, and the identification of new forms of dangerous and social threatening criminals, on the other.[27] It is also, crucially, explored in the area of gender, where Lacey has explored the ways in which women's agency has been denied or distorted in criminal law doctrine and practices.[28] Criminal law thus does not serve or reflect economic interests directly but equally neither can it be seen (as much liberal criminal law theory would have it) as being neutral between interests. The fact that criminal law is disproportionately enforced against particular groups or social classes or ethnic communities—the practice of criminalization—must be central to any attempt to build a theory of the criminal law.[29] This focus on power also informs the normative focus of Lacey's work. If criminal law excludes and discriminates, the challenge is that of confronting these exclusions. This is so both in the sense that a theory of criminal law should engage with what has traditionally been excluded as not theoretically interesting or relevant, and in the related sense that the recognition of those who have been or are excluded is the necessary precursor to building a fairer and more inclusive criminal law. In Lacey's words:

> We can only think about how best to protect and pursue [the ideals of equality, legality and human rights] by trying to understand their conditions of existence, and hence the practical and political context in which we are operating.[30]

The idea of political economy plays two roles in Lacey's account, linking it to academic movements of 'law in context' and critical legal studies. On the one hand, it refers to the political and economic context in which the criminal law operates. In this sense it is an approach which locates itself in the tradition of 'law in

[27] Lacey, *In Search of Responsibility* (n. 3) ch. 5 and 'The Resurgence of Character' (n. 22).

[28] Nicola Lacey, *Unspeakable Subjects. Feminist Essays in Legal and Social Theory* (Hart Publishing 1998).

[29] Nicola Lacey, 'Historicising Criminalisation: Conceptual and Empirical Issues' (2009) 72 Modern Law Review 936; Lacey, *In Search of Responsibility* (n. 3) ch. 6

[30] Lacey, *In Search of Responsibility* (n. 3) 192.

context' studies, appealing to the understanding that law cannot be understood solely in terms of an internal doctrinal logic, but is shaped by, and shapes, social, political, and economic relations. In Lacey's work this is done specifically by reference to recent writings on varieties of capitalism, but it is also part of a broader tradition which argues that law is shaped by social context.[31] Political economy from this approach is something external to the object of study, be it criminal law or punishment—we must understand the political economy *of* criminal law, or *of* punishment, in the sense of bringing something external into the analysis. On the other hand, political economy references a tradition of critique which seeks to challenge conventional understandings of law, politics, or economy as each operating with an internal logic and as developing independently of each other.[32] This critical tradition seeks to understand both the theory and practice of law as the products of a historical process, and thereby to explore the internal contradictions of the theory and its relation to its object. This is part of longer tradition of critique of political economy inaugurated by Karl Marx in which he argued that the abstract generalizations of bourgeois political economists had to be analysed in terms of the material relations of production.[33] Thus, use of a category such as population masked the fact that 'population' comprised different social classes, different types of wage labour, and different relations of production. Law, likewise, obscured material class relations by appealing to abstract universal categories which in fact expressed and maintained the hegemony of a particular class.[34] This tradition of critique seeks in different ways to put the political back into political economy by pointing to the ideological effects of the categories of law and economy and to open up new ways of engaging with them.

Important as these are, I want to argue here that the uses of political economy as context and critique do not exhaust the ways that we might understand the relation between criminal law and political economy. Indeed, by seeing political economy only as something external to the criminal law, I will argue that we have obscured certain features of the earlier development of the criminal law—notably that the scope and function of the modern criminal law was shaped by early understandings of political economy. In the next section I shall thus go on to explore the history and development of theories of political economy in the work of Adam

[31] E.g. Philip Selznick, '"Law in Context" Revisited' (2003) 30 Journal of Legal Studies 177: '[T]he phrase 'law in context' points to the many ways legal norms and institutions are conditioned by culture and social organization.' (at 177). See now e.g. *Law and Political Economy Blog: A Manifesto* at <https://lpeblog.org/2017/11/06/law-and-political-economy-toward-a-manifesto/>.

[32] For discussion of the tradition of critique, see Emilios Christodoulidis, 'Critical Theory and the Law: Reflections on Origins, Trajectories and Conjunctures' in Christodoulidis et al., *Research Handbook in Critical Legal Theory* (Edward Elgar 2019). See also Alan W Norrie, *Crime, Reason and History. A Critical Introduction to Criminal Law* (3rd edn, Cambridge University Press 2014) ch. 1.

[33] Karl Marx, *Capital. Critique of Political Economy* (1867) (3 vols) (Penguin 1990).

[34] See e.g. Marx's critique of rights in Karl Marx, 'On the Jewish Question' in David McLellan, *Karl Marx. Selected Writings* (Oxford University Press 1977). See generally Hugh Collins, *Marxism and Law* (Oxford University Press 1982).

Smith, Jeremy Bentham, and John Stuart Mill, and their understanding of the role of criminal law.

3. Political Economy and the Criminal Law in Historical Perspective

a. Adam Smith

Modern understandings of political economy begin with Adam Smith.[35] For Smith, political economy was, as the title of his most famous work has it, the study of the 'nature and causes of the wealth of nations' or the laws governing the production and distribution of wealth.[36] These causes were not to be sought exclusively in economic rationality or practices, but in the relationships between these practices and political and legal institutions, in the sense of how the institutions contributed to or hindered the accumulation of wealth. The *Wealth of Nations* can thus be read as a wide-ranging examination of the factors that had contributed to the relative wealth of nations over time, including an account of what governments might do to contribute to current and future national prosperity. As is well known, Smith defended the idea that the pursuit of individual self-interest through the market, based on man's natural propensity to 'truck, barter, and exchange' produced the greatest prosperity.[37] Individuals in society depended on the continuing cooperation and assistance of others, but this was not achieved by design or through the benevolence of others but through the pursuit of self-interest. This gave rise to the division of labour as individuals specialized in developing their own talents and then exchanged any surplus production to satisfy their other needs. As each individual pursued their own self-interest they were 'led by an invisible hand to promote an end which was no part of his intention'—notably the general or collective welfare and prosperity.[38] Much of his work was thus devoted to explaining the growth of the division of labour, and the emergence of commercial society in terms of an emerging economic rationality. However, he also argued that progress and wealth of any society was determined by 'the nature of its laws and institutions' and that if these favoured any particular group then the development of that society towards a civilized state would be hindered.[39]

[35] I do not, of course, want to imply that Smith had no intellectual precursors, only that he was generally taken as a foundational figure for the thinkers I am discussing here. For a discussion of those precursors and the intellectual context in which Smith wrote, see Emma Rothschild, *Economic Sentiments. Adam Smith, Condorcet and the Enlightenment* (Harvard University Press 2001) ch. 1.

[36] Adam Smith, *An Inquiry into the Nature and Causes of the Wealth of Nations* (*WN*) (2 vols) (1776) (Penguin 1999).

[37] *WN*, I,ii, 117.

[38] Ibid., IV.ii.32.

[39] Ibid., I.ix.197. See also Jerry Evensky, 'The *Wealth of Nations*' in Ryan P Hanley, *Adam Smith. His Life, Thought and Legacy* (Princeton University Press 2016).

His defence of the market was thus linked to a distinctive account of the role of government and law which he described as 'a branch of the science of a legislator'.[40] Some understanding of the 'science of a legislator' can be found in the notes of his lectures on jurisprudence, delivered at the University of Glasgow in the early 1760s.[41] Smith conceived of jurisprudence as the theory of the 'general principles of law and government', with the 'four great objects of law' being justice, police, revenue, and arms—thus extending beyond questions of private law and right narrowly conceived to the production of wealth, revenue and war and conflict.[42] This had both a normative and a historical dimension, the aim being to show, on the one hand, 'the rules by which civil governments ought to be directed' and, on the other, the ways in which the laws of particular countries were prevented from achieving the ends of natural justice.[43] His account of the general principles of justice built on the moral theory developed in the *Theory of Moral Sentiments* (1759), notably his account of the impartial spectator, but in the *Lectures*, he applied his moral theory to the analysis of law. Here he analysed rights as either natural or acquired.[44] Natural rights, such as rights to life, bodily integrity, and social identity arose from social life and, if not universal, were viewed as fundamental to any kind of social relationships and could be found in most societies. Acquired rights, such as property or contracts, arose from an individual's relationships with things or with other people. These were not necessary to all social relationships—and indeed might be absent from certain kinds of society—and the extent and complexity of such rights would thus depend on the state of development of a particular society. This opened up his historical analysis as he explored the emergence of different kinds of rights and law in each of the four stages he identified in the development of society (hunter/gatherer, pastoral/nomadic, agricultural, and commercial).[45] A primary aim of government was to secure natural rights and property, without which people had 'no motive to be industrious'.[46] But beyond this he examined different ways in which

[40] *WN*, IV.ii.45.

[41] Adam Smith, *Lectures on Jurisprudence* (eds Ronald L Meek, DD Raphael, and Peter G Stein) (Liberty Fund 1982). Notes from two sets of lectures have survived. The lectures from 1762–63 are referred to as *LJ(A)*, and those from 1766 as *LJ(B)*. For broader discussions of the lectures and their place in Smith's work see David Lieberman, 'Adam Smith on Justice, Rights and Law' in Knud Haakonssen, *The Cambridge Companion to Adam Smith* (Cambridge University Press 2006); Knud Haakonssen, 'The *Lectures on Jurisprudence*' in Hanley (ed.), *Adam Smith*; Andrew Skinner, 'Adam Smith: Society and Government' in Elspeth Attwooll, *Perspectives in Jurisprudence* (University of Glasgow Press 1977).

[42] *LJ(B)* 5.

[43] *LJ(A)* i.1. See also Adam Smith, *The Theory of Moral Sentiments* (TMS) (1759) (Penguin 2009) 401–3.

[44] *LJ(B)* 8; *LJ(A)* i.12 calling these rights 'adventitious'. This latter terminology is followed by Haakonssen, 'Lectures' (n. 41) 53–6.

[45] On the four stages of society see Peter G Stein, *Legal Evolution. The Story of an Idea* (Cambridge University Press 1979) ch. 2; John Salter, 'Adam Smith on Feudalism, Commerce and Slavery' (1992) 13 History of Political Thought 219.

[46] *LJ(B)* 287. See also TMS 104: 'Justice . . . is the main pillar that upholds the whole edifice. If it is removed, the great, the immense fabric of human society . . . must in a moment crumble into atoms.'

government and laws had hindered the development of wealth and commerce, whether through the law of entails or inefficient and unjust forms of taxation, or through his famous criticisms of the corrupt practices of colonial merchants.[47] Thus, the science of a legislator aimed both to identify principles of natural justice and to integrate these with aims of government in providing security and developing wealth (that is to say, with the principles of political economy).[48]

His analysis of criminal law fitted within this general framework.[49] The primary role of criminal law was to secure justice where man's rights in his person, property, or reputation had been injured.[50] Although he understood rights in person as natural rights, the scope of these rights was wide, including not only injury to the person by some sort of physical harm or restraint, but also what he called a right to free commerce, or to do what was not detrimental to another.[51] His discussion here thus concerned some of the basic ways in which the criminal law protected the body of the person. By contrast, property rights and rights to reputation were acquired rights, and so the form and extent of protection depended on the type of social organization.[52] His discussion of these areas was thus a more critical historical examination of the different ways in which property had been protected by the criminal law depending on the type of social organization. He thus noted, for example, that while theft did not appear to merit harsh punishment according to principles of natural justice, it was in practice punished severely because of the weakness of civil government.[53] It is also important to note that the discussion of police—one of the principle objects of the law—did not include discussion of criminal law. Police, for Smith, meant the conditions for the development of wealth and so in this section of the lectures he was thus mapping out the arguments that were to become the *Wealth of Nations*. To the extent that there was a relationship between commerce and security, he argued that the 'best police for preventing crimes' is the establishment of commerce.[54] Thus, when he later moved on to consider obstacles to the improvement of commerce, amongst these was the

[47] See *LJ(B)* 285ff. The whole of Book III of *The Wealth of Nations* was devoted to this topic.

[48] His 'overriding ambition was to integrate the theory of rights with the theory of law and government' (Haakonssen, 'Lectures' (n. 41) 60).

[49] There has been little academic discussion of Smith on criminal law, and most has focused on Smith's theory of punishment rather than the substantive criminal law. For a survey see Chad Flanders, 'Adam Smith's Jurisprudence: Resentment, Punishment, Justice' in Hanley, *Adam Smith* (n. 39). See also J Ralph Lindgren, 'Adam Smith's Treatment of Criminal Law' in Robin P Malloy and Jerry Evensky (eds), *Adam Smith and the Philosophy of Law and Economics* (Kluwer 1994) 63; Chloe Kennedy, 'Declaring Crimes' (2017) 37 Oxford Journal of Legal Studies 741, 754–7; Vincenzo Ruggiero, 'On Liberty and Crime: Adam Smith and John Stuart Mill' (2009) 51 Crime, Law & Soc. Change 435.

[50] For Smith's discussion of criminal law see *LJ(A)* ii.88–180; *LJ(B)* 181–201. Smith also recognized that criminal law played a role in the protection of the state, and his discussion of forms of government included discussion of treason, though this was separate from his main discussion of criminal law. See *LJ(A)* v.54–85 and *LJ(B)* 80–6.

[51] *LJ(A)* i.12–13.

[52] *LJ(A)* ii.93.

[53] *LJ(A)* ii.147–55.

[54] *LJ(B)* 205.

criminalization of forestalling, or the withholding of goods from market in order to drive up the price.[55]

We can thus note some central features of Smith's account of the relationship between political economy and law. First, it is marked by the continual movement between normative general principles and historical evidence that was central to his jurisprudence.[56] These normative principles shaped both the concept of justice that underpinned the justification of punishment and his account of the scope of the criminal law. Second, however, the scope of the criminal law was also shaped by the general principles of political economy, putting questions of power and special interests at the heart of his legal analysis. His historical account of the development of the law demonstrated again and again the role played by powerful social elites in preserving their own interests, to show how certain laws were contrary to reason and were anachronistic survivals.[57] Smith's interest here was to show how laws which might appear to facilitate commerce in fact obstructed it, and were thus inconsistent with political economy, and how laws which might appear to protect the welfare of all might in fact favour a particular group. In relation to property he argued that:

> Civil government, so far as it is instituted for the security of property, is in reality instituted for the defence of the rich against the poor, or those who have some property against those who have none at all.[58]

Third, in doing this Smith linked liberty and commerce both in the sense that the spread of commerce developed liberty, and in that he saw the right to free commerce as an element of individual liberty.[59] This was not an uncritical defence of free trade, though, as he also drew attention to the inequalities and injustices of a commercial society. In a striking passage in the *Lectures*, for example, he notes the dulling effect of repetitive labour on the mind of the individual worker and how rich commercial nations neglect education.[60] Overall, then, this was a science of government and society that combined the idea of general principles of natural justice with an empirical understanding of the social laws governing the production of wealth.

[55] *LJ(B)* 304–5. See also *WN* Bk. IV 102–14. For discussion see Lindsay Farmer, 'Civil Order, Markets and the Intelligibility of the Criminal Law' (2020) 70 University of Toronto Law Journal 123.

[56] See *TMS*, VII, iv, 36–7

[57] *LJ(B)* 326–33; *WN* Bk. IV. See also Lieberman, 'Adam Smith' (n .41) 231.

[58] *WN*, Bk. V 302.

[59] See Skinner, 'Adam Smith' (n. 41) 213; Lieberman, 'Adam Smith' (n .41) 240.

[60] *LJ(B)* 328–30.

b. Political Economy beyond Adam Smith: Bentham and Mill

Political economy quickly became highly influential, part of the intellectual landscape of late eighteenth- and early nineteenth-century Britain. The major English universities established Chairs in political economy and a knowledge of political economy was considered essential for politicians and statesmen.[61] Going beyond this, popularizations of political economy were produced to educate working people in the laws of society, to the extent that authors of these 'moral' tracts were satirized by writers such as Dickens.[62] The important point to note here is that, notwithstanding theoretical differences between particular writers or economists, political economy had a 'taken for granted' quality that shaped virtually all thought of the era. It was understood as a 'body of speculation which formed part of the expertise required for the proper administration of the modern state'.[63] It is thus important to look at the work of both Jeremy Bentham and John Stuart Mill, well known as utilitarian philosophers who had a particular interest in, and influence on, the criminal law, but who both also wrote on political economy to explore how their understanding of political economy impacted on their thought about criminal law.

Bentham's best-known contribution to political economy was his *Defence of Usury* (1787) in which he both praised Adam Smith and took him to task for his support of legal limitations on the rates of interest that might be charged.[64] He also attempted two more systematic treatments in his *Manual of Political Economy* (1793–95) and *Institute of Political Economy* (1801–04). As Lieberman has shown, in these works Bentham largely accepted Smith's account of the 'science' (or theory) of political economy but distinguished this from the 'art' of political economy, or its practical application in legislation.[65] The 'art' was focused on the role of government in directing social conduct. In some areas of social life such as wages for labour, Bentham directly endorsed the arguments of political economy, arguing for liberty of competition.[66] In other areas, however, the science of political economy

[61] See Boyd Hilton, *The Age of Atonement. The Influence of Evangelicalism on Social and Economic Thought, 1795–1865* (Clarendon 1988) ch. 2; David Eastwood, 'Tories and Markets: Britain 1800–1850' in Mark Bevir and Frank Trentmann, *Markets in Historical Contexts. Ideas and Politics in the Modern World* (Cambridge University Press 2004).

[62] Geoffrey Searle, *Morality and the Market in Victorian Britain* (Oxford University Press 1998) 36–43 on the popularizations of political economy.

[63] David Lieberman, 'Economy and Polity in Bentham's Science of Legislation' in Stefan Collini et al., *Economy, Polity and Society: British Intellectual History 1750–1950* (Cambridge University Press 2000) 110.

[64] This has now been reprinted, together with Bentham's other writings on political economy in Michael Quinn, *Writings on Political Economy Vol. I. The Collected Works of Jeremy Bentham* (Oxford University Press 2016).

[65] Lieberman, 'Economy and Polity' (n. 63) 111–12. The argument presented here draws heavily on Lieberman. See also Elie Halévy, *The Growth of Philosophic Radicalism* (Beacon Press 1955) 107–8.

[66] *The Rationale of Reward* (1825), discussed in Lieberman, 'Economy and Polity' (n. 63) 112.

was only one of a number of factors to be taken into consideration by the legislator. Bentham's own legislative science was not derived from political economy, but from his utilitarian psychology and philosophy which saw the role of the legislator as that of promoting general happiness, through the promotion of the subsidiary ends of subsistence, abundance, equality and, above all, security—and the 'art' of political economy sat within this broader framework.[67] Security meant the maintenance of a stable social order so that individuals could pursue their own interests, as they conceived them. As a result, he advocated social institutions designed to give individuals incentives to act so as to promote the general happiness, which might sometimes require that the promotion of wealth be sacrificed in favour of other ends. This was the project developed in the *Introduction to the Principles of Morals and Legislation*, which set out the basis for a code of criminal laws.[68] It should, though, be noted that his challenge to false or mistaken justifications of criminal laws on occasion drew on arguments from political economy—as with the critique of criminal laws on usury where these interfered with free competition.[69] Overall, though, his project was a broader 'utilitarian reconstruction of public institutions' in which the science of political economy might be utilized for insight into certain spheres of conduct.[70]

The distinction between the art and science of political economy was also central to John Stuart Mill's work on political economy. For Mill the 'science' of political economy was empirical—discovering the internal laws of a phenomenon—while the 'art' was addressed to designing a system of practical rules of conduct to promote general welfare. This in turn was a component of a liberal utilitarian 'art of life' aimed at preserving security, subsistence, and individuality.[71] These rules of conduct, then, for Mill, were not science, but were the result of science:

> Political economy does not instruct how to make a nation rich; but whoever would be qualified to judge of the means of making a nation rich must first be a political economist.[72]

He discussed these rules, or the functions of government, in Book V of his massive *Principles of Political Economy*, first published in 1848.[73] Against those who saw the

[67] See Ross Harrison, *Bentham* (Routledge 1983) 244–62.

[68] Jeremy Bentham, *Introduction to the Principles of Morals and Legislation* (Clarendon 1996) (ed. JH Burns and HLA Hart).

[69] These were in fact repealed in 1854. Though note Lieberman's point that Bentham's argument against laws on usury did not really engage political economy ('Economy and Polity' (n. 63) 117–18).

[70] Lieberman, 'Economy and Polity' (n. 63) 117.

[71] See Jonathan Riley, 'Mill's Political Economy: Ricardian Science and Liberal Utilitarian Art' in John Skorupski, *The Cambridge Companion to Mill* (Cambridge University Press 1998) 294–6. See also John Stuart Mill, 'On the Definition of Political Economy' (1836) London and Westminster Review (October) 1, 3–4; 'System of Logic' in *Collected Works vol. VIII* (Routledge & Kegan Paul 1974) 944–5.

[72] Mill, 'Definition' (n. 71) 4.

[73] *Principles of Political Economy* (*POPE*) (ed. WJ Ashley) (7th edn, Longmans, Green and Co. 1909) at >https://oll.libertyfund.org/titles/101>. He was clear that the question of the role of

functions of government as limited only to the protection of person and property, he defended a broad conception:

> The ends of government are as comprehensive as those of the social union. They consist of all the good, and all the immunity from evil, which the existence of government can be made, either directly or indirectly.[74]

He began by distinguishing between those functions of government that were necessary and those that were merely optional. Necessary functions were those such as taxation, maintaining the security of person and property, and the administration of justice and police.[75] However, he also noted the essential importance of the 'moral influences of the law', such as its ability to encourage integrity and trustworthiness or discourage idleness and prodigality.[76] Optional functions of government were discussed in terms of the grounds and limits of the principle of laissez-faire, with his starting point being that 'laissez-faire . . . should be the general practice: every departure from it, unless required by some great good, is a certain evil'.[77] This, then, operated on the basis of an understanding of the market as self-regulating and which could provide more effectively than government in all but a limited set of circumstances. In practice this meant that 'authoritative interference' by government should be limited as it amounted to the infringement of liberty. Instead he favoured measures which would help individuals to develop practical experience and judgment (or character) so as to pursue their own interests.[78] He finally went on to discuss situations where law or legal intervention might still be necessary. Here he argued that this might be necessary for the purposes of education, or to protect the collective interests of a particular group, for example by setting a maximum number of working hours, or where the interests of government went beyond purely economic considerations, as was the case with colonization which 'involves the future and permanent interests of civilisation itself'.[79] He concluded:

> It may be said generally, that anything which it is desirable should be done for the general interests of mankind or of future generations, or for the present interests of those members of the community who require external aid, but which is not of

government, which he discussed here, should be distinguished from the constitution, or construction, of government (Bk. V, ch. 1 § 1 at <https://oll.libertyfund.org/titles/101#Mill_0199_1388>.

[74] *POPE*, Bk. V, ch. 2 §2 at <https://oll.libertyfund.org/titles/101#Mill_0199_1415>.

[75] *POPE*, Bk. V, ch. 1 §3 at <https://oll.libertyfund.org/titles/101#Mill_0199_1399>.

[76] *POPE*, Bk. V, ch. 8 §3 at <https://oll.libertyfund.org/titles/101#Mill_0199_1559>.

[77] *POPE*, Bk. V, ch. 11 §7 at <https://oll.libertyfund.org/titles/101#Mill_0199_1654>. See also the discussion in Paul Johnson, 'Market Disciplines' in Peter Mandler (ed.), *Liberty and Authority in Victorian Britain* (Oxford University Press 2006)

[78] *POPE*, Bk. V, ch. 11 §5 at <https://oll.libertyfund.org/titles/101#Mill_0199_1649>.

[79] *POPE*, Bk. V, ch. 11, §8–14.

> a nature to remunerate individuals or associations for undertaking it, is in itself a suitable thing to be undertaken by government.[80]

Criminal law was part of this general framework, though his scattered remarks have also to be read in the light of the more general framework for the constitution of liberty set out in works such as *On Liberty* (1863).[81] This, as is well known, was framed in terms of the harm principle: 'that the only purpose for which power can be rightfully exercised over any member of a civilized community, against his will, is to prevent harm to others'.[82] A similar principle was expressed, indeed, in the very last sentence of the *Principles*:

> It is the proper end of government [to take] such measures as shall cause the energies now spent by mankind in injuring one another, or in protecting themselves against injury, to be turned to the legitimate employment of the human faculties, that of compelling the powers of nature to be more and more subservient to physical and moral good.[83]

However, a closer reading also shows how Mill saw the principles of political economy having an impact on the scope of the criminal law. The *Principles*, for example, contained a detailed discussion of the question of bankruptcy and the imprisonment of debtors, which was a major concern in Victorian Britain.[84] Here Mill was highly critical of moves to relax laws around the imprisonment of debtors, which he characterized as being motivated by concerns of humanity rather than justice. He argued that to remove the possibility of all imprisonment for debt would produce demoralizing effects, encouraging fraud and embezzlement, because the consequences of bankruptcy were insufficiently severe. He concluded that 'It is the business of law to prevent wrong-doing, and not simply to patch up the consequences of it when it has been committed'.[85] Mill then went on to discuss other kinds of interventions by government in the market, described as economically injurious acts of governance or interferences based on erroneous theories.[86] His examples here, following in the footsteps of Smith and Bentham, included the criminal prohibitions on usury, regulating the price of food, and workers

[80] *POPE*, Bk. V, ch. 11, §15 at <https://oll.libertyfund.org/titles/101#Mill_0199_1697>.

[81] John Stuart Mill, *On Liberty and Other Essays* (Oxford University Press 1991). It is also worth noting that he did not develop a typology of rights such as those developed by Smith and Bentham.

[82] Ibid., 14. For discussion see Farmer, *Making the Modern Criminal Law* (n. 4) 48–55.

[83] *POPE*, Bk. V, ch. 11, §16 at <https://oll.libertyfund.org/titles/101#Mill_0199_1699>.

[84] *POPE*, Bk. V, ch. 9 §8. See generally V Markham Lester, *Victorian Insolvency: Bankruptcy, Imprisonment for Debt and Company Winding-up in Nineteenth-Century England* (Oxford University Press 1995) ch. 3 arguing that the concern was less that entrepreneurs might be discouraged from taking risks than the potential losses to creditors from fraudulent bankruptcy.

[85] *POPE*, Bk. V, ch. 9 §8 at <https://oll.libertyfund.org/titles/101#Mill_0199_1596>.

[86] *POPE*, Bk. V, ch. 10.

combinations, all of which were characterized as inappropriate laws.[87] It is also significant to note that Mill addressed the general theme of the relationship between the doctrine of free trade (political economy) and the principle of individual liberty in *On Liberty*, in a passage that is often overlooked.[88] He argued that these rested on different foundations, as restraints on trade could be justified if they promoted the social end (the accumulation of wealth) for which they were designed, while political liberty was understood in more absolute terms as a right of the individual to be free from government interference.[89] On Mill's account, then, most questions of the limits of free trade did not engage principles of individual liberty, and government might justifiably intervene in economic relations if justified by the principles of political economy. In general terms this recognized a distinction between the sphere of economic activity, governed by principles of political economy, and a broader idea of individual liberty—reflecting the distinction between the science of political economy and the broader art of utilitarian government.

***

What emerges from this brief survey is a nuanced picture of the theory of political economy and its relevance to understandings of the role of government and to the criminal law in the writings of Smith, Bentham, and Mill. Notwithstanding some differences between the three, it is possible to identify some important continuities and common themes. The first important theme is their understanding of the scope of political economy and the underlying conception of society that this was based on. Political economy as a science was understood as relating to the production and distribution of wealth. This, however, was emphatically not seen as coterminous with all social activity. The production of wealth was socially important, with benefits for the whole of society, but the market (or commercial activity) was understood to operate within a socially restricted sphere and according to its own logic. The theory of political economy was thus to be a guide for the legislator when deciding whether or not to regulate certain spheres of social activity. While this led all three to criticize certain laws for obstructing commercial activity, all were vocal supporters of the need for law to protect the rights of the individual and the security of society. This leads to the second theme, which was the recognition and centrality of the role of government. While the terminology shifted, between Smith's science of a legislator and Bentham and Mill's art of legislation, there was

[87] See also Kennedy, 'Declaring Crimes' (n. 49) 753–4 and 760–3. It is striking that Sir James Fitzjames Stephen used the same examples when discussing offences against trade and labour. See JF Stephen, *History of the Criminal Law of England* (3 vols) (Macmillan 1883) III, ch.XXX.

[88] *On Liberty*, ch. V Applications. See also Riley, 'Mill's Political Economy' (n. 71) 317.

[89] Cf. *POPE*, Bk. V ch. 11 condemning 'authoritative interferences' by government. See also Jon P Parry, 'Liberalism and Liberty' in Mandler (ed.), *Liberty and Authority* (n. 77) arguing that political liberalism was concerned with integrating different sections of the community, checking vested interests, and the development of character.

a common understanding that knowledge of the laws of political economy only provided the raw material for the legislator, and that this was only something to be taken into account in the framing of practical rules. The role of government was not necessarily limited by political economy; as Mill commented, 'the ends of government are as comprehensive as those of the social union'.[90] The factors governing intervention in different areas might be different. All three drew attention to areas which government had regulated on the basis of erroneous understanding of the commercial benefits of certain laws and attacked corrupt laws which served the interests of particular groups, but they also recognized that there might be pragmatic reasons for government to intervene in the market for reasons of security, as well as the existence of factors—be it justice or utility—that stood outside political economy and which overrode its ends. This sheds important light on the idea of government in the age of laissez-faire and its relationship to political liberalism. Laissez-faire, at least for these theorists, was not the same as neglect, as the proper understanding of political economy left space for active government. It is also important to note that economic and political liberalism were not identical as someone like Mill was careful to distinguish between the different scope of political and economic liberty.[91]

This leads to the third point, which is the question of the relationship between political economy and utilitarianism, particularly as these two theories understood the scope and function of criminal law in society. For Bentham and Mill there was a clear difference between the two: the science of political economy might contribute to legislation where it was appropriate for government to intervene, but utilitarianism as a moral philosophy was broader in scope (and of wider social application). Notwithstanding this, the two theories interacted with each other, not least in marking out reasonably distinct spheres of application—or at least seeing the market as a distinct sphere which operated according to its own laws. This had implications for the criminal law in the sense that traditional laws regulating market conduct and prices were seen as obstacles to free trade. This fitted with the gradual re-ordering of criminal law in the course of the nineteenth century to be primarily focused on the protection of individual interests.[92] There was, though, a clear affinity between the two theories. Both took individuals and their interests as the starting point for understanding social conduct—though, as Mill was at pains to point out, it was not the case that 'any political economist was ever so absurd as to suppose that mankind are really thus constituted, but because this is the mode in which science must necessarily proceed'.[93] Society was understood as being composed of individuals who in different spheres of social activity pursue their own

[90] See n. 69 above.

[91] See the more detailed discussion in the essays in Mandler (ed.), *Liberty and Authority* (n. 77)

[92] See Farmer, *Making the Modern Criminal Law* (n. 4) ch. 3.

[93] Mill, 'Definition' (n. 71) 13. See also the discussion of Bentham in Lieberman, 'Economy and Polity' (n. 63) 118–24.

interests—and socially complex conduct could be reduced to the interaction of self-interested individuals. The self-interested, acquisitive, economic actor might pursue those interests in a slightly different way from the pleasure seeking individual of utilitarian theory, but both are understood as rational and calculating—and the problem of government intervention was understood in terms of when individuals could be trusted to recognize their own true interests. Both then were models of individual conduct, which enabled the legislator to frame general rules to govern that conduct and saw the role of government as being centrally concerned with building character through the moral influences of the criminal law.

4. Conclusion

> To give a systematic account of criminal responsibility in modern English law is . . . to theorize a concept which is strongly inflected by a particular political, intellectual, and institutional history.[94]

My argument in this chapter has been that political economy is not merely the context in which modern conceptions of criminal responsibility and criminal law have developed but is in fact central to the intellectual and institutional history invoked by Lacey. Theories of political economy as a new way of thinking about society spread rapidly in the early nineteenth century and shaped thought about the role of government and the criminal law. On this approach, as we have seen, political economy is not 'external' to law or government—a 'context' which shapes legal rules—but played a key role in the making of the institutions of law and government. Political economy was framed as a 'science' which should inform the legislator in the formulation of practical rules—as well as providing a valuable resource for the critique of inefficient and corrupt practices.

In concluding, the first point that I want to make is that this is not something that should be regarded as of merely historical interest. While it is unquestionably important, in terms of our understanding of the historical development of the modern criminal law, to reconstruct the place and impact of theories of political economy, this is an argument that also has a broader significance for our understanding of the relationship between law and society. Theories of political economy were not only foundational to the making of modern legal institutions, the criminal law amongst them, but also to our understanding of modern society.[95] Central to this was the fundamental distinction that we still live with—between the market

[94] Lacey, *In Search of Responsibility* (n. 3) 201.

[95] See e.g. Patrick S Atiyah, *The Rise and Fall of Freedom of Contract* (Oxford University Press 1979) Pt II; Paul Johnson, *Making the Market. Victorian Origins of Corporate Capitalism* (Cambridge University Press 2010).

and the rest of society.[96] The market was a dimension of society, but was defined by the absence of institutional structures. It was no longer understood as a particular location where buying and selling took place but was conceived of as a generalized form of social relation with its own laws and rationality. This then underpinned, as we have seen above, understandings of the role and function of government. For the criminal law it has clear implications for thinking about criminalization: the proper scope of the criminal law is, at least in part, defined by the boundaries of the self-regulating market. It also sheds light on the relationship between individualism and the criminal law for while it complicates the easy assumption that there was a relationship between *homo economicus* and the responsible individual of criminal law, it opens up important questions about ways of thinking about society in terms of individuals and their interests. The question of the scope of political economy is, to be sure, one that has a complex history. Political economy had its contemporary critics, from Carlyle to Marx, and we should not assume that theoretical writings automatically translated into practice. The principles identified by those such as Smith and Mill frequently led to harsh and exploitative practices. Equally, the history of the market and its regulation by criminal law in the nineteenth century is a complex one, and it is clear that legal regulations did not always match the ideals defended by the theorists and promoters of political economy.[97] However, that does not detract from the need to understand the place that the market occupied in the modern social imagination to engage with its significance for all areas of the law.

This kind of work requires precisely the kind of political, intellectual, and institutional history that Lacey has argued for in her sustained engagement with, and critique of, an analytical jurisprudence that neglects historical and institutional dimensions of law.[98] I have tried to show in this chapter how the potential resources for this kind of institutional jurisprudence can be found in the work of theorists such as Smith, Bentham, and Mill. For Adam Smith, the role of criminal law was already to be seen within a different kind of jurisprudence focused on 'the general principles of law and government'.[99] Smith, Bentham, and Mill's work sought to develop an understanding not only of the market, but also of the relationship of government to the market and the rest of society. Their understanding of jurisprudence can be characterized by their attention to institutions and government as well as to normative concepts such as justice and liberty. What this suggests is that the kind of institutional jurisprudence championed by Lacey can be further developed by attending to the history of government and criminal law in this tradition.

[96] Charles Taylor, *Modern Social Imaginaries* (Duke University Press 2003).
[97] Searle, *Markets and Morality* (n. 62).
[98] Lacey, *In Search of Responsibility* (n. 3) ch. 6; 'Institutionalising Responsibility'.
[99] *LJ(B)* 5.

Her work has played a key role in raising these questions and, hopefully, as we move forward, in renewing interest in these neglected traditions of thought.

Bibliography

Atiyah, PS, *The Rise and Fall of Freedom of Contract* (Oxford University Press 1979)

Bentham, J, *Writings on Political Economy* (2 vols) (ed. M Quinn) (Oxford University Press 2016 and 2019)

Bentham, J, *Introduction to the Principles of Morals and Legislation* (ed. JH Burns and HLA Hart) (Oxford 1996)

Christodoulidis, E, 'Critical Theory and the Law: Reflections on Origins, Trajectories and Conjunctures' in Christodoulidis et al., *Research Handbook in Critical Legal Theory* (Edward Elgar 2019)

Collins, H, *Marxism and Law* (Oxford University Press 1982)

de Giorgi, A, *Re-Thinking the Political Economy of Punishment. Perspectives on Post-Fordism and Penal Politics* (Routledge 2006)

Duff, RA, *The Realm of the Criminal Law* (Oxford University Press 2018)

Eastwood, D 'Tories and Markets: Britain 1800–1850' in M Bevir and F Trentmann, *Markets in Historical Contexts. Ideas and Politics in the Modern World* (Cambridge University Press 2004)

Evensky, J, 'The *Wealth of Nations*' in RP Hanley, *Adam Smith. His Life, Thought and Legacy* (Princeton University Press 2016)

Farmer, L, 'Civil Order, Markets and the Intelligibility of the Criminal Law' (2020) 70 University of Toronto Law Journal 123

Farmer, L, *Making the Modern Criminal Law. Criminalization and Civil Order* (Oxford University Press 2016)

Flanders, C, 'Adam Smith's Jurisprudence: Resentment, Punishment, Justice' in RP Hanley (ed.), *Adam Smith* (Princeton University Press 2016)

Gallo, Z, 'Punishment, Authority and Political Economy: Italian Challenges to Western Punitiveness' (2015) 17 Punishment & Society 598

Garland, D, *The Culture of Control. Crime and Social Order in Contemporary Society* (Oxford University Press 2001)

Haakonssen, K, 'The *Lectures on Jurisprudence*' in RP Hanley, *Adam Smith. His Life, Thought and Legacy* (Princeton University Press 2016)

Halévy, E, *The Growth of Philosophic Radicalism* (Beacon Press 1955)

Hall, PA and Soskice, D, *Varieties of Capitalism: The Institutional Foundations of Comparative Advantage* (Oxford University Press 2001)

Harrison, R, *Bentham* (Routledge 1983)

Hilton, B, *The Age of Atonement. The Influence of Evangelicalism on Social and Economic Thought, 1795–1865* (Clarendon 1988)

Johnson, P, *Making the Market. Victorian Origins of Corporate Capitalism* (Cambridge University Press 2010)

Johnson, P, 'Market Disciplines' in P Mandler, (ed.), *Liberty and Authority in Victorian Britain* (Oxford University Press 2006)

Kennedy, C 'Declaring Crimes' (2017) 37 Oxford Journal of Legal Studies 741

Lacey, N, *In Search of Responsibility. Ideas, Interests and Institutions* (Oxford University Press 2016)

Lacey, N, 'The Rule of Law and the Political Economy of Criminalisation: An Agenda for Research' (2013) 15 Punishment & Society 349

Lacey, N, 'What Constitutes Criminal Law?' in RA Duff et al. (eds), *The Constitution of the Criminal Law* (Oxford University Press 2013)

Lacey, N, 'The Resurgence of Character' in RA Duff and S Green, *Philosophical Foundations of Criminal Law* (Oxford University Press 2011)

Lacey, N, 'American Imprisonment in Comparative Perspective' (2010) 139 Daedalus 102

Lacey, N, 'Psychologising Jekyll, Demonising Hyde: The Strange Case of Criminal Responsibility' (2010) 4 Criminal Law & Philosophy 109

Lacey, N, 'Historicising Criminalisation: Conceptual and Empirical Issues' (2009) 72 Modern Law Review 936

Lacey, N, *The Prisoners' Dilemma. Political Economy and Punishment in Contemporary Democracies* (Cambridge University Press 2008)

Lacey, N, *Women, Crime and Character: From Moll Flanders to Tess of the D'Urbevilles* (Oxford University Press 2008)

Lacey, N, 'In Search of the Responsible Subject: History, Philosophy and the Social Sciences in Criminal Law Theory' (2001) 64 Modern Law Review 350

Lacey, N, 'Responsibility and Modernity in Criminal Law' (2001) 9 Journal of Political Philosophy 249

Lacey, N, *Unspeakable Subjects. Feminist Essays in Legal and Social Theory* (Hart Publishing 1998)

Lacey, N and Soskice, D, 'Crime Punishment and Segregation in the United States: the Paradox of Local Democracy' (2015) 17 Punishment & Society 454

Lester, VM, *Victorian Insolvency: Bankruptcy, Imprisonment for Debt and Company Winding-up in Nineteenth-Century England* (Oxford University Press 1995)

Lieberman, D, 'Adam Smith on Justice, Rights and Law' in K Haakonssen, *The Cambridge Companion to Adam Smith* (Cambridge University Press 2006)

Lieberman, D, 'Economy and Polity in Bentham's Science of Legislation' in S Collini et al., *Economy, Polity and Society: British Intellectual History 1750–1950* (Cambridge University Press 2000)

Lindgren, JR, 'Adam Smith's Treatment of Criminal Law' in RP Malloy and J Evensky (eds), *Adam Smith and the Philosophy of Law and Economics* (Kluwer 1994)

Loughnan, A, *Self, Others and the State. Relations of Criminal Responsibility* (Cambridge University Press 2020)

Marx, K, *Capital. Critique of Political Economy* (1867) (3 vols) (Penguin 1990)

McLellan, D, *Karl Marx. Selected Writings* (Oxford University Press 1977)

Mill, JS, *On Liberty and Other Essays* (Oxford University Press 1991)

Mill, JS, *System of Logic*, in *Collected Works vol.VIII* (Routledge & Kegan Paul 1974)

Mill, JS, 'On the Definition of Political Economy' (1836) London and Westminster Review (October) 1

Mill, JS, *Principles of Political Economy* (John W Parker 1848)

Norrie, AW, *Crime, Reason and History. A Critical Introduction to Criminal Law* (3rd edn, Cambridge University Press 2014)

Parry, JP, 'Liberalism and Liberty' in P Mandler, (ed.), *Liberty and Authority in Victorian Britain* (Oxford University Press 2006)

Quinn, M, *Writings on Political Economy Vol.I. The Collected Works of Jeremy Bentham* (Oxford University Press 2016)

Riley, J, 'Mill's Political Economy: Ricardian Science and Liberal Utilitarian Art' in J Skorupski, *The Cambridge Companion to Mill* (Cambridge University Press 1998)

Rothschild, E, *Economic Sentiments. Adam Smith, Condorcet and the Enlightenment* (Harvard University Press 2001)
Ruggiero, V, 'On Liberty and Crime: Adam Smith and John Stuart Mill' (2009) 51 Crime, Law & Social Change 435
Salter, J, 'Adam Smith on Feudalism, Commerce and Slavery' (1992) 13 History of Political Thought 219
Searle, G *Morality and the Market in Victorian Britain* (Oxford University Press 1998)
Selznick, P, '"Law in Context" Revisited' (2003) 30 Journal of Legal Studies 177
Skinner, A 'Adam Smith: Society and Government' in E Attwooll, *Perspectives in Jurisprudence* (University of Glasgow Press 1977)
Smith, A, *The Theory of Moral Sentiments* (TMS)(1759)(Penguin 2009)
Smith, KJM, *Lawyers, Legislators and Theorists. Developments in English Criminal Jurisprudence, 1800–1957* (Oxford University Press 1998)
Smith, A, *An Inquiry into the Nature and Causes of the Wealth of Nations* (*WN*) (2 vols) (1776) (Harmondsworth 1999)
Stein, PG, *Legal Evolution. The Story of an Idea* (Cambridge University Press 1979)
Stephen, JF, *History of the Criminal Law of England* (3 vols) (Macmillan 1883)
Tadros, V, *Criminal Responsibility* (Oxford University Press 2005)
Taylor, C, *Modern Social Imaginaries* (Duke University Press 2003)
Wacquant, L, 'Deadly Symbiosis: When Ghetto and Prison Meet and Mesh' in D Garland (ed), *Mass Imprisonment in the United States: Social Causes and Consequences* (Sage 2001)
Wiener, M, *Reconstructing the Criminal. Culture, Law and Policy in England, 1830–1914* (Cambridge University Press 1990)
Young, J, *The Exclusive Society. Social Exclusion, Crime and Difference in Late Modernity* (Sage 1999)

10
Punishment and Comparative Political Economy
An Exposition and Critique

David Garland

1. Introduction[1]

This chapter is an exposition and critical assessment of Nicola Lacey's work on punishment and comparative political economy. This project, which Niki has been pursuing for more than a decade now, has made her a leading figure in the sociology of punishment and comparative penology—an achievement that is all the more remarkable considering that punishment and political economy is only one strand in the Lacey oeuvre, which includes books and articles in the philosophy of punishment; criminal law theory; the history of criminal responsibility; histories of law's depictions of women; feminist and communitarian theory; comparative work on criminal justice in Germany and the United Kingdom; and a brilliant, beautifully written biography of legal philosopher HLA Hart. My aim in this chapter is to trace the trajectory of Lacey's work in this specific field, describe how it has developed, engage with it critically, and then sum up its achievement.

The first results of her thinking in this field were published in 2008 in *The Prisoners' Dilemma*[2] where she introduced the 'varieties of capitalism' (VoC) framework as a basis for explaining penal system development and variation. The book begins by observing a widespread transformation of penal practice in the period since the 1970s, with policy in many nations moving in a punitive, populist direction. According to Lacey, the fundamental cause of this transformation was the collapse of Fordism and the emergence of the knowledge economy, a technology regime change that affected all the developed industrial nations. But she insists that this widespread change was experienced and managed differently by

[1] David Garland is Arthur T Vanderbilt Professor of Law and Professor of Sociology at New York University.

[2] Nicola Lacey, *The Prisoners' Dilemma: Political Economy and Punishment in Contemporary Democracies* (Cambridge University Press 2008).

David Garland, *Punishment and Comparative Political Economy* In: *On Crime, Society, and Responsibility in the Work of Nicola Lacey.* Edited by: Iyiola Solanke, Oxford University Press (2021).
DOI: 10.1093/oso/9780198852681.003.0011

different nations—these varied patterns of adjustment reflecting one or other of the varieties of capitalism identified by the VoC framework.

VoC is an institutionalist theory of comparative political economy. Originally focused on differences in production regimes and labour market institutions—and on the extent to which these regimes were 'coordinated'—the theory was later expanded to embrace differences in welfare state regimes and in political systems. In *The Prisoners' Dilemma*, Lacey leaned on the early version of VoC theory and pointed to the likely impact of coordinated production regimes on patterns of punishment. But in subsequent work, she stresses the different political institutions associated with the two varieties of capitalism, pointing to the moderating penological effects of proportional representation and coalition politics in contrast to the more punitive effects of first-past-the-post majoritarian systems.

The Prisoners' Dilemma is a work of comparative penology, seeking to explain variation across national penal systems. But beginning in 2010, Lacey's work began to focus on the specific issue of 'American penal exceptionalism'—that is the question of why US rates of imprisonment are so much higher than those of other nations, including other nations with 'liberal market economies', minimal welfare states, and majoritarian voting systems. And although she continues to locate her work within the VoC problematic, her new focus is on the impact of America's weak political parties, its radically decentralized polity, and home ownership—which, she argues, sharply limits redistributive politics and militates against an inclusive penal policy.

In this body of work, Lacey is, I think, trying to do several things. *First*, she is seeking to move away from generalized accounts of penal change towards a more differentiated analysis that acknowledges persistent national differences in punishment and in political economy. Against the claim that there is a single trajectory, with penal systems being transformed by the effects of some generalized development (such as late modernity, a culture of control, governing through crime, neoliberalism, or whatever), Lacey insists that the institutional configurations of specific nations shape the impact of global forces—and that these configurations approximate to one or other of two basic models. *Second*, Lacey argues for a theory of the middle range, focused on how specific institutional ensembles and national histories generate national differences that are reproduced over time. Her concern is to fill in what she calls the 'explanatory space' between macro-structures and micro-outcomes, and to do so by providing 'a systematic, mid-level institutional account'.[3] *Third*, her turn to the VoC literature introduces into the sociology of punishment a framework that has been influential in comparative political economy but which has been absent from comparative penology. In doing so, she aims to move penological scholarship beyond the observation of correlations

[3] Nicola Lacey, 'Punishment, (Neo)Liberalism and Social Democracy' *The SAGE Handbook of Punishment and Society* (SAGE 2013) 267.

towards a 'genuinely explanatory model'. *Fourth*, following engagement with the question of American exceptionalism, she expanded her focus to take account of America's high levels of violent crime and social disadvantage. Addressing these broader issues leads her to link the sociology of punishment with sociological criminology and research on the causes of violence. *Finally*, throughout this project, Lacey poses scientific questions aiming to explain variation and develop comparative theory but she also poses normative, reform-oriented questions that ask how to counter mass incarceration and establish a more humane criminal justice. This normative inquiry is most explicit in *The Prisoners' Dilemma*, less so in the later work. However, a concern to deploy scholarly analysis in the service of liberal penal reform is present throughout.

2. Lacey on Punishment and Political Economy: An Exposition

a. The Varieties of Capitalism (VoC) Framework

Lacey's signature contribution to comparative penology is her introduction of the VoC framework and her deployment of its arguments in the penal domain. I will offer a brief exegesis of VoC theory before describing how Lacey uses that framework to explain systematic variation in national systems of punishment.[4]

VoC theory begins from the premise that capitalist forms of economic action are always embedded in specific institutional frameworks—that is to say, specific 'political economies'. It presents a comparative analysis of what it sees as the two most common varieties of capitalism currently in existence—*Coordinated Market Economies* (CMEs) and *Liberal Market Economies* (LMEs)—and explores whether these different forms can explain differences in productivity, employment, education and vocational training, inequality, literacy rates, and other social and economic outcomes. The result is a powerful, empirically grounded account of the costs and benefits of the two modes of capitalist political economy that characterize the advanced democracies.

The central claim of VoC theory is that capitalist societies can be distinguished by the degree to which a political economy is, or is not, 'coordinated'—hence the fundamental distinction between CMEs (with Germany being the paradigmatic example) and LMEs (of which the exemplary instance is the United States). In societies with a coordinated market economy (an institutional achievement that is brought about over time by an enabling state that actively fosters cooperation and

[4] The *locus classicus* of VoC theory is Peter Hall and David Soskice, (eds), *Varieties of Capitalism* (Oxford University Press 2001). For a review of the VoC literature, see Chris Howell, 'Varieties of Capitalism: And Then There Was One' (2003) 36(1) Comparative Politics 103.

facilitates investment) firms cooperate as well as compete, assisted by (i) negotiated agreements between the social partners; (ii) long-term commitments regarding finance and investment; and (iii) a system of education and training that provides employers with workers with specific skill-sets. The planned, long-term orientation of the system, backed up by powerful unions and a supportive welfare state, encourages workers to invest in skills acquisition, confident that they will receive a return on their investments in the form of secure, well-paid employment. At the same time, it enables firms to plan and invest within a more predictable environment and to benefit from a trained workforce and improved labour relations.

According to the theory, these institutional supports provide CMEs with the 'comparative institutional advantage' of an improved capacity for strategic coordination, enabling long-term development and high-quality production. They also encourage industrial relations that are less hierarchical, with an emphasis on industrial citizenship and power-sharing within firms; inter-firm agreements; and forms of corporate governance that encourage 'patient capital' rather than the short-term maximization of shareholder value.

These forms of coordination and cooperation are much less present in LMEs, where firms—encouraged by a more hands-off 'free-market' state—engage in arms-length, competitive relations and formal contracting, basing their decision-making not on plans and agreements but on market prices and patterns of supply and demand. As a consequence, LMEs exhibit (i) highly competitive, insecure labour markets; (ii) less powerful unions and limited collective bargaining; and (iii) a short-term orientation—all of which give rise to a greater degree of flexibility and innovation.

Underpinning VoC theory is a conception of the rational, calculating, self-interested capitalist firm. Institutions—such as government, finance, education and training, welfare state regimes, and industrial relations—become crucial for the theory to the extent that they structure interaction between economic actors; enable firms to solve coordination problems; and stamp national economies with a specific *modus operandi* that shapes the interests of social and economic actors. As Lacey[5] explains, VoC theory is 'based on the methods of ... rational choice theory, historical institutionalism, and the analysis of comparative institutional advantage'.

Another of the theory's central assumptions is that the various institutions that compose LMEs and CMEs are interlocking ensembles that cluster tightly together, interacting in complementary and mutually supporting ways. These institutional relations provide the overall assemblage with a functional integrity as well as an ability to resist change or disruption.

VoC theory assumes that CMEs and LMEs are distinct institutional configurations that are, in effect, alternative forms of capitalist equilibria. Each one is

[5] Lacey, 'Punishment, (Neo)Liberalism and Social Democracy' (n. 3) 274.

marked by complementarity, integration, and coherence; and each is driven by rational firms seeking profitability, albeit by different means. These are alternative forms of capitalist organization, each of which allows firms to prosper, each of which has comparative institutional advantages, each of which has costs and benefits accruing to different economic actors.

b. Varieties of Capitalism and Varieties of Penal Systems

Lacey was not the first scholar to utilize political economy to explain patterns of punishment: Rusche and Kirchheimer (1968), Melossi (1998), and De Giorgi[6] (2006) had all presented arguments of that kind. But their work was mostly historical rather than comparative, pointing to economic changes as the cause of correlative shifts in penal practice. By contrast, John Sutton's work on punishment and political economy was certainly comparative in nature[7] but Sutton's impressive empirical studies stopped short of offering a theoretical model, concluding instead that 'incarceration rates are higher in countries where capacities for regulating the macro-economy and containing inequality are weak'.[8] It was not until Cavadino and Dignan published *Penal Systems: A Comparative Approach*[9] in 2006 that we find comparative political economy being utilized to analyse cross-national variations in punishment. Using a four-fold taxonomy that built on Esping-Andersen's influential typology of welfare state regimes,[10] Cavadino and Dignan classified the penal systems of twelve countries into four types—neoliberal; conservative corporatist; social democratic; and oriental corporatist.

But Cavadino and Dignan's work, for all its programmatic importance, remained at the level of empirical correlation—observing associations between the four types of political economy on the one hand, and the rates of imprisonment, penal rhetoric, and youth justice exhibited by their sample of national penal systems on the other. It had little to say about the institutional linkages that connect political economy with punishment and it stopped short of identifying specific causal mechanisms. Lacey's work, in contrast, stands out as she seeks to locate these correlations within a developed theoretical framework—VoC theory—and

[6] Dario Melossi (ed) *The Sociology of Punishment: Socio-Structural Perspectives* (Dartmouth Publishing Co.); D Melossi, 'Neoliberalism's "Elective Affinities": Penality, Political Economy and International Relations' in D Melossi (ed.), *Travels of the Criminal Question* (Hart 2011) 45; A De Giorgi, *Rethinking the Political Economy of Punishment: Perspectives on Post-Fordism and Penal Politics* (Ashgate 2006).

[7] J Sutton, 'Imprisonment and Social Classification in Five Common-Law Democracies, 1955–1985' (2000) 106 American Journal of Sociology 350; J Sutton, 'The Political Economy of Imprisonment in Affluent Western Democracies, 1960–1990' (2004) 69 American Sociological Review 170.

[8] Sutton (2004) 109.

[9] M Cavadino and J Dignan, *Penal Systems: A Comparative Approach* (SAGE 2006).

[10] Gøsta Esping-Andersen, *The Three Worlds of Welfare Capitalism* (Polity Press 1990).

to identify actors, patterns of action, and causal mechanisms that can form the basis for an explanation.

c. Lacey on Punishment and Political Economy

Lacey first announced this project in *The Prisoners' Dilemma*, a book based on the Hamlyn Lectures she delivered in 2007. She begins by questioning the idea that penal systems everywhere are growing increasingly populist, abandoning penal welfarism, and becoming less committed to humanity, fairness, and effectiveness. Her objection to this sweeping claim was not to the direction of change that it alleged but to the implicit assumption that these illiberal trends were affecting all western nations equally. Against this generalization, she stresses the fact of variation across national penal systems and insists that we should attend not just to the macro-structural causes of cross-national change but also to the institutional sources of national variation.

In her review of prior 'political economy and punishment' literature, she pays respectful attention to the pioneering work of Rusche and Kirchheimer (1968) and to De Giorgi's 2006 analysis of how penality has been reformulated in the wake of the shift to a post-Fordist, post-Keynesian world. But for all its illumination of the role of macro-level structures, this literature has little to say about variation, tending to assume, as Sutton puts out, 'that all capitalist economies are the same and that business cycles are wholly exogenous to other kinds of social processes'.[11]

Lacey finds more value in James Whitman's[12] work—especially his focus on long-term historical pathways as a basis for understanding contemporary national differences and his invoking of the classic distinction between strong states and weak states as a basis for understanding policy choices. And she commends Downes[13] for conceptualizing the Dutch 'culture of tolerance' not as an indigenous sensibility but instead as a corollary of specific institutional arrangements that organize, incentivize, and reinforce tolerant attitudes towards offenders.

Finally, she turns to Cavadino and Dignan.[14] Unlike other comparatists who focus on the peculiarities of cultural difference and are inattentive to structural similarities, Cavadino and Dignan strive for systematic comparison and classification. However, their work remains 'diagnostic'—marking patterns of association without identifying the causal processes that generate them.

[11] Quoted in Lacey, *The Prisoners' Dilemma* (n. 2) 51.
[12] James Whitman, *Harsh Justice* (Oxford University Press 2003).
[13] David Downes, *Contrasts in Tolerance* (Clarendon Press 1988).
[14] Cavadino and Dignan, *Penal Systems* (n. 9).

An explanatory theory must identify the causal processes by means of which the institutions of political economy determine the institutions on criminal punishment. Here is how Lacey approaches this issue:

> [A coordinated market economy], which functions in terms primarily of long-term relationships and stable structures of investment . . . and which incorporates a wide range of social groups and institutions into a highly coordinated governmental structure, may be more likely, other things being equal, to generate incentives for the relevant decision-makers to opt for a relatively inclusive criminal justice system. For it is a system which is premised on incorporation, and hence on the need to reintegrate offenders into society and economy. Such a system is, we might hypothesize, structurally less likely to opt for degradation or exclusionary stigmatization in punishment.[15]

In contrast, societies organized as LMEs, which are more individualistic and depend less on coordination, long-term investments, and trust-based relationships are, Lacey suggests, more liable to 'harsh, exclusionary criminal justice' because they are more unequal; because they frequently have surplus populations of unskilled labourers; and because the costs of social exclusion are lower.[16] The underlying assumption is that investment in socially inclusive practices fosters higher levels of trust, integration, and solidarity—whereas promoting competition fosters lower levels—and that the resulting social relations will, in turn, shape the character of penal systems.

Part of any theory's value lies in its ability to focus attention on processes and relationships that might otherwise have seemed irrelevant to the phenomenon we seek to understand. To the extent that the VoC framework highlights processes that have not been prominent in 'punishment and society' literature, it demonstrates its usefulness. Production regimes—the structured ensembles of labour markets and associated institutions such as employer coordination, education, training and apprenticeships—are clearly relevant to crime and punishment insofar as they enable (or inhibit) social order through secure employment, family formation, and the social integration of individuals. We know, for example, that in the United States—the paradigmatic LME—high-school non-completion is among the highest in the OECD and that a majority of black males who fail to complete high school spend time in prison. The situation in CME countries such as Germany is very different, with correspondingly high rates of school completion and low rates of imprisonment. VoC theory brings into sharp focus the American school-to-prison pipeline, contrasting it with the German school-to-employment pattern, while indicating the institutional arrangements that produce these contrasting life

[15] Lacey, *The Prisoners' Dilemma* (n. 2) 58.
[16] Ibid., 59.

course pathways.[17] As Lacey[18] observes, VoC theory motivates research on 'the impact of education, training and general skills-formation [on] criminogenic and penal dynamics'—an area that has heretofore been surprisingly underdeveloped.

If differences in production regimes form the fundamental basis of the CME/LME distinction and the original focus of VoC theory, subsequent work in that tradition has pointed to the importance of other institutional contrasts.[19] In particular, it has highlighted how the associated *welfare states* (more extensive and solidaristic in CMEs; more minimalist in LMEs) and *political systems* (Proportional Representation (PR) systems in CMEs; First Past the Post (FPTP) systems in LMEs) provide additional institutional contrasts between these two kinds of society. After a discussion of these institutions and their implications for punishment, Lacey sums up her thesis as follows:

> [I]n liberal market economies with majoritarian electoral systems . . . the unmediated responsiveness of politics to popular opinion in the adversarial context of a two party system makes it harder for governments to resist a ratcheting up of penal severity.[20]

And she continues:

> Co-ordinated systems which favour long-term relationships—through investment in education and training, generous welfare benefits, long-term employment relationships—have been *able to resist* the powerfully excluding and stigmatizing aspects of punishment. By contrast, liberal market systems oriented to flexibility and mobility *have turned inexorably* to punishment as a means of managing a population consistently excluded from the post-Fordist economy.[21]

d. American Imprisonment in Comparative Perspective

In 2010, Lacey's focus began to shift towards the question of why America maintains a higher rate of incarceration than other nations. She points out that although global economic changes—deindustrialization, post-Fordism, welfare state retrenchment, and insecure work—have produced more crime and more

17 B Western, *Punishment and Inequality in America* (Russell Sage 2006)
18 Lacey, *The Prisoners' Dilemma* (n. 2) 168.
19 See e.g. T Iversen,. and D Soskice 'Electoral Institutions and the Politics of Coalitions: Why Some Democracies Redistribute more than Others' (2006) 100 American Political Science Review 165; and D Soskice, 'American Exceptionalism and Comparative Political Economy' in C Brown. C., C Eichengreen, and M Reich (eds), *Labor in the Era of Globalization* (Cambridge University Press 2009)
20 Lacey, *The Prisoners' Dilemma* (n. 2) 76
21 Lacey, *The Prisoners' Dilemma* (n. 2) 109

punishment everywhere, that general pattern nevertheless exhibits marked variation. Despite these pressures, nations such as Denmark, Germany, and Sweden have retained moderate and inclusionary criminal justice systems, while others, such as the United States and the United Kingdom, have become much more punitive and exclusionary.

To explain this pattern, Lacey again invokes VoC theory, asserting that '[v]arieties of capitalism either favor or inhibit penal tolerance and humanity in punishment'.[22] But here she states her thesis more precisely, highlighting the structural patterns and functional needs that predispose CMEs to more moderate patterns of punishment:

> In a political-economic system premised on incorporation, and hence on the need to reintegrate offenders into society and the economy, decision-makers are more likely to opt for an inclusionary criminal justice system and less likely to favor exclusionary stigmatization in punishment.[23]

By contrast, LMEs—of which the United States is the most extreme example—with their 'ever-increasing disparities of wealth and *de facto* status distinctions' generate political and economic forces 'that favor harsh and extensive punishment'.[24]

Lacey next considers aspects of political structure and organization that might explain America's penological distinctiveness. In contrast to PR systems—which foster negotiation and consensus; electoral bargains that ensure governments stick to their policy promises; and 'institutional buffers' that deflect popular demands—America's majoritarian electoral system is more polarizing and more open to populist currents. Moreover, the highly decentralized nature of American federalism, the frequency of elections, and the fact that so many criminal process actors are elected—are all potential factors linking American penal exceptionalism to the equally distinctive structure of American political institutions.

The following year, Lacey defended her approach against critics who suggested that her reliance on the VoC's typology led her to miss the distinctiveness that characterizes every penal system when viewed up close. Lacey replied that although the use of models may sometimes lead to simplification, reductivism, and determinism, this is by no means inevitable, particularly if theoretical frameworks are made 'answerable to local knowledge' and brought into a dialogue with detailed empirical research.[25] She acknowledged that models, like maps, 'simplify the terrain they chart' and that they are more revealing in respect of 'paradigmatic' cases

[22] Nicola Lacey, 'American Imprisonment in Comparative Perspective' (Summer 2010) Daedalus 102, 104.
[23] Ibid., 104.
[24] Ibid., 105.
[25] Nicola Lacey, 'Why Globalization Doesn't Spell Convergence' in A Crawford (ed.), *International and Comparative Criminal Justice and Urban Governance* (Cambridge University Press 2011) 214, 246.

and less accurate in 'penumbral' ones. But the pay-off of her approach is, she says, that models provide a vital 'orienting framework' without which we are unable to interpret the data. She concludes that, despite its relative simplicity, her 'two-families model' has already succeeded in identifying the theoretical relevance of a number of areas 'thus far barely addressed by criminal justice scholars'.[26]

In 2013, in an essay on 'neoliberalism' published in the *SAGE Handbook on Punishment and Society*,[27] Lacey argued that the advantage of her theory, as compared to the 'neoliberal penality thesis', is its greater ability to identify the 'institutional linkages' that mediate between macro-social structures and penal system outcomes. Her main objection to the neoliberal thesis is that it offers 'no systematic, mid-level institutional account to fill the explanatory space between the macro account ... and the micro examples'.[28] By contrast, Lacey's theory operates precisely in this space, seeking to trace the interlinking processes by means of which the structures of political economy shape the patterns of penal practice.

The articles and book chapters in the five years following *The Prisoner's Dilemma* mostly refined her thesis and applied it to specific cases such as Scotland, New Zealand, England and Wales, and Canada. But in 2015, Lacey (now with co-author David Soskice) published an article[29] that marked a major advance in thinking about the causes of American penal exceptionalism. Here, for the first time, Lacey extended her analysis to discuss not just punishment but also crime and violence, their links with political economy, and their role in prompting punitive policies. This, it seems to me, was a big step forward. In prior work, Lacey had not excluded crime from her explanatory framework but she tended to suggest that western societies had faced similar problems of rising crime. Here she insists that (i) the United States has had a qualitatively different experience with crime, violence, racial segregation, and social dislocation; (ii) that these social problems are a result of America's political economy and political system; and (iii) that these exceptional problems are directly linked to America's exceptional levels of punishment.

More significantly, the 2015 article identifies a new causal mechanism that, according to Lacey and Soskice, has the potential to explain the American difference. This mechanism—which centres on the voting preferences of home owners in local elections—is, like VoC theory, quite well established in political science but altogether new to the sociology of punishment. As a result of Lacey's initiative, a promising new line of inquiry has been opened up.

Pointing to the greater institutional capacity of CMEs 'to temper crime and to retain stable penal policy and moderation in punishment',[30] Lacey and Soskice

[26] Ibid., 246.

[27] Lacey, 'Punishment, (Neo)Liberalism and Social Democracy' (n. 3).

[28] Ibid., 267.

[29] Nicola Lacey and David Soskice, 'Crime, Punishment and Segregation in the United States: The Paradox of Local Democracy' (2015) 17(4) Punishment & Society 454.

[30] Ibid., 455.

begin their analysis by observing that LME institutional structures generally explain elevated penal levels. But even among LME nations, the United States is a clear outlier, inviting the question: what distinguishes the United States from other LMEs that might explain this? The answer they propose points to America's unique system of locally elected government—an institutional characteristic that sets the United States apart from the other LMEs. 'It would be hard' they write, 'to exaggerate the distinctiveness of the US tendency to organize government and executive power through electoral mechanisms at the local level.'[31] Because in the US locally elected representatives (and not national politicians as in other nations) make key decisions about residential zoning, education, policing, and criminal justice, it becomes plausible to hypothesize that political processes at the local level have a causal impact upon patterns of crime and punishment—the outcomes their theory seeks to explain. As Lacey and Soskice put it:

> We focus on the exceptional direct and indirect role of local democracy in key policy areas including law and order and beyond that in residential zoning, in public education, and in incorporation of suburbs, which has no parallel in the other Anglo-Saxon polities, and which magnifies through residential and educational segregation and concentrated poverty the social problems caused by socio-economic developments.[32]

The new hypothesis is that America's peculiar system of local democracy magnifies the social problems caused by deindustrialization and prompts an exceptionally punitive response. Radical local democracy is, they hypothesize, an institutional structure that helps explain American penality:

> Our suggestion is that these decentralization effects, though they vary according to specific state structures, are sufficiently pervasive to constitute a key part of the explanation of American exceptionalism.[33]

'Homevoters'—voters who own their homes and vote in ways intended to preserve the value of their property—are the key actors in this account, the hypothesis being that their self-interested actions tend to sustain racial segregation, concentrated poverty, and associated social problems. Since homevoters participate strongly in low-turnout local elections, they often become the median voters whose interests shape policy outcomes. And since their primary concern is to maintain property

[31] Ibid., 461.

[32] Lacey and Soskice offer a synoptic historical account of the emergence of America's exceptional political and economic institutions. Nicola Lacey and David Soskice, 'American Exceptionalism in Inequality and Poverty: A (Tentative) Historical Explanation' (2019) *LSE International Inequalities Institute Working Paper* 32

[33] Lacey and Soskice, 'Crime, Punishment and Segregation in the United States' (n. 29) 472.

values, homevoters often vote to sustain housing and educational segregation, keep taxes low, and limit social spending, especially where spending involves redistributive transfers to other groups. Lacey and Soskice hypothesize that the reliable preferences of homevoters, repeated in local elections across the country, serve to reproduce racialized segregation and concentrated poverty, leading those affected to be disproportionately crime-prone. When poor black communities consequently exhibit high rates of criminal violence, the response by white voters is to hold individual offenders responsible and demand that they be imprisoned.

This new version of the Lacey thesis still operates within a VoC framing but the focus is now more pointed and precise. It directly addresses just one nation—the United States —and foregrounds just one mechanism—the patterned action of median voters in local elections and its consequences for racial disadvantage, crime, and punishment. As the authors put it, in a follow-up book chapter published in 2018: 'Our core argument focuse[s] on the institutional structure of the political system' and its 'distinctive degree of local autonomy'.[34] As for the mechanisms that link this institutional structure to patterns of crime and punishment, these are clearly set out in a 2019 paper:

> Our broad argument is that violent crime came from the poverty, lack of welfare, limited education, and lack of effective policing, in the tracts into which zoning policies segregated the disadvantaged losers—a group which is moreover strongly racially patterned—from the collapse of Fordism, policies which favoured median local voters by bolstering house process and reducing taxation ... as well as distributing local public goods in radically unequal ways ... These very same dynamics shaped a distinctive, and toxic, politics of punishment.[35]

The 2018 chapter also makes the very interesting observation that 'mass imprisonment' (perhaps the defining feature of American penality today) 'looks dispiritingly like the extreme policy manifestation of a much more widespread institutional ... dynamic'.[36] I take them to mean by this that mass incarceration is, in itself, a form of zoning and segregation: the end-point of a wider logic that

[34] Nicola Lacey and D Soskice, 'American Exceptionalism in Crime, Punishment, and Disadvantage' in K Reitz (ed.), *American Exceptionalism in Crime and Punishment* (Oxford University Press 2018) 4. They stress that the polarizing dynamics generated by local political processes 'have become particularly strong since the collapse of Fordist industrial production' (ibid., 4). This is an important qualification, since they would otherwise be explaining a variable (America's rate of incarceration) by what they take to be a constant (the conservative preferences of local home-voters). Nicola Lacey and David Soskice, 'American Exceptionalism in Crime, Punishment, and Disadvantage' in K Reitz (ed.), *American Exceptionalism in Crime and Punishment* (Oxford University Press 2018).

[35] Nicola Lacey and David Soskice 'Political Systems, Technology Regime Change and Institutional Capacity to Manage Social Stress: Crime, Punishment and Welfare in the Era of the Knowledge Economy' (2019) Unpublished paper, 15.

[36] Lacey and Soskice, 'American Exceptionalism in Crime, Punishment, and Disadvantage' (n. 34) 34.

runs through American society's treatment of poor people of colour. *Mass incarceration as zoned segregation* is not just a metaphor whereby a characteristic of one domain is figuratively applied to another: it follows directly from their analysis of the causes of the phenomenon. The mass incarceration of poor people of colour, like the racial segregation of schools and housing, are separate points on a racial fault-line that cuts across the American social structure.

Comparative penology remains at an early stage of development. But within this new field, Nicola Lacey's work stands at the very forefront, setting a new standard, and opening up new horizons. She exhibits an encyclopedic knowledge of the existing literature and research findings, together with a discerning sense of which theories are promising and which are empirical dead-ends. Her interdisciplinary expertise has enabled her to introduce into comparative penology a set of theoretical resources drawn from political science; to develop plausible hypotheses, specify mechanisms, and identify the kinds of empirical studies that will have to be carried out in order to confirm or disconfirm the emerging theory. No one else has made this kind of contribution.

Admittedly, much of the work remains programmatic: we do not yet have the case studies or the comparative data that these analyses will require if they are to be substantiated. But she has already elevated the quality of scholarship in this field and generated a powerful set of ideas and hypotheses. The excitement surrounding her work is palpable, which is why it has been the subject of high-profile conferences, workshops, and review symposia.

3. Lacey on Punishment and Political Economy: A Critique

a. Varieties of Capitalism Theory

Turning from exegesis to critique, we might begin by raising some questions about the theoretical framework upon which Lacey relies. VoC theory has been very influential in political science but it is by no means uncontested, and some of the criticisms of the VoC model may carry over into Lacey's use of it.

A frequent criticism of VoC theory is that the two-variety typology upon which it is based is overly simple, grouping together political economies that share a high or low degree of coordination but which are differentiated by much else. Thus the Nordic nations, with their egalitarian, Social Democratic, welfare state regimes are classified as CMEs together with more conservative Continental European nations that have more stratified, more gendered Christian Democratic modes of welfare. Similarly, at the level of industrial relations, there are important within-type differences: with quite different levels of unionization, corporatism, and social partnership all included within the categories. The binary classification of political systems is also rather crude, leading VoC theory to classify the United States and the United Kingdom together as majoritarian, FPTP systems, typical of LMEs—despite the very important differences between the two polities. (A difference that Lacey and Soskice acknowledge when they highlight the peculiarities of the American case.)[37]

Why so few varieties? As Hall and Soskice[38] admit, several important countries such as France, Italy, and Spain do not easily fit into either ideal-type. And when analysis shifts from paradigmatic case (such as Germany or the United States) to 'penumbral' or 'hybrid' cases, the weakness of the binary distinction becomes apparent.[39] Indeed, in the view of some commentators, such as Thelen,[40] VoC theory is not even about *two* types of capitalism: its real interest being the coordinated form of CME with the liberal market form functioning as a residual category characterized largely in negative terms.

A different criticism, most forcibly made by Wolfgang Streeck,[41] is that the conception of capitalist society implicit in VoC theory is altogether too static, too unified, and too coherent. VoC theorists are certainly attuned to the importance of change, but their conception of societies—particularly of 'coordinated' ones—tends to depict them as stable, functional, integrated systems in which institutions mesh and mutually reinforce each other. According to Streeck, this model overstates the rationality of capitalist economies and downplays their vulnerability to political and economic disruption. Where Hall and Soskice conceive of historical change in terms of punctuated equilibrium,[42] Streeck insists that change in capitalist society is a continuous, subterraneous process that constantly undermines efforts to create a stable and predictable investment environment.[43] Politics can modify and, for a time, counteract capital's tendency towards 'creative destruction', as Schumpeter famously called it. But this is a continual struggle with no guarantee of success. There are no settled equilibria—just ongoing political struggles and economic competition that are sometimes managed for a period of time. 'Order'

[37] The United Kingdom now has PR systems for European Union and devolved assembly elections in Scotland and Northern Ireland. FPTP continues as the system for electing MPs to the national parliament in Westminster.

[38] Peter Hall and David Soskice, 'An Introduction to Varieties of Capitalism' in Peter Hall and David Soskice (eds), *Varieties of Capitalism* (Oxford University Press 2001).

[39] For details, see Howell, 'Varieties of Capitalism' (n. 4) (2003).

[40] Katheleen Thelen, 'Varieties of Labor Politics' in Hall and Soskice (eds), *Varieties of Capitalism* (n.38).

[41] Wolfgang Streeck, 'Order is an Exception, not the Rule': An interview with Wolfgang (2016) at <https://www.versobooks.com/blogs/2807-order-is-an-exception-not-the-rule-an-interview-with-wolfgang-streeck>.

[42] See Hall's famous account of policy paradigm shifts, which assumes that policy development is a matter of one settled equilibrium being replaced by a different one—Peter Hall, 'Policy Paradigms, Social Learning and the State' (1993) 25(3) Comparative Politics 275.

[43] Wolfgang Streeck and Katheleen Thelen (eds), *Beyond Continuity: Institutional Change in Advanced Political Economies* (Oxford University Press 2005).

Streeck insists, 'is the exception, not the rule.' Viewed in this light, VoC theorists put too much stress on the idea of a static functioning system, too little on power, politics, and disruption. VoC theory foregrounds rational action, institutional complementarity, and integrated equilibrium but in doing so it understates the importance of contingency, crisis, patch-work solutions, and irrational, unstable outcomes.

A final concern is that VoC's commitment to a binary CME/LME division makes it reluctant to acknowledge processes of convergence between the two forms of political economy. But over the last forty years, powerful economic actors (ranging from the World Bank, the IMF and the EU to multi-national corporations and the financial markets) have been pressing neoliberal policies on CME nations and moving them, however reluctantly, in the direction of LMEs. Meanwhile, there has been virtually no pressure on LMEs to change in the other direction. What was once a sharp division of type is becoming more of a continuum.

b. VoC Theory in the Penal Realm

How well does VoC theory apply to questions of comparative penology? Can its success in explaining different economic outcomes be reproduced when we try to explain penological differences? There are, I think, three issues to consider: (i) again, the binary, two-model typology; (ii) the interdependency (or lack thereof) of the institutions of political economy and the institutions of punishment; and (iii) the causal mechanisms that VoC identifies.

Two varieties of penal systems

How much explanatory power is generated by the distinction between two 'varieties of capitalism' when applied to the penal systems of the western world? Are there really just 'two families' of penal systems, each of them relatively stable and reproduced over time? And if so, what are the characteristics that distinguish these two types?

In the original VoC literature, the binary division is between market economies that are *coordinated*, and market economies that are not. But in Lacey's work, the presence or absence of coordination is not the principle that divides the penal systems of CMEs from the penal systems of LMEs.[44] In fact, coordination in criminal justice is barely mentioned.[45] As far as I can tell, Lacey does not explicitly identify any structural principle that distinguishes one kind of penal system from another—other than being situated in one or other of the two varieties of capitalism. The effect of being

[44] On the question of coordination in criminal justice, see Samuel Walker, *Taming the System: The Control of Discretion in Criminal Justice* (Oxford University Press 1993).

[45] At one point in Lacey, *The Prisoners' Dilemma* (n. 2)she notes that Downes, *Contrasts in Tolerance* (n. 13) describes how Dutch criminal justice actors to work together to produce low rates of imprisonment. But the question of criminal justice coordination plays no role in the rest of her work.

situated in one or other of these political economies is, she asserts, *either* the generation of high rates of incarceration and harsh, exclusionary punishment (in LMEs), *or* the maintenance of low levels of incarceration and inclusive, reintegrative penal measures (in CMEs). If there is a suggestion of a principle that distinguishes the two families, it is perhaps the principle of *incorporation*—but this is not a logic of action for which Lacey provides evidence but rather an inference drawn from the fact of higher or lower rates of incarceration.

Are two varieties enough to capture the variation exhibited by contemporary penal systems? Or might there be several types of penal systems, distinguishable on several dimensions? In some comparative studies[46] the penal systems of the Social Democratic Nordic nations are regarded as a distinct type, marked off by exceptionally low levels of incarceration, humane conditions of confinement, and well-developed forms of reintegration. But Lacey's theory groups the Nordic systems together with those of Continental Europe, many of which have markedly higher imprisonment rates and quite different institutional cultures.

Even if it is true, as Lacey insists, that there are systematic differences between the penal systems of CME and LME nations, it seems unlikely that a binary divide will capture all of this variation. Indeed, Lacey acknowledges when she notes that Canada's penality is exceptionally moderate for an LME nation[47] (and that the US rates are exceptionally high (Lacey 2011). The question then is whether this intra-type variation is both significant and systematic, in which case we ought to distinguish these variants and acknowledge the existence of additional types. Perhaps Lacey is doing something of the kind when she treats US penality as an 'exceptional' case (a stand-alone type?) that is better explained by reference to its peculiar system of local democracy than to its market-oriented political economy?

The test of any ideal type model is, as Weber[48] pointed out, a pragmatic one. How much does it explain and would a different typology explain more? In Lacey's work, the two-type VoC classification has been remarkably generative—suggesting fruitful hypotheses and identifying causal processes—but I suspect that future researchers will want to develop a more extended scheme of classification. A key question is always: what are the proper dimensions along which penal systems ought to be compared? Because VoC theory provides a ready-made basis upon which to distinguish penal systems—that is those embedded in LMEs versus those embedded in CMEs—the question of how best to distinguish penal systems is deferred rather than foregrounded. But given that penal systems are complex, internally differentiated, and multi-dimensional, it seems to me that comparative penology will eventually develop models that are better able to capture these patterned differences and dimensions.

[46] Cavadino and Dignan, *Penal Systems* (n. 9); Anna Erikkson and John Pratt (eds), *Contrasts in Punishment: An Explanation of Anglophone Excess and Nordic Exceptionalism* (Routledge 2013).

[47] Lacey, *The Prisoners' Dilemma* (n. 2) 142 Lacey, "Why Globalization Doesn't Spell Convergence".

[48] Weber, *Methodology of the Social Sciences* (1949)

c. How Well-integrated Are Penal Systems in the Larger Political Economy?

In the comparative political economy literature, there is some debate about the extent to which national political economies actually cohere and form close-knit, interlocking institutional systems. Do such systems possess a functional unity that provides a source of resistance to change and a tendency to stable reproduction? Are social systems so tightly bound and well-integrated that no one part can be changed without major changes elsewhere in the system? Or are these merely the assumptions of VoC theorists—derived from an implicit functionalism?

This question becomes especially relevant when VoC theory is applied to the institutions of punishment. Do we know for sure that there is a tight coupling of political-economic institutions and penal policy? Are penal systems so closely integrated into the structures of political economy that the latter always determine the former? Or is it possible that penal systems—especially small penal systems that affect only a tiny fraction of the working age population—are relatively independent of these larger structures and are shaped by quite other causal processes? Here we bump up against some basic conceptual issues: should we assume that societies are tightly-knit, functional totalities? Or are relations across societal subsystems looser and more variable?

Are there compelling reasons to assume a high degree of institutional complementarity and mutual entailment linking a society's penal system to its economy? In my view, the answer to this question is generally 'no', except where a penal system becomes so large that it produces non-negligible economic impacts—as in the United States.[49] Even if we accept that political economic institutions tend, in a well-managed polity, to be interdependent and mutually calibrated, it is not obvious that these need be coordinated with criminal justice. Rather, it seems likely that a nation's penal institutions and policies can develop relatively independently, not least because powerful economic actors such as large corporations, financial institutions, and labour unions, are little affected by criminal justice. That there has sometimes been very significant penal change over a short time-period—for example in Finland or the Netherlands[50]—without corresponding changes in the larger structures of political economy reinforces this thought.

To make this point is not to deny that there may be structural alignments, or perhaps elective affinities, between production regimes, welfare states, and political systems on the one hand, and penal systems on the other. It is simply to suggest that there is no a priori reason to assume that these different domains are always

[49] Bruce Western and Katherine Beckett, 'The US Penal System as a Labor Market Institution' (1999) 104 American Journal of Sociology 103.

[50] T Lappi-Seppala, 'American Exceptionalism in Comparative Perspective' in Kevin Reitz (ed.), *American Exceptionalism in Crime and Punishment* (Oxford University Press 2018) 195.

tightly interlocked and incapable of independent change or policy divergence. If this is to be a theoretical premise, it is one that needs to be explicitly argued and empirically evidenced, not just assumed.

d. The Question of Causal Mechanisms 1

Lacey introduced the VoC framework into comparative penology in 2008 in order to develop an explanatory theory that could advance beyond empirical correlations and specify the causal processes whereby the structures of political economy shape patterns of punishment. Does she succeed in this regard?

As I noted earlier, Lacey's work is still at a programmatic stage and its proper evaluation will have to wait for the requisite empirical research and comparative case studies. But it is not too early to assess the clarity and plausibility of the causal mechanisms that she specifies. How, according to her theory, does political economy shape penal outcomes? And how do such processes vary between LMEs and in CMEs so as to produce such different penal outcomes? If, as she insists, different varieties of capitalism 'favour or inhibit penal tolerance and humanity in punishment'[51] what are the mechanisms that produce these effects?

At this point in Lacey's project, the answer to this question is not altogether clear. Or rather, it only becomes clear when she moves from general claims about the differential penal effects of LMEs and CMEs to more specific claims about the behaviour of home-owning voters in American elections. I will discuss these specifically American mechanisms in a moment, but let me first discuss her general account of how political economy shapes patterns of punishment.

The question Lacey seeks to answer here is fundamental to any social science explanation—and one that presents real difficulty for the analyst. Observed correlations make it appear that certain social, or economic, or political structures (in this case, LME and CME varieties of capitalism) co-vary with a certain pattern of action and outcome (in this case, more or less harsh forms of punishment). The analytical conjecture is that one is causing the other. The research question is: what are the action sequences through which one set of institutions (political economy) affects the shape of another apparently distinct institution (the penal system)? Who are the relevant actors (policy-makers, officials, firms, organizations, etc.) and what are the considerations (opportunities, values, beliefs, reasons, interests, incentives, and so on) that pattern their choices, shape their actions, and cumulatively produce the outcome of interest? In short, what are the recurring sequences of meaningful action that reproduce the observed outcomes?[52]

[51] Lacey, 'Punishment, (Neo)Liberalism and Social Democracy' (n. 3) 52.

[52] An ancillary question concerns the *conditions* under which these action processes are liable to occur. It may be that the requisite actions will be undertaken only by certain kinds of individuals, in

Looking closely at Lacey's engagement with this fundamental question, it seems to me that she indicates several different possibilities. In the excerpts below, I highlight passages where one or other mechanism is identified:

In 2008 Lacey wrote that:

> My suggestion is that ... [a CME], which functions in terms primarily of long-term relationships and stable structures of investment ... and which incorporates a wide range of social groups and institutions into a highly coordinated governmental structure, may be more likely ... **to generate incentives for the relevant decision-makers to opt for a relatively inclusive criminal justice system.** For it is **a system which is premised on incorporation**, and hence on **the need to reintegrate offenders into society and economy.** Such a system is, we might hypothesize, structurally less likely to opt for degradation or exclusionary stigmatization in punishment.[53]

On the next page, and by way of contrast, she observes that for LMEs,

> **the costs of a harsh, exclusionary criminal justice system are less** than they would be in a CME.[54]

Finally, an additional mechanism is introduced in 2010 when she writes that

> the interlocking institutions of [CMEs] **conduce to an environment of relatively extensive informal social controls**, which in turn **supports the cultural attitudes** that underpin and stabilize a moderated approach to formal punishment.[55]

I think these passages specify three kinds of processes. One has to do with 'incentives' and 'costs'; the second talks of a system's 'premises' and 'needs'; and a third points to 'social controls' and 'cultural attitudes'.[56] The first and third of these are,

certain kinds of circumstances—with the result that the operation of the causal mechanism will be conditional rather than automatic: and the theory will have to incorporate this qualification.

[53] Lacey, *The Prisoners' Dilemma* (n. 2) 58. See also Lacey, 'American Imprisonment in Comparative Perspective' (n. 22) 104 and Lacey, 'Why Globalization Doesn't Spell Convergence' (n. 25) 220 where these claims are repeated.

[54] Lacey, *The Prisoners' Dilemma* (n. 2) 59.

[55] Lacey, 'American Imprisonment in Comparative Perspective' (n. 22) 104.

[56] Elsewhere Lacey notes that LMEs generally have higher levels of inequality and that, as Richard Sennett has pointed out, it is difficult to show 'mutual respect across the boundaries of inequality' (*The Prisoners Dilemma* (n. 2) 83). This suggests a different mechanism, produced not by the variety of capitalism but indirectly by the effects of inequality and status differentials on patterns of human interaction. See also Lacey, 'American Imprisonment in Comparative Perspective' (n. 22) 105 where she talks about how LMEs with their 'ever-increasing disparities of wealth and *de facto* status distinctions' feed into 'political and economic forces that favor harsh and extensive punishment'. This too, hints at an undeveloped claim about the penal effects of inequality.

I think, underspecified and will require more detailed description before they can be confirmed or disconfirmed by research; the second, is, I think, less persuasive and may need to be rethought.

Incentives and costs

When Lacey refers to 'incentives' that encourage 'relevant decision-makers' to 'opt for' an inclusive criminal justice—or to the lower 'costs' that make exclusionary justice more likely, what are these costs and benefits and which actors experience them? As far as I can see, she never directly answers these questions but, in light of VoC theory, we might surmise that these incentives and costs have something to do with differential social investments in human capital that lead penal policy-makers and justice officials in CMEs to behave differently than their LME counterparts. Thus exclusionary policies such as imprisonment might seem wasteful in a CME insofar as they destroy prior societal investments in educating and training individuals who later became offenders. Moreover, the general availability of secure jobs and welfare support might enable (and thereby 'incentivize') prosecutors and judges to choose penal sanctions—such as community penalties—that promote reintegration. In contrast, penal decision-makers in LMEs might correctly assume that offenders have had little education and poor job prospects and consequently judge that nothing much will be lost if they are sentenced to imprisonment.

Both of these incentive stories seem plausible, but we should not take them as established mechanisms until we have evidence that criminal justice actors in the different political economies really do think in these contrasting ways. And we should bear in mind that even in CMEs with generous welfare states and education systems many offenders coming before the courts possess very little human capital. This is certainly true of non-nationals and migrants, who form a large proportion of the prison population in European nations but even among citizens, it is a rare offender who has a good education and employment record and is free of addictions and health problems. Is a concern to safeguard societal investment in human capital really a motivating consideration for criminal justice officials? In the absence of empirical data, we cannot say.

It may be that it is not a cost-benefit calculation that is operating in these settings, but instead a feeling of solidarity. And it may be that the relative strength of social bonds is greater in egalitarian, cooperative societies than in competitive liberal-market societies. But if so, we are talking about cultural and ideological processes, and Lacey's deployment of VoC theory was intended, in part, to displace vague cultural claims with more specific mechanisms.

The other consideration Lacey mentions has to do with relative costs: the idea that it is more costly for a CME to adopt exclusionary punishments and less costly for an LME to do so. But what does this mean exactly? Perhaps when she observes that it is less costly for an LME to use exclusionary punishments she does not mean less costly compared to a CME. Perhaps she means it is less costly for an LME to opt for harsh punishment than it would be for that same LME to opt for more reintegrative, more supportive penal sanctions—because LMEs tend to have meagre welfare states and insecure, competitive labour markets, making it more difficult for them to deal with offenders in rehabilitative ways. If this is the claim, then it also seems quite plausible, though again we would need supportive evidence.

Needs

The second kind of mechanism Lacey specifies has to do with a specific characteristic of the CME system. She suggests that in a CME, 'incorporation' is a societal principle and that this system logic creates a 'need' to reintegrate offenders that is somehow felt, and acted upon, by key decision-makers in criminal justice. The suggestion seems to be that a principle of 'incorporation' runs through all the CME society's institutional domains, originating in corporatist economic policies and coalition politics but also reaching down into the penal system, where offenders benefit from the same urge to include rather than exclude.

This certainly seems possible. There may well be a societal imperative that presses towards inclusion rather than exclusion and shapes institutional behaviour in every social sphere. But it would seem to be a theoretical assumption rather than a proven fact. And it draws on an implicit functionalism that assumes that complex societies can be understood as cohesive, fully integrated totalities. If we grant that assumption, then it is plausible to suppose that a CME (defined by extensive patterns of coordination and the incorporation of the social partners into corporatist forms of cooperation) will project that integrative logic onto its penal system. But outside of functionalist theory, why should we think of modern complex societies as unified, integrated systems, driven by a singular logic or imperative? Lacey insists that a CME 'system' that is 'premised on incorporation' has a 'need' to reintegrate offenders. But perhaps this 'system need' is merely a theoretical premise—a functionalist conceit—rather than an empirically observed fact.

What would happen if this 'need' were not fulfilled? What repercussions might follow if a CME such as Germany or Sweden became harshly punitive in its treatment of offenders? Would the larger political economy of these nations fall apart? Would serious costs be borne by important social groups or economic actors? These outcomes seem unlikely—which raises questions about the functionalist premises that support Lacey's hypotheses.

The claim that coordinated market capitalism produces moderate punishment because of its principle of incorporation and inclusion is more plausible, I think, if it is understood as a claim about ideology, social values, and attitudes and not about functional imperatives. The ideology of 'inclusiveness'—of solidarity and fellowship—may be a dominant value in a particular society, reinforced by institutional structures and extending to the treatment of offenders. Criminal justice actors may be imbued with an inclusive approach to deviants, or a 'culture of tolerance',[57] which may prompt them to avoid harsh imprisonment and resist pressure to exclude criminals.

But even here there are doubts. Why assume that there is just one single, hegemonic ideology that shapes the action of penal legislators, prosecutors, and judges? Why assume an ideological coherence that stretches across all policy domains? Why assume that offenders are viewed and valued and treated in the same way as prospective employees, or voters, or law-abiding citizens? Is it not equally likely that values and ideas are contested and differentially influential in different domains? In which case, why not assume value pluralism across policy domains? Why not consider that penal policy might be driven by values and imperatives that are relatively distinctive, and that penal policy is relatively autonomous?

Moreover, if patterned penal action is to be explained by ideology and attitude, it is more likely that criminal justice officials learned this in law school or from their professional peers, as Downes[58] describes, rather than from 'the system' of political economy and its corporatist arrangements. Criminal justice decision-makers in CME societies may think inclusively, prefer to reintegrate, and resist the urge to degrade offenders, etc. But if these penal attitudes exist, they are likely to have been reproduced within the penal policy realm—and adjacent spheres like the welfare state—rather than being imposed from outside by the supposed 'needs' of the political economy. In modern, functionally differentiated societies, the different institutional spheres generally have their own processes of education, training, and appointment and their own (often contested) value sets. And while the value orientations of different institutions have to coexist and somehow correspond, there is no need to assume a singular uncontested value set that ensures a uniform policy orientations across the range of differentiated domains.

Informal social controls

The third mechanism identified by Lacey, which points to the more extensive web of informal social controls associated with CMEs—and presumably operating within their extensive welfare states—seems both plausible and promising. A relatively more effective network of informal social controls in the institutions of civil society (such as the family, the school, the neighborhood, and the community) might operate to produce low levels of crime and deviance and also provide resources for non-penal, non-state responses to social problems when they do arise.[59] But having pointed to this mechanism, Lacey does not elaborate on its operation or character, so it remains a suggestion to be developed in future.

[57] Downes, *Contrasts in Tolerance* (n. 13).

[58] Ibid.

[59] D. Garland, 'Penal Controls and Social Controls' in Punishment and Society (2020) vol 22(3) pp 321–352.

e. The Question of Causal Mechanisms 2

In her most recent papers, which address the question of American exceptionalism, Lacey identifies a new mechanism unmentioned in her earlier work—a mechanism that appears peculiarly American and is unlikely to account for observed differences between CME and LME-based penal systems.

Lacey begins from the premise that LME countries have elevated levels of imprisonment compared to CMEs, and that this difference can be explained by the mechanisms mentioned above: that is incentives, costs, system imperatives, and informal social controls. But the fact that America is an outlier *even among LMEs* means that its extraordinary imprisonment rates are to be explained by a specifically American mechanism, namely the political dynamics of a radically localized system of government. Here VoC ideas about political economy recede into the background and Lacey's focus shifts to the dynamics of local political processes.

It is true that as early as 2008 Lacey had pointed to political systems as a cause of penal difference in political mechanisms, but the mechanism remained rather general and under-specified. As she put it: 'in liberal market economies with majoritarian electoral systems ... the unmediated responsiveness of politics to popular opinion in the adversarial context of a two party system makes it harder for governments to resist a ratcheting up of penal severity'.[60] In 2015, this claim about the impact of majoritarian political systems is developed into a more detailed argument about a distinctive feature of American democracy—its peculiar system of decentralized, devolved government and electoral democracy:

> Local democracy, especially in the large northern and mid-western cities, we hypothesize, may help to explain the USA's distinctive patterns of crime and punishment in the late 20th century because it magnified through residential and educational segregation and concentrated poverty the social problems caused by deindustrialization and the collapse of Fordism.[61]

As noted above, 'home-voters' are the key actors in this account, and it is their self-interested voting conduct that has, Lacey and Soskice claim, given rise to the social circumstances that underpin mass incarceration. What are we to make of this distinctive mechanism?

It certainly has plausibility, particularly in a socio-economic context defined by an exceptionally unequal market society with weak social protections and a deeply engrained history of racial subordination. And Lacey's focus on the structure of American political institutions aligns with much scholarship in this field that

[60] Lacey, *The Prisoners' Dilemma* (n. 2) 76.
[61] Lacey and Soskice, 'Crime, Punishment and Segregation in the United States' (n. 29) 457.

makes similar connections.[62] But precisely because the United States is the only nation exhibiting this kind of political institutional structure, we are dealing with a single case that is unlikely to generate a comparative theory with more general application.

One might also question whether the causes of mass incarceration in America are mostly located at the local level: after all, sentencing law is enacted by the states and the federal government, not by local municipalities, and most scholars agree with Tonry[63] that, but for the revolution in sentencing law that occurred in the 1980s and 1990s, mass incarceration could not have occurred. Federal funding for local law enforcement has also been a crucial enabler of these processes—suggesting that the mechanism Lacey identifies is only one of several.[64] One would also want to ask whether the policy choices of home-voters are always the same and always win out, in a nation that exhibits great geographical diversity and local variation.[65] Fortunately, the United States has thousands of local government constituencies where such elections occur, so internal comparisons in US jurisdictions would seem to be a viable research strategy to test this hypothesis.

f. The Problem of Theoretical Capaciousness

Lacey's intellectual reach is remarkable, stretching across multiple disciplines, giving her work an impressive richness and depth. But every virtue has its corresponding vice and the drawback of this impressive erudition is that it sometimes tends to expand and complicate Lacey's theoretical claims. Her conceptual framework sometimes grows too compendious, incorporating so much of the relevant scholarship that her own thesis slips out of focus, becoming too hung about with qualifications and conditions. (In this respect, it parallels VoC theory, which tends in a similar direction, particularly in its later restatements.)

Reductive simplification is certainly a problem in theoretical work, but so too is its opposite. Parsimony, clarity, crisp precision in causal statements—these are all virtues in theoretical work. Without these characteristics, theory can become so all-encompassing that it reduces its ability to offer sufficient guidance. We see this most clearly when Lacey turns to the discussion of specific cases, such as the penal systems of the United States, Canada, or New Zealand.[66] At these moments

[62] Joachim Savelsberg, 'Knowledge, Domination and Criminal Punishment' (1994) 99 American Journal of Sociology 911; Lisa Miller, *The Perils of Federalism: Race, Poverty, and the Politics of Crime Control* (Oxford University Press 2008).

[63] M. Tonry, *Sentencing Fragments* (Oxford University Press 2016).

[64] M. Campbell and H. Schoenfeld, 'The Transformation of America's Penal Order: A Historicised Political Sociology of Punishment' (2013) 118(5) American Journal of Sociology 1375–423.

[65] Vanessa Barker, *The Politics of Punishment* (Oxford University Press 2009); Emily Bazelon, *Charged: The New Movement to Elect Progressive Prosecutors and End Mass Incarceration* (Random House 2019).

[66] Lacey, *The Prisoners' Dilemma* (n. 2) 168 and 82.

her argument shifts imperceptibly away from theoretical modelling towards a historical recounting of multiple converging processes, circumstances, and contingencies. After a while, these qualifications tend to crowd out her model's central thesis, with the result that the work begins to read more like economic, political, and social history and less like theory.

There is, of course, nothing wrong with writing history and it may be that historical institutional analysis is the most appropriate and effective form of explanation currently available in this domain. But Lacey explicitly presents this work as a project of modelling and theory-building and, at least on occasion, it does not always live up to this billing.

Already capacious in its original 2008 version, Lacey's model has tended to expand as her research has proceeded, embracing more and more arguments, processes, and variables, each one folded in as a condition or a modification of the underlying VoC theory. So even though she indicates that she is deploying VoC theory to explain specific penal systems, she frequently does so in a way that adds a series of exogenous factors to the causal account. For example, in 2011[67] she sets out the (already quite complex) causal claim, to the effect that a specific variety of capitalism—involving a production regime, a welfare state, and a political system—determines the character of punishment, only to insist that 'to this picture we must add three further features' which turn out to be race, the war on drugs, and sentencing reform, each of which contains multiple dimensions and processes of its own.

Sometimes, these additional, extra-theoretical factors are characterized as 'conditions' which, it seems, modify the causal operations predicted by the theory. Thus in Lacey (2008) she writes:

> [I]n liberal market economies with majoritarian electoral systems, *particularly under conditions of relatively low trust in politicians, relatively low deference to the expertise of criminal justice professionals, and a weakening of the ideological divide between parties as they become increasingly focused on the median voter* and correspondingly less able to make commitments to a stable party base, the unmediated responsiveness of politics to popular opinion in the adversarial context of a two party system makes it harder for governments to resist a ratcheting up of penal severity.[68] (Emphasis added)

The problem, it seems to me, is that these 'conditions'—and not her VoC theoretical model—may do most of the explanatory work. And if this is the case, why can we not simply rely on these lower-level causal processes to explain outcomes? Why should we assume that these conditioning processes are bundled together in the

[67] Lacey, 'Why Globalization Doesn't Spell Convergence' (n. 25).
[68] Lacey, *The Prisoners' Dilemma* (n. 2) 76.

larger structures of an LME or a CME and that the larger structures are causally determinative? Is there any need to retain the higher-level determinations when the lower-level processes are generating the relevant penal effects?

g. A Normative Approach

The final issue I want to raise concerns the relationship between Lacey's inquiry into the determinants of punishment and the normative purpose with which she invests this investigation. Lacey states very clearly that one of her aims in undertaking this project is to identify the institutional conditions that make for moderate punishment and, particularly in the US context, to counter the forces producing mass incarceration.[69] Explanation and reform are viewed as interlinked because 'only by understanding the institutional preconditions for a tolerant criminal justice system . . . can we think clearly about the possible options for reform'.[70]

It is no secret that Lacey's sympathies lie with the moderate, humane, reintegrative policies that she takes to be characteristic of CME systems. Indeed, the surfaces of her texts are liberally sprinkled with normative interjections commenting on what she takes to be the objectionable features of the penal policies associated with LMEs.[71] There is, of course, nothing wrong in seeking to combine social scientific analysis with a reform orientation. And it seems correct to assume that reform efforts will be better directed when reformers have a sound understanding of the forces and conditions that shape penal policy. But it seems to me that Lacey's structural, VoC account of the institutional determinants of penal policy may be less encouraging for reformers than one might hope.

Consider that Lacey's theory insists that the fundamental causes of penal policy flow from the structures of political economy—that is that penal systems are embedded in tightly knit institutional configurations (LMEs or CMEs) that are designed to serve the interests of powerful economic actors—and that the functional imperatives of these varieties of capitalism lead either to humane or harsh penal systems. If we accept these arguments and the causal processes they imply, does this theory not tend to limit the possibility of discrete penal reform initiatives? Does it not suggest that substantial change in patterns of punishment will only be possible if prior changes are made in the structures of political economy? And is it not improbable to suppose that major changes will be made in a society's fundamental

[69] Lacey, 'Why Globalization Doesn't Spell Convergence' (n. 25) 2008.

[70] Nicola Lacey, 'The Rule of Law and the Political Economy of Criminalization: An Agenda for Research' (2013) Punishment & Society 352.

[71] Policy developments are described as 'worrying' (Lacey, *The Prisoners' Dilemma* (n. 2) 117); 'depressing' (ibid., 137; 'alarming' (ibid., 145); 'terrifyingly dystopian' (ibid., 156); and 'baleful' ('American Imprisonment in Comparative Perspective' (n. 22) 102).

political and economic arrangements in order to facilitate changes in the treatment of offenders?

Of course, it might be argued that significant changes in penal policy can be achieved *without* corresponding changes in political economy—as occurred in Finland between 1960 and 2000 and the Netherlands in 1980s.[72] But if that is the case, it throws into doubt the theory's supposed linkage between varieties of capitalism and systems of punishment. Either these political-economic structures *determine* penal policy, in which case they are unlikely to be changed just to improve the treatment of offenders—or, they do not, in which case there is no need to focus on the structures of political economy.

One response to this challenge might be to accept that a causal account of penal policy will not facilitate short-term penal reform and to recognize that major political and economic change will be required if we are to transform how societies punish. Another would be to relax the theory's assumption that punishment and political economy are functionally integrated and mutually determining and to allow that penal policy may have a degree of relative autonomy.

Those of us influenced by Lacey's scholarship and excited by its possibilities will look forward to seeing how her future work addresses these questions and responds to these concerns. In the meantime, we can continue to utilize the new theoretical resources she has provided to us and to reflect on the impressive body of work that she has produced.

Bibliography

Barker, V, *The Politics of Punishment* (Oxford University Press 2009)

Bazelon, E, (2019) *Charged: The New Movement to Elect Progressive Prosecutors and End Mass Incarceration* (Random House 2019)

Campbell, M and Schoenfeld, H, 'The Transformation of America's Penal Order: A Historicized Political Sociology of Punishment' (2013) 118(5) American Journal of Sociology 1375

Cavadino, M and Dignan, J, *Penal Systems: A Comparative Approach* (SAGE 2006)

De Giorgi, A, *Rethinking the Political Economy of Punishment: Perspectives on Post-Fordism and Penal Politics* (Ashgate 2006)

Downes, D, *Contrasts in Tolerance* (Clarendon Press 1988)

Esping-Andersen, G, *The Three Worlds of Welfare Capitalism* (Cambridge University Press 1990)

D. Garland, 'Penal Controls and Social Controls' in Punishment and Society (2020) vol 22(3) pp 321–352.

Hall, P, 'Policy Paradigms, Social Learning and the State' (1993) 25(3) Comparative Politics 275

[72] See T Lappi-Seppala, 'Explaining Imprisonment in Europe' (2011) 8(4) European Journal of Criminology 303.

Hall, P. and Soskice, D (eds), *Varieties of Capitalism* (Oxford University Press, 2001)
Hall, P. and Soskice, D, 'An Introduction to Varieties of Capitalism' in Hall and Soskice (eds), *Varieties of Capitalism* (Oxford University Press 2001)
Howell, C, 'Varieties of Capitalism: And Then There Was One' (2003) 36(1) Comparative Politics 103
Iversen, T and Soskice, D, 'Electoral Institutions and the Politics of Coalitions: Why some Democracies Redistribute More than Others' (2006) 100(2) The American Political Review 165
Lacey, N, 'Companions on a Serendipitous Journey' (2017) 44(2) Journal of Law and Society 283
Lacey, N, 'Punishment, (Neo)Liberalism and Social Democracy' *The SAGE Handbook of Punishment and Society* (SAGE 2013)
Lacey, N, 'The Rule of Law and the Political Economy of Criminalization: An Agenda for Research' (2013a) Punishment & Society
Lacey, N, 'Political Systems and Criminal Justice' (2012) 65(1) Current Legal Problems 203
Lacey, N, 'Punishment in the Perspective of Political Economy' (2012) 44 Kriminologische Journal 9
Lacey, N, 'Why Globalization Doesn't Spell Convergence' in A Crawford (ed.), *International and Comparative Criminal Justice and Urban Governance* (Cambridge University Press 2011) 214
Lacey, N, 'American Imprisonment in Comparative Perspective' (Summer 2010) Daedalus 102
Lacey, N, *The Prisoners' Dilemma: Political Economy and Punishment in Contemporary Democracies* (Cambridge University Press 2008)
Lacey, N and Soskice, D, (2019) 'American Exceptionalism in Inequality and Poverty: a (Tentative) Historical Explanation' *LSE International Inequalities Institute Working Paper* 32
Lacey, N and Soskice, D, 'American Exceptionalism in Crime, Punishment, and Disadvantage' in K Reitz (ed.), *American Exceptionalism in Crime and Punishment* (Oxford University Press 2018)
Lacey, N and Soskice, D, 'Crime, Punishment and Segregation in the United States: The Paradox of Local Democracy' (2015) 17(4) Punishment & Society 454
Lacey, N and Soskice, D, (2019) 'Political Systems: Technology Regime Change and Institutional Capacity to Manage Social Stress: Crime, Punishment and Welfare in the Era of the Knowledge Economy' *Unpublished Paper.*
Lacey, N, Soskice, D, and Hope, D, 'Understanding the Determinants of Penal Policy: Crime, Culture and Comparative Political Economy' (2018) Annual Review of Criminology 1195
Lappi-Seppala, T, 'American Exceptionalism in Comparative Perspective' in K Reitz (ed.), *American Exceptionalism in Crime and Punishment* (Oxford University Press 2018) 195
Lappi-Seppala, T, 'Explaining Imprisonment in Europe' (2011) 8(4) European Journal of Criminology 303
McAra, L, 'Global Politics and Local Culture' Review Symposium on *The Prisoners' Dilemma* (2011) 13 Punishment & Society 1
Melossi, D, 'Neoliberalism's "Elective Affinities": Penality, Political Economy and International Relations' in D Melossi (ed.), *Travels of the Criminal Question* Bloomsbury 2011) 45
Miller, L, *The Perils of Federalism: Race, Poverty, and the Politics of Crime Control* (Oxford University Press 2008)

Nelkin, D, 'Explaining Differences in European Prison Rates' Review Symposium on *The Prisoners' Dilemma* 2011 Punishment & Society 104
Savelsberg, J, 'Knowledge, Domination and Criminal Punishment' (1994) 99 American Journal of Sociology 911
Soskice, D, 'American Exceptionalism and Comparative Political Economy' in C Brown, C Eichengreen, and M Reich (eds), *Labor in the Era of Globalization* (Cambridge University Press 2009)
Streeck, W, 'Order Is an Exception, not the Rule': An interview with Wolfgang (2016) <https://www.versobooks.com/blogs/2807-order-is-an-exception-not-the-rule-an-interview-with-wolfgang-streeck>
Streeck, W and Thelen, K, (eds), *Beyond Continuity: Institutional Change in Advanced Political Economies* (Oxford University Press 2005)
Sutton, J, 'The Political Economy of Imprisonment in Affluent Western Democracies, 1960–1990' (2004) 69 American Sociological Review 170
Sutton, J, 'Imprisonment and Social Classification in Five Common-Law Democracies, 1955–1985.' (2000) 106 American Journal of Sociology 350
Thelen, K, 'Varieties of Labor Politics' in PA Hall and D Soskice (eds), *Varieties of Capitalism* (Oxford University Press 2001)
Tonry, M, Sentencing Fragments: Penal Reform in America, 1975–2025 (Oxford University Press 2016)
Wacquant, L, *Punishing the Poor: The Neoliberal Governance of Social Insecurity* (Duke University Press 2009)
Walker, S, *Taming the System: The Control of Discretion in Criminal Justice* (Oxford University Press 1993)
Max Weber, *Methodology of the Social Sciences* (1949) New York: Free Press.
Western, B, *Punishment and Inequality in America* (Russell Sage 2006)
Western, B and Beckett, K, 'The US Penal System as a Labor Market Institution' (1999) 104 American Journal of Sociology 103
Whitman, J, *Harsh Justice* (Oxford University Press 2003)

Professor Nicola Lacey—Full List of Publications

Books

In Search of Criminal Responsibility: Ideas, Interests and Institutions (Oxford University Press 2016) (This book was the subject of a symposium in *Critical Analysis of Law* 4(2) (2017) <http://cal.library.utoronto.ca/index.php/cal/index>)

Women, Crime and Character: From Moll Flanders to Tess of the d'Urbervilles (Oxford University Press 2008) (The Clarendon Law Lectures)

The Prisoners' Dilemma: Political Economy and Punishment in Contemporary Democracies (Cambridge University Press 2008) (The Hamlyn Lectures: this book was the subject of a *Punishment and Society* Special Issue in 2011 (Issue 13 (1))

A Life of HLA Hart: The Nightmare and the Noble Dream (Oxford University Press 2004) (Winner of the RSA's Swiney Prize 2004 and shortlisted for the James Tait Black Prize for Biography and for the British Academy Book Prize) (Translated into Chinese, 2006; Japanese translation under contract)

Regulating Law edited by Christine Parker, Colin Scott, Nicola Lacey, and John Braithwaite (Edited collection including introduction co-authored with the other editors and one article) (Oxford University Press 2004)

with Celia Wells and Dirk Meure, *Reconstructing Criminal Law: Critical Perspectives on Crime and the Criminal Process* (Weidenfeld and Nicolson, Law in Context Series 1990) (2nd edn with Celia Wells, Butterworths 1998; 3rd edn with Celia Wells and Oliver Quick, Cambridge University Press 2003)

Unspeakable Subjects: Feminist Essays in Legal and Social Theory (Hart Publishing 1998) (This book was the subject of a 20th anniversary symposium at SOAS in April 2018, papers from which were published in autumn 2018 in the open access journal feminists@law <https://journals.kent.ac.uk/index.php/feministsatlaw/article/view/661>)

with Elizabeth Frazer, *The Politics of Community: A Feminist Analysis of the Liberal Communitarian Debate* (Harvester Wheatsheaf/University of Toronto Press 1993)

State Punishment: Political Principles and Community Values (Routledge 1988)

Criminal Justice: A Reader (Oxford University Press 1994) (Edited collection: original introduction, 1–36)

Journal Articles

'Approaching or Rethinking the Terrain of Criminal Law?' (2019) Criminal Law and Philosophy DOI 10.1007/s11572-019-09516-6

'Populism and the Rule of Law' (2019) 15 Annual Review of Law and Social Science <https://www.annualreviews.org/doi/10.1146/annurev-lawsocsci-101518-042919>

'Women, Crime and Character in the Twentieth Century' (2018) 6 Journal of the British Academy <https://www.thebritishacademy.ac.uk/publications/women-crime-and-character-20th-century?_ga=2.58965157.965165179.1543163740-1138102987.1543163740>

with Hanna Pickard, 'A Dual-Process Approach to Criminal Law: Victims and the Clinical Model of Responsibility without Blame' (2018) Journal of Political Philosophy DOI: 10.1111/jopp.12160

with David Soskice and David Hope, 'Understanding the Determinants of Penal Policy: Crime, Culture and Comparative Political Economy' (2018) 1 Annual Review of Criminology 195

'Theorising Criminalisation through the Modalities Approach: A Critical Appreciation' (2018) 7(3) International Journal for Crime, Justice and Social Democracy 122

'Companions on a Serendipitous Journey' (2017) 44(2) Journal of Law & Society 283

'Socializing the Subject of Criminal Law: Criminal Responsibility and the Purposes of Criminalization' (2016) 99(3) Marquette Law Review 541

'The Metaphor of Proportionality' (2016) 43(1) Journal of Law and Society 27–44 ISSN 1467–6478

'Rechtswissenschaft, Geschichte und die institutionelle Natur des Rechts' (2016) Deutsche Zeitschrift für Philosophie ISSN 0012–1045 (trans. Frieder Vogelman)

'Responsibility without Consciousness' (Summer 2016) 36(2) Oxford Journal of Legal Studies 219

with David Soskice, 'Crime, Punishment and Segregation in the United States: The Paradox of Local Democracy' (2015) 17(4) Punishment & Society 454 DOI: 10.1177/1462474515604042

'Jurisprudence, History, and the Institutional Quality of Law' (2015) 101 Virginia Law Review 919

with Hanna Pickard, 'To Blame or to Forgive? Reconciling Punishment and Forgiveness in Criminal Justice' (2015) Oxford Journal of Legal Studies DOI: 10.1093/ojls/gqv012

with Hanna Pickard, 'The Chimera of Proportionality: Institutionalising Limits on Punishment in Contemporary Social and Political Systems' (2015) 78(2) Modern Law Review 216

'Comparative Criminal Justice: An Institutional Approach' (2014) 24 Duke Journal of Comparative and International Law 501

'Gouvernement-Manageur et Citoyens-Consommateurs' (2014) 27 Tracés 183 (translated and adapted paper previously published in the *Modern Law Review* in 1994, with introduction by Pierre Thévenin)

'The Path Not Taken: H.L.A. Hart's Harvard Essay on Discretion' (2013) 127 Harvard Law Review 636

'The Rule of Law and the Political Economy of Criminalisation: An Agenda for Research' (2013) 14(4) Punishment and Society

'Institutionalising Responsibility: Implications for Jurisprudence' (2013) 4(1) Jurisprudence 1

'Humanizing the Criminal Justice Machine: Re-Animated Justice or Frankenstein's Monster?' (2012) 126(5) Harvard Law Review 1299 (review article)

with Hanna Pickard, 'From the Consulting Room to the Court Room? Taking the Clinical Model of Responsibility Without Blame into the Legal Realm' (2013) 33 Oxford Journal of Legal Studies 1 doi: 10.1093/ojls/gqs028;

'Reflections on Brian Simpson' (2012) 3 Transnational Legal Theory 161

'Reflections on the Philosophy of Law' (2012) *Rivista di filosofia del diritto* 91

'Political Systems and Criminal Justice: The Prisoners' Dilemma After the Coalition' (2012) Current Legal Problems DOI: 10.1093/clp/cus002

'Punishment in the Perspective of Comparative Political Economy' ('Bestrafung in der Perspektive der Komparativen Politischen Ökonomie') (2012) 44 Kriminologische Journal 9

'The Way We Lived Then: The Legal Profession and the Nineteenth Century Novel' (2011) 33 Sydney Law Review 599

'The Prisoner's Dilemma and Political Systems: The Impact of Proportional Representation on Criminal Justice in New Zealand' (2011) Victoria University of Wellington Law Review 1

'Differentiating among Penal States' (2010) 61(4) British Journal of Sociology 778

'Psychologising Jekyll, Demonising Hyde: The Strange Case of Criminal Responsibility' (2010) 4(2) Criminal Law and Philosophy 109

'American Imprisonment in Comparative Perspective' (2010) 139(3) Daedalus (Summer 102

'Historicising Criminalisation: Conceptual and Empirical Issues' (2009) 72(6) Modern Law Review 936

'Philosophy, Political Morality and History: Explaining the Enduring Resonance of the Hart-Fuller Debate' (2008) 83 New York University Law Review 1059

'H.L.A. Hart's Rule of Law: The Limits of Philosophy in Historical Perspective' (2007) XXXVI Quaderni Fiorentini 1159

'Space, Time and Function: Intersecting Principles of Responsibility across the Terrain of Criminal Justice' (2007) 1 Criminal Law and Philosophy 233

'Analytical Jurisprudence versus Descriptive Sociology Revisited' (2006) 84 Texas Law Review 945

'In Search of the Responsible Subject: History, Philosophy and Criminal Law Theory' (2001) 64 Modern Law Review 350

'Social Policy, Civil Society and The Institutions of Criminal Justice' (2001) 26 Australian Journal of Legal Philosophy 7

'Responsibility and Modernity in Criminal Law' (2001) 9 Journal of Political Philosophy 249

'Violence, Ethics and Law: Feminist Reflections on a Familiar Dilemma' (2000) 1 Figurationen: Gender, Literatur, Kultur: Special Issue on Women and Law 43

'Bentham as Proto-feminist?' (1998) Current Legal Problems 441

'Philosophy, History and Criminal Law Theory' (1998) 1 Buffalo Criminal Law Review 295

'Unspeakable Subjects, Impossible Rights: Sexuality, Integrity and Criminal Law' (1998) Canadian Journal of Law and Jurisprudence 47

with Lucia Zedner, 'Community in German Criminal Justice: A Significant Absence' (1998) 7 Social and Legal Studies 7

'Unspeakable Subjects, Impossible Rights' (1997) 8(2) Women: A Cultural Review

'Feminism and the Tenets of Conventional Legal Theory' (1996) 11 Humboldt ForumRechts <http://www.rewi.hu-berlin.de/HFR/11-1996>

'Normative Reconstruction in Socio-Legal Theory' (1996) Social and Legal Studies 131

'Feminist Legal Theory Beyond Neutrality' (1995) Current Legal Problems 1

with Lucia Zedner, 'Discourses of Community in Criminal Justice' (1995) Journal of Law and Society 93

'Community in Legal Theory: Idea, Ideal or Ideology?' (1995) 15 Studies in Law, Politics and Society 105

'In(de)terminable Intentions' (1995) 58 Modern Law Review 692

'Community, Identity and Power: Some Thoughts on Women and Law in Central and Eastern Europe' (1995) UCLA Women's Law Journal 15

with Elizabeth Frazer, 'Politics and the Public in Rawls' Political Liberalism' (1995) 43 Political Studies 233 (review article)
'Abstraction in Context' (1994) Oxford Journal of Legal Studies 255 (review article)
'Mapping Modernities' (1994) Law and Critique 209 (review article)
'Government as Manager, Citizen as Consumer' (1994) 57 Modern Law Review 534
with Elizabeth Frazer, 'Blind Alleys: Communitarianism' (1994) Politics 75
'Theory into Practice? Pornography and the Public/Private Dichotomy' (1993) Journal of Law and Society 93
(Special Issue, also published as *Feminist Theory and Legal Strategy*, eds A Bottomley and J Conaghan (Blackwell 1993))
(Reprinted in F Olsen (ed.), *Feminist Legal Theory Volume 1: Foundations and Outlooks* (Dartmouth 1995) Chapter 13, 355)
'A Clear Concept of Intention: Elusive or Illusory?' (1993) 56 Modern Law Review 621.
'Feminist Legal Theory' (1989) Oxford Journal of Legal Studies 383 (review article)
'Are Rights Best Left Unwritten?' (1989) Political Quarterly 433
'Legislation against Sex Discrimination: Questions from a Feminist Perspective' (1987) Journal of Law and Society 411
(Reprinted in C. McCrudden (ed.), *Anti-Discrimination Law* (Dartmouth 1991) 437)
'The Territory of the Criminal Law' (1985) Oxford Journal of Legal Studies 453 (review article)
'Dangerousness and Criminal Justice: The Justification of Preventive Detention' (1983) Current Legal Problems 31
'Capital Punishment: Objections from Principle and Practice' (1983) Government and Opposition 407

Contributions to Books

with David Soskice, 'American Exceptionalism in Crime, Punishment, and Disadvantage: Race, Federalization, and Politicization in the Perspective of Local Autonomy' in KR Reitz (ed.), *American Exceptionalism in Crime and Punishment* (Oxford University Press 2018) 53
with Zelia Gallo and David Soskice, 'Comparing Serious Violent Crime in the United States and England and Wales: Why it Matters, and How It Can be Done' in KR Reitz (ed.), *American Exceptionalism in Crime and Punishment* (Oxford University Press 2018) 332
with Lucia Zedner, 'Criminalization: Historical, Legal and Criminological Perspectives' in A Liebling, S Maruna, and L McAra (eds), *The Oxford Handbook of Criminology* (6th edn, Oxford University Press 2017) 57
'Do the Persistent Questions Persist?' in L Duarte d'Almeida, J Edwards, and A Dolcetti, *Reading HLA Hart's The Concept of Law* (Hart Publishing 2013) 269
'Could He Forgive Her? Gender, Agency and Women's Criminality in the Novels of Anthony Trollope' in MC Nussbaum and A Lacroix (eds), *Subversion and Sympathy: Gender, Law and the British Novel* (Oxford University Press 2013) 176
'What Constitutes Criminal Law?' in RA Duff, L Farmer, S Marshall, M Renzo, and V Tadros (eds), *The Constitution of the Criminal Law* (Oxford University Press 2013) 12
'Punishment, (Neo)Liberalism and Social Democracy' in J Simon and R Sparks (eds), *The Sage Handbook of Punishment and Society* (Sage Publishing 2012) 260
'Principles, Policies and Politics of Criminal Law' in J Roberts and L Zedner (eds), *Principles and Values in Criminal Law and Criminal Justice* (Oxford University Press 2012) 19

with Lucia Zedner, 'Legal Constructions of Crime' in M Maguire, R Morgan, and R Reiner, *The Oxford Handbook of Criminology* (5th edn, Oxford University Press 2012) 159

'Community, Culture and Criminalisation' in R Cruft, MH Kramer, and MR Reiff (eds), *Crime, Punishment and Responsibility: The Jurisprudence of Antony Duff* (Oxford University Press 2011) 292; reproduced in modified form in

W Kymlicka, C Lernestedt, and M Matravers (eds), *Criminal Law and Cultural Diversity* (Oxford University Press 2014) 47

'Why Globalisation Doesn't Spell Convergence: Models of Institutional Variation and the Comparative Political Economy of Punishment' in A Crawford (ed.), *International and Comparative Criminal Justice and Urban Governance* (Cambridge University Press 2011) 214

'The Resurgence of Character: Criminal Responsibility in the Context of Criminalisation' in A Duff and S Green (eds), *Philosophical Foundations of Criminal Law* (Oxford University Press 2011) 151

'Out of the Witches' Cauldron?: Reinterpreting the Context and Re-assessing the Significance of the Hart-Fuller Debate' in P Cane (ed.), *The Hart-Fuller Debate Fifty Years On* (Hart Publishing 2010) 1

'Escaping the Prisoners' Dilemma: Strategies for a Moderated Penal Policy in England and Wales' in J Collins and S Siddiqui (eds), *Transforming Justice: New Approaches to the Criminal Justice System* (Criminal Justice Alliance 2009) 15

'The Prisoners' Dilemma in England and Wales' in M Hough et al. (eds), *Tackling Prison Overcrowding* (Policy Press 2008) 9

P Cane and J Conaghan (eds), *The New Oxford Companion to Law* (member of the advisory editorial committee and contributor of three entries) (Oxford University Press 2008)

'Interview' in ME Juul Nielson, *Legal Philosophy: Five Questions* (Automatic Press 2007) 124

'Criminal Justice' in R Goodin and T Pogge (eds), *Blackwell Companion to Political Philosophy* (Blackwell 2007) 511

'Character, Capacity, Outcome: Towards a Framework for Assessing the Shifting Pattern of Criminal Responsibility in Modern English Law' in M Dubber and L Farmer (eds), *Modern Histories of Crime and Punishment* (Stanford University Press 2007) 14

'Crime, Responsibility and Institutional Design' in M Smith, R Goodin, and G Brennan (eds), *Common Minds* (Oxford University Press 2007) 182

'Legal Constructions of Crime' in M Maguire, R Morgan, and R Reiner (eds), The Oxford Handbook of Criminology (4th edn, Oxford University Press 2007) 179

'Denial and Responsibility' in C Chinkin, D Downes, C Gearty, and P Rock (eds), *Crime, Social Control and Human Rights* (Willan Publishing 2007)

'Historicising Contrasts in Tolerance' in T Newburn (ed.), *The Politics of Crime Control* (Oxford University Press: Clarendon Studies in Criminology 2006) 197

'Criminalization as Regulation: The Role of Criminal Law' in C Parker et al. (eds), *Regulating Law* (Oxford University Press 2004) 144

'The Constitution of Identity: Gender, Feminist Legal Theory and the Law and Society Movement' in A Sarat (ed.), *The Blackwell Companion to Law and Society* (Blackwell 2004) 471

'Feminist Legal Theories and the Rights of Women' in K Knop (ed.), *Gender and Human Rights* (Oxford University Press 2004) 13

'Interpreting Doctrines of Privacy: A Comment on Anita Allen' in B Roessler (ed.), *Privacies: Philosophical Evaluations* (Stanford University Press 2004) 40

'Penal Theory and Penal Practice: A Communitarian Approach' in S McConville (ed.), *The Use of Punishment* (Willan Publishing 2003) 175

'Principles, Politics and Criminal Justice' in L Zedner and A Ashworth (eds), *The Criminological Foundations of Penal Policy* (Oxford University Press 2003) 79

'Modern Positivism: HLA Hart and Analytical Jurisprudence', and with Emily Jackson, 'Introducing Feminist Legal Theory' in J Penner, D Schiff, and R Nobles (eds), *Jurisprudence and Legal Theory: Commentary and Materials* (Butterworths 2002) 143 and 779 respectively

'Legal Constructions of Crime' in M Maguire, R Morgan, and R Reiner (eds), The Oxford Handbook of Criminology (3rd edn, Oxford University Press 2002)

'Violence, Ethics and Law: Feminist Reflections on a Familiar Dilemma' in S James and S Palmer (eds), *Visible Women* (Hart Publishing 2002)

'Partial Defences to Murder: Questions of Power and Principle in Imperfect and Less Imperfect Worlds' in A Ashworth and B Mitchell (eds), *The Law of Homicide* (Oxford University Press 2000)

'General Principles of Criminal Law: A Feminist Perspective' in L Bibbings and D Nicolson (eds), *Feminist Perspectives on Criminal Law* (Cavendish 2000)

with Lucia Zedner, '"Community" and Governance: A Cultural Comparison' in S Karstedt and K-D Bussmann (eds), *Social Dynamics of Crime Control* (Hart Publishing 2000) 157

'Philosophical Foundations of the Common Law: Social Not Metaphysical' in J Horder (ed.), *Oxford Essays in Jurisprudence* (4th series, Oxford University Press 2000)

'Penal Philosophy and Practices of Punishment: An Agenda for Dialogue' in M Matravers (ed.), *Punishment and Political Theory* (Hart Publishing 1999)

'Contingency and Conceptualism: Reflections on an Encounter between Critique and Philosophical Analysis of Criminal Law' in RA Duff (ed.), *Philosophy and the Criminal Law* (Cambridge University Press 1998)

'Criminal Justice and the Humanities in England' in K Luderssen (ed.), *Enlightened Policy in Criminal Law or Struggle against Evil* (Suhrkamp Verlag 1998)

'Criminal Law, Criminology and Criminalisation' in M Maguire, R Morgan, and R Reiner (eds), *The Oxford Handbook of Criminology* (2nd edn, Oxford University Press 1997)

'On the Subject of Sexing the Subject . . .' in N Naffine and R Owens (eds), *Sexing the Subject of Law* (Law Book Company 1997) 65

'Contingency and Criminalisation' in I Loveland (ed.), *Frontiers of Criminality* (Sweet and Maxwell 1995) 1

'Missing the Wood . . . Pragmatism versus Theory in the Royal Commission' in M McConville and L Bridges (eds), *Criminal Justice in Crisis* (Edward Elgar 1994) 30

with Elizabeth Frazer, 'MacIntyre, Feminism and the Concept of Practice' in J Horton and S Mendus (eds), *After MacIntyre* (Polity Press 1994) 265

'Sexual Harassment and Legal Strategy in the U.K.' in S Jagwanth, PJ Schwikkasd, and B Grant, *Women and the Law* (HSRC 1994) 55

'Closure and Critique in Feminist Jurisprudence' in A Norrie (ed.), *Closure or Critique: New Directions in Legal Theory* (Edinburgh University Press 1993) 194

'Escaping the Legal Paradigm' in K Hawkins (ed.), *The Uses of Discretion* (Oxford University Press 1992) 361

'Theories of Justice and the Welfare State' in G Sprenger (ed.), *Proceedings of the IVR World Congress, 1991* (A.R.S.P. 1992) 20 (also published in (1992) Social and Legal Studies 323)

'From Individual to Group?' in BA Hepple and E Szyszczak (eds), *Discrimination: the Limits of Law* Papers from the W.G. Hart Workshop, 1990 (Mansell 1992) 99

'Do We Need a Bill of Rights?' in R Hoggart (ed.), *Liberty and Legislation* (Frank Cass 1989) 149 (edited versions of this paper appeared in New Society and in Marxism Today in 1986).

'Justice and Efficiency in Criminal Justice' in WE Butler (ed.), *Justice and Comparative Law, Anglo-Soviet Perspectives on Criminal Law, Evidence, Procedure and Sentencing Policy* (Martinus Nijhofff 1987) 91

'Discretion and Due Process at the Post-Conviction Stage' in I Dennis (ed.), *Criminal Law and Justice* Essays from the W.G. Hart Workshop, 1986, (Sweet and Maxwell 1987) 221

'Obligations, Sanctions and Obedience' in N MacCormick and P Birks (eds), *The Legal Mind, Essays for Tony Honore* (Clarendon Press 1986) 219

'Responsibility: Law, Medicine or Morals?' in P Byrne (ed.), *Rights and Wrongs in Medicine* King's College Studies, 1985–6 (Oxford University Press 1986) 139

'Punishment and Discretion in the English Legal System' in J Broekman et al. (ed.), *Social Justice and Individual Responsibility in the Welfare State* (Franz Steiner 1985) 251

'Punishment, Justice and Consequentialism: A Reply to Professor Eckhoff' in A Duff and N Simmonds (eds), *Philosophy and the Criminal Law* (Franz Steiner 1984) 21

'The Place of the Distinction between Momentary and Non-momentary Legal Systems in Legal Analysis' in WE Butler (ed.), *Anglo-Polish Legal Essays* (Transnational 1982) 15

Index

For the benefit of digital users, indexed terms that span two pages (e.g., 52–53) may, on occasion, appear on only one of those pages.